T0354116

"The Morning Echo"

An Observation of Nature and Science

Javed Naseer

iUniverse, Inc.
Bloomington

The Morning Echo
An Observation of Nature and Science

iUniverse books may be ordered through booksellers or by contacting:
iUniverse
1663 Liberty Drive
Bloomington, IN 47403
www.iuniverse.com
1-800-Authors (1-800-288-4677)

ISBN: 978-1-4759-5707-5 (sc)
ISBN: 978-1-4759-5708-2 (e)
ISBN: 978-1-4759-5709-9 (dj)

Printed in the United States of America

iUniverse rev. date: 10/22/2012

Dedication

I dedicate my book to the Honor'able President
of the "Republic of India".

Contents

· ·

Preface:

. . . .

This book is about the phenomenal beauty that manifests itself in nature and how we are inspired with love, kindness, and good will only by watching the phenomenal beauty of nature. The facts presented in this book are not only based on experimentations and comprehensible speculations but also on mathematical computations, derivations, and extrapolations. This manuscript is mostly about me, what I know, and what I am capable of comprehending. In other words, this book is about numerous projects that I took up randomly at various stages of my life from early childhood, in 1968, when my mother, my brother, my sister, and I boarded Boeing 707 Jumbo Jet in New Delhi for New Orleans, Louisiana, via Air France Airlines, to the time I grew up to be a man. Hence various topics have been randomly selected in this marvelous book, which is entitled, "The Morning Echo". In this book, I have described how India emerged as a free democratic republic after dethroning British from positions of authority in the Indian subcontinent and I have presented a brief introduction to a ruling democratic government and its methods of implementing justice. I have described the Apollo 11 mission to the moon and the first man viz. Niel A. Armstrong on the moon. I have discussed the issues involving the ever growing world population and the pollution crisis that plagues our planet. I have also momentarily brought to light one of the cheapest resources of energy, viz. hydropower. I have presented, in this book, the top ten universities of the world, and finally I have included an elaborate discussion on "Einstein's Special Relativity" and "Newton's Laws of Motion".

Greetings

· ·

Hello, I am Physicist Javed Naseer. I was born in the state of Uttar Pardesh, (UP), in India. I have crossed gigantic bodies of water, a gigantic landscape, and unexplored, and uncultivated vast deserts to come to the United States of America for India happens to be on the opposite corner of this indeterminable, unfathomable, and immensely blessed earth.

In the present times, every unearthly phenomenon is viewed through the observations of science. The most incomprehensible experiences in life are accounted for in the light of science. It seems the modern age, somewhat, resembles with the primitive era except for the most fundamental laws of science. To argue why things happen in a certain scientific fashion is a useless debate. Things happen because we are inclined to feel most comfortable with them exactly the way they are happening. We have made a great stride in transforming this world into, what it looks like today as, a most advanced and developed world, and we have harnessed tremendous amounts of energy to meet our needs. We have built great towns and cities and we have greatly increased in number, that is, our population has grown tremendously, during the past few decades. We have not only built great nations but we have also built an amazing transportation network. We have increased our population growth and have hoisted thousands of flags all over the surface of the earth, each representing a distinct nation.

We have increased our food production as well as our technological production. We have subdued nature to serve our most significant and profound purpose, and simultaneously we have also firmly believed that we are a minute part of God's creation, and in God we trust. Sometimes, nature is subdued to serve mankinds most significant, and profound purpose. This implies different kinds of natural resources are explored and exploited to serve mankind, which, as a consequence, leads to the beginnings of new civilizations on earth and other parts of the world. We have harnessed nuclear energy and we have built great canals and pipelines and we have built great railway lines and we have launched huge satellites in earth's orbits in space and we have also sent space rockets into outer space.

Our culture, no doubt, has become very rich but we have to, at the same time, keep our morale and self-esteem in check. We have to observe etiquettes and mind our language and culture and we must also make effort to be courteous and soft-spoken. We must try not to look down upon the highly majestic and the highly ranked human tribe. We must also not forget our actual purpose in life which is to love and cherish life and share the best things in life together, and live in peace and harmony with other individuals and nations. Humanity has been genetically and traditionally surviving, along with timeless passing generations, here on the surface of the planet earth, since the dawn of civilization. Certain restrictions had been imposed by ancient traditions because ancient traditions forbid class rivalry and opposition and narrow mindedness. The world is much older and much humongous than what human mind is capable of speculating but we must try to remain steadfast and be bold enough to face the challenges of the world and mind our territories and protect mankind on earth from meeting with a misfortune or a horrible tragedy in the face of disaster.

1)

··

a) The Pasteurized Cow Milk

The cow grazes on green grass in the grassland meadow, which is herbage for animals, and produces huge quantities of milk.

The homosapiens drink cow milk and this is called a dairy product because it is stored, processed, distributed, and sold in dairy stores.

The cows are milked on a dairy farm and the cow milk is used to make many other dairy products like cream, cheese, and butter.

These dairy products are distributed all over the world and sold in grocery stores everywhere.

There are two kinds of groceries, namely, "perishable" grocery and "non-perishable" grocery, according to a certain type of a classification.

Grains, for example, are non-perishable groceries and dairy products are perishable groceries.

When you buy a dairy product, like cream, cheese, and butter that has been packed, sealed, and priced, look for the date of expiration on it also and buy it in accordance with it.

Dairy products are therefore perishable groceries and must be used within a fixed period of time otherwise they become putrefied with bacteria.

Hence cow milk, butter, and cheese are the dairy products that help young homosapiens grow strong and intelligent and must not be disregarded.

Pasteurized cow milk is composed of many ingredients that are useful in the development of a growing body of a homosapien. For example, it contains Calcium with Vitamin D, which plays a great role in the development of the skeleton system. The skeleton system of a homosapien comprises of bones structured together in the body.

Pasteurized cow milk is that milk which has been heated to 145°F (63°C) for 30 minutes or to 161°F (72°C) for 15 seconds. This treatment kills disease-producing microorganisms and many of the bacteria that cause spoilage. Ultra-pasteurized cow milk is heated to 300°F (149°C) for 3 seconds. Ultra-pasteurized cow milk is vacuum packed and well sealed. Most United States cities and states require pasteurization of all milk sold.

b) A Monday, the 13th, Wedding Ritual

It was Monday, the 13th, in late afternoon, when all the neighborhood kids were playing in a ruin that had been abandoned since time immemorial. Among them were small boys and small girls, who were playing with beautiful dolls that they had loved a lot and the dusky twilight still seemed hours away.

These boys and girls were dressing their dolls with garments, combing their artificial golden hair, and were occupied in making conversations on behalf of their magnificent and awe-inspiring dolls. They were exchanging presents and embracing each other, once again, on behalf of their beloved and wonderful dolls. Suddenly somebody announced the wedding of a couple of beautiful dolls. There were two young local girls who owned these dolls. One of these girls provided a groom doll designed with an expensive fabric and the other girl provided a bride doll also designed with an expensive fabric. They had decorated their dolls in a wonderful and fashionable way. One party of the kids joined with the groom doll and the other party of the kids joined with the bride doll.

The wedding ceremony took place, all the essential ritual formalities were completed and the couple of beautiful dolls were at last wedded. It all began in late afternoon but now evening was approaching. At sun down, the parents of the neighborhood kids arrived to take their off springs back home because it was getting late in the night and everybody left the frightful ruins, taking their dolls with them. It was a doll's wedding ceremony in an old, abandoned, a frightful, and quite a rundown ruin on Monday, the 13th.

2)

· ·

a) Inside - concealing Sky Blue Curtains

There is an international panorama of nations scattered all over the surface of planet earth outside the inside - concealing sky blue curtains. There are starving homosapiens, and human desires dying of hunger, epidemic, and malnutrition outside the inside - concealing sky blue curtains.

There are acts of terrorism being committed with great patented schemes and ostensive demonstrations, and there are communal tensions, disturbances, and rivalry taking place outside the inside-concealing sky blue curtains. There are bloody battles and horrible wars being fought between hostile armies and a great Armageddon taking place outside the inside - concealing sky blue curtains.

There are banks being robbed and there are caravans being looted outside the inside-concealing sky blue curtains. There are acts of forgery and fraudulent crimes being committed outside quite an unsophisticated and ordinary sky blue curtain. There is dishonesty, disorderliness, and corruption rampant everywhere and the whole world is in a state of agitation and turmoil outside the inside-concealing sky blue curtains.

The whole world, including each and every nation of the world, is in dire need of an adequate, and an urgent leadership, and a more appropriate, efficient, organized, and well established authority as well as a pragmatic, a more dependable and honest public administration. The public, however, needs certificates, diplomas, and degrees to run these departments of authority and administration.

b) In Praise of my Mother

My mother is an extraordinary intellectual. She is not only a verse immortalizing poet, she is also a philosopher. Her compositions are a combination of philosophy and poetry both. Through her prose and poetic writings, she has touched the very length and breadth of

3

philosophy. Her philosophical expression and poetic elegance in lyrical prose writing is truly a genius.

My mother is also a science graduate from a prestigious university from India, like myself. She likes to participate in all kinds of organized activities and functions. She never misses an appointment or a telephone call. She likes to keep herself involved in social activities, which are essential for a healthy life.

She has inspired political thinkers with a new radiance of a democratic administration in this politically enterprising, rapidly advancing, and technologically developing world. She is the kind of mother, who has touched our hearts and souls and we adore her a lot, indeed! She says that one hour's clear thinking is better than a whole night's devotion and we have always believed in her, like her eternally devoted off springs, forever enslaved to her for her noble ideals.

May my mother live a long and a blessed life on the soil of the same old Mother Earth! Furthermore, may the township, in which she was born and raised, be blessed and may the heavens and the earth, both, be blessed, for her sake, through Almighty God's infinite bounty, and finally may my mother be blessed as well. May the All Forgiving God have mercy on us! Amen!

c) Unani Philosophers

Suqrat, Aflatoon, and Arastu

Ancient Unani philosophy is dominated by three very famous men: Suqrat, Aflatoon, and Arastu. All three of these lived in Athens for most of their lives, and they knew each other. Suqrat came first, and Aflatoon was his student, around 400 B.C. Suqrat was killed in 399 B.C. and Aflatoon began his work by writing down what Suqrat had taught, and then continued by writing down his own ideas and opening a school. Arastu, who was younger, came to study at Aflatoon's school, and ended up starting his own school as well.

In the years after Aflatoon and Arastu died, in the 200's B.C, three famous kinds of philosophy started up in the schools that Aflatoon and Arastu had started. These are the Stoics, the Skeptics, and the Epicureans. Each of these continued to be important ways of thinking about the world all the way through the Roman Empire, until people converted to Christianity in the 300's A.D, and even after that.

Suqrat

Suqrat was the first of the three great Athenian, Unani philosophers (the other two are Aflatoon and Arastu). Suqrat was born in Athens, Unan in 469 B.C, so he lived through the time of Pericles and the Unani Empire, though he was too young to remember Marathons or Salamis. He was not from a rich family. His father was probably a stone – carver, and Suqrat also worked in stone, especially as a not very good sculptor. When Peloponnesian War began, Suqrat fought bravely for Athens, Unan. When Suqrat was in his forties or so, he began to feel an urge to think about the world around him, and try to answer some difficult questions. He asked, "What is wisdom?" and "What is beauty?" and "What is the right thing to do?" He knew that these questions were hard to answer, and he thought it would be better to have a lot of people discuss the answer together, so that they might come up with more ideas. So he began to go around Athens asking people he met these questions: "What is wisdom?" and "What is piety?" and so forth. Often this made people angry and sometimes they even tried to hurt him.

Suqrat soon had a group of young men who listened to him and learned from him how to think. Aflatoon was one of these young men. Suqrat never charged them any money. But in 399 B.C, some of the Athenians got mad at Suqrat for what he was teaching the young men. They charged him in court with impiety (not respecting the gods) and corrupting the youth (teaching young guys bad things). People thought he was against democracy, and he probably was – he thought the smartest people should make the decision for everyone. The Athenians couldn't charge him with being against democracy because they had promised not to take revenge on anyone after the Peloponnesian War. So they had to use these vague religious charges instead. It, however, causes a lot of embarrasement to the authorities to incriminate and punish a faculty of intellectuals, having important colleagues, for any kind of accusations, other than what they really deserve. Suqrat had a big trial in front of an Athenian jury. He was convicted of these charges and sentenced to death, and he died soon afterwards, when the guards gave him the potion of death to drink. Suqrat never wrote down any of his ideas but after his death Aflatoon did write down.

Aflatoon

Aflatoon is known today as one of the greatest philosophers of all times. He was born about 429 B.C close to the time when Pericles died, and he died in 347 B.C, just after the birth of Sikandarai Azam. Aflatoon was born in Athens, to a very wealthy and aristocratic family. Many of his relatives were involved with Athenian politics, though Aflatoon himself was not. When Suqrat was killed in 399 B.C, Aflatoon was very upset (He was 30 years old when Suqrat died). Aflatoon began to write down some of the conversations he had heard Suqrat have. Practically everything we know about Suqrat comes from what Aflatoon wrote down. (Remember Aflatoon was from a rich aristocratic family so he probably considered himself among the best people).

Arastu

Arastu's father was Nicomachus, a doctor who lived near Macedon, in the north of Unan. So unlike Suqrat and Aflatoon, Arastu was not originally from Athens. He was not from a rich family like Aflatoon though his father was not poor either. When Arastu was very young around 350 B.C he went to study at Aflatoon's Academy. Aflatoon had grown quite old at that time, and when he died, the people at the Academy did not choose Arastu as their leader but picked some body else. For this reason Arastu became upset and soon returned to Macedonia to become the tutor of young Sikandarai Azam. Sikandarai Azam was not interested in learning but he became a good friend of Arastu. When Sikandarai Azam became king, Arastu went back to Athens and opened his own school there which continued to impart education and various disciplines for hundreds of years.

3)

a) The Familiar Footpath, (Phantom, the ghost, who walks, by Lee Falk)

Leon Harrison Gross, more known by the alias of Lee Falk (April 28, 1911 – March 13, 1999) was an American writer, best known as the creator of the popular comic strip superheroes, The Phantom and Mandrake, the Magician, who at the height of their popularity secured him over a hundred million readers every single day. He was also a playwrite and theatrical producer and contributed to a series of novels based on the Phantom. Leon was born in St. Louis, where he spent his childhood and youth. His mother was called Elanore Aleina (a name he would later on, in some form, use in both Mandrake and Phantom stories), and his father was Benjamin Gross. Both his parents were Jewish. However Albert Gross died when Leon was a small homosapien. Elanore married Albert Epstein, who became Leon's father figure in life. Leon reportedly changed his surname after leaving college. It is not known why he took the name "Falk", but "Lee" had been his nickname since childhood. His brother, Leslie, also took the name "Falk". During World War II, Lee also worked as chief propaganda for the new radio station, KMDX, in Ilinois, where he became the leader of the radio foreign language division of the Office of War Information.

Lee died because of heart failure in 1999. He lived the last years of his life in New York, in a luxury apartment not far from Central Park. He also had a summer house on Cape Cod. He literally wrote his comic strips from 1934 to the last days of his life, when in hospital he took off his oxygen mask to dictate his stories.

b) The Familiar Footpath,
Frankenstein, by Mary Shelley)

Frankenstein; or, The Modern Prometheus is a novel about a failed artificial life experiment that has produced a monster, written by Mary Shelley. Shelley started writing the story when she was eighteen, and the novel was published when she was twenty one. The first edition was published anonymously in London in1818. Shelley's name appears on the second edition, published in France in 1823. It is common to refer to the monster itself as "Frankenstein", but in the novel the monster is identified via words such as "monster", "fiend", "wretch", "vile insect", "daemon", and "it". Shelley herself called it "Adam".

Shelley had travelled the region in which the story takes place, and the topics of galvanism and other similar occult ideas were themes of conversation among her companions. The actual storyline took place from a dream. Shelley was talking with her three writer colleagues and they decided they would have a competition to see who could write the best horror story. After thinking for weeks about what her possible storyline could be Shelley dreamt about a scientist who created life and was horrified by what he created. Then "Frankenstein" was written.

Frankenstein is infused with some elements of the Gothic novel and the Romantic Movement and is also considered to be one of the earliest examples of science fiction. It is partially based on Giovanni Aldini's electrical experiments on dead and (sometimes) living animals and was also a warning against the expansion of modern man in the Industrial Revolution, alluded to in its subtitle, The Modern Prometheus. It had had a considerable influence across literature and popular culture and spawned a complete genre of horror stories and cinema.

4)

. . . .

a) Motion in One Dimension

Concepts

1. 1) Displacement: - The displacement is a vector that points from the object's initial position to its final position and has a value that equals the shortest distance between the two positions.

    $\Delta x = (x - x_0) = $ displacement

    SI unit of displacement = meter or designated by (m)

2. 2) Speed and Velocity: - The average speed is the distance travelled divided by the time required to cover the distance.

    Average Speed = distance / elapsed time (m/s)

    The average velocity is the displacement Δx divided by the elapsed time $\Delta t = t - t_0$

    SI unit of average velocity is meters/second or (m/s)

    $\overline{v} = (x - x_0)/ (t - t_0) = \Delta x/\Delta t$

    Instantaneous Velocity: - The instantaneous velocity, "v", of an object in motion indicates how fast the object is moving and its direction of motion at each instant of time. The value of the instantaneous velocity is the instantaneous speed. If Δt, the time interval, is small enough the instantaneous velocity becomes approximately equal to the average velocity. In the limit Δt becomes infinitesimally small, the instantaneous velocity and average velocity become equal, so that: -

    $v = \lim_{\Delta t \to 0} (\Delta x/\Delta t)$

    In our discussion we will use the word velocity to mean instantaneous velocity and speed to mean instantaneous speed.

3. 3) Acceleration: - Acceleration is defined as the rate at which the velocity is changing. It is a vector like velocity and force.

Average acceleration = Change in velocity/Elapsed time

$\bar{a} = (v - v_0)/(t - t_0) = \Delta v/\Delta t$

Hence average acceleration $\bar{a}$ is a vector that points in the same direction as Δv, the change in velocity.

Instantaneous acceleration is the limiting case of the average acceleration when Δt approaches zero and is defined as follows: -

$a = \lim_{\Delta t \to 0} (\Delta v/\Delta t) = \bar{a}$

When Δt approaches zero in the limit given above, the instantaneous acceleration and average acceleration become equal. In our discussion we will use the word acceleration to mean instantaneous acceleration.

Equations of Kinematics for Constant Acceleration: - In the equations, $v = (v_0 + at)$ and $x = \frac{1}{2}(v + v_0) t$, there are five kinematic variables involved, viz. (1) x = displacement, (2) $a = \bar{a}$ = acceleration (constant), (3) v = final velocity at time t, (4) v_0 = initial velocity at time $t_0 = 0$ seconds, and (5) t = time elapsed since $t_0 = 0$ seconds.

The equations of kinematics for constant acceleration are as follows:
-

1) $v = v_0 + at$
2) $x = \frac{1}{2}(v_0 + v) t$
3) $x = v_0 t + (\frac{1}{2})at^2$
4) $v^2 = v_0^2 + 2ax$

Freely Falling Bodies: - The idealized motion of an object falling from a height, in which air resistance is neglected and the acceleration is approximately constant, is known as free fall. Since the acceleration is constant in a free fall, the equations of kinematics can be used.

The acceleration of a freely falling body is called its acceleration due to gravity and its value without any algebraic sign is denoted by the symbol g. The acceleration due to gravity is directed downward towards the center of the earth. Near the surface of the earth, g is approximately $g = 9.8$ m/s^2.

In reality, however, g decreases with increasing altitude and varies slightly with latitude. The acceleration due to gravity on the surface of the moon is one sixth as large as that on the earth.

The equations of Kinematics for constant acceleration for freely falling bodies are as follows: -

1) $v = v_0 + gt$
2) $y = \frac{1}{2}(v + v_0) t$
3) $y = v_0 t + (\frac{1}{2}) gt^2$
4) $v^2 = v_0^2 + 2gy$

In these equations, the x-axis becomes the y-axis and the constant acceleration, "a", becomes the acceleration due to gravity, "g".

Motion in One Dimension

Numerical Problems: -

Displacement, Speed, and Velocity: -

1. A whale swims due east for a distance of 7km, turns around and goes due west for 2km and finally turns around and heads 4km due east. (a) What is the total distance travelled by the whale? (b) What are the magnitude and direction of the displacement of the whale?

    Solution

    (a) S = total distance

    S = 7km + 2km + 4km = 13km

    (b) d = total displacement

    d = 7km – 2km + 4km = 11km due east

2. A woman and her husband are out for a morning run to the river, which is located 5km away. The woman runs at 3m/s in a straight line. The husband runs back and forth at 5m/s between his wife and the river, until the wife reaches the river. What is the total distance run by the husband?

    Solution: -

    $t = d/v = 5km/3m/s = 5000m/3m/s = 1.667 \times 10^3$ s

    $d = vt = 5m/s \times 1.667 \times 10^3$ s $= 8.333 \times 10^3$ m

    $d = 8.333 \times 10^3 m$

    Hence the total distance run by the husband is 8.333 km.

3. A plane is sitting on a runway, awaiting take off. On an adjacent parallel runway, another plane lands and passes the stationary plane at a speed of 55m/s. The arriving plane has

a length of 50m. By looking out of a window (very narrow), a passenger on the stationary plane can see the moving plane. For how long a time is the plane visible?

Solution: -

$t = d/v = 50m/55m/s = 0.909$ seconds

$t = 0.909$ secs.

Hence the plane is visible for 0.909 seconds only.

4. A tourist being chased by an angry bear is running in a straight line towards his car at a speed of 5m/s. The car is a distance d away. The bear is 30m behind the tourist and running at 8m/s. The tourist reaches the car safely. What is the maximum possible value for d?

Solution: -

The speed of the tourist relative to the bear is given by the following:

$v` = 8m/s - 5m/s = 3m/s$

$t = d`/v` = 30m/3m/s = 10$ seconds

$d = vt = 5m/s \times 10s = 50m$

Hence the maximum possible value for d is 50m.

Acceleration: -

5. A motorcycle has a constant acceleration of $4m/s^2$. Both the velocity and acceleration of the motorcycle point in the same direction. How much time is required for the motorcycle to change its speed from (a) 15 to 40m/s and (b) 40 to 70m/s?

Solution: -

$v = v_0 + at$ $t = (v - v_0)/a$

a) $t = (40m/s - 15m/s)/4m/s^2 = 25m/s / 4m/s^2 = 6.25$ seconds.

b) $t = (70m/s - 40m/s)/ 4m/s^2 = 30m/s/ 4m/s^2 = 7.5$ seconds

Hence the answers are (a) $t = 6.25$ seconds and (b) $t = 7.5$ seconds.

6. A runner accelerates to a velocity of 6m/s due west in 2 secs. His average acceleration is $0.7m/s^2$, also directed due west. What was the velocity when he began accelerating?

Solution: -

$v = v_0 + at$ $v_0 = v - at$

$v_0 = 6m/s - 0.7m/s^2 \times 2s = 6m/s - 1.4m/s = 4.6m/s$

Hence the velocity of the runner when he began accelerating has been 4.6m/s.

Equations of kinematics for constant acceleration, Application of the equations of kinematics: -

7. The speed ramp at an airport is basically a large conveyor belt on which you can stand and be moved along. The belt of one ramp moves at a constant speed such that a person who stands still on it, leaves the ramp 80 seconds after getting on. Jack is in a real hurry, however, and skips the speed ramp. Starting from rest with an acceleration of 0.4ms⁻², he covers the same distance as the ramp does, but in one-fourth the time. What is the speed at which the belt of the ramp is moving?

Solution: -

$x = (½) at^2 = vt$

$x = (½) (0.4ms^{-2}) (80s/4)^2 = 80m$

$x = vt = 80m = v (80s)$

$v = 80m/ 80s = 1ms^{-1}$

Hence the speed at which the belt of the ramp is moving is 1 ms⁻¹.

8. A car is travelling at a constant speed of 25m/s on a highway. At the instant this car passes an entrance ramp, a second car enters the highway from the ramp. The second car starts from rest and has a constant acceleration. What acceleration must it maintain so that the two cars meet for the first time at the next exit which is 3km away?

Solution: -

$x = x_0 + vt = 3000m = 25m/s \times t(s)0$

$t = 3000/25 = 120 seconds$

$x = (1/2) at^2 \quad a = 2x/t^2$

$a = (2 \times 3000)/ (120)^2 = 6000/ (120)^2$

$a = 0.41666667m/s^2$

Hence the second car must maintain an acceleration of 0.41666667m/s² if it wants to meet the first car for the first time at the next exit 3km away.

9. A train has a length of 100m and starts from rest with a constant acceleration at time t = 0 seconds. At this instant, a car just reaches the end of the train. The car is moving with a constant velocity. At a time t = 15 seconds, the car

just reaches the front of the train. Ultimately, however, the train pulls ahead of the car and at t = 30 seconds, the car is again at the rear of the train. Find the value of (a) the car's velocity and (b) the train's acceleration.

Solution: -

(a) v/2 = 100m / 15s v = 200/15 = 13.3m/s

v = 13.3m/s

(b) acc. = v/t = 13.3/15 = 0.88m/s^2

a = 0.88m/s^2

Hence (a) the car's velocity is 13.3m/s and (b) the train's acceleration is 0.88m/s^2

10. A jetliner, travelling northward, is landing with a speed of 70m/s. Once the jet touches down, it has 800m of runway, in which to reduce its speed to 7m/s. Compute the average acceleration of the plane during landing.

Solution: -

$v^2 - v_0^2 = 2\bar{a}x$

$\bar{a} = (v^2 - v_0^2)/2x$

$\bar{a} = \{(7)^2 - (70)^2\}/ (2 \times 800)$

$\bar{a} = (49 - 4900)/1600$

$\bar{a} = -4851/1600 = -3.03m/s^2$

$\bar{a} = -3.03m/s^2$ northward

Hence the average acceleration of the plane during landing has been computed and its value is $-3.03m/s^2$.

Freely Falling Bodies: -

11. An astronaut on a distant planet wants to determine its acceleration due to gravity. The astronaut throws a rock straight up with a velocity of 21m/s and measures the time of 18 seconds before the rock returns to his hand. What is the acceleration due to gravity on this planet?

Solution: -

v = 21m/s

t = 18s/2 = 9s

$v = v_0 + gt = 9g$

v = 21m/s = 9g

g = 21m/s/9s = 2.33m/s^2

Hence the acceleration due to gravity on this planet is 2.33m/s^2 directed towards the center of this planet.

12. A stone is dropped from a sea cliff and the sound of it striking the ocean bed is heard 2 seconds later. How high is the cliff, assuming the speed of sound to be 343m/s?

Solution: -

$h = (1/2) gt^2$ and $t = (2 - h/343)$ s

$h = (1/2) g (2 - h/343)^2$

$h = (1/2) g \{4 + h^2/ (343)^2 - 4h/343\}$

$h = 2g + gh^2/2(343)^2 - 2gh/343 = h$

$h^2 - 4(343) h - 2(343)^2h/g + 4(343)^2 = 0$

$h^2 - 1372h - 24010h + 470596 = 0$

$h^2 - 25382h + 470596 = 0$

Now this is a quadratic equation in h and therefore it can be solved for h. The value thus found comes out to be 18.55m or approximately 18.6m. It is left as an exercise for the student to solve.

$\Rightarrow h = 18.55m$

13. A ball is thrown straight upward and rises to a maximum height of 9m above its launch point. At what height above its launch point has the speed of the ball decreased to one third of its initial value?

Solution: -

$v = \sqrt{(2gh)} = \sqrt{(2 \times 9.8 \times 9)} = \sqrt{(176.4)} = 13.28156617$m/s

$v = 13.28$m/s

$v^2 - v_0^2 = 2gh$

$v^2 - (v/3)^2 = v^2 - v^2/9 = 2gh$

$8v^2/9 = 2gh$

$h = 8v^2/18g = 8 \times (13.28)^2/18g = 7.99m$

$h = 7.99m$

Hence it will rise to a height of 7.99m above its launch point when its speed has decreased to one third of its initial value.

14. A woman on a bridge 80m high sees a raft floating at a constant speed on the river below. She drops a stone from rest in an attempt to hit the raft. The stone is released when the raft has 8m more to travel before passing under the bridge. The stone hits the water 5m in front of the raft. Find the speed of the raft.

Solution: -

$v = (8 - 5)/t = 3/t$

$t = \sqrt{(2h/9.8)} = \sqrt{(2 \times 80/9.8)}$

$v = 3/t = 3\sqrt{(9.8/160)} = \sqrt{(9 \times 9.8/160)}$

$v = \sqrt{(88.2/160)}$

$v = \sqrt{(0.55125)}$

$v = 0.74246212 m/s$

$v = 0.742 m/s$

Therefore the speed of the mentioned raft is $v = 0.742 m/s$.

15. Two identical pallet guns are fired simultaneously from the edge of a cliff. These guns impart an initial speed of 20m/s to each pallet. Gun A is fired straight upward, with the pallet going up and then falling back down, eventually hitting the ground beneath the cliff. Gun B is fired straight downward. In the absence of air resistance, how long after pallet B hits the ground does pallet A hit the ground?

Solution: - The time it takes for the pallet A to return to the level of the cliff is how long it will take for pallet A to hit the ground after pallet B has already hit the ground.

$v^2 - v_0^2 = 2gh$

$(20)^2 - (0)^2 = (20)^2 = 2gh$

$h = (20)^2/2g = 20.40816327 m$

$h = (1/2) gt^2 \ t = \sqrt{(2h/g)} = \sqrt{(2 \times 20.4040816327 /9.8)}$

$t = 2.040816327$

$t` = 2t = 2 \times 2.040816327 = 4.081632653$ seconds

Hence the required time $t` = 4.081632653$ seconds.

Miscellaneous: -

16. A stone is dropped at rest from the top of a cliff and it takes 3 seconds for it to hit the ground below. Determine the height of the cliff.

Solution: - $h = (1/2) gt^2$

$\Rightarrow h = (1/2) (9.8 \ m/s^2) (3 \ s)^2 = 44.1 \ m$

$\Rightarrow h = 44.1 \ m$

17. A motorcycle starts from rest and has a constant acceleration. In a certain time interval its displacement triples. In the same time interval, by what factor does its velocity increase?

Solution: - $v^2 = v_0^2 + 2ax$

Now $v_0 = 0$ at $t = 0$

$\Rightarrow v^2 = 2ax$ and

$v`^2 = 2a (3x) = 6ax$ when $x` = 3x$

$$\Rightarrow v^2 / v^2 = 6ax/2ax = 3$$
$$\Rightarrow v` = v\sqrt{3} = 1.73v$$
Hence the velocity will increase by a factor of 1.73.

Motion in Two Dimensions

Concepts: -

Displacement, Velocity and Acceleration: - The displacement has been defined in Chapter No.2 along x and y axes. The displacement vector, however, may lie anywhere in the plane.

Displacement $= \Delta r = r - r_0$

The average velocity of a moving object is a vector and may lie anywhere in the x-y plane.

$$\nabla = (r - r_0)/ (t - t_0) = \Delta r/\Delta t$$

The velocity of a moving object at an instant of time is its instantaneous velocity. The average velocity becomes equal to the instantaneous velocity, "v", in the limit that Δt becomes infinitesimally small and approaches zero.

$$v = Lim\Delta_t \rightarrow_0 (\Delta r/\Delta t)$$

The average acceleration, "ā", is defined as the change in velocity divided by the elapsed time.

$$\bar{a} = (v - v_0)/ (t - t_0) = \Delta v/\Delta t$$

The average acceleration, "ā", becomes equal to the instantaneous acceleration, "a", when Δt becomes infinitesimally small.

$$\backslash a = Lim\Delta_t \rightarrow_0 (\Delta v/\Delta t)$$

The acceleration may have a vector component, "a_x", along the x-direction and a vector component, "a_y", along the y-direction.

Equation of Kinematics in Two Dimensions: -

For the motion in two dimensions, we may have x and y components of the vector variable and these may have positive or negative signs. The x and y components are scalars and comprise five kinematic variables.

Serial Number: Variable: -

1) Displacement: -

　　x - Component: - x

　　y - Component: - y

2) Acceleration: -

　　x - Component: - a_x

　　y - Component: - a_y

3) Final Velocity: -

　　x - Component: - v_x

y - Component: - v_y

4) Initial Velocity: -

    x - Component: - v_{ox}

    y - Component: - v_{oy}

5) Elapsed Time: -

    x - Component: - t

    y - Component: - t

The following are the equations of kinematics for constant acceleration in two dimensions: -

    For the x-component we may have the following equations: -

    1) $v_x = v_{ox} + a_x t$

    2) $x = (\frac{1}{2})(v_{ox} + v_x) t$

    3) $x = v_{ox} t + (1/2) a_x t^2$

    4) $v_x^2 = v_{ox}^2 + 2a_x x$

For the y-component we may have the following equations: -

    1) $v_y = v_{oy} + a_y t$

    2) $y = (1/2)(v_{oy} + v_y)t$

    3) $y = v_{oy} t + (1/2) a_y t^2$

    4) $v_y^2 = v_{oy}^2 + 2a_y y$

Projectile Motion: -

A projectile is any object which is fired on the surface of the earth, through the barrel of cannon. We shall now study the angle θ that the projectile makes with the horizontal while it is fired, the speed v of the projectile, the x-component and the y-component of its speed, the height H reached by a projectile, the range R covered by a projectile, and the time t, the projectile is in the air, etc.

a) The fall time of a projectile can be calculated as follows: -

    $y = v_{oy} t + (1/2) a_y t^2$

    $t = \sqrt{(2y/ a_y)}$ where $v_{oy} = 0$ m/s

b) The velocity of a projectile is determined from the equations which are given below: -

    $v_y = v_{oy} + a_y t$

    $v = \sqrt{(v_x^2 + v_y^2)}$

    $\theta = \cos^{-1}(v_x /v)$

c) The height of a projectile is calculated as follows: -

    $v_{oy} = v_o \sin\theta$

    $y = H = (v_y^2 - v_{oy}^2)/2a_y$

d) The time of flight of a projectile is determined from the equations which are given below: -

$$y = v_{oy}t + (1/2) a_yt^2 \Rightarrow y = 0$$
$$v_{oy}t = (1/2) a_yt^2$$
$$t = 2v_{oy}/a_y$$

e) The range of a projectile is measured as follows: -

$$v_{ox} = v_o \cos\theta = v_x$$
$$x = R = v_xt = v_{ox}t$$

f) The final parameters can be used to calculate initial parameters from the same kind of equations that we have already given, viz.

$$v_o = \sqrt{(v_{ox}^2 + v_{oy}^2)} \quad \theta = \tan^{-1}(v_{oy}/v_{ox})$$
$$v_{ox} = v_x = v_o \cos\theta$$
$$v_y^2 = v_{oy}^2 + 2a_yy \text{ or } v_{oy} = \sqrt{(v_y^2 - 2a_yy)}$$

There are two ways of throwing an object from a cliff. It can be thrown either with an angle θ above the horizontal or with the same angle θ below the horizontal. In any case it will strike the ground beneath with the same velocity.

Relative Velocity: -

Along one direction, the relative velocity can be understood by the equation: -

$$v_{AB} = v_{AC} + v_{CB}$$

Along perpendicular directions the relative velocity, "v_{AB}" is given by the equation of Pythagoras as follows: -

$$v_{AB} = \sqrt{(v_{AC}^2 + v_{CB}^2)}$$
$$\theta = \tan^{-1}(v_{CB}/v_{AC})$$

Note, "v_{CB}" is the velocity along the vertical direction and, "v_{AC}" is the velocity along the horizontal direction. Note also while the velocity of object A relative to object B is v_{AB} that of object B relative to object A is $v_{BA} = -v_{AB}$ along the same axis.

Motion in Two Dimensions

Numerical Problems: -

Displacement, Velocity, and Acceleration: -
1) In diving to a depth of 800m, an elephant seal also moves 500m due east of his starting point. What is the value of the seal's displacement?
Solution: -

$$R = \sqrt{(x^2 + y^2)} = \sqrt{[(500)^2 + (-800)^2]}$$
$$R = \sqrt{890000}$$

$R = 9.43 \times 10^2$ m

2) A jetliner is moving at a speed of 300m/s. The vertical component of the plane's velocity is 50m/s. What is the value of the horizontal component of the plane's velocity?

Solution: -

$v^2 = \sqrt{(v_x^2 + v_y^2)}\ v_x = \sqrt{(v^2 - v_y^2)}$

$v_x = \sqrt{[(300m/s)^2 - (50m/s)^2]} = \sqrt{87500} = 295.8$m/s

$v_x = 295.8$m/s

3) A dolphin leaps out of the water at an angle of 40^0 above the horizontal. The horizontal component of the dolphin's velocity is 8.8m/s. Find the value of the vertical component of the velocity.

Solution: -

$v_x = v\cos\theta\ v = v_x/\cos\theta = (8.8m/s)/\cos40^0$

$v_y = v\sin\theta = [(8.8/\cos40^0]\sin40^0 = 8.8\tan40^0$

$v_y = 7.38$m/s

4) An object moves around a circular orbit of radius 2×10^{10}m. It moves ¼ of the circumference of this great circle in a period of 8×10^5seconds. (a) What is the average speed of this object for the given period? (b) What is the value of the average velocity of the object during this period?

Solution: -

(a) Average Speed = distance/time

$\bar{S} = (C/4)/t = (1/4)(2\pi \times 2 \times 10^{10}m)/(8 \times 10^5 s)\ S = 3.9 \times 10^4$m/s

(b) Average Velocity = displacement/time

$\bar{V} = \sqrt{(R^2 + R^2)}/t = R(\sqrt{2})/t = (2 \times 10^{10}m)(\sqrt{2})/(8 \times 10^5 s)$

$\bar{V} = 3.5 \times 10^4$m/s

Equation of Kinematics in Two Dimensions, Projectile Motion: -

5) A tennis ball is struck such that it leaves the racket horizontally with a speed of 30m/s. The ball hits the court at a horizontal distance of 20m from the racket. What is the height of the tennis ball when it leaves the racket?

Solution: -

$v_{ox} = 30$m/s, $x = 20$m, $h = ?$

$x = v_{ox}t = v_x t\ t = x/v_{ox}$

$t = 20m/30m/s = (2/3)\ s = 0.66666$s

$h = (½)gt^2 = (1/2) \times 9.8m/s^2 \times (0.66666s)^2 = 2.177$m

$h = 2.177$m

6) A diver runs horizontally with a speed of 2m/s off a platform that is 8m above the water. What is his speed just before striking the water?

Solution: -

$v_y = \sqrt{(2gh)} = \sqrt{(2\times9.8\times8)} = \sqrt{(156.8)} = 12.52198067$

$v = \sqrt{(v_x^2 + v_y^2)} = \sqrt{[(2)^2 + (12.52198067)^2]} = \sqrt{(4 + 156.8)}$

$v = \sqrt{(160.8)} = 12.68m/s$

$v = 12.68m/s$

7) A horizontal rifle is fired at a bull's eye. The muzzle speed of the bullet is 700m/s. The barrel is pointed directly at the center of the bull's eye but the bullet strikes the target 0.015m below the center. What is the horizontal distance between the end of the rifle and the bull's eye?

Solution: -

$h = (\frac{1}{2}) gt^2 = 0.015m$

$t = \sqrt{(2h/g)} = \sqrt{[(2\times0.015)/9.8]} = \sqrt{(0.003061224)}$

$t = 0.055328334s$

$x = R = v_x t = (700m/s) (0.055328334s) = 38.72983346m$

$x = 38.7m$

8) An Olympic long jumper leaves the ground at an angle of 30^0 and travels through the air for a horizontal distance of 9m before landing. What is the take off speed of the jumper?

Solution: -

$x = 9m,$

$y = x \tan\theta = 9 \tan 30^0 = (1/2) gt^2$

$t = \sqrt{[(2\times9\tan30^0)/9.8]} = 1.02977632s$

$d = \sqrt{(x^2 + y^2)} = \sqrt{[(9m)^2 + (9\tan30^0)^2]} = 9\sqrt{(1+\tan^230^0)}$

$d = 10.39230485m$

$v = d/t = 10.39230485m/1.02977632s = 10.09180795m/s$

$v = 10.09m/s$

Therefore the take off speed of the Olympic jumper, when he leaves the ground, is 10.09 m/s.

9) The two stones have identical initial speeds of $v_0 = 14m/s$ and are thrown at an angle $\theta = 40^0$, one below and one above the horizontal. What is the distance between the two points where the two stones strike the ground?

Solution: -

$h = (\frac{1}{2}) gt^2 = v_y^2/2g = (v_0\sin\theta)^2/2g = (14\sin40^0)^2/(2\times9.8)$

$h = 4.131759112m$

$t = \sqrt{(2h/g)} = \sqrt{(2\times4.131759112/9.8)} = 0.918268014s$

$t` = 2t = 2\times0.918268014 = 1.836536028s$

$v_x = v \cos\theta = 14 \cos40^0 = 10.7246222m/s$

$x = v_x t` = 10.7246222m/s \times 1.836536028s = 19.69615506m$

x = 19.696m

Therefore the distance between the two points where the two stones strike the ground is x = 19.696m.

10) An eagle is flying horizontally at 7m/s with a fish in its claws. It accidentally drops the fish. (a) How much time passes before the fish's speed triples? (b) How much additional time would be required for the fish's speed to triple again?

Solution: -

(a) $v = \sqrt{[(3\times7)^2 - (7)^2]} = \sqrt{(441 - 49)} = \sqrt{(392)}$

$v = 19.79898987m/s = 19.8m/s$

$t = v/g = 19.79898987m/s /9.8m/s^2 = 2.020305089s$

$t = 2.02s$

(b) $v = \sqrt{[(3\times21)^2 - (7)^2]} = \sqrt{(3969 - 49)} = \sqrt{(3920)}$

$v = 62.60990337m/s$

$t` = v/g = 62.60990337m/s /9.8m/s^2 = 6.38876565s$

$t`` = t` - t = 6.38876565 - 2.020305089 = 4.368460561s$

$t`` = 4.368s$

11) A fire hose rejects a stream of water at an angle of 40^0 above the horizontal. The water leaves the nozzle with a speed of 30m/s. Assuming that the water behaves like a projectile, how far from a building should the fire hose be located to hit the highest possible fire?

Solution: -

$h = v_y^2/2g = (v\ sin\theta)^2/2g = (30sin40^0)^2/2g$

$h = 18.97236327m$

$h = (\frac{1}{2})\ gt^2\ t = \sqrt{(2h/g)}$

$t = \sqrt{[2(30sin40^0)^2/2g^2]} = 30sin40^0/g = 19.28362829/9.8$

$t = 1.967717173s$

$v_x = v\ cos\theta = 30cos40^0 = 22.98133329m/s$

$x = R = v_x t = 22.98133329m/s \times 1.967717173s = 45.22076418m$

$x = R = 45m$

12) Suppose a ball is kicked on the moon where the acceleration due to gravity is one sixth that on earth. If the velocity of the ball is $v_0 = 30m/s$ and the angle above the horizontal is 30^0 find (a) the height of the ball and (b) the range of the ball.

Solution: -

(a) $h = v^2/2g` = (30sin30^0)^2/2g` = (30sin30^0)^2/ (2g/6)$

$h = 68.87755102m$

$h = 68.877m$

(b) $x = v_x t = R = (v_0 cos\theta)\ t$

$v_x = v_0\cos\theta = 30\cos30^0 = 25.98076211 \text{m/s}$
$t = \sqrt{(2h/g)} = \sqrt{[(2\text{x}68.87755102)/9.8]} = 3.749218994\text{s}$
$x = v_x t = 25.98\text{x}3.749 = 97.40756678\text{m}$
$x = R = 97.4\text{m}$

Therefore (a) the height of the ball is 68.877m and (b) the range of the ball is 97.4m respectively.

Relative Velocity: -

13) Two passenger trains are passing each other on adjacent tracks. Train A is moving east with a speed of 15m/s and train B is travelling west with a speed of 30m/s. (a) What is the velocity of train A as seen by passengers in train B? (b) What is the velocity of train B as seen by passengers in train A?

Solution: -

    (a) Train A as seen by passengers in train B: -
    $V_{WE} = V_W + V_E = 30\text{m/s} + 15\text{m/s} = 45\text{m/s}$ due east.
    (b) Train B as seen by passengers in train A: -
    $V_{EW} = V_E + V_W = 15\text{m/s} + 30\text{m/s} = 45\text{m/s}$ due west.

14) At some airports there are speed ramps to help passengers get from one place to another. A speed ramp is a moving conveyor belt that you can either stand or walk on. Suppose a speed ramp has a length of 200m and is moving at a speed of 3m/s relative to the ground. In addition, suppose you can cover this distance in 100s when walking on ground. If you walk at the same rate with respect to the speed ramp that you walk with respect to the ground, how long does it take for you to travel the 200m using the speed ramp?

Solution: -

    $V_{PG} = V_{PR} + V_{RG}$

Note that V_{PG} is the velocity of the person with respect to the ground, V_{PR} is the velocity of the person with respect to the ramp, and V_{RG} is the velocity of the ramp with respect to the ground.

    $V_{PR} = \text{Length/time} = 200\text{m}/100\text{s} = 2\text{m/s}$ and $V_{RG} = 3\text{m/s}$
    $V_{PG} = V_{PR} + V_{RG} = 2\text{m/s} + 3\text{m/s} = 5\text{m/s}$
    $t = \text{Length}/V_{PG} = 200\text{m}/5\text{m/s} = 40\text{s}$

Hence it takes, for that person, 40 seconds to travel 200m using the speed ramp.

15) A swimmer capable of swimming at a speed of 2m/s in still water (i.e. the swimmer can swim with a speed of 2m/s relative to the water), starts to swim directly across a 3km wide river. However, the current

is 1m/s and it carries the swimmer downstream. (a) How long does it take the swimmer to cross the river? (b) How far downstream will the swimmer be upon reaching the other side of the river?
Solution: -

(a) t = distance/velocity = 3000m/2m/s = 1500 seconds

t = 1.5×10^3 seconds

(b) s = vt = 1m/s x 1500s = 1500m

s = 1.5×10^3m

Hence it takes 1500s for the swimmer to cross the river and he is 1500m downstream upon reaching the other side of the river.

b) Simple Pendulum and Simple Harmonic Motion

The intricacies and the complexities of nature are hard to explore, but the apparatus is always there almost aligned with the floor.

The simple pendulum is a string tied to a round metallic bob, performing simple harmonic motion.

The metallic bob as it moves to and fro, like a simple pendulum, executes in its wonderful frequency, the simple harmonic motion.

The use of the constant, "π" is made to evaluate the value of, "g", the acceleration due to gravity.

The time for each oscillation is determined with the help of a stop watch, which is called the period.

The length of the pendulum is meticulously measured and finally the value of "g" is evaluated.

Now the length of the pendulum is multiplied by $4\pi^2$ and then divided by the square of the period to calculate the value of, "g", the acceleration due to gravity.

Hence the theory of simple harmonic motion is quite phenomenal for it allows the value of, "g", the acceleration due to gravity to be determined.

The equation used is given below:-

$1/f = 2\pi \sqrt{[L/g]} = T$

Where, "L", is the length of the pendulum, "g", is the acceleration due to gravity, "f", is the frequency, and, "T", is the period.

$\Rightarrow g = 4\pi^2 L / T^2$

The value of the acceleration due to gravity, "g", at most locations on the surface of the earth has been experimentally found to be 9.8m/s^2.

According to Newton's Law of Universal Gravitation, the value of g is calculated from the following equation: -

$$F = GMm/R^2 = mg$$
$$\Rightarrow g = GM/R^2$$

The symbol G is the Universal gravitational constant with a value of 6.673×10^{-11} N-m^2/kg^2, M is the mass of the earth with a value of 5.98×10^{24}kg, and R is the equatorial radius of the earth with a value of 6.38×10^6m.

$$g = (6.673 \times 10^{-11}\text{N-m}^2/\text{kg}^2)(5.98 \times 10^{24}\text{kg})/(6.38 \times 10^6\text{m})^2$$
$$g = 9.803495445\text{m/s}^2 = \text{acceleration due to gravity}$$
$$\Rightarrow g = 9.8 \text{ m/s}^2$$

A quantum unit of gravitational force field called, the "graviton" has not yet been discovered.

5)

. . . .

a) Inverse Square Law

This law applies to the intensity of light. Inverse Square Law states that the intensity of a power source is inversely proportional to the square of the distance. Hence the intensity I of a power source P of light or sound or any type of wave at a distance R away from the source is given by the following equation: -

$I = \text{Intensity} = P/A = P/4\pi R^2 = E/tA$

Where $A = 4\pi R^2$ is the total area of the sphere around the source of power and P is the total power of the source of energy.

Note E (energy)/t (time) = P (power) i.e. 1 Joule/second = 1 Watt.

The SI unit of intensity is therefore W/m^2.

Consider two distances R_1 and R_2 from a source of light, then the intensities I_1 and I_2 are given by the following: -

$I_1 = P/4\pi R_1^2$
$I_2 = P/4\pi R_2^2$
$I_2/I_1 = R_1^2/R_2^2$

Hence according to Inverse Square Law, the intensity, I, decreases as the square of the distance from the power source of light or sound or any type of wave.

$\Rightarrow I = P/4\pi R^2$

b) University Terrace Elementary School

The school that my brother, my sister, and I joined, when we arrived in Baton Rouge, Louisiana, during the winter of 1968, was called "University Terrace Elementary School".

I had joined the highest class in that elementary school, which was the sixth grade, my younger sister had joined the fifth grade, and our youngest brother had joined the third grade.

We used to take our own lunch boxes and we purchased our own milk from the vending machine, which had been installed close to the school cafeteria.

We were very fortunate about attending a great school in the USA. My class teacher was a white American. He used to take all the classes in a single class room which was assigned to all the sixth graders. All class work and most of the school activities took place in that same old class room which had been allocated to all the sixth graders.

We soon mastered math and science. We also read history and literature. In our spare time, we even learned how to sing when our music teacher, who had been appointed for the whole school, made a round of our class rooms, at least once in a fortnight.

We were very young in those days. It had seemed to us, life will continue forever without end. Time seemed to have been an insignificant parameter.

We were forever and the world, we had lived in, was forever. There had been no issues (big or small) involved in our lives, in those days when we were attending school at a very young age.

But our stars seemed to have been in charge of our young and pathetic lives. Change is the tradition of this unfortunate world. The world had been destined to change, once again.

Once, during recess hour, I had a fight with a fat school kid. He almost defeated me in wrestling that morning because I had slight nausea. Those were good old school days and the fights that we had, did not matter because we were delinquents.

We passed our examinations with a list of straight A's in our report cards, and I was also awarded a "Courtesy Award" as a gesture of good will by the school.

We left Baton Rouge, Louisiana, in the winter of 1970 only to be despised by jealous relatives and friends but we came back exactly ten years later, in the winter of the year 1980, after having graduated from a university with a degree in Theoretical and Applied Physics.

6)

. . . .

a) The Memoirs of a Physicist

The Friend's Colony was well developed and was situated close to the university campus in a town called Aligarh. The people living in Friend's Colony were mostly retired and senior most professors. Some graduating and undergraduating students had also lived there as desperate boarders.

Some professors liked to call that community as Friend's Colony because the people living up there were supposedly friendly and brotherly.

Right in the back of the boundaries of Friend's Colony laid the Farmers' village. It was an undeveloped village. The houses in this village were made of mud and clay and no really good construction had taken place up there.

The Friend's colony was a pleasant area to live in. We lived at 4/582 Friend's Colony. This was our house number. It was situated right behind Professor Ansari's lodge but within the development, that was called Friend's Colony.

The boundaries of our house were, somewhat, triangular when we had moved in. Then a time came when I talked to the farmers in the village, from whom we had bought the land at the very beginning, about buying more farmland to bring in symmetry to our property and change the triangular shape of our land into a rectangular piece of land.

It didn't take much effort to convince them to agree on selling their piece of farmland to us. We soon bought the land and had a beautiful boundary around our house.

One night, I remember, we were sleeping in our veranda when a storm had hit our house. That night we had slept comfortably without anything to worry about but the next morning when we woke up we found that our boundary had fallen down and we had been exposed to the whole outside world right from our backyard. This had happened during a summer night of an academic year.

Then we had to rebuild our boundary and so building construction took place at 4/582 Friend's Colony.

We had a big water tank right at the top of the roof of our house and had the pleasure of enjoying running water. We even had a hand pump in our backyard where our maid servant did our laundry for us.

The janitor came everyday to clean up our house. The cook always washed the dishes and prepared meals for us.

We enjoyed life a lot at Friend's Colony. We had a slide projector that we had bought from the USA. We even had a movie projector and we had a red Volkswagen, Station Wagon, parked in our garage that my parents had imported from Europe.

One morning, my brother was in a strange mood. He left the house in the early morning hours and came back a little before sunset. When we asked him where he had been, all day, he had a long story to narrate about his dangerous and arduous journey into the woods. He told us he had been to the countryside and that he had fired at a mad buffalo there with his rifle to save the lives of the villagers. It was a long story in which he had narrated his adventures, how he had interacted with those illiterate country folks, and how he was able to escape from those rural dwellings.

One sad day, one of my relatives in a nearby town had died and we were having a religious conference on her behalf. Many neighbors were invited to come and attend the conference. This took place, probably during the summer season, of late 1970s.

The neighbors attended the conference and then refreshments were served to everyone and snacks were handed out in small bags.

The neighbors were overjoyed, and they became gratified and they left with spiritual contentment.

We had a big lawn in front of our house that we used to spray water with a water sprinkler during summer holidays. The water sprinkler was one of the things that we were able to purchase from the Downtown Shopping Plaza in Aligarh. We once had tried to purchase an electric shaver but the shop keepers up there made fun of us and we never thought about buying it again. It was available; they were just not familiar with the term, "electric shaver".

Our house was like a tourist attraction spot. Many senior most professors and many retired professors and their families and many newly wedded married couples, living in our neighborhood, came to visit our house when we were just about to leave that country and come to the United States.

We lived at 4/582 Friend's Colony and close to our backyard was a newly established Dairy. During early hours of the morning after Morning Prayer we used to go there to buy a whole carton of milk.

Life had seemed so pleasant in Friend's Colony. It was so calm and quite up there and we were able to relax and take a nap any time of the day without any kind of interruptions.

b) The Prehistoric Monkey

The monkey is man's only friend in the wild. The monkey is probably the only friendly and brother like creature in the wild.

The monkeys eat from the topmost branches of trees. The monkeys do not roar or make an obnoxious sound.

The monkeys are the most divine of all creatures that live in the wild. If one desires to communicate with the wild life, monkeys would serve as good specimens. The monkeys eat nectar and they also eat dandruff from the old woman's head. The monkeys drink from the clean covered pots arranged in an orderly fashion.

The monkeys seem to be our only link with prehistoric times. The dear monkey seems to have missed a compartment of a train of time. The monkeys are our only link with our prehistoric ancestors.

May God bless the intelligent, the modest, the friendly, the beautiful, divinely and spiritually motivated, very lovely, quite romantic, and the most perfect and upright monkey. Amen.

The monkey is the only wild life creature who shows signs of human intelligence and fortunately these monkeys are not an endangered forest wildlife species. These prehistoric monkeys support scientific evidence that evolution did take place in mankind, as man evolved from primitive ape like monkeys.

7)

. . . .

a) The Pursuit of Happiness

A person always feels great about being happy. It is divinely ordained.

So, when a person is happy, he is just fortunate that he is happy.

Happiness is not about precious possessions and it is not about a sound and a healthy mind. It is something the angel writes down in one's destiny at the time one is about to come into this world as a living homosapien.

So, when we are involved in pursuing happiness, we are only invoking destiny to become kind to us and bring forth what it has already divinely ordained for us.

If happiness is not divinely ordained, the pursuit of happiness will be a futile attempt to attain happiness, even if one tried hard enough.

So, happiness is divinely ordained and it is something the heavens write down in one's destiny when one is about to have a birth in the material world.

Happiness, therefore, is spiritual. It pertains to the spiritual world rather than the material world.

b) The Thundering Clouds

It's raining, it's pouring. The sky seems to have become overburdened with thundering clouds.

The sight of the rain drops and the busy street is quite a phenomenon to behold. It's extremely damp out there, with privately owned automobiles passing by on the roads.

The rain drops do not allow you even a moment's rest. It's as hectic as ever down here and the streets are crowded with wet and fuming people.

The raindrops create a melody of an immortal existence, the immortality that's an arm's length away while it's raining. The rain drops are from the thundering clouds in the sky up above.

During summer season, when it rains at night, it seems the whole world is dancing before our eyes with rhythm of immortality.

A cool breeze of freshly scented air in summer and warm rain are the phenomena of nature that I like a lot. I am also very fond of taking a shower in the warm water of the rain during summer.

8)

· ·

a) The Friendship

We may have big issues in life, within our own community, which we may resolve only through politics or an intimate friendship.

Friendships are developed to research upon the romantic aspects of a human being's intellectual instincts.

Friends do provide one another the apparatus for researching on the lovely and romantic aspects of the development of their youth.

Friendship is a great commitment of life and it is also a great pursuit of happiness. It is a commitment of life, full of innovations and also a desire to fulfill certain challenging ambitions in life, together.

Friendship is a social relationship which is based on patience, trust and loyalty. It encourages cooperation between the two loyal and intimate friends.

Love that we share as friends is of the highest order because it is a concept which has a deeper meaning than anything else in the whole wide world. It is not an obligation and it does not demand forfeiture or a relinquishment.

b) The Entertainment Industry

The entertainment industry keeps on scattering all over the surface of the planet Earth, and spreading, and expanding throughout the world like a de-escalating world war without any signs of a peaceful outcome.

Life would seem dull and quite monotonous without entertainment. We do not discourage entertainers. As a matter of fact, we do not discourage any individual in any profession, business, or trade.

But we are out of funds and have no extra capital to pay them. We, however, do not wish to discourage them but at the same time we also want our peace of mind. Silence, no doubt, is golden, but it is a concept that has been missing from us.

Let the entertainers entertain the audience and make their living if that's what they wish to do. Life would seem dull and quite monotonous without entertainment but some guys just cannot afford entertainment. We, however, do not wish to discourage them but at the same time, we want to keep our integrity.

For our own involvement in social community matters, we sometimes, try to have a hobby, like a coin collection or a stamp collection. To keep ourselves occupied we play games. We also read the daily newspaper, weeklies, and sometimes we read the comic section to keep ourselves entertained.

Sometimes for the sake of joining the mainstream of national life, we buy membership of a club or an association. We meet new acquaintances and join certain reputable organizations to keep ourselves occupied.

So the world keeps spinning around on its axis and it never really gets that monotonous and gloomy around here. Entertainment and occupation are part of the fun that we have in living together.

I do not wish to persuade the entertainment industry or people having other occupations in life to quit their federal jobs and excuse us from the burden of spending huge sums of money on trifle matters.

I do not mind spending money when it is available and I hope I am not too miserly about spending little of my income on entertainment and other types of recreation. Money must, most certainly, be safely deposited for the well-being of the future generations. The money must not be allowed to become a disastrous toy in the hands of an insincere, unfaithful, immoral, and corrupt faculty of mindless delinquents.

9)

a) My Sensitive Immune System

I am a man of an extremely sensitive body and mind, and my immune system is not efficient enough. I easily become unbalanced. I cannot live on a farm in the country side, where epidemic infection is on the rampage. I cannot live in an unpleasant environment. My immune system is wanting in many ways and that adds to my sensitive mind and delicate body. I am also sensitive to most medicines and hospitals because these stink of dying and decaying human bodies and corpses. If I were persuaded by my senior colleagues to live in an undeveloped village, I would probably die before anyone found out about it. I cannot conform to the idea of being exiled to a country, where animals roam about without a leash. I cannot conform to the idea of relishing a lot of cooked and garnished old fashioned food catered and served in birthday parties and wedding parties. I cannot conform to the idea of being in the company of big, overweight, and obese people. These strange and peculiar manifestations and interruptions in life make me extremely unbalanced, exhausted, and extremely starving and spoil my taste. These unnatural disturbing manifestations in life also give me nightmares and I wind-up with nausea, with my head spinning like a cyclotron, completely devastated. I have the physiology of a man and not the physiology of a prehistoric ape or a monster from outer space. I am not much of a youth. I am more like a brain wave, that is, an influence on the minds of my colleagues. In spite of my weak and unique immune system and my sensitive body, I'm an advocate of radical reform and I have a strong mind and even a stronger heart. I like to accept the challenges of life and confront the dangers that are involved therein all by myself. In other words, I am good at remedying my own social upheavals.

b) The Dream

The experience of dreaming is actually a live experience, in which you are able to gaze deep into the cosmic space.

The dream portrays before you a live scene of the deep outer space and it's a phenomenon much similar to the one that occurs in an optical observatory, where an astronomer tries to goggle deep into outer space through his giant telescope.

The human mind that materializes the sensation of dreaming is like an optical observatory, in which deep outer space is extended unobstructed, before the visionary eyes of the person who is dreaming.

Through a dream, you are able to tour the most amazing and wonderful of the worlds that exist in the universe. Through a dream, you may actually visit the dwellings of the most fascinating and the most astonishing personalities of the universe in deep outer space because space exists in our imagination also.

Dreaming is a human experience in which the planet earth and the heavenly space are brought together, dimensionally encountered by the dreamer, as in a vision. Dreams are not always good and evil, they are astronomical also, and that is, they are scientific and mathematical.

10)

. . . .

a) The Barometer

Whether it is over the ground or in the sky up above, the pressure keeps rising up. The barometer determines the atmospheric pressure, which is the standard one atmosphere. The standard temperature is 273.15 K. At standard temperature and pressure one mole of every Ideal gas occupies 22.4 litters by volume, according to the Ideal Gas Law, which is given below:-

$\Rightarrow PV = n \, RT$

Note P, V, and T are the pressure, volume, and the temperature of the ideal gas, and R is the Universal Gas Constant with a value of R $= 8.314472J/$ (mol. K), and n is the number of moles of the ideal gas present, and 1 liter $= 10^{-3} \, m^3$.

The weather is reported with the help of a barometer, which is an instrument for measuring atmospheric pressure, where one atmosphere is given by $P_0 = 1.013 \times 10^5$ Pascal or Newton per square meter. Inside the water, the absolute pressure P is related to the gauge pressure $P - P_0$ as follows: -

$\Rightarrow P - P_0 = \rho gh =$ gauge pressure

$\Rightarrow P = P_0 + \rho gh =$ absolute pressure

Note $\rho = 1 \times 10^3 \, kg/m^3$ is the density of water, $g = 9.8 m/s^2$ is the acceleration due to gravity and h is the depth of water in meters.

The metereologists depend a lot on the barometer for their weather report.

The Navigational Compass

The navigational compass is all what we need, to find the direction to our own friend's house of horrifying nightmares.

The navigational compass is a reality not perceived, like a kite flying at our uncle's feet.

The directions and angles are all measured beneath our eyes, as soon as a navigational compass comes in handy.

At the Magnetic Equator, however, the dipping needle has no inclination and lies horizontal because the attraction of the Magnetic North Pole is the same as the attraction of the Magnetic South Pole.

Mankind is weak. They cannot face the calamities of nature on their own. They rely on the blunders made by their own hands.

Navigational compass is all what we need, to find the friend we have lost during our long journey of life through a memory beguiling maze of a 4-dimensional space-time continuum.

b) The Global Positioning System (GPS)

When you are driving your car at night or in the day, and you've lost your way, GPS (Global Positioning System) comes to your assistance. Global positioning system is a breakthrough in satellite communication technology and you are able to receive instructions on how to follow directions in order to arrive at your car's destination.

The kinetic energy of the car is given by the equation:

Kinetic Energy $= (1/2)\ mv^2$

Note that m is the mass of the car and v is the velocity of the car.

The velocity of the radio wave is the product of its frequency and wavelength. It is an electromagnetic wave and has a velocity of C = 299,792,458 m/sec. in vacuum space.

The car is not a UFO (unidentified flying objects) flying at the speed of light. The speed of the car is so slow, compared to the speed of light, that relativistic effects do not play any role.

Now the car is a man-size object and quantum effects are not applied. In other words, the size of the car is so big, compared to the size of the atomic and sub-atomic particles, that quantum considerations are not applicable.

There are several satellites and several radio-stations and you are in contact with the system on a one on one basis.

There are numerous frequencies and numerous wavelengths of electromagnetic radio-waves on which the system works.

There is a representative standing by who is ground-based and with him you are in contact through the satellite system.

This representative is able to communicate to you how to arrive at your car's destination.

Hence science and technology are rapidly coming to everybody's assistance during nights as well as during day light hours.

11)

. . . .

a) The Ranga Billa Kidnapping Case

The Ranga Billa Kidnapping Case was a notorious crime in New Delhi in 1978. Two teenagers, Geeta and Sanjay Chopra, were kidnapped by two young boys, Ranga Khus (Kuljeet Singh) and Billa (Jasbir Singh), who planned to demand ransom from the parents of the teenagers. Their plan went awry when the car they were in was involved in a traffic accident with a public bus. They subsequently murdered the teenagers and fled from Delhi. They were arrested in a train a few months later, tried, and hanged for the crime, in 1982. The crime was an important psychological turning point for residents of Delhi in changing their perceptions of living in a reasonably safe city to one of living with crime.

The Kidnapping: - The teenagers were reported missing on 26 August, 1978 and their bodies were discovered on 29 August, 1978. It later transpired that they had been kidnapped while asking for a ride from outside Gol Dak Khana near Connaught Place.

The Trial: - Both culprits were found guilty and the court gave death sentence to them. Both were hanged later on.

Aftermath: - In 1978, the Indian Council for Child Welfare instituted two bravery awards for children under age 16, the Sanjay Chopra Award, and Geeta Chopra Award given each year along with National Bravery Award. The Janta Party, which was the ruling party in New Delhi, was defeated in 1978 elections, partly because of its handling of the Ranga Billa Kidnapping Case.

b) Short Sightedness and Far Sightedness

A far sighted (hyperopic) person can usually see distant objects clearly but cannot focus on those nearby, whereas the near point of a young and normal eye is located about 25 cm from the eye, the near point of a far sighted eye may be considerably farther away than that, perhaps as far as several hundred centimeters. When a far sighted person focuses on a book held closer than the near point it accommodates and shortens its focal length as much as it can. However, even at its shortest, the focal length is larger than it should be. Therefore the light rays from the book would form a sharp image behind the retina if they could so. In reality no light passes through the retina, but a blurred image does form on it.

Far sightedness can be corrected by placing a converging lens (convex lens) in front of the eye. The lens refracts the light rays more towards the principal axis before they enter the eye. Consequently when the rays are refracted even more by the eye, they converge to form an image on the retina.

Suppose the far sighted person has a near point at 125cm from the eyes. The focal length of a converging lens in a pair of contacts that can be used to read a book held 25cm from the eyes will be:

$1/f = 1/d_o + 1/d_i = 1/25 + 1/(-125) = 4/125$

This implies $f = 125/4$ cm = 31.25cm

Similarly the refractive power of a lens (in diopters) is the reciprocal of the focal length (in meters).

This implies $1/f$ (in meters) = the refractive power of a lens in units of diopters.

$1 diopter = 1/(f = 1meter)$

A person who is near sighted (myopic) can focus on nearby objects but cannot clearly see objects far away. For such a person the far point of the eye is not at infinity and may even be as close to the eye as three or four hundred centimeters. When a near sighted eye tries to focus on a distant object, the eye is fully relaxed like a normal eye. However the near sighted eye has a focal length that is shorter than it should be. So rays from a distant object form a sharp image in front of the retina and blurred vision results.

The near sighted eye can be corrected with glasses or contacts that use diverging lens (concave lens). The rays from the object diverge after leaving the eye-glass lens. They are subsequently refracted toward the principal axis by the eye. A sharp image forms further back and falls on the retina.

Suppose a near sighted person has a far point located 603cm from the eye. Assuming the eye glasses are to be worn 3cm in front of the eyes, the focal length for the diverging lens of the glasses, so that the person can see distant objects would be:

$1/f = 1/d_o + 1/d_i = 1/\alpha + 1/(-600) = -1/600$

This implies $f = -600$cm

The value of f (the focal length) is negative as expected for a diverging lens.

In traversing the complex structure of the eyes, a ray of light encounters cornea, pupil, lens, and finally vitreous humour.

12)

· ·

a) The Banner like Spectrum of Visible Light

Behold, a banner like spectrum of visible light has been exploited in the present day modern scientific world.

The seven colors of the visible spectrum of solar radiation which are violet, indigo, blue, green, yellow, orange, and red have been split asunder as a consequence of the dispersion of light through a prism.

The spectrum of visible light begins after ultraviolet region and continues till infrared region of the spectrum of electromagnetic radiation.

The seven colors of the visible light in the spectrum of electromagnetic radiation have distinct frequencies and distinct wavelengths.

The visible spectrum of light begins with 4×10^{14} Hz and continues till 7.9×10^{14} Hz of frequencies or their wavelengths lie between 750nm and 380nm, respectively.

Hence a panorama of the seven colors of the visible spectrum of light has become an essential component in the overdeveloped mechanics of the present day scientifically advancing and rapidly developing modern world. It's but a small world and all men are created equal without regard to color, creed, caste or national origin.

b) Half-lives for Radio-active Decay

We define half-life $T_{1/2}$ of a radioactive isotope as the time required for one-half of the nuclei present to disintegrate. For example the half life of Radon $^{222}_{86}Rn$ is 3.83 days, the half-life of Radium $^{226}_{88}Ra$ is 1.6×10^3 years, and the half-life of Uranium $^{238}_{92}U$ is 4.47×10^9 years. The activity is the number of disintegrations per second that occur. Activity is the magnitude of $\Delta N/\Delta t$, where ΔN is the change in the number N of the nuclei present and Δt is time interval during which the change occurs. Activity is therefore $|\Delta N/\Delta t|$. The SI unit of activity is bacquerel (Bq), 1 bacquerel being equal to 1 disintegration per second.

Radio-active decay obeys the following relation: -

$\Delta N/\Delta t = -\lambda N$

In the above equation λ is the decay constant. This equation can be solved by the method of integral calculus to show that the following equation holds: -

$N = N_0 e^{-\lambda t}$

In this equation N_0 is the original number of nuclei. The decay constant λ is related to the half-life $T_{1/2}$ according to the following equation: -

$\lambda = 0.693/T_{1/2}$

Example

In 6 days, the number of radioactive nuclei decreases to one-fourth the number present initially. What is the half-life (in days) of the material?

Solution: -

$N = N_0 e^{-\lambda t}$

$\Rightarrow N/N_0 = e^{-\lambda t}$

$\Rightarrow 1/4 = e^{-\lambda \times 6}$

Taking natural log of both sides of the equation, we arrive at the following relation: -

$\lambda = \ln 4/6 = 1.386294361/6 = 0.23104906$

$\Rightarrow T_{1/2} = \ln 2/\lambda = 0.693147181/ 0.23104906 = 3$ days

$\Rightarrow T_{1/2} = 3$ days

Hence the half-life of the given radio-active material is 3 days.

13)

∙∙∙

a) Tobacco Products

There are five tobacco products that are generally sold in the market. These are viz. (1) cigarettes, (2) cigars, (3) smoking tobacco, (4) chewing tobacco, and finally (5) snuff. More than 80% of the tobacco consumed in the United States is in the form of cigarettes.

All tobacco used in cigars is air cured and is classified according to its use in the cigar as filler, binder or wrapper. The filler is used to make the core of the cigar; the binder is wrapped around the filler to give shape to the cigar. A reconstituted tobacco sheet (made from powdered tobacco that is wetted and formed into flat sheets) is often used as a less expensive substitute for natural binders. Most cigars and cigarettes are produced by machines.

Smoking tobacco mostly refers to the pipe tobacco but it is also used for hand rolled cigarettes. Most smoking tobacco is treated with materials that prevent loss of moisture and contribute to mildness and aroma. All types of tobacco can be used in making chewing tobacco. There are four principle kinds of manufactured chewing tobacco viz. (1) plug, (2) twist, (3) fine cut, and (4) scrap.

Snuff is a tobacco that has been ground into fine powder. At one time, snuff was sniffed through the nostrils and its use was considered the mark of a gentleman. Currently, however, snuff accounts for the smallest percentage of tobacco products. Snuff is made primarily from fire cured tobacco. There are many forms of snuff, including plain, toasted, and sweet.

Various Brands of American Cigarettes

1. Alternative Cigarettes: -Brands: - Glory, Herbal Gold, Lewiston, Magic, and Pure.
2. Brown and Williamson Tobacco: -Brands: - American, Barclay, Belair, Capri, Carlton, GPC, Herbert Tareyton, Kool, Lucky Strike, Misty, Pall Mall, Prime, Private Stock,

Raleigh, Raleigh Extra, Richmond, Silva Thins, State Express, Summit, Tall, Tareyton, and Viceroy.

3. Commonwealth Brands: - Crown, Malibu, Montclair, Natural Blend, Riviera, Sonoma, and USA Gold.

4. Cig Tec Tobacco: -Brand: - CT

5. Farmer's Tobacco: -Brand: - Kentucky's

6. Forsyth Tobacco Products: - Brands: - Austin, Bargain Buy, Beacon, Best Choice, Best Value, Brentwood, Cavalier, Charter, Cimarron, Citation, Courier, Director's Choice, Extra Value, First Choice, Focus, Gold Coast, Highway, Jacks, Legend, Marker, Monaco, Mustang, Pilot, Premier, Price Master, Quality Smokes, Scotch Buy, Sebring, Signature, Slim Price, Smoke 1, Smoker Friendly, Stockton, Sundance, Tempo, Tri Brand, Value Time, Value Quality, Value Pride, Value Sense, Worth.

7. Liggett Group Inc. Brands: - Class 'A', Eve, Epic, Kinsport, Liggett, Meridian, Pyramid, Omni, Sincerely Yours, and Yours. (Chesterfield, L&M, and Lark were sold to Philip Morris)

8. Lignum – 2 Inc. Brand: - Rave.

9. Lorillard: - Brands: - Kent, Maverick, Max, Newport, Old Gold, Satin, Triumph, and True.

10. Native Trading Association: -Brand: - Native.

11. Nat Sherman: -Brands: - Black & Gold, Cigarettellos, Classics, Fantasia Lights, Havana Ovals, Hint of Clove, Hint of Mint, MCDs, Naturals, Phantom, Slims, Turkish Ovals, Virginia Circles.

12. Omaha Nation Tobacco: -Brand: - Omaha.

13. Philip Morris Companies: -Brands: - Alpine, Basic, Best Buy, Benson & Hedges, Bristol, Bucks, Cambridge, Chesterfield, Collector's Choice, Commander, English Ovals, Lark, L & M, Marlboro, Merit, Parliament, Players, Saratoga, Super Slims, and Virginia Slims.

14. Premier Marketing: -Brands: - 1st Class and Ultra Buy.

15. R. J. Reynolds: -Brands: - Best Value, Camel, Century, Doral, Magna, Monarch, More, Now, Salem, Sterling, Vantage, and Winston.

16. Santa Fe Natural Tobacco Company: -Brand: - American Spirit.

17. S & M Brands: - Bailey's
18. Seneca Smoke: -Brands: - Seneca
19. Seneca – Cayuga Tobacco: -Brands: - Seneca (Note: - There are two brands called Seneca)
20. Smokin Joes: -Brands: - Exact, Lewiston, and Smokin Joes.
21. Sovereign Tobacco Company: -Brands: - Niagara.
22. Sparrow Maker Natural Technologies: -Brand: - Sparrow.
23. Star Scientific Inc.: -Brands: - G Smoke, Main Street, Sport, and Vegas.
24. Tobacco Holidays: -Brands: - Bridge Port, Calon, Jim Porter.

Narcotics

Narcotics is a drug that in moderate doses causes insensibility, relieves pain, and produces profound sleep but in poisonous doses causes stupor, coma, and convulsions. Several drugs fit this description, and various organizations have somewhat different lists of drugs they identify as narcotics. To physicians, opium and its derivatives (morphine, codeine, heroin, and other opiates) are narcotics. US government agencies also consider as narcotics the drug obtained from coca leaves (especially cocaine) and the synthetic drugs chemically related to the opiates and the coca drug. (The government lists LSD and marijuana as "dangerous drugs" but not as narcotics.)

Narcotics are used in medicine as anodynes to relieve pain, and as hypnotics and soporifics to induce sleep. Some persons use narcotics to use other effects, since small doses tend to make the user forget his troubles, dream beautiful dreams, and experience pleasant sensations. However it is dangerous to take narcotics for pleasure and large doses can be fatal.

Improperly used narcotics are a hazard to the health of the user and to society because such drugs cause people to become addicted or habituated to them. Chiefly, the body seems to develop a physiological need for the drug. When the addict is unable to get more of it he experiences a severe physical reaction called withdrawal symptom. The opium and cocaine when used with opiates cause addiction. Narcotics can be obtained legally with a prescription for medicine or with a license for manufacture of medicine.

b) Philosophy or Metaphysics

Philosophy is a discipline all by itself. It is not only the discipline but the very concept of being an academic discipline.

It is the study of the concepts of being, knowing, cause, identity, time, and space. Furthermore it is the study of the fundamental nature of knowledge, reality, and existence.

Philosophy is the study of the vastness of the universe as well as the study of the state of timelessness, which is, eternity.

Philosophy is also termed, "meta-physics", by certain enlightened academia of intellectuals.

Philosophy strives to combine and generalize the concepts that pertain to the gigantic world of the macrocosm and the tiny world of the microcosm.

Philosophy is the study of the microcosm, the macrocosm and it is also the study of a general concept obtained by inference from these specific cases.

Hence metaphysics is the philosophy of the concepts of being, knowing, cause, identity, time, and space and philosophy is the study of the fundamental nature of knowledge, reality, and existence, as an academic discipline.

14)

. . . .

a) The Illuminating Candles

Candles are made of wax and when these are lighted they burn, converting the wax that these are composed of, into carbon dioxide and water.

Candles are lighted at night and these illuminate the whole house. When the lights go out and there is a power failure, candles are found very convenient to use.

During stormy nights, when there is heavy rain with gusty winds and sometimes snow and when there is lightening, bolts, and thunder, the candles come in practical use because there is a power cut. Candles are used to light up the whole house, including the bed rooms, living room, family room, dining room, kitchen, hall ways, as well as the powder room.

Sometimes candles are used at night to read love letters and other private messages by lightening them up with a match light.

When there are guests at night and you are playing a certain game of cards with them, candles illuminate your table during a power cut which may be due to a stormy weather.

You may illuminate the whole environment by burning candles with a match light.

b) The Drinking Fountain Water

The drinking fountain water is a blessing of God. It functions like an enzyme, assisting in the digestion of food, in the process of digestion. It is the most common way of extinguishing an aggravating thirst. The drinking water quenches thirst and it is not an intoxicant and has no side effects. After drinking water one may take a short nap or sleep for long hours without having nightmares. The drinking fountain water induces sleep without making you feel drowsy. On a hot and dry summer day, it is vital that one take small amounts of cold drinking water. It relieves man of anguish and pain and curtails his abnormal behavior and clears away his confounded head of misconceptions and misunderstandings when he feels stressed and tired and is not in his right mind during a hot and a dry summer day.

The drinking fountain water also relieves man of anxiety that may be associated with certain financial deadlock in his family because intoxicants cost a lot of money and we are here to avoid all kinds of intoxications. It also enhances love and affection. It has never been the cause for a broken heart or a broken friendship. It does not cause madness or prejudice or envy or a fit of anger or a desire to hurt one's best friend. Actually the drinking fountain water does not cause evil human notions, like hate, envy, or prejudice, to become apparent in one's life. It does not drive a man crazy. It is blessed and promulgates goodness in mankind and frees mankind of evil human desires, like lust. It is a valuable commodity which suits most mankind. All praises are due to God who showers such wonderful blessings upon mankind and his environment. Long live the wonderful rain forests, and long live the endangered forest wildlife species, whose survival also depends on good clean spring water.

15)

. . . .

a) The Transfer of Heat

There are precisely three ways by which heat is transferred from one place to another and these are referred to as convection, conduction, and radiation, respectively. One point which should be clear is the fact that heat flows from a hot region to a cold region. We shall now approach convection, conduction, and radiation, sequentially.

Convection

Convection is the process in which heat is carried from place to place by the bulk movement of a fluid.

During natural convection, the warmer, less dense part of a fluid is pushed upward by the buoyant force provided by the surrounding cooler and denser part.

Forced convection occurs when an external device, such as a fan or a pump, causes the fluid to move.

The amount of heat energy a substance gains or loses is given by the following expression: -

$Q = C m (\Delta T)$

Note Q is the amount of heat gained or lost by a substance; c is the specific heat capacity of a substance, defined as the amount of heat required to raise the temperature of 1g of a substance through 1°C, (eg. $C = 4186 J/kg.C^0$ or $1 kcal/kg.C^0$ or $1 cal/g.C^0$ for water); m is the mass of the substance; and ΔT is the difference between initial and final temperatures.

Conduction

Conduction is the process whereby heat is transferred directly through a material, with any bulk motion of the material playing no role in the transfer.

Materials that conduct heat well, such as most metals, are known as thermal conductors. Materials that conduct heat poorly, such as wood, glass, and most plastics, are referred to as thermal insulators.

The heat Q conducted during a time t through a bar of length L and cross-sectional area A is given by the expression: -

$$Q = (kA\Delta T)t / L$$

Now ΔT is the temperature difference between the ends of the bar and k is the thermal conductivity of the material.

Radiation

Radiation is the process in which energy is transferred by means of electromagnetic waves.

All objects, regardless of their temperature, simultaneously absorb and emit electromagnetic waves. Objects that are good absorbers of radiant energy are also good emitters, and objects that are poor absorbers are also poor emitters.

An object that absorbs the entire radiation incident upon it is called a perfect blackbody. A perfect blackbody, being a perfect absorber, is also a perfect emitter.

The radiant energy Q emitted during a time t by an object whose surface area is A and whose Kelvin temperature is T is given by the Stefan-Boltzmann law of radiation as follows:-

$$Q = e\sigma T^4 At$$

Now $\sigma = 5.67 \times 10^{-8} J/(s.m^2.K^4)$ is the Stefan-Boltzmann constant and e is the emissivity, a dimensionless number characterizing the surface of the object. The emissivity lies between 0 and 1, being zero for non-emitting surface and one for a perfect blackbody.

The net radiant power is the power an object emits minus the power it absorbs. The net radiant power P_{net} emitted by an object of temperature T located in an environment of temperature T_0 is given by the expression: -

$$P_{net} = e\sigma A (T^4 - T_0^4)$$

Hence the three agencies through which heat is transferred from one place of a hot region to another place of cold region viz. convection, conduction, and radiation have been meticulously elaborated.

b) Hobby

Hobby is almost anything that a person likes to do in his spare time. Almost everyone wants to make things, do things, learn things, or collect things. Hobbies bring pleasure to people because they satisfy their wants.

There are almost as many hobbies as there are interests in the world. Occupation at which some people earn a living may be leisure – time activities to other. Some hobbies cost almost nothing while others are expensive. Some call for a great deal of activity while others are suitable for hospital patients. Since almost any human interest can become a hobby, everyone, rich or poor, sick or well, young or old can enjoy a hobby.

Generally, a hobby selects itself, that is, a person encounters an activity that he finds interesting and pursues it further. Such activities may grow out of a person's occupation or school work, or may be totally unrelated. The best way to find a hobby is to expose oneself to a variety of activities. Organizations, such as YMCA or YWCA, school clubs, summer camps, park districts, senior citizen councils at community centers offer activities that arouse interests. Libraries and museums also encourage pursuit of hobbies. These organizations publish pamphlets and encourage interests. Certain organizations often sponsor shows or conventions to arouse interests in people in picking a hobby.

16)

. . . .

a) Nawab Ali Yavar Jung (A National Administrator)

Ali Javar Jung (February, 1906 – December, 1976) was an eminent administrator of India. He was governor of Maharashtra from 1971 to 1976. He studied at Queen's College, Oxford and thereafter at Paris in 1927.

He served as the Vice Chancellor of the Osmania University from 1945 to 1946 and again from 1948 to 1952. Thereafter he served as Indian ambassador to Argentina 1952 – 54, Egypt 1954 – 58, Yugoslavia 1958 – 61, France 1961 – 65, and the USA 1968 – 70.

He was appointed as Governor of Maharashtra state in 1971. He was born in Hyderabad and died serving as governor at Raj Bhavan, Mumbai in December, 1976.

He was awarded the Padma Bhushan in 1956 and the Padma Vibhushan in 1977. The stretch of the Mumbai – Ahmadabad Highway (NH 8, commonly called "Western Express Highway") in the suburb of Bandra in Mumbai and The National Institute for the Hearing Handicapped located up there are named after him.

b) The Plane Mirror and the Curved Mirrors

The plane mirror reflects your image, like your cousin, greeting you with a salutation, from the top of your balcony.

The plane mirror is like a remarkable high school science project and it is quite phenomenal in beauty and elegance.

The reflection from a plane mirror is an echo of our own image.

It is quite like a sea farer who has not arrived at his destination yet, and he still has miles to cover.

The reflections from a plane mirror are an obstacle in the path to freedom, like a generalist, who has ominously defected from his freedom high sounding democratic republic.

The radiance through a plane mirror is an imprisonment of our own personality, like Commerce Bank declaring bankruptcy.

The real images that can be viewed on a screen are formed by concave mirrors and also by convex or converging lenses and the virtual images that only appear to come from at a distance are formed by concave as well as convex mirrors. The virtual images are also formed by concave and convex lenses. The convex mirror and the concave lens, also called a diverging lens, form only virtual images. The image that the plane mirror reflects is a virtual image because it appears to come from behind the mirror. The virtual image, which we see in the plane mirror, however, is a case of mind over matter, that has held mankinds fascination since time immemorial and it became a good excuse for beholding your own silly reflection. The plane mirror does not reflect my best intellectual panorama but it is rather essential and is a junction where the imagination and the reality meet each other. May the blessed mirror guide all humankind to become more organized, civilized, vigilant, and disciplined?

17)

. . . .

a) Himalayan Mountains

Himalaya Mountain is a mountain range extending 1500 miles on the border between India and Tibet, the world's highest.

i) Sitsang Thibet, Tibet, Xizang – an autonomous region of the People's Republic of China, located in the Himalayas.

ii) Anapurna, Annapurna – a mountain in the Himalayas in Nepal (26,500 feet high).

iii) Changtzu – a mountain in the central Himalayas on the border of Tibet and Nepal (24,780 feet high)

iv) Daulagiri – a mountain in the Himalayas in Nepal (26,820 feet high)

v) Everest, Mt. Everest – a mountain in the central Himalayas on the border of Tibet and Nepal; the highest mountain peak in the world (29,028 feet high)

vi) Gosainthan – a mountain in the Himalayas in Tibet (26,290 feet high)

vii) Kamet – a mountain in the Himalayas in northern India (25,450 feet high)

viii) Mount Kanchenjunga – a mountain in the Himalayas on the border between Nepal and Tibet (28,208 feet high).

ix) Lhotse – a mountain in the central Himalayas on the border of Tibet and Nepal (27,890 feet high)

x) Makalu – a mountain in the Himalayas in Nepal (27,790 feet high)

xi) Nanda Devi – a mountain in the Himalayas in northern India (25,660 feet high)

xii) Nanga Parbat – a mountain in the Himalayas in Kashmir (26,660 feet high)

xiii) Nuptse – a mountain in central Himalayas on the border of Tibet and Nepal (25,726 feet high)

b) Time, a Paradox

The time has no physical existence of its own. It is regarded as something that happens in the three dimensional space. The motion of heavenly bodies in space causes time to happen as a consequence of their motion, which is relativistic. By relativistic, we mean it may happen at a quicker pace for one person compared to a second person in a different inertial frame of reference in the four-dimensional world.

When heavenly bodies, like the earth, move in space, nights and days are fashioned due to their relative positions in space at different intervals. Various seasons, which are generally longer than a day, like those on Earth, pass by in succession, again due to the relative positions of planets, satellites, and other heavenly bodies in space, which are in continuous relative motion to one another. Hence we see a link between space and motion. When nights and days alternate and the seasons change, the human mind becomes conscious of a fourth dimension in the universe and this fourth dimension is time, which is in consequence of motion.

Hence the universe is a four dimensional space-time continuum. The space itself is three dimensional, (x, y, and z-axes), and the motion of material objects in space causes a fourth dimension, which is a physical parameter, to predominate. This fourth dimension is time, a relativistic phenomenon.

In this passage, I would briefly like to quote Einstein. According to Einstein, "One of the most beautiful and one of the most profound emotions one can comprehend is the sensation of the mystical".

According to a psychiatrist, one may interpret time as a form of emotion which causes the eyes of a young virgin to dance with joy, as she contemplates the prospect of becoming a bride. According to the scientist, time is the phenomenon of the transformation of matter into energy, given by $E = mc^2$. When a material object of mass m travels in the void of space at the velocity of light c, it is transformed into energy of magnitude E in the equation $E = mc^2$. The time may also be regarded as an increase in the entropy of the universe i.e. randomness because this phenomenon also pertains to time, like in the Big Bang Theory, according to which, the universe had a definite beginning in a cataclysmic event, sometimes called the "Primeval Fireball".

Now one second, which is a unit of time, is the time it takes a ray of light to travel 2.99792458×10^8 m through the vacuum of space.

Furthermore it is the fourth dimension besides the x, y, and z-dimensions of space and it is again a phenomenon which is relativistic. When an object travels through the void of space at a velocity v which is close to the constant velocity of light c, the time dilation equation is given as follows: -

$$\Delta t = \Delta t_0 / \sqrt{[1 - v^2/c^2]}$$

Note that Δt_0 is the proper time interval for the astronaut in space and Δt is the dilation of time which means lengthening of time for an observer on earth, as the spacecraft travels deep into the void of space at a velocity v close to the constant velocity of light c, in vacuum. To experience, an adequate amount of relativity in deep outer space at a speed close to the speed of light does not seem feasible. This, however, is called the relativity of time.

18)

∙∙

a) Elasticity and Modulus of Elasticity

The modulus of elasticity is defined as follows: -
Stress/Strain = constant (i.e. modulus of elasticity)

$$F/A = Y (\Delta L / L_0)$$
$$F/A = S (\Delta X / X_0)$$
$$\Delta P = - B (\Delta V / V_0)$$
$$\Rightarrow \text{Stress} = \text{constant (Strain)}$$

Note Y, S, and B are called the Young's modulus, Shear modulus, and Bulk modulus of elasticity respectively and may have different constant values for different materials. Note that L_0, X_0, and V_0 are the original length, original surface area, and original volume respectively. Note F is the force, applied to an area A, and F/A is the stress and ΔP is the change in pressure. Note that $\Delta L/L_0$, $\Delta X/X_0$, and $\Delta V/V_0$ are the length strain, area strain, and volume strain respectively. Hence the modulus of elasticity has been defined with the help of symbols.

According to Hooke's Law stress (units N/m^2) eg. F/A, ΔP is directly proportional to strain (a unitless quantity) eg. $\Delta L/L_0$, $\Delta X/X_0$, $\Delta V/V_0$.
$$\Rightarrow \text{Stress /Strain} = \text{Constant}$$

This constant of proportionality is defined as Young's modulus, Shear modulus, and/or Bulk modulus, depending on wheather we are considering length, surface area, or the volume of an object undergoing stretching, compression, and/or deformation.

b) Anti-Matter

Nuclear reactions are of two types. There is fission, in which an atomic particle undergoes decay, and there is fusion, in which two atomic or subatomic particles combine to form a single particle.

In either case, that is fission or fusion, vast amounts of energies are released. Gernally fission releases more energy than fusion.

In a radioactive decay, there is α-decay, β-decay, and γ-decay, besides other kinds of radioactive decay.

In an α-decay helium nuclei which are also called, α-particles, are released. For example, when $^{238}_{92}U$ decays into $^{234}_{90}Th$, $^{4}_{2}He$ (helium nuclei) are released.

In a radio-active β-decay, $^{234}_{90}Th$ decays into $^{234}_{91}Pa$ and $^{0}_{-1}e$. Now $^{0}_{-1}e$ is the β^{-1} particle and is also called the electron.

Sometimes a positron, $^{0}_{1}e$, is released, as a result of β^{+} decay. The Nuclear Proton, $^{A}_{Z}P$, is transformed into a Neutron, $^{A}_{Z-1}D$, and a Positron, $^{0}_{1}e$. Hence Positrons are released.

In a radio-active γ-decay, a photon is emitted. In this γ-decay, the Nucleus, $^{A}_{Z}P^{*}$, changes from an excited energy state to a lower energy state $^{A}_{Z}P$, and γ-ray particles also called photons are released.

Experimentally, however, it is found that most β-particles do not have enough kinetic energy to account for all the energy released. If β-particle carries away only part of the energy, where does the remainder go?

Scientists believe that this remainder of energy is carried away by a particle called Neutrino.

Hence when $^{234}_{90}Th$ decays into $^{234}_{91}Pa$ and $^{0}_{-1}e$, there is also an anti-neutrino that is produced. This Anti-Neutrino ($\boxtimes$) is Anti-Matter.

An Anti-Neutrino has zero electric charge and is extremely difficult to detect, because it interacts very weakly with matter. For example an average Neutrino can penetrate 1 light year (9.5×10^{15}m) of lead without interacting with it.

The emission of Neutrinos and β-particles involves a force, called the Weak Nuclear Force because it is much weaker than Strong Nuclear Force. Now this Weak Nuclear Force and the Electro-magnetic Force are two different manifestations of a single more Fundamental Force, the Electro-Weak Force.

The Theory of Electro-Weak Force has recently been developed by Abdus-Salaam (1926 – 1996), who shared Nobel Prize for his achievement in 1979.

Hence Electro-Weak Force, the Gravitational Force, and the Strong Nuclear Force are the three Fundamental Forces in nature.

19)

··

a) The Gateway of India

The Gateway of India is a monument in Mumbai (formerly Bombay), India. Located on the waterfront in Apollo Bunder area in South Mumbai, the Gateway is a basalt arch, which is 26 m (85 ft) high. It was a crude jetty used by fisher folks and was later renovated and used as a landing place for British governors and other distinguished personages. In earlier times, the Gateway was the monument that visitors arriving by boat would have first seen in the city of Bombay.

Its design is a combination of both Hindu and Muslim architectural styles. The arch is in Muslim style while the decorations are in Hindu style. The Gateway is built from yellow basalt and reinforced concrete. The stone was locally obtained, and the perforated screens were bought from Gwalior.

The central dome is 15 m (49 ft) in diameter and is 26 m (85 ft) above ground at its highest point. The whole harbor front was realigned in order to come in line with a planned esplanade which would sweep down to the center of the town. The cost of the construction was 2.1 million rupees, borne mostly by the government of India. For lack of funds, the approach road was never built, and so the Gateway stands at an angle to the road leading up to it.

History of the Gateway of India

The Gateway of India was built to commemorate the visit of King George V and Queen Mary to Bombay, prior to Delhi Durbar, in December, 1911. The foundation stone was laid on 31 March, 1911, by the Governor of Sydenham Clarkes with the final design of George Wittet sanctioned in August, 1914. Between 1915 and 1919 work proceeded on reclamation of Apollo Bunder (Port) for the land on which the Gateway and the New Sea Wall would be built. The foundation was completed in 1920, and the construction was finished in 1924. The Gateway was opened on 4 December, 1924, by the Viceroy, the Earl of Reading.

Gammon India claims that it did India's first pre-cost reinforced concrete job for the foundation of the Gateway of India.

The last British troops to leave India, the First Battalion of the Somerset Light Infantry, passed through the Gateway in a ceremony on 28 February, 1948.

From here, people can visit Elephanta Caves by ferry boats. There are luxury boats which take visitors around the harbor for a couple of hours. In front of the Gateway of India, there is a statue of Hindu religious significance.

b) Hindustan

In this small passage, we briefly present an account of Kohinoor, a diamond of royal historical significance.

Kohinoor

This royal diamond which had belonged to a royal dynasty, stood for the tremendous powers manifested by the royal dynasty, called the Mongol dynasty.

The royal Mongol dynasty had ruled over the Sultanate of Hindustan for over quarter of a millennium from 1526 till 1857.

Kohinoor was the symbol of vigor and energy with which the Mongol dynasty executed authority and manifested suzerainty upon the sultanate of Hindustan.

The Sultanate of Hindustan had occupied all territory lying between Khyber Pass and the outskirts of the eastern provinces.

The diamond called Kohinoor revives the past, and brings back to the mind, old memories of a lost and forgotten civilization that has become a dazzling fantasy today.

Kohinoor reminds us of the romantic moments of love and affection that we had shared together in the beautiful valley of Hind, which has been called the sultanate of tranquility.

Situated in the heart of Asia, Hindustan is a country of diverse cultures and the following is a brief account of Taj Mahal, one of the Seven Wonders of the World.

Taj Mahal

Taj Mahal is one of the new 7 wonders of the world.

After seven years of campaigning and one hundred million votes received, the results of the global ballet were announced on July 7, 2007, in Lisbon, Portugal during a spectacular gala show in the "Estadio da Luz" in the presence of 50,000 spectators and watched by hundreds of millions of T.V viewers worldwide, the new 7 wonders of the world were revealed:-

1. The Pyramid at Chichen Itza (Pre 800 A.D), Yucatan Peninsula, Mexico.
2. Cristo Rendentor (1931), Rio De Janeiro, Brazil.
3. The Colosseum (A.D 70-82), Rome, Italy.
4. The Great Wall of China, (220 B.C and A.D 1368-1644), China.
5. Machu Picchu (1460-70), Peru.
6. Petra (9 B.C – A.D 40), Jordan
7. The Taj Mahal (A.D 1630), Agra, India.

The Taj Mahal was built in the seventeenth century. It took 20 year's hard labor to fully construct it and about 20,000 royal construction workers had worked very hard to complete it.

The Taj Mahal is a tomb made of white marble stone. It was built by a Mogul king named Shah Jahan, in loving memory of his beloved wife Mumtaz Mahal in the year 1630 A.D.

When you look at the Taj Mahal, you feel deeply inspired with the radiance of love, courage, and sacrifice and you immediately realize what a great legacy the Mogul Kings have left behind in the Sultanate of Hindustan. We shall always cherish these great legacies of the Great Mogul Kings and never condemn them or vandalize their historical projects in the Sultanate of Hindustan, now called the Indian Subcontinent. Taj Mahal, a monument of a great historical significance, is not just a conception but it is also quite phenomenal in beauty, and elegance.

The Taj Mahal stands for the symbol of peace, unity, and solidarity for all mankind and that true love shall not perish from the face of the Earth but rather conquer all frontiers and become immortal and radiant for all times to come.

The beauty that is inherent in the Taj Mahal inspires wisdom and enlightenment and enhances the development of conceptions and a guide to comprehending the complexities and intricacies of the universe.

The Jantar Mantar (an ancient observatory), in New Delhi

The Yantra Mantra (literally the "instrument and formula" and often called the Jantar Mantar) is located in the modern city of New Delhi. It consists of 13 architectural astronomy instruments, built by a Mogul Emperor named Muhammad Shah for revising the calendar and astronomical tables. There is a plaque fixed on one of the structures in Jantar Mantar Observatory in New Delhi that was placed there in 1910 mistakenly dating the construction of the complex to the year 1710. Later research, though, suggests 1724 as the actual year of construction.

The main purpose of the observatory was to compile astronomical tables, and to predict the times and movements of the sun, moon, and the planets.

Purpose of Individual Structures: -

There are four distinct instruments within the observatory of Jantar Mantar in New Delhi viz. the Samrat Yantra, the Ram Yantra, the Jayaprakash Yantra, and the Mishra Yantra.

1. Samrat Yantra: - The Samrat Yantra, or Supreme Instrument, is a great triangle that is basically an equal hour sundial. It is 70 feet high, 114 feet long at the base, and 10 feet thick. It has a 128 foot long (39m) hypotenuse that is parallel to the earth's axis and points towards the North Pole. On each side of the triangle is a quadrant with graduations indicating hour, minutes, and seconds.

    At the time of the Samrat Yantra's construction, sundials already existed but the Samrat Yantra turned the basic sundial into a precision tool for measuring declinations and other relative coordinates of various heavenly bodies.

2. Jayaprakash Yantra: - The Jayaprakash consists of hollowed out hemisphere with marking on their concave surfaces. Cross wires were stretched between points on their rim. From inside the Ram, an observer could align the position of a star with various markings on a window's edge.

3. Ram Yantra: - It is one of the four distinct instruments within the observatory of Jantar Mantar, in New Delhi.

4. Mishra Yantra: - The Mishra Yantra's were able to indicate when it was noon in various cities all over the world and was the only structure in the observatory not invented by the Emperor's engineer.

The Jantar Mantar, in New Delhi, is an observatory without a telescope. The numerous astronomical evaluations are made by studying the rays of the sun that strike our planet earth with the naked human eye without the use of telescopes, in this ancient observatory built during the days of the Great Mogul Dynasty.

Other Observatories: - In all between 1727 and 1734, five similar observatories, Yantra Mantra in West Central India, all known by the same name, were built. Today the observatory is mainly a tourist attraction and is significant in the history of Astronomy.

20)

· ·

a) Hindustan

The Majestic Mongol Sultanate

The Mogul Empire or Mongol Sultanate was an Indian imperial power that ruled a large portion of the Indian subcontinent. It began in 1526, invaded and ruled most of India by the late 17th and early 18th centuries, and ended in the mid 19th century.

The Mogul emperors were descendants of the Timurids, and at the height of their power around 1700, they controlled most of the Indian Subcontinent – extending from Bengal in the east to Baluchistan in the west, Kashmir in the north to Kaveri basin in the south. Its population at that time had been estimated to be between 110 and 150 million, over a territory of over 3.2 million square kilometers (1.2 million square miles).

The "classical period" of the Empire started in 1556 with the accession of Jalaluddin Muhammad Akbar, better known as Akbar, the Great. It ended with the death and defeat of Emperor Aurangzeb in 1707 by the rising of Hindu Maratha Empire, although the dynasty continued for another 150 years. During this period, the Empire was marked by a highly centralized administration connecting the different regions.

All the significant monuments of the Moguls, their most visible legacy, date to this period which was characterized by the expansion of Persian cultural influences in the Indian subcontinent, with brilliant literary, artistic, and architectural results.

Following 1725 the empire declined rapidly, weakened by wars of succession, agrarian crisis fueling local revolts, the growth of religious intolerance, the rise of the Maratha, Durrani, and Sikh empires and finally the British colonialism. The last King, Bahadur Shah Zafar II, whose rule was restricted to the city of Delhi, was imprisoned and exiled by the British after the Indian Rebellion of 1857.

The name Mogul is derived from the original homelands of Timurids, Central Asian Steppes, once conquered by Changez Khan and hence known as Moghulists, "Land of Moguls". Although early Moguls spoke the Chagatai language and maintained Turko-Mongol practices, they were essentially persianized. They transferred the Persian literature and culture to India, thus forming the base for the Indo – Persian culture.

The Early History

Zahiruddin Muhammad Babur learned about the riches of Hindustan and conquest of it by his ancestor Timur Lang in 1503 at Dikh Kat, a place in the Transoxiana region. At that time he was roaming as a wanderer after losing his principality, Farghana. In his memoirs he wrote that after he had acquired Kabul (in 1514), he desired to regain the territories in Hindustan held once by Turks. He started his exploratory raids from 1519 when he visited the Indo – Afghan borders to suppress the rising by Yusufzai tribes. He undertook similar raids up to 1524 and had established his base camp at Peshawar.

In 1526, Babur defeated the last of the Delhi sultans, Ibrahim Shah Lodi, at the first Battle of Panipat. To secure his newly founded kingdom, Babur then had to face Rajput Rana Sanga of Chittor, at the Battle of Khanwa. Rana Sanga offered stiff resistance but was defeated.

Babur's son Humayun succeeded him in 1530, but suffered reversals at the hands of the Pashtun Sher Shah Suri and lost most of the fledgling empire before it could grow beyond a minor regional state. From 1540 Humayun became ruler in exile, reaching the court of the Safavid rule in 1554 while his force still controlled some fortresses and small regions. But when Pashtuns fell into disarray with the death of Sher Shah Suri, Humayun returned with a mixed army, raised more troops, and managed to conquer Delhi in 1555.

Humayun crossed the rough terrain of the Makran with his wife. The resurgent Humayun then conquered the central plateau around Delhi, but months later died in an accident, leaving the realm unsettled and in war.

Akbar succeeded his father on 14 February, 1556, while in the midst of a war against Sikandar Shah Suri for the throne of Delhi. He soon won his eighteenth victory at age 22. He became known as Akbar, as he was a wise ruler, setting high but fair taxes. He was born in a Hindu Rajput household. He was more inclusive in his approach to the non – Muslim subjects of the Empire. He investigated the production in a certain area and taxed inhabitants one-fifth of their agricultural produce.

"The Morning Echo"

He also set up an efficient bureaucracy and was tolerant of religious differences which softened the resistance of the locals. He made alliance with Rajputs and appointed Hindu general administrators. Later in life, he devised his own brand of religion based on tolerance, and inspired by viewpoints of Hinduism and Islam. After his death, this religion did not become popular, but it is still remembered for its noble intentions of bringing people and minds together.

Jahangir, son of Emperor Akbar, ruled the Empire from 1605 – 1627. In October, 1627, Shah Jahan, son of Emperor Jahangir succeeded to the throne, where he inherited a vast and rich empire. At mid-century this was perhaps the greatest empire in the world.

Shah Jahan commissioned the famous Taj Mahal (1630-1653) in Agra, which was built by the Persian architect Ustad Ahmad Lahauri as a tomb for Shah Jahan's beloved wife Mumtaz Mahal, who died giving birth to their 14th child. By 1700 the empire reached its peak under the leadership of Aurangzeb Alamgir with major parts of present day India, Pakistan, and most of Afghanistan under its domain. Aurangzeb was the last of what are now referred to as the Great Mogul Kings, living a shrewd life but dying peacefully.

Mogul Dynasty

The Mogul Empire was the dominant power in the Indian subcontinent between the mid 16th century and the early 18th century. Founded in 1526, it officially survived until 1858, when it was supplanted by the British Raj. The dynasty is sometimes referred to as the Timurid dynasty because Babur was descended from Timur.

The Mogul dynasty was founded when Babur, hailing from Farghana (Modern Uzbekistan), invaded parts of northern India and defeated Ibrahim Shah Lodi, at the First Battle of Panipat, in 1526. The Mogul Empire superseded the Delhi Sultanate as rulers of northern India.

In time, the state thus founded by Babur far exceeded the bounds of Delhi Sultanate, eventually encompassing a major portion of India and earning the appellation of Empire. A brief interregnum (1540-1555) during the reign of Babur's son, Humayun, saw the rise of the Afghan Suri Dynasty under Sher Shah Suri, a competent and efficient ruler in his own right, and Hindu King, Hem Chandra Vikramaditya, also called Hemu. However Sher Shah's untimely death and the military incompetence of his successors enabled Humayun to regain his throne in 1555. However Humayun died a few months later, and was succeeded by his son the 13 year old Akbar, the Great. The greatest portion of the Mogul expansion was accomplished during the reign of Akbar (1556-1605). The empire was maintained as the dominant force of the present day Indian subcontinent for a hundred years further by his successors Jahangir, Shah Jahan, and Aurangzeb. The first six emperors, who enjoyed power both de jure and de facto, are usually referred to by just one name, a title adopted upon his accession by each emperor.

Akbar, the Great initiated certain important policies, such as religious liberalism (abolition of Jizya tax), inclusion of Hindus in the affairs of the empire, and political alliance/ marriage with the Hindu Rajput caste, that were innovative for his milieu; he also adopted some policies of Sher Shah Suri, such as the division of the empire into Sarkar Rajs, in his administration of the empire.

These policies, which undoubtedly served to maintain the power and stability of the empire, as the Hindu populace had shown resistance to the Islamic conquest in its years in the Indian subcontinent. These were preserved by his two immediate successors but were discarded by Aurangzeb, who followed a more strict interpretation of Islam and followed a stricter policy of intolerance to the practice of religions than his own. Furthermore, Aurangzeb spent nearly his entire career seeking to expand his realm into the Deccan and South India, Assam in the east, this venture sapped the resources of the empire while provoking strong resistance from the Marathas, Rajputs, Sikhs of Punjab, Ahoms of Assam successfully resisted the Mogul invasion, the last battle being the Battle of Saraighat. It is interesting to note in this regard that while Mogul ruled India for nearly three hundred years, they never ruled the complete geographical mirror of the Indian subcontinent. The power was mostly centered on Delhi, which was for historical reasons, considered a strategic stronghold.

Decline

After Emperor Aurangzeb's death in 1707, the empire fell into decline. Beginning with Bahadur Shah I, the Mogul emperors progressively declined in power and became figureheads, being initially controlled by courtiers and later by various rising warlords.

In the 18th century, the empire suffered depredations of invaders like Ahmad Shah Abdali of Afghanistan, who repeatedly attacked Delhi, the Mogul capital. The greater portion of the empire's territories in India passed to the Marathas, who attacked Delhi, reducing the once powerful and mighty empire to just an isolated city before falling to the British. Other adversaries included the Sikh Empire and the Hyderabad Nizam. In 1804, the blind and powerless Shah Alam II formally accepted the protection of the British East India Company. The British had already begun to refer to the weakened emperor as "King of Delhi", rather than "Emperor of India". The once glorious and mighty Mogul army was defeated in 1805 by the British; only the guards of the Red Fort were spared to serve with the king of Delhi, which avoided the uncomfortable implication that the British governing body was outranked by the Indian monarch. Nonetheless, for a few decades afterwards, the British East India Company continued to rule the areas under its control as the nominal servants of the emperor and in his name. In 1857, even these courtesies were abolished.

After some rebels in the Sepoy Rebellion declined their allegiance to Shah Alam's descendant, Bahadur Shah Zafar, the British decided to abolish the institution altogether. They deposed the last Mogul emperor in 1857 and exiled him to Burma, where he died in 1862. Hence Mogul Dynasty came to an end, which opened a new chapter in the history of India.

There are still many Moguls living in the Indian subcontinent. The term Mogul in the current socio-political context also does not have decisive meaning, as the blood lines of the original Moguls are now mixed with the other Muslim populations of India and have South Asian identities which are stronger than any Turkish or Mongolian origin.

The Legacy of the Great Mogul Emperors: -

A) Zahiruddin Muhammad Babur: - He was born on February 23, 1483; his period of reign lasted 1526-1530; he died on December 26, 1530; and he is known as the "Founder of the Mogul Dynasty".

B) Nasiruddin Muhammad Humayun: - He was born on March 6, 1508; his period of reign lasted 1530-1540 and 1555-1556; he died on Jan, 1556. His reign was interrupted by Suri dynasty. It was once again restored during 1555-1556, leaving a unified empire for his son Akbar.

C) Jalaluddin Muhammad Akbar: - He was born on November 14, 1542; his period of reign lasted 1556-1605; and he died on October 27, 1605. One of his most famous construction marvels was the Lahore Fort.

D) Nooruddin Muhammad Jahangir: - He was born on October, 1569; his period of reign lasted 1605-1627; and he died 1627. Jahangir set the precedent for sons rebelling against their emperor father. He first opened relations with the British East India Company. Reportedly he was an alcoholic and his beloved wife Empress Noor Jahan became the real power behind the throne and completely ruled in his place.

E) Shahabuddin Muhammad Shah Jahan: - He was born on January 5, 1592; his period of reign lasted 1627-1658; and he died 1666. Under Shah Jahan, Mogul arts and crafts, and architectures reached their zenith; constructed the Taj Mahal, Jama Masjid, Red Fort, Jahangir mausoleum and Shalimar Garden in Lahore.

F) Mohiuddin Muhammad Aurangzeb Alamgir: - He was born on October 21, 1618; his period of reign lasted 1658-1707; and he died on March 3, 1707. Emperor Aurangzeb made two copies of the Koran using his own calligraphy.

So this ends our brief introduction of Mogul history. What transpired afterwards is discussed under the topic subtitled, "Republic of India", which follows after "Industrial Revolution".

b) Chandni Chowk

Chandni Chowk, originally meaning moonlit square or market, is one of the oldest and busiest markets in Old Delhi, now in central north Delhi, India.

Chandni Chowk is the major street in the walled city of Old Delhi, which was originally called Shahjahanabad. The walled city, which includes the Lal Qila or Red Fort of Delhi, was established in 1650 AD by the Mughal Emperor Shah Jahan. It was designed by his daughter Jahanara Begum Sahib, who also made significant contributions in the landscaping of her father's new capital.

Chandni Chowk runs through the middle of the walled city, from the Lahori Darwaza (Lahore Gate) of the Red Fort to Fatehpuri Masjid. Originally a canal ran through the middle of the street as part of the water supply scheme. It was initially divided into three sections.

1. Lahori Darwaza to Chandni Chowk: - This section closest to the imperial residence, was called Urdu Bazar i.e encampment market. The language Urdu got its name from this encampment.

2. Chowk Kotwali to Chandni Chowk: - The term Chandni Chowk originally referred to the square that initially had a reflecting pool. It was replaced by a clock tower (Ghantaghar) that was damaged and demolished in 1960's. This section was originally called Johri Bazar.

3. Chandni Chowk to Fatehpuri Masjid: - This was called Fatehpuri Bazar. It is said that moonlit reflecting on its canal, earned its name, Chandni (moonlit). Chandni Chowk was once the grandest of the markets in India. The Mughal imperial processions used to pass through Chandni Chowk.

4.

c) Industrial Revolution

Industrial revolution was the change from the use of hand methods of manufacturing to machine methods. This change, which began in England in about 1750 and later spread to other countries, is called a "revolution" because it brought vast transformation in the way people work and live. It created an industrialized society – one in which large-scale mechanized manufacturing replaced farming as the main source of employment. Instead of growing their own food and making at home the products they use, a great many persons in an industrialized society work for wages and buy their food and other essential commodities. They live in towns and cities rather than in the countryside.

Progress in technology and in industrial development has been almost continuous since the industrial revolution began. Since 1900, and particularly since World War II, industry and technology have advanced at an ever increasing rate. In a sense the revolution that began around 1750 has never ended.

When using the words "Industrial Revolution" in this broad context, it is proper to divide the revolution into a number of "ages". The dates of these ages are approximate and several of them overlap.

Some of these ages (each named for its principal fuel, product, or source of power) are the Wood Age (1750-1840); the Age of Steam (1769-1900); the Age of Coal and Iron (1840-1860); the Age of Steel (began 1860); and the atomic age (began 1942). The Industrial Revolution can also be divided into the first revolution (1750-1860) and the second revolution (began 1860). During this second period came such major developments as modern steel making processes, electrical machinery and communication devices, internal-combustion engines, automation, and atomic energy.

In a more restricted sense, "Industrial Revolution" refers to the transformation of a country from an agricultural and commercial economy to an industrial economy. This process was completed in England by about 1850. In other countries the process began later and ended later. It did not reach some nations, such as those of Africa, until the middle of the 20th century.

Effects of the Industrial Revolution: -

On the one hand, the Industrial Revolution brought masses of people from the countryside to the city. It led to higher standards of living, as inexpensive manufactured goods came on the market. It increased trade between nations. On the other hand, the revolution, in its early days; brought exploitation of workers; slums; and great suffering as a result of periodic unemployment.

The wonders of modern science are a result of the Industrial Revolution, but so are the horrors of modern war. In economics, the Industrial Revolution brought on the rise of Capitalism – and also of Socialism and Communism. Labor unions, social legislation, government regulation – all are outgrowth of Industrial Revolution.

Background

Ground had been prepared for the Industrial Revolution in England over a long period. During the crusades (12th through 13th century), trade routes were opened to faraway lands and a merchant class developed. In the 17th century, overseas trade increased greatly as a result of voyages of exploration and colonization of the Americas. Merchants grew prosperous, and a large middle class developed that wanted and could afford a higher standard of living.

England excelled in the making of woolen and cotton cloth. The new demand at home as well as in the colonies caused steady growth of English textile manufacturing. The method of manufacture at the beginning of Industrial Revolution was the cottage, domestic, or putting out, system that had largely replaced the guild system of the Middle Age. Merchants brought raw wool or cotton and "put it out" in the cottages of workers who spun it into thread and wove it into cloth. Each process required a different set of laborers, who did the work on their own spinning wheels or hand looms.

With the decline of feudalism and the growth of the cottage system of manufacturing, small scale farming declined in importance. Enclosure Acts made it possible for the wealthy to buy up scattered strips of land formerly farmed by villagers and to consolidate them into large holdings. Many villagers had to turn to the cities to seek work.

By the middle of the 18th century, the cottage system was beginning to decline as a result of a series of important inventions. Hand equipment could not compete with the costly new machines, which were power operated, and had to be installed in large buildings called factories. Spinners and weavers were hired to work in factories instead of at home. The factory system of Capitalism was therefore developing, with the means of production owned by the person who hired workers.

Industrialization of England: -

Textiles: - The first of the developments that revolutionized the textile industry was the invention of the flying shuttle in 1733. This was a mechanism on a loom that projected the shuttle carrying the wool back and forth across the warp. Weaving was so much faster on looms with flying shuttle that a yarn shortage soon developed.

The spinning wheel in use at that time turned only a single spindle, which twisted the fiber into yarn. Inventors started designing machines to replace the spinning wheel. About 1764, spinning jenny was introduced. It was a machine that could turn several spindles at the same time.

Yarn spun by jenny was fine but weak. Spinning frame (often called water frame because it was operated by water power) was patented in 1769. It stretched cotton fibers so that they spun it into a yarn that was stronger than the one produced by a jenny but coarser. Spinning mule, perfected in 1779, was able to spin many fine, strong yarns at the same time. It was called spinning mule because it was a hybrid combining the features of spinning jenny and spinning frame.

Edmund Cartwright's mechanical loom (1785) was too clumsy to be widely used, but was improved by other inventors until in the 1820's power-driven looms were adopted throughout the textile industry. In 1793 Eli Whitney invented the cotton gin, which separated fiber from seeds 50 times faster than could be done by hand. This machine made a vast supply of United States cotton available to the English mills.

Beginnings of the Factory System: - The factory system that replaced the cottage system in the cotton industry was extended later to the manufacture of woolen, lace, and knitted hosiery.

Metal working also transformed from a cottage industry to a factory industry. Hastily built factory towns sprang up. Most workers were housed in ugly communities that, after the introduction of steam power, lay under a constant pall of coal smoke and soot.

The textile factories employed mostly women and children, who could easily handle the machine and would work for very low pay. There were no laws controlling wages, hours, or working conditions. The working day might be 16 hours long. Orphans and children of the poor were often apprenticed to the textile manufacturers, and were sometimes chained to their machines. The factories were drafty and insanitary. When workers became ill or were injured by a machine, they received no pay. Their earnings barely kept them alive.

The Steam Engine: - Steam power was first used in industry when the steam pump was introduced in the early 18th century to remove water from mines. In 1776, an improved steam engine designed by James Watt was installed in John Wilkinson's wrought-iron works to pump air to the furnace. Hence, so far, the steam engine was only a pump. When Watt had worked out a system by which it could turn wheels, Wilkinson brought a second engine to roll iron. In 1784, a steam engine was used in a deep coal mine to lift coal to the surface. In 1785 Arkwright installed a steam engine in one of his cotton mills. The use of steam power in the iron and textile industries and in mining soon became popular.

Iron and Coal: - In early iron furnaces, charcoal was used as fuel. By the 17th century, timber was becoming scarce in England. In the early 18th century it was found that coke (the residue from carbonized coal) burned with enough heat to smelt the iron. The pig iron produced in a coke furnace, however, had a high carbon content that made it weak and brittle.

The new textile machinery and the steam engine required a tougher metal. In 1783 Peter Onion and Henry Cort introduced a process called puddling. Puddling removed most of the carbon and produced wrought iron, a metal that was tough and malleable. A system for rolling the iron into shape was developed, and methods of making machine parts to precise measurements were worked out. The use of iron increased rapidly, and called for more coal to furnish coke for fuel.

Working conditions in coal mines were even worse than in factories. Because of the low height of the mine tunnels, women and technicians were often employed to pull the coal carts. Small children were used as door tenders. The working day was 12 to 16 hours. Coal mining was unhealthful work, but it became less dangerous with the invention of the miner's safety lamp by Sir Humphry Davy in 1815.

Transportation and Communication: - In the mid 17th century, the only highways in England were those built by the Romans 14 centuries before.

A series of turnpike laws brought construction of some toll roads. Good transportation became a necessity as industry grew and a road building program was started in the late 1700's. In the early 19th century John Mc Adam developed a crushed stone process of surfacing (macadamizing) that helped construct a good highway system.

Coal and iron were too heavy to be transported by road. A Canal Act was passed in 1759 and by 1830 there were 4,000 miles of canals and improved rivers. Meanwhile, the steamboat was being perfected by Robert Fulton in the United States. Regional transatlantic steam navigation began in 1838.

The canal system provided cheap, efficient transportation for heavy freight but was too slow for such perishable goods as food. What was needed was a means of adjusting the steam engine to land transportation. The problem was solved by George Stephenson, who built his first steam locomotive in 1814 and helped establish the first two English railways in 1825 and 1830. Trains replaced canal boats in transport of many products. Iron and coal production increased to meet the needs of railways.

Good roads made it possible to intoduce penny postage, the first cheap mail service, in 1840. A decade later, the railways began carrying the mail. The telegraph came into use in Great Britain in 1837 when Charles Wheatstone made the first practical installation. In 1851 a cable was laid beneath the English Channel to France.

Political and Social Transformation: - During the first part of the Industrial Revolution, the government policy was laissez faire (noninterference in business and industry). Britain's parliament was dominated by aristocrats and capitalists, who benefited from cheap labor. Protests about the plight of the working people were so great by the end of the 18th century, however, that Parliament was forced to act. The first two Factory Acts (1802 and 1819) were designed to regulate the employment of children. Since no enforcement procedure was set up, however, the laws were not observed.

Between 1811 and 1816 a bunch of workingmen, calling themselves Luddites, staged a series of riots protesting unemployment caused by the introduction of machines. The demands for political and social reform, coming from many quarters, became so insistent that Parliament at last took action. In 1832 a Reform Bill was passed that gave increased parliamentary representation to the new industrial cities. This marked the beginning of a reform era in which the principle of government regulation for the welfare of the people was accepted by most British leaders.

In 1834 a new Poor Law made employed men ineligible for public aid. Employers, who had depended on their workmen getting relief payment in addition to their earnings, were forced to pay a living wage.

Reforms in working conditions were accomplished by passage of Fatory Acts in 1833, 1844, and 1847, and of a Mines Act in1842. The parliamentary leader of the reform cause was Lord Ashley (who later became earl of Shaftesbury). In 1846 the Corn Law imposing heavy duties on the import of grain was repealed, and local prices, which had been exorbitant, gradually were lowered.

During this period trade unionism began to grow. It was outlawed by acts passed in 1799-1800, but became legal in 1824. The social reformer Robert Owen formed a Consolidated Trade Union in 1834, which led to some labor strikes. The government, alarmed, took legal action against strikers under a law prohibiting secret oaths. An outgrowth of unionism was the establishment of co-operatives, beginning in 1844.

Another working-class movement, chastism, tried to bring about further political reform during 1838-48. It died out because of increasing prosperity and betterment of workingmen's condition.

Spread of the Industrial Revolution: -

United States: - At the time of the Revolutionary War, the American colonies were importing factory made goods and luxury products from Great Britain. In 1790, Samuel Slater built the first cotton mill in the United States, and in 1793 Eli Whitney patented the cotton gin. New England soon had a flourishing cotton textile industry.

The manufacture of iron developed more slowly because of the lack of soft coal. A process for using anthracite coal, which was plentiful, was introduced in about 1830. Later both iron ore and soft coal were found in western Pennsylvania. The great expanse of American farm land encouraged the mechanization of agriculture. Inventions of a successful reaper e.g. Cyrus Mc Cormick, in 1834, was followed by the development of other types of farm machinery.

As the nation expanded, the almost unlimited supply of raw materials and of customers brought a rapid growth of industry. The steamboat, which came into general use in about 1817, provided transportation on inland waterways. A railroad system was built up after the introduction of steam locomotives in the 1830's.

The principles of mass production, based on use of interchangeable parts, were developed by Eli Whitney in the early 19th century. These were widely adopted at the time of the Civil War, when the need for supplies brought a great increase in manufacturing. Another development during the Civil War was the use of the sewing machine, perfected during the 1840's and '50's, to mass-produce ready made uniforms. Postwar growth and a vast supply of immigrant factory workers made the United States a leading industrial nation.

During the early part of the Industrial Revolution, social legislation did not keep pace with the rapid development of industry. Workers had no means of protecting themselves for long hours, low wages, and loss of employment. Beginning in 1813, some states passed laws regulating child labor. After the Civil War, a national organization of industrial workers, called knights of labor, rose momentarily to prominence, but declined without accomplishing any political or economic reform.

France: - By the start of the French Revolution in 1789, France had begun to adopt some of the new English manufacturing methods. The political confusion of the next several decades, however, held back industrial development. Hard labor and small enterprise continued to dominate until the middle of the 19th century, when a revival of commerce brought a gradual changeover to mechanical production. After formation of the Third Republic, 1870-71, France entered its modern industrial era.

Other Countries: - The first Asian nation to become industrialized was Japan. After restoration of imperial power in 1868, Emperor Mutsuhito sent Japanese scholars to study western industry. Quickly and methodically Japan became a highly industrialized nation.

China and India largely retained their ancient primitive systems of agriculture and handicrafts until after World War II. The governments of the countries then began the slow process of teaching their farmers modern agriculture and industrial methods.

Russia under the Czars was also a peasant society. After the Russian Revolution in 1917, the Communist leaders moved first to gain control of agriculture and production. In 1928, the First Five Year Plans went into effect. Its aim was to transform Russia from an agricultural society to an industrial society. Under a continuing series of five year plans Russia became second only to the United States in industrial power.

Industrialization in Latin America came largely in the 20th century, due in many cases to foreign investments. Unstable governments and lack of effective social legislation, however, hindered progress in many countries.

21)

. . . .

a) India (or Republic of India)

Introduction: - India or Republic of India is a country in southern Asia and is a member of the British Commonwealth of Nations. India is an English word derived from the Sanskrit Sindhu, which means river and was originally applied to the part of the Indus River which is now in Pakistan. In Hindi, the official national language established by the Indian Constitution, the nation is called Bharat.

With some 1.147 billion people representing many different languages and ethnic groups, India is an extremely diverse country. It is held together largely by centuries-old religious and social customs. India is the home of one of the world's oldest civilizations-dating back more than 3,000 years and the birth place of two great religions, Hinduism, still the faith of most Indians, and Bhuddism, now little practiced in the land of its origin. A century and a half of British rule, ending with independence in 1947, left its mark in various ways, including widespread use of the English language and a parliamentary system of government.

Since becoming independent, India has followed a neutralist policy in world affairs, avoiding alignment with either the communists or the West. The nation has made a great stride in relieving the extreme poverty of the vast majority of its people.

Physical Geography: -

Location and Size: - India occupies the greater part of a peninsular subcontinent fronting on two great arms of the Indian ocean- the Arabian Sea on the west and the Bay of Bengal on the east. Just off its southern coast lies the island nation of Ceylone (Sri Lanka), separated from the mainland by the narrow Palk Strait. Land boundaries are shared with Pakistan, China, Nepal, Bhutan, Burma, and Bangladesh. On the northwestern frontier is the disputed territory of Kashmir, the southern part occupied by India, the northern part by Pakistan. India has an area of 1,237,205 square miles; including Indian occupied Kashmir (The official Indian government figure of 1,269,344 square miles includes all of Kashmir). It is the third largest country in Asia, after the Soviet Union and China, and is about one-third the size of the United States. Maximum dimensions are about 2000 miles north-south and 1,700 miles east-west.

Land: - India has three distinct physical regions; the Himalayas, the Ganges Plain, and the Deccan Plateau.

The Himalayas: - These Mountains extend along the nation's northern border, forming a high mountain wall, 100 to 150 miles wide, which separates the Indian subcontinent from Asia's interior. The region consists of a complex system of mountain ranges that divide into three roughly parallel mountain chains: the Great, Middle, and Outer Himalayas. Several related ranges strike off from the main Himalayan arc along the Burmese border. In the towering snow-covered ranges of the Great Himalayas are many of the world's highest peaks. Although the greatest summits are in Nepal and China, numerous peaks in India exceed 20,000 feet above sea level. Nanda Devi, the nation's highest, records 26,645 feet. Heights of 5,000 to 15,000 feet mark the Middle Himalayas, which in turn, give way to low foothills of less than 4,000 feet in the Outer Himalayas.

Huge glaciers and snow fields on the flanks of the higher ranges feed rivers that flow southward through deep gorges and narrow steep-sided valleys to the Ganges Plains.

The Ganges Plain: - It is a broad, alluvial low land, 100 to 300 miles wide, spanning the country south of the Himalayas. It consists mainly of the fertile basin of the Ganges River, which together with the adjoining Indus basin, forms one of the largest alluvial plains in the world. The land is generally flat, with a slight eastward tilt. Much of India's farm land and many of its largest cities are concentrated on the plains, one of the most densely settled areas on earth. Only the Thar (The Great Indian) Desert, an almost barren area in the southwest is sparsely populated and little used.

The Deccan Plateau: - It is often called simply the Deccan and is a complex system of plateaus and hills occupying the peninsula south of the Ganges Plain. It is roughly triangular in shape, and consists of a series of eroded uplands topped by rolling hills and broken by river valleys. The land slopes towards the east.

A rugged maze of low mountains, reaching elevations of 3,000 to 4,000 feet in the Vindhya and Satpura ranges, separates the Deccan from the Ganges Plain. Elsewhere the plateau is bordered by escarpments, known as ghats. The Western Ghats, 3,000 to 5,000 feet high, form a wall that drops abruptly to a narrow coastal plain fringing the Arabian Sea. The Eastern Ghats, in contrast, consist of low, disconnected ranges that slope gently toward a broader coastal plain along the Bay of Bengal. At the southern end of the peninsula, connecting the Eastern and Western Ghats, are the Nilgiri, Anaimalai, and Cardamom hills, with elevations of more than 8,000 feet.

Water: - India's principal river is the Ganges. It flows from the western Himalayas to the Bay of Bengal-a distance of more than 1,500 miles. Together with such tributaries as the Yamuna (Jumna), Son, Ghaghara, and Gandak, the Ganges drains most of the mountains and the plains and part of the plateau region. In the northeast the Brahmputra River follows a tortuous course through the Assam Valley from China and merges with the Ganges to form a vast common delta, lying partly in India and partly in Bangladesh. The Ravi and Sutlej rivers, part of the Indus system, cross northern India on their way to Pakistan.

The Deccan is drained primarily by the eastward-flowing Mahanadi, Godavari, Krishna, and Cauvery rivers. They form large, fertile deltas at their mouths on the Bay of Bengal. The Narmada and Tapti are the only sizable rivers flowing to the Arabian Sea.

India's rivers are used extensively for irrigation; they also provide hydroelectric power and limited navigation. Of particular importance is the Indus River system, which provides water for the dry Punjab region of India and Pakistan. The Indus Waters Treaty of 1960 allocates the waters of the Ravi and Sutlej to India and the waters of the Indus and its other major tributaries to Pakistan. Bhakra Dam, on the Sutlej River, is the largest of many dams in India and one of the highest in the world.

Climate: - Sheltered by the Himalayas from the climatic extremes of Asia's interior, most of India has a tropical or subtropical climate, strongly influenced by the monsoonal wind system of southern Asia. In India the monsoons are characterized by an outward flow of relatively cool, dry air from Central Asia during winter and a reverse flow of warm, moist air from the sea in summer. Other factors-such as latitude, elevation, nearness to the oceans, and location on the windward or the leeward side of the mountain-help determine the climate of any given area. In the Himalayas, for example, climate changes from humid subtropical in the eastern foothills to perpetually cold in the highest ranges.

Three seasons are generally recognized in India, the cool, the hot, and the rainy.

The cool season lasts from October or November until early March, the period of winter monsoon. Average temperatures in Decemmber and January, the coolest months vary from about 55^0F on the northern edge of the Ganges Plain to the mid-70 in the coastal cities of the south.

For most of the country this is the dry season. A notable exception is the northeast coast, which receives much of its annual rainfall in October, November, and December. There is heavy snowfall in the Himalayas.

The hot season prevails from about mid March until June; it is extremely dry. Temperatures rise rapidly over most of the country, reaching averages of 85^0 to 95^0F in May, the hottest month. Daytime highs often exceed 100^0F, especially on the Ganges Plain. Nights bring only slight relief from the intense heat.

The rainy season begins in June with the onset of the summer or southwest monsoon and continues through September. Most of India receives more than 80% of its annual rainfall during this period. In addition to rain, the summer monsoon brings a reduction in the heat but causes high, often oppressive humidity. The heaviest rain that total more than 100 inches a year, occur in the northeast and along the Malabar Coast in the southwest. At Cherrapunji, in the Assam Hills, the annual average is about 425 inches - one of the highest in the world. Elsewhere rainfall usually varies from 20 to 80 inches a year. Only the Thar Desert receives less than 10 inches.

The summer monsoon is vital to India's agriculture. The timing and the amount of the rain can mean the difference between a successful harvest and widespread crop failure and famine.

In New Delhi the average temperatures vary between 67^0F in January to 92^0F in May and the precipitation is 25 inches. In Bombay the average temperatures vary between 75^0F in January and 85^0F in May and the precipitation is 71 inches.

Vegetation: - Little remains of India's natural vegetation except in the more remote mountains and hill regions. The original forest land of the plains and plateaus was cleared long ago for farming and grazing, leaving only scrubby grassland and scattered trees.

Forests cover about a fifth of the country. They grow mainly on the slopes of the Himalayas and Western Ghats and along the northern edge of the Deccan. Differences in climate and elevation produce many kinds of forests. The most widespread is the deciduous monsoon type, which grows in areas receiving 40 to 80 inches of rainfall a year. It contains such valuable timber trees as sal, teak, ebony, and rosewood. Dense typical rain forests occur in parts of the northeast and southwest. In the Himalayas temperate forests of pine, spruce, fir, oak, poplar, and birch predominate. Bamboo, which grows throughout much of India, is widely used for making furniture, household items, and paper.

Wildlife: - India has rich and varied wildlife, though most of the larger animals have been greatly reduced in number and range. Tigers, elephants, and rhinoceroses, once widespread, are now restricted mainly to remote mountain and forest regions.

Lions have become extremely rare; they are found only in the Gir Forests of Gujarat. Large animals, less affected by the trained hunters, include bears, wolves, leopards, cheetahs, hyenas, and deers. Monkeys and mongooses are the most numerous of India's many small mammals. The monkeys, seldom killed because they are held sacred by Hindus, have become serious pests, destroying valuable food crops.

Economy: - India, having many of the natural resources necessary to develop a modern diversified economy, is a nation of great economic capability. Although some industrialization has taken place, most of the people still depend for a livelihood on a classical kind of agriculture little modified since historic times. Per capita income is one of the lowest in the world.

Efforts to raise India's extremely low standard of living have been hindered mainly by rapid growth of inhabitants, which offsets increases in economic manufacturing. Progress towards a modern industrial economy has also been hampered by hundreds of years old communal traditions, widespread illiteracy, and heavy military expenditures brought on by conflicts with Pakistan.

Since the early 1950's, India has had a planned economy based on the philosophy of democratic socialism.

Private enterprise predominates, but is combined with government, or public, independence of certain basic industries and financial institutions. In general the government has expanded its economic role by achieving new enterprises rather than by nationalizing existing ones. Only the transportation, communication, banking, and insurance industries have been largely or completely nationalized. Since 1951 economic development has been guided by a series of five year plans, designed to stimulate industrialization and improve production.

Agriculture: - The success of India's development plans depend heavily on the nation's ability to nationalize its agriculture, which supports about 70% of the people and provides nearly half the gross national product (GNP). Most of India's food and industrial raw materials come from farming; yet that is the least developed portion of the economy.

Most farmers work small family plots of less than five acres (2 hectares), using primitive methods and growing only what they themselves need. Food production for the nation as a whole fails to meet domestic requirements and must be supplemented by imports.

Agricultural reform has been given top priority in the five-year-plans. Government programs stress land reforms, improved irrigation and rural transportation, formation of farmer's cooperatives, and introduction of fertilizers, pesticides, and high yielding seed.

Roughly half of India's area, or about 400 million acres (162 million hectares) is cultivated – an amount exceeded only in the United States and Soviet Union. Crop yields, however, are among the lowest in the world. The nation's vast irrigation system, one of the largest on earth, serves a fourth of the farmland, the rest receives virtually all its water from the monsoon rains, which are highly variable in amount.

Cereals and other staples take up about three-fourth of the cropland. India grows more rice than any country except China and is also a major wheat producer. Rice predominates on the lower Ganges Plains, in Assam, and along eastern and southwestern coasts. Wheat is grown mainly on the drier central and western plains, which are unsuited to rice. Other cereals produced in large quantities include barley, millet, sorghum, and corn. Chick-pea, lentils, and dry beans are the principal non-cereal foods grown. They constitute the main source of protein in India, where meat consumption is restricted by poverty and by religious beliefs.

The remaining one-fourth of the farmland is devoted to commercial crops. India is one of the world's leading producers of tea, peanuts, cotton, sugarcane, and tobacco. Rubber, coffee, and spices are also important. The commercial crops, grown on both small farms and large plantations, provide raw materials for domestic industries, and as exports, earn much of the nation's foreign exchange.

India has a huge domestic animal population with cattle and water buffaloes the most numerous. They are widely used as draft animals and provide milk, fuel (dried dung), and manure for fertilizer. Because cattle are sacred to Hindus, they are rarely slaughtered and eaten. Millions of weak, undernourished animals roam the countryside competing with humans for the nation's meager food supply. Large numbers of sheep and goats are raised for meat, milk, wool, hair, and skins.

Production: - Except for textile milling, that was started, on a large scale, in the 1850's India had little modern production prior to independence in 1947. Since then industrialization has progressed rapidly, drawing on the nation's relatively abundant raw materials and aided by public and private investment. Great emphasis has been placed on the development of heavy industry, much of which is controlled wholly or partly by the government. The manufacturing of consumer goods has also increased but at a slower rate. Except for some metallurgical industries, located near the source of the raw materials, production is concentraded in and around major cities, especially Bombay, Calcutta, and Madras.

In addition to supporting modern factory development, the government has encouraged the expansion of custom-old handicraft or cottage industries. These small-scale operations employ some 20 million workers – four times the number employed by factories – and provide many of the items used in everyday life.

Textile milling remains India's largest and best developed industry, in both employment and value output. The nation is one of the world's leading producers of cotton and jute textiles and also produces woolen, silk, and synthetic goods. Mechanized mills contribute most of the textile output; however nearly half the cotton cloth and virtually all the wool and silk are produced by cottage industries.

The iron and steel industry – next to textile milling in importance – has expanded rapidly, more than tripling production since 1950. Government – owned steel mills built under the five – year – plans, account for slightly more than half the steel produced. The rest comes from privately owned plants established before independence, notably the Tata Iron and Steel Works at Jamshedpur – one of the largest in the world. Other prominent heavy industries include petroleum refining and production of chemicals and fertilizers, transportation equipment, machinery, electrical products and aluminum.

India's food processing industry is based primarily on sugar refining and the production of vegetable oils, although relatively small, it is an important part of the economy. Also significant are metal fabricating, printing, and publishing, and the making of rubber goods, tobacco products, and paper.

Mining: - India has abundant and varied mineral resources, and mining is an increasingly important industrial activity. Like most other heavy industries, mining is divided between the public and private sectors of the economy, with new development the responsibility of the government. Many mines are relatively primitive and only partially mechanized.

Coal and iron ore are the nation's principal mineral resources, contributing about 80% of the value of all minerals produced. India's iron ore deposits constitute a fourth of the world's known reserves. Other minerals that rank high in both production and value include manganese, mica, and bauxite. Some copper, lead, and zinc are mined but production falls short of domestic needs. Oil fields in Assam and Gujrat supply substancial amounts of petroleum, however, most of the crude oil for the nation's refineries is imported.

Fishing: - Although fishing has quite an economic capability, it is not a major activity in India. Fish make up a major part of the Indian diet, being wildely eaten only in coastal areas and the island territories. A small, but growing commercial fishing industry yields mainly shrimp for export.

Transportation: - India's transportation system consists chiefly of a 37,000 mile railway network, built by the English and now owned and operated by the government. The railways serve all major cities and carry about 70 % of the nation's freight and passenger traffic.

The road system is poorly developed, especially in rural areas, where roads often are little more than widened footpaths. Of the country's 600,000 miles of roads more than 99% are only one lane wide and less than a third are paved. Most of the better roads are the result of a building program begun in 1961.

Inland waterways total 5,000 miles, about a third of which are navigable by power vessels. The Ganges, Brahmaputra, Godavari, and Krishna rivers carry most of the water borne traffic. Also important are canals in the delta areas of the east coast.

Ocean shipping is concentrated at eight major seaports – Calcutta, Paradip, Vishakhapatnam, and Madras on the east coast and Kandla, Bombay, Mormugao, and Cochin on the west coast. These ports handle nearly all of India's foreign trade. More than 100 smaller ports are engaged in the extensive coastal trade.

Air transportation is well developed and is provided chiefly by two government–owned corporations. Indian Airlines serves scores of cities within India and also flies to adjacent countries. Air–India is the long distance international airline. Numerous foreign carriers also provide international service through airports at Bombay, Calcutta, Madras, and Delhi.

Use of motor vehicles and bicycles in India has increased tremendously since 1947 but is confined largely to cities.

Trade: - India depends heavily on foreign trade for food and for industrial equipment essential to continued growth. As in most developing countries, imports exceed exports by a large margin. Grains, chemicals, and machinery make up more than half the nation's imports by value. Major exports include agricultural commodities, metal ores, textiles, and iron and steel products. The United States is India's principal trading partner, followed by England, the Soviet Union, and Japan.

Communication: - The government owns and operates all postal, telephone, and telegraph services. Radio and television broadcasting is also a government monopoly. The All India Radio network (AIR), the largest in Asia, broadcasts in more than 40 languages and dialects. Because of the nation's high rate of illiteracy, radio is an extremely important means of getting educational material to the people. Television, still in early stages of development, is limited to the major cities.

The People: - Most Indians are Caucasian stock belonging to two main subdivisions – the fairer skinned Aryans and the darker skinned Dravidians. The Aryans, who entered the country from the north, settled in northern India sometimes between 2000 and 1500 B.C. The Dravidians of southern India may be descendants of the people of the ancient Harappa Culture that flourished in the north around the Indus Valley before the Aryans arrived.

Indian society, highly diverse, is divided into a great number of cultural groups, officially called communities, which are based chiefly on religion, language, caste, and subcaste. Rigid caste lines determine from infancy the actions of each individual. There are about 3,000 castes and subcastes. All stem from four chief castes of which Brahmins are the highest. Below the castes are the "untouchables". The Indian government has outlawed discrimination against untouchables but it continues.

The family is still one of the strongest social institutions, mainly in rural areas. It is traditionally large, tightly knit, and under the authority of the oldest male.

Population: - With an estimated population of 1.2 billion, India is the world's second most populous country. The last 50 years have seen a rapid increase in population due to medical advances and massive increase in agricultural productivity due to the green revolution. The % of Indian population living in urban areas has grown from 1991 to 2001, India's urban population increased by 31.2 %. In 2001 about 285 million Indians lived in urban areas, while more than 70% of India's population resided in rural areas. As per the 2001 census, there are 27 million – plus cities with the largest cities being Bombay, Delhi, and Calcutta.

The human sex ratio is 944 females per 1000 males. Indian's age is 24.9 and the population growth rate is 1.38 % per annum, there are 22.01 births per 1000 people per year.

Literacy: - India's literacy rate is 64.8% (53.7% for females and 75.3% for males). The state of Kerala has the highest literacy rate at 91% while Bihar has the lowest literacy rate at 47%.

Medical: - Though India has one of the world's most diverse, and modern health care system, the country continues to face several public health related challenges. According to the World Health Organization, 900,000 Indians die each year from drinking contaminated water and breathing in polluted air. There are about 60 physicians per 1000 people in India.

Religion: - The Indian constitution recognizes 212 scheduled tribal groups which together constitute about 7.5 % of the countrie's population. As per the 2001 census, over 800 million Indians (80.5 %) were Hindus. Other religious groups include Muslims, (13.4 %); Christians, (2.3 %); Sikhs, (1.9 %); Budhists, (0.8 %); Jains, (0.4 %). Jews, Zoroastrians (also called Parsis), and Bahais are also found in India but their total population is approximately negligible. India has the world's third largest Muslim population and the largest Muslim population for a non-Muslim majority country.

Languages: - India has more than 800 languages and dialects. The constitution declares Hindi as the national language but English is also an official language in government and is widely used. The constitution recognizes 14 other major languages – Assamese, Bengali, Gujurati, Kannada, Kashmiri, Malyalam, Marathi, Oriya, Punjabi, Sanskrit, Sindhi, Tamil, Telegu, and Urdu.

Culture: - India has a very rich and ancient cultural heritage. Its Sanskrit literature, dating back to about 1500 B.C. ranks among the world's greatest literary achievements. In the forefront of a modern Hindu literature are the works of Tagore, whose poetry won the Nobel Prize for literature in 1913.

Traditional art is highly religious in content. Ancient Hindu paintings and sculpture has a very exotic and vigorous style. Under Islamic influence, India created some of the world's most beautiful architectures. The Taj Mahal is an example.

Sports and Recreation: - Field hockey is India's national game, and the country regularly wins world championship in this sport. Soccer and cricket are other important spectator sports. Polo is popular with India's upper classes.

For much of the population there is little involvement in sports. Generally, Indian social life is dominated by religious events and holidays and ceremonies surrounding family births, marriages, and deaths.

Government: -

Under its 1950 constitution India is a democratic republic. It is a federal union of 22 states and a number of union territories. The states have only limited powers. The president, who is only a ceremonial head of state, is elected for a five year term by an electoral college.

Executive power is exercised by the cabinet, headed by the prime minister. The cabinet is responsible to Parliament, which consists of the Council of States or Upper House and the House of the People or Lower House. Members of the Council of States are chosen by the members of the State Legislative Assemblies. There are more than 200 council members who serve six year terms; about one-third are replaced every two years. The House of the People has more than 500 members elected directly for a five year term.

The Supreme Court of India consists of the chief justice and not more than 13 judges appointed by the president. Each state has a governor appointed by the president, a council of ministers (cabinet) and a legislature.

History: -Early Conquests in India: - The civilization of India is very ancient. In the Indus Valley are ruins of a civilization of high order, known as the Harappa Culture that flourished from about 2300 B.C. to 1750 B.C. It probably was destroyed by the Aryans, people of the Indo-European language family who entered through the northwest mountain passes between 2000 and 1000 B.C. The Aryans first settled in the Punjab and Indus Valley, and from there spread eastward and southward. They introduced the Sanskrit language, the Hindu religion, and the caste system into Indian culture.

In the sixth century B.C. the Persians made northwest India part of their empire. Alexander the Great of Macedonia conquered the Persian district in 326 B.C. Macedonian control lasted only a few years, but trade was established between India and Mediterranean countries. The Roman world knew India as the exotic land from which came spices, drugs, and cotton fabrics.

After the Macedonians, control of northern India was held in turn by native dynasties and invading tribes from beyond the mountains. India became known by the Persian name, Hindustan (land of the Hindus). The most famous of the native dynasties were the Maurya and the Gupta. The Gupta fell before White Hun invasions in the later part of the fifth century A.D. Northern India, like the southern part of the country, became a land of many independent states.

The Muslim and Mogul Empires: - Invasions by the Turks, who were Muslims, began about 1000 A.D. A Muslim empire with Delhi as its capital was established about 1200 A.D. The empire flourished until 1398, when it was destroyed by Tamerlane, a Tater chieftain of Turkestan who sought to revive the Mongol Empire in Western Asia. Tamerlane's empire did not survive his death in 1405, and northern India broke up into small warring Muslim and Hindu states.

In 1526 Baber, ruler of a small kingdom in Turkestan conquered all northern India. Baber traced his ancestry back to Tamerlane and as a result his domain was called the Mogul (Mongol) Empire.

The Mogul rulers helped establish the Muslim religion firmly in the north, although the majority of the people remained Hindu.

The greatest Mogul emperor was Akbar (ruled 1556 – 1605), who subdued some of the strongest Hindu states. Akbar's grandson Shah Jahan (ruled 1628 – 58), was the builder of the Taj Mahal. He was deposed by his son, Aurangzeb (Alamgir) (1658 – 1707), who extended the Mogul domains, but aroused fierce resistance by the Maratha Confederacy, a group of Hindu states in central India. Shortly after Aurangzeb's death the Persians invaded India and trampled over Delhi. Many Indian states declared their independence, and Mogul power gradually dwindled away, although the empire survived in name until 1858.

Europeans in India: - In1498 the Portuguese reached India by sea and established trading posts. For a century they had no competition from Europe. Then the Dutch, English, and French East India companies began gaining footholds in India.

In the intense commercial rivalry that followed, English company was victorious. About 1700 it started its conquest of the country, extending control from its three major bases, Madras, Calcutta, and Bombay. British East India Company forces, under the leadership of Robert Clive, expelled the French from Bengal in 1757, and put down Indian rebellions, 1756 – 64. The expansion of company authority was continued under Warren Hastings and Richard (later Marquess) Wellesley.

Much of India was brought under the direct control of the East India Company. The Mogul emperor and the native princes of independent states retained nominal rule under British supervision. In 1857 a native rebellion, the Indian (or Sepoy) Mutiny, broke out among Bengal troops, who seized Delhi. When it was put down in 1858, the Mogul emperor was deposed and administration of the country, including the nominally independent states, was transferred from the East India Company to the British government. With the exception of a few remaining French and Portuguese coastal communities, India was, for the first time in its history, politically united. In 1876 Queen Victoria was proclaimed empress of India.

Struggle for Independence: - In 1885 a group calling itself the Indian National Congress, consisting largely of Hindus, was organized to work for Indian participation in government. Britain responded by permitting Indian representation in legislative councils. In 1905 the Muslims fearing Hindu control, formed the Muslim League.

India supported the British cause during World War I. In 1919, however, the Congress party began a campaign for self-government. Party leader Mohandas K. Gandhi led a non-cooperation (or civil disobedience) movement, in which British courts and other institutions were boycotted and taxes withheld. Gandhi was jailed in 1922, but the independence movement continued.

An investigation-committee report and a series of conferences led to the Government of India Act of 1935. The provinces were given elective government, but neither Hindus nor Muslims were satisfied with the method of representation.

Independence and Partition: - During World War II Indian troops fought for the Allies, and the country united to repulse a threatened Japanese attack through Burma. Gandhi, however, renewed his non-cooperation campaign, and he and the president of the Congress party, Jawaharlal Nehru were imprisoned for several years. The Muslim League, led by Muhammad Ali Jinnah, demanded a separate Muslim state. At the close of the war the British announced that India would be granted independence.

The Congress party reluctantly agreed to the separate Muslim state of Pakistan, and in August, 1947, the two countries became fully independent British dominions, with Nehru as India's first prime minister. Violent conflict broke out immediately between Hindus and Muslims, where either was found in hostile territory, and thousands of persons were killed. In 1948 Gandhi, who had worked for peace, was assassinated by a Hindu fanatic.

The Republic of India: - Most of the princely states were absorbed by India without conflict. In 1947, however, warfare broke out between Pakistani and Indian forces in Kashmir. A ceasefire in 1949 left the eastern part of the state occupied by India. In 1950 India proclaimed itself a republic. During the next 11 years it absorbed the French and Portuguese enclaves.

Under Nehru India adopted a neutralist policy in world affairs. However, armed conflict with China over disputed border areas developed in 1962 and continued intermittently. In 1965 fighting broke out again in Kashmir between India and Pakistan. The United Nations Security Council affected a ceasefire and a troop-withdrawal agreement was signed in 1966.

Indira Gandhi, Nehru's daughter became prime minister in 1966, at a time of widespread internal conflict. There were demands for new states based on ethnic and linguistic lines. Although several were created, the demands of all groups were not met. Many of the states had unstable governments, and a number of governments were dissolved and replaced by federal rule.

India's large; rapidly growing population was a major problem. Although family-planning measures had long received government support, results were disappointing. Agricultural production was unable to keep up with the population growth throughout much of the 1960s, and India experienced chronic food shortages.

In 1971 a rebellion in East Pakistan against West Pakistan caused some 10 million Bengalis to flee to India. Partly to relieve this refugee burden, India attacked and destroyed the West Pakistani forces in East Pakistan; East Pakistan became the independent nation of Bangladesh. In 1972 India signed a treaty with Pakistan (the former West Pakistan).

In 1975, Indira Gandhi, in response to a number of setbacks, assumed dictatorial powers, abolishing basic liberation. Mrs. Gandhi, seeking a popular mandate, restored some freedom and called for national elections in 1977. Her party, however, was defeated by a coalition of opponents and she had to step down. The new leadership restored all democratic freedoms. The coalition against Gandhi soon splintered, and in the election of 1980 Gandhi was returned to power. The third prime minister of India, Mrs. Indira Gandhi, daughter of the first prime minister of India, Jawaharlal Nehru, was assassinated in 1984, by a Sikh security guard, in New Delhi.

Kingdom of Nepal

Nepal is a country in the Himalayas in southern Asia. It is bounded by India and the Tibetan regions of China. Nepal has an area of 54,362 square miles, slightly more than that of North Carolina. Roughly rectangular in shape, it is slightly more than 500 miles long and up to 150 miles wide.

Physical Geography: - Most of Nepal consists of high, rugged mountain ranges and deep, steep-sided valleys. The towering, snow-covered peaks of the Great Himalayas, more than 20,000 feet above sea level, mark Nepal's northern frontier. On or near Tibetan border 8 of the world's 10 highest peaks, including 29,028 feet high Mount Everest, the world's highest. Lower ranges of the Himalayas, up to 15,000 feet high, and fertile river valleys cross central Nepal. The main one is the Kathmandu Valley. In the south, foothills merge with the Terai, a narrow lowland less than 1,000 feet above sea level. It is part of the high Ganges Plain, which lies mainly in India. Nepal is drained primarily by the headstreams of the Ghaghara, Gandak, and Sapt Kosi rivers, which flow to the Ganges River in India.

Nepal's climate varies from extremely cold in the highest mountains to warm and humid in the eastern Terai. The Kathmandu Valley has warm summers, cool winters, and an annual rainfall of about 60 inches. Natural vegetations consist essentially of forests, which cover a third of the country.

Tropical hardwoods predominate in the Terai, mixed oak and pine on the lower mountain slopes, and conifers at higher elevations. The forests shelter a variety of wildlife, including rhinoceroses, bears, tigers, leopards, elephants, and buffaloes.

Economy: -Nepal's economy is largely agricultural. Most of the people live by subsistence farming, growing crops on terraced slopes and in mountain valleys. Rice is the staple food, supplemented by wheat, corn, and millet. Cash crops, grown mainly in the eastern Terai, include jute, tea, oilseeds, tobacco, and sugarcane. Buffaloes are the most numerous farm animals; next to poultry, sheep, and goats. Manufacturing is little developed and consists almost entirely of cottage and handicraft industries. The government operates rice and jute mills and few factories producing basic consumer goods.

Forests are Nepal's most valuable natural resources, yielding wood for domestic use and export, dyes, medicine, and herbs. Though a variety of minerals are known to exist, only small amounts of iron ore, copper, mica, coal, and tate are mined.

Except for air travel, which is fairly well developed, transportation in Nepal is poor. Surfaced roads are few but are being extended; railways are limited to short lines linking towns in the Terai with railheads in India. Nepal's foreign trade is primarily with India.

The People: -Nepal has many different peoples, most of whose ancestors migrated either from India or Tibet. Those of Indian origin, the Indo-Nepalese make up about 80% of the population. The largest Indo-Nepalese groups are the Pahari, Newars, and Tharu. Those of Tibetan origin, the Tibeto-Nepalese include the Gurungs, Magars, Tamang, and Sherpas. It is predominantly rural and heavily concentrated in the central valleys, especially the Kathmandu Valley, and in the eastern Terai. Less than 10% people live in urban areas. Kathmandu is the capital and largest city. Other sizable cities include Patan, Bhadgaon, and Biratnagar.

About 80% of the people speak Nepali, the Sanskrit-based national language. Hindi and several Tibeto-Burmese languages are also spoken. Hinduism is the main religion and the professed faith of the majority of Nepalese. Buddhism is also widely practiced. Education is not compulsory, and only about 16% of the population is literate. A university was founded in Kathmandu in 1959.

Government: - Nepal is a monarchy under a hereditary king. Under the constitution of 1962, the king has sole executive powers, and appoints the council of ministers (from the legislature) and executive officials of all administration units. The one-chamber legislature is called the National Panchayat (council).

About one fifth of the members are appointed by the king; the rest are elected by zonal Panchayats, whose members are in turn elected by district Panchayats. Local government is controlled by the town and the village Panchayats, which also elect members to the district Panchayats.

History: - Much of Nepal's early history is known only by legend. Apparently there were migrations from surrounding area and small tribal principalities established. It is thought that by the seventh century the Newar tribes controlled Nepal, which then consisted only of the Kathmandu Valley. The region came under Tibetan domination for a time. In the 11th century, control passed to India. In the late 18th century a ruler of Gurkha (a country west of Kathmandu) seized control of the Kathmandu Valley and most of the area that is now Nepal.

The Gurkhas established friendly relations with the British in India, but in 1814 they went to war with them as a result of border dispute. A peace treaty in 1816 granted Great Britain territorial concessions. The Ranas, a family of court officials seized power in the 1840's and established themselves as hereditary prime ministers, reducing the king to figurehead. Following a successful invasion of Tibet in 1854, Nepal gained territory and forced Tibet to send an annual tribute (which continued until stopped by the Chinese in 1953).

A popular revolution in 1950-51 overthrew the Rana prime ministers and restored all power to the king. In 1959 King Mahendra issued a constitution, and the country's first parliament government was elected. However, the king suspended the constitution in 1960 and resumed authoritarian rule. In 1972 King Mahendra died, and his son, Birenda Bir Bikram Shav Dev, succeeded to the throne. During the 1970's the new king's reign was beset with considerable political unrest as supporters of democracy agitated and rioted for a greater role in the government.

b) The Incongruous Mother Earth

The world is disproportionate. It lacks harmony and it lacks symmetry. It is not proportionately symmetrical. The concept of symmetry is a beautiful idea but the standards are not always in harmony with symmetry and proportions.

The concept of a perfectly, proportionately, spherical world is a dazzling fantasy and not a scientific fact. Mankind likes to believe in a faultless world without errors and distortions but the incongruous Mother Nature is full of distortions, disorderliness, incongruity, and disproportions.

God created us not as symmetrical beings but as quite disproportionate buffoons whose behavior is even more incongruous and deflected than their obvious psychology. We are not complaining about the color of the world but only its distorted, quaky, and tumultuous shape.

It is a privilege for mankind to decorate the Earth with beauty, charm, and souvenirs and it is again a privilege for mankind to bring joy to the world. It is desired by mankind to proclaim faith and fight injustice and discrimination and it is again desired by mankind to effortlessly and continuously work in peace and harmony with nature.

22)

a) Tennis

Tennis is sometimes confused with badminton. Therefore it is also referred to as long tennis.

Tennis is an outdoor game in which two or four players use rackets to hit a ball back and forth over a net. Two players play singles, four in two pairs, that is doubles. Tennis is one of the world's most popular amateur sports.

Service: At the start of the game the ball is served by tossing it in the air and hitting it. The server stands behind the baseline or the right side of his court and serves the ball diagonally into the receiver's right service side. After the first point is scored he serves from the left side of the court into the left service court.

Scoring: The first point won by a player is called "15", the second is called "30" and the third is called a "40". Zero is called "love". A tie of three points or more each is called a "deuce". The score is called after each point by the scorer or an official, the server score being given first.

If the score is a deuce they must score two more points in succession to win. A set is won by the first player to win six games. There should be a margin of two games in order to win. A match is usually two out of three sets but may be three sets out of five in men's play.

Baseball

While on defense, a team has nine players on the field: pitcher and a catcher, (both together are called the battery), four infielders, namely (first baseman, second baseman, shortstop, and the third baseman), and three outfielders, namely (right fielder, center fielder, and left fielder).

A game is supervised by one or more umpires. Normally there are four umpires, one (umpire-in-chief) behind the catcher at home plate and one near each of the other three bases.

A baseball field is diamond shaped, with the first baseman, second baseman, shortstop, and the third baseman placed on the four corners of the diamond shaped baseball field.

The object of each team when it is on offense is to score runs; when it is on defense, to prevent opponents from scoring.

A run is scored when an offensive player legally advances from home plate to first, second, and third base and back to home plate.

A turn at bat for each team makes up an inning. Normally a game consists of eight and a half or nine innings.

b) Intelligence Quotient Tests or simply IQ Tests

The Intelligence Quotient, IQ, is defined as the ratio of the mental age (MA) to the chronological age (CA) and multiplied by 100 to avoid decimals.

$$IQ = (MA/CA) \times 100$$

For example a child whose chronological age (CA) is 5 and whose mental age (MA) is 5 has an intelligent quotient (IQ) of 100 indicating average mental ability. A 10 years old child whose mental age (MA) is 12 has an IQ given by:-

$$IQ = 12/10 \times 100 = 120$$

This value of IQ is above average. A 10 years old child whose mental age (MA) is 8 ½ has an IQ given by:-

$$IQ = 8 \text{ ½} /10 \times 100 = 85$$

This value of IQ is below average. The ratio IQs in the present times are called deviation IQs which is a mean of a child's score in the test that deviates or differs from the average for a representative group of children of his age.

Although deviation IQs are not derived in the same way as the original ratio IQs but these scores are interpreted in the same way as traditional IQs.

23)

······································

a) Fundamental Concepts of Mechanics

Introduction

Units: - The SI system of units includes the meter (m), the kilogram (kg), and the second (s) as the base units for length, mass, and time, respectively.

One meter is the distance that light travels in a vacuum in a time of 1/299,792,458 seconds.

One kilogram is the mass of a standard cylinder of platinum-iridium alloy kept at the International Bureau of Weights and Measures.

One second is the time for a certain type of electromagnetic wave emitted by cesium-133 atoms to undergo 9,192,631,770 wave cycles.

The Role of Units in Problem Solving: - To convert a number from one unit to another, multiply the number by the ratio of the two units. To convert 559 meters to feet, multiply 559 meters by the factor (3.281foot/1meter). Use conversion factors to change from one unit into another.

The dimension of a quantity represents its physical nature and the type of unit used to specify it. Three such dimensions are length [L], mass [M], and time [T]. Dimensional analysis is a method for checking mathematical relations for the consistency of their dimensions.

Scalars and Vectors: - A scalar quantity is described completely by its size, which is also called its magnitude. A vector quantity has both a magnitude and a direction. Vectors are often represented by arrows, the length of the arrow being proportional to the magnitude of the vector and the direction of the arrow indicating the direction of the vector.

Vector Addition and Subtraction: - One procedure for adding vectors utilizes a graphical technique, in which the vectors to be added are arranged in a tail to head fashion. The resultant vector is drawn from the tail of the first vector to the head of the last vector. The subtraction of a vector is treated as the addition of a vector that has been multiplied by a scalar factor of – 1. Multiplying a vector by – 1 reverses the direction of the vector.

The Components of a Vector: - In two dimensions, the vector components of a vector A are two perpendicular vectors A_x and A_y that are parallel to the x and y axes, respectively, and that add together vectorially so that $A = A_x + A_y$. The scalar component A_x has a magnitude that is equal to that of the vector A_x and is given a positive sign if A_x points along the + x axis and a negative sign if A_x points along the – x axis. The scalar component, A_y, is defined in a similar manner.

Addition of Vectors by Means of Components: - If two vectors A and B are added to give a resultant vector C such that C = A + B, then $C_x = A_x + B_x$ and $C_y = A_y + B_y$ where C_x, A_x, and B_x are the scalar components of the vector C_X along the x-direction, and C_y, A_y, and B_y are the scalar components of the vector C_Y along the y-direction.

$$C = C_X + C_Y = \sqrt{[C_x^2 + C_y^2]}$$

Newtonian Mechanics

Introduction and Mathematical Concepts: -
Physics: - Physics is that branch of science which deals with matter and motion.
Units: - There are three systems of units that are widely used, viz. "Le Systeme International d' Units", or simply SI system, Cgs units, and finally British Engineering System BE (the Gravitational version).

System SI Cgs BE
Length meter (m) centimeter (cm) foot (ft)
Mass kilogram (kg) gram (g) slug (sl)
Time second (s) second (s) second (s)
The Conversion of Units: -
1. 1 meter = 3.281 feet
2. 1 mile = 5280 feet
3. 1 hour = 3600 seconds
4. 1 day = 8.64×10^4 seconds
5. 1 year = 3.156×10^7 seconds
6. 1 slug = 14.59 kg
7. 9.8 m/s^2 = 32.1538 ft/s^2 = acceleration due to gravity
8. F = mg = 1 kg x 9.8 m/s^2 = 9.8 N
   F = ma = 1 kg x 1 m/s^2 = 1N

9. 1mile/s = 1.609 km/s

Dimensional Analysis: -

In Physics, the term dimension is used to refer to the physical nature of a quantity and the type of units used to specify it. Dimensional analysis is used to check mathematical relation for the consistency of their dimensions.

Example: -

(a) $h = (1/2) gt$

$[L] = \{[L] / [T]^2\} \times [T] = [L] / [T]$

Hence this is dimensionally incorrect.

(b) $h = (1/2) gt^2$

$[L] = \{[L] / [T]^2\} \times [T]^2 = [L]$

Hence this is dimensionally correct.

Trigonometry: -

Suppose hp = hypotenuse, al = altitude and ba = base of a right angled triangle, then we may have the following relations: -

$Sin\ \theta = al\ /hp\ \theta = Sin^{-1}\ (al /hp)$

$Cos\ \theta = ba\ /hp\ \theta = Cos^{-1}\ (ba /hp)$

$Tan\ \theta = (Sin\theta / Cos\theta) = al\ /ba\ \theta = Tan^{-1}\ (al /ba)$

$Sin^2\theta + Cos^2\theta = 1$

$Sin\ (\alpha \pm \beta) = Sin\alpha\ Cos\beta \pm Cos\alpha\ Sin\beta$

$Sin\ 2\beta = 2Sin\beta\ Cos\beta$

$Cos\ (\alpha \pm \beta) = Cos\alpha\ Cos\beta \mp Sin\alpha\ Sin\beta$

$Cos\ 2\beta = Cos^2\ \beta - Sin^2\ \beta = 1 - 2\ Sin^2\ \beta$

Law of Cosines: $C^2 = A^2 + B^2 - 2AB\ Cos\gamma$

Law of Sines: $A / Sin\alpha = B / Sin\beta = C / Sin\gamma$

Note that in the Law of Cosines and the Law of Sines A, B, and C are the three sides of the triangle, and the angles α, β, and γ are the three angles of the same triangle, respectively.

Scalars and Vectors

Scalars are physical quantities that have only a value, e.g. (mass and temperature). Vectors, on the other hand, are physical quantities that not only have a value but a direction also, e.g. (force, acceleration, velocity, and displacement). The fact that a quantity is negative or positive does not necessarily imply it is a scalar or a vector.

Mathematically a vector is represented by an arrow, in which, the length of the arrow specifies the value of the vector and the angle that the arrow makes with respect to the x, y, or z axis specifies the direction of the vector.

Vector Addition and Subtraction

The negative of a vector is the same vector with its direction reversed. There are two methods of adding or subtracting vectors, viz. (1) the Component Method and (2) the Law of Cosines Method.

The Component Method

$C_x = A_x + B_x$
$C_y = A_y + B_y$
$C = \sqrt{(C_x^2 + C_y^2)}$
$\theta = \tan^{-1}(C_y/C_x)$
Furthermore we may have as follows: -
$C_x = C \cos\theta$
$C_y = C \sin\theta$

The Law of Cosines Method

The Law of Cosines is as follows: -
$C^2 = A^2 + B^2 - 2AB \cos\gamma$
Note that γ is the angle between vector A and vector B.

Introduction and Mathematical Concepts: -

Numerical Problems: -

Units, the Role of Units in Problem Solving: -

1. The mass of the parasite wasp Caraphractus Cintus can be as small as 6×10^{-7}kg. What is this mass in (a) gram (g), (b) milligram (mg), and (c) microgram (μg)?
Solution: -
(a) Mass = 6×10^{-7}kg = 6×10^{-4}g
(b) Mass = 6×10^{-7}kg = 6×10^{-1}mg
(c) Mass = 6×10^{-7}kg = $6 \times 10^{2}\mu$g
2. How many seconds are there in (a) 2 hours and 25 minutes, and (b) half a day?
Solution: -

(a) 2 hours x 60 minutes/hour x 60 seconds/minute + 25 minutes x 60 seconds/minute = 7.2 x 10^3 + 1.5 x 10^3 = 8700 seconds

(b) (½) day x 24 hours/day x 60 minutes/hour x 60 seconds/minute = 12 x 3.6 x 10^3 = 4.32 x 10^4 seconds

3. The following are the dimensions of various physical parameters that will be discussed later in the text. Here [L], [T], and [M] denote respectively the dimensions of length, time, and mass.

e.g. Acceleration = a = [L] / $[T]^2$

Force = F = ma = [M] [L] / $[T]^2$

Energy = E = (1/2) mv^2 = mgh = [M] $[L]^2$ / $[T]^2$

Speed = v = [L] / [T]

Find out if the following statements are dimensionally correct.

(a) F = mv = [M] {[L]/ [T]} Incorrect

(b) E = (1/2) mv^2 = [M] {$[L]^2$/ $[T]^2$} correct

(c) E = mgh = [M] {[L]/ $[T]^2$} [L] correct

(d) v = √(Ex/m) = √{([M]$[L]^2$/ $[T]^2$) [L]/ [M]}

v = {[L]√[L]}/[T] Incorrect

(e) x = (1/2) at^2 = {[L]/ $[T]^2$}$[T]^2$ = [L] correct

Hence (b) E = (1/2) mv^2, (c) E = mgh, and (e) x = (1/2) at^2 are dimensionally correct.

4. The depth of the ocean is sometimes measured in fathoms (1fathom = 6 feet). Distance on the surface of the ocean is sometimes measured in nautical miles (1nautical mile = 6076 feet). The water beneath a surface rectangle, 3.4 nautical miles by 4.5 nautical miles has a depth of 15 fathoms. Find the volume of water (in cubic meters) beneath this rectangle.

Solution: -

V = 3.4 x 4.5 x 15 x 6/6076 (nautical mile)³

= .226629361 (nautical mile)³

V = .226629361 x (6076 feet)³

= 5.083577755 x 10^{10} cubic feet

V = 5.083577755 x 10^{10} x (.3048 meter)³

= 1.439508914 x 10^9 cubic meters

Hence the answer is 1.4395 x 10^9 m³.

Trigonometry: -

5. What is the angle θ that the diagonal of a cube makes with the diagonal of the opposite face of the cube if the length of one of the edges of the cube is 0.342 nm?

Solution: -

$S = 0.342$ nm x 10^{-9} m/nm $= 0.342$ x 10^{-9} m

$S` = \sqrt{(S^2 + S^2)} = S\sqrt{2}$

Tan θ = perpendicular / base $= S / S\sqrt{2} = 1 / \sqrt{2}$

$\theta = \tan^{-1} (1/\sqrt{2}) = 35.26^0 = 35.3^0$

Hence $\theta = 35.3^0$, which is the required angle.

6. What is the value of each of the angles of a triangle whose sides are 80m, 120m, and 180m in length respectively? (Hint: Consider using the law of cosines.)

Solution: -

$C^2 = A^2 + B^2 - 2AB \cos\theta$

The above given is the Law of Cosines.

(a) $(80)^2 = (120)^2 + (180)^2 - 2(120)(180) \cos \alpha$

Cos $\alpha = \{(120)^2 + (180)^2 - (80)^2\} / 2(120)(180)$

Cos $\alpha = 0.935185185$

$\alpha = \cos^{-1}(0.935185185)$

$\alpha = 20.7^0$ opposite 80m side

(b) $(120)^2 = (80)^2 + (180)^2 - 2(80)(180) \cos \beta$

Cos $\beta = \{(80)^2 + (180)^2 - (120)^2\} / 2(80)(180)$

Cos $\beta = 0.847222222$

$\beta = \cos^{-1}(0.847222222)$

$\beta = 32.1^0$ opposite 120m side

(c) $(180)^2 = (80)^2 + (120)^2 - 2(80)(120) \cos \gamma$

Cos $\gamma = \{(80)^2 + (120)^2 - (180)^2\} / 2(80)(120)$

Cos $\gamma = - 0.604166667$

$\gamma = \cos^{-1}(- 0.604166667)$

$\gamma = 127.2^0$ opposite 180m side

We may check the result by adding $\alpha + \beta + \gamma = 180^0$.

Vector Addition and Subtraction: -

7. A car is being pulled out of the mud by two forces that are applied by two ropes. The value of each force applied by each rope is 3000N. The two ropes make an angle of $\theta = 9^0$ with respect to a perpendicular line that bisects the car into two equal halves. (a) How much force would a single rope have to apply to accomplish the same effect as that due to the combined effect of the two ropes? (b) How would the

single rope be directed with respect to the perpendicular line that bisects the car into two equal halves?

Solution: -

(a) $F = 2F_1\cos\theta_1 = 2F_2\cos\theta_2$

Note $F_1 = F_2 = 3000N$, and $\theta_1 = \theta_2 = 9^0$

$F = 2 \times 3000N \times \cos9^0 = 5926.13$ N

(b) The single rope will be directed along the perpendicular line that bisects the car into two equal halves.

8. Vector A has a value of 10 units and points due west and vector B points due north. (a) What is the value of vector B if A+B has a value of 20 units? (b) What is the direction of A+B relative to due west? (c) What is the value of vector B if A-B has a value of 20 units? (d) What is the direction of A-B relative to due west?

Solution: -

(a) A+B = 20 units & A = 10 units

$B = \sqrt{\{(20)^2 - (10)^2\}} = \sqrt{300} = 17.32050808$ units

(b) $\theta = \tan^{-1}(B/A) = \tan^{-1}(17.32050808/10) = \tan^{-1}(1.732050808)$

$\theta = 60^0$ North of West

(c) A-B = 20 units & A = 10 units

$B = - \sqrt{\{(20)^2 - (10)^2\}}$

$B = - 17.32050808$ units

(d) $\theta = \tan^{-1}(B/A) = \tan^{-1}(-17.32050808/10)$

$\theta = \tan^{-1}(-1.732050808)$

$\theta = - 60^0$ South of West

The Components of a Vector: -

9. The value of the force vector F is 90N. The x- component of this vector is directed along the +x-axis and has a value of 60N. The y-component points along the +y-axis. (a) Find the direction of F relative to the +x-axis. (b) Find the component of F along the +y-axis.

Solution: -

$F = \sqrt{(F_x^2 + F_y^2)}$

$F_x = F \cos\theta$

$F_y = F \sin\theta$

(a) $F_x/F = \cos\theta$

$\theta = \cos^{-1}(F_x/F) = \cos^{-1}(60/90) = \cos^{-1}(0.666666667) = 48.2^0$

$\theta = 48.2^0$

(b) $F_y = \sqrt{(F^2 - F_x^2)} = \sqrt{\{(90)^2 - (60)^2\}} = \sqrt{(4500)}$

$F_y = 67.1N$

10. The speed of an object and the direction in which it moves constitutes a vector quantity known as velocity. An ostrich is running at a speed of 20m/s in a direction of 70° N of W. What is the magnitude of the ostrich's velocity component that is directed (a) due north and (b) due west?

Solution: -

(a) $v_N = 20$m/s x $\sin70^0 = 18.79385242$ m/s

(b) $v_W = 20$m/s x $\cos70^0 = 6.840402867$ m/s

Addition of Vectors by Means of Components: -

11. 11) Vector A has a value of 10 units and points due east and vector B points due north. (a) What is the value of B, if the vector (A+B) points 30° north of East? (b) Find the value of the vector (A+B).

Solution: -

(a) $\tan \theta = B/A$ $B = A \tan \theta$

$B = 10$ units $(\tan 30^0) = 5.77$ units

(b) $R = A + B = \sqrt{[(10)^2 + (10 \tan 30^0)^2]}$

$R = 10\sqrt{(1 + \tan^2 30^0)} = 11.547$ units

12. You are driving into a metropolis and in the distance you see the famous Gateway-to-the-arch. This monument rises to a height of 180m. You estimate your line of sight with the top of the arch to be 3° above the horizontal. Approximately how far (in km) are you from the base of the arch?

Solution: -

$\tan \theta = $ height/ base $= h/ b$

base $=$ height/ $\tan\theta = 180$m / $\tan 3^0 = 3434.604604$m

base $= 3.4$km

13. A highway is to be built between two towns, one of which lies 40km south and 80km west of the other. What is the shortest length of highway that can be built between the towns, and at what angle would the highway be directed with respect to due west?

Solution: -

$AB = \sqrt{[(40km)^2 + (80km)^2]} = \sqrt{[1600 + 6400]} = \sqrt{[8000km^2]}$

$AB = 89.4$ km

$\theta = \tan^{-1}(40/ 80) = \tan^{-1}(0.5) = 26.6^0$

$\theta = 26.6^0$ south of west

14. 14) A chimpanzee sitting against his favorite tree gets up and walks 60m due east and 45m due south to reach a termite mound, where he eats his lunch. (a) What is the shortest distance between the tree and the termite mound? (b) What angle does the shortest distance make with respect to due west?

Solution: -
$R = [(60m)^2 + (45m)^2] = \sqrt{[3600 + 2025]} = \sqrt{[5625]} = 75m$
$R = 75m$
$\theta = \tan^{-1}(45/60) = \tan^{-1}(0.75) = 36.86989765^0$
$\theta = 37^0$ south of east

15. The x-vector component of a displacement vector r has a magnitude of 200m and points along the negative x-axis. The y-vector component has a magnitude of 250m and points along the negative y-axis. Find the magnitude and direction of r; specify the direction with respect to negative x-axis.

Solution: -
$r = \sqrt{[x^2 + y^2]}$
$r = \sqrt{[(200m)^2 + (250m)^2]}$
$r = \sqrt{[40000 + 62500]}$
$r = \sqrt{[102,500]}$
$r = 320.1562119m$
$r = 320m$
$\theta = \tan^{-1}(y/x)$
$\theta = \tan^{-1}(250/200)$
$\theta = \tan^{-1}(1.25) = 51.34019175^0$
$\theta = 51.3^0$ below the negative x-axis.

Miscellaneous: -

16. The x-component of a vector r is $+4m/s$ and the y-component of that same vector r is $+8$ m/s. What is the magnitude and direction of vector r? Give the direction with respect to $+$ x-axis.

Solution: -
$r = \sqrt{[x^2 + y^2]}$
$r = \sqrt{[(4 \text{ m/s})^2 + (8 \text{ m/s})^2]} = \sqrt{[16 + 64]} = \sqrt{[80]} = 8.94427191$ m/s
$\Rightarrow r = 8.9$ m/s
$\tan \theta = y/x = 8/4 = 2 \Rightarrow \theta = \tan^{-1}[2] = 63.4^0$

Hence r = 8.9 m/s and $\theta = 63.4^0$ are the magnitude and direction of the vector r.

b) Pigeon

The adult of the nominate subspecies of the Rock Pigeon is 32–37 cm (12–14.5 inch) long and a 64–72 cm (25–28 inch) wingspan. The weight for Rock Pigeon ranges from 238 to 380 grams (8.4–13.4 oz). It has a dark bluish-gray head, neck, and chest with glossy yellowish greenish and reddish-purple iridescence along its neck and wing feathers. The iris is orange, red or golden with pale inner ring, and the bare skin round the eye is bluish grey. The bill is grey-black with a conspicuous off white cere, and the feet are puplish-red.

The adult female is almost identical to the male, but the iridescence on the neck is less intense and more restricted to the rear and sides, while that on the breast is often very obscure.

The white lower back of the pure Rock Pigeon is its best identification character, and the two black bars on its pale grey wings are also distinctive. The tail has a black band on the end and the outer web of the tail feathers are margined with white. It is strong and quick on the wing, dashing out from sea caves, flying low over sea water, its lighter grey rump showing a lot.

Young birds show a little luster and are duller. Eye color of the pigeon is generally orange but a few pigeons may have white-gray eyes. The eyelids are orange in color and encapsulated in a grey-white eye ring. The feet are red to pink.

When circling overhead, the white underwing of the birds becomes conspicuous. In its flight, behavior, and voice, which is more of a dovecot coo than the phrase of the Wood Pigeon, it is typical pigeon. Although it is a relatively strong flier, it also glides frequently, holding its wings in a very pronounced V-shape as it does. Though fields are visited for grain and green food, it is nowhere so plentiful as to be a pest.

Pigeons feed on the ground in flocks or individually. They roost together in buildings or on walls or statues. When drinking, most birds take small amounts of water and tilt their heads backwards to swallow the water. Pigeons are able to dip their bills into the water and drink continuously without having to tilt their heads back. When disturbed, a pigeon in a group will take off with a noisy clapping sound.

Pigeons, especially homing or carrier breed, are well known for their ability to find their way home from long distances. Despite these demonstrated abilities, wild Rock Pigeons are sedentary and rarely leave their local areas, etc.

24)

a) The Luxurious Motor Car

The imported or exported luxurious motor car is like a compact room in a random or haphazard motion with an endless destination. Its wheels are like thunderbolts of lightning, crashing through hail and storm and running like typhoons of magnanimous speeds. It's as if, the yesteryear's bulldozer has been incorporated in its newly developed breakthrough advanced technology.

The carburetor, the alternator, the regulator, the starter, the cylinders, the shock absorbers, the exhaust manifold, the intake manifold, the crank shaft, the pistons, the ignition coils, the accelerator, the indicator, the steering wheel, the catalytic converter and the suspension system are together like an incredible rocket with speed and momenta beyond imagination.

It is a heat engine and it is also called a thermodynamic system.

The gasoline is the only fuel which is essential for its efficient functioning and you may drive around anywhere you like. The efficiency, "e", of the engine is given by the equation: -

$e = $ Work done / Input Heat $ = W / Q_H$

$e = (Q_H - Q_C) / Q_H = 1 - Q_C/Q_H$

Note that Q_C is the amount of heat rejected into the cold reservoir, Q_H is the quantity of heat in the hot reservoir, which is the input heat and $W = Q_H - Q_C$ where W is the amount of work done.

Its technology is based on the exploitation of conventional forms of natural resources and there is no nuclear waste, but there are deadly toxic fumes from the exhaust pipes of the cars, involved. Thanks to Pep Boys who work quite hard on cars and trucks to save the environmental pollution from spreading.

The Top 10 Most Dependable Cars in the World: -

1. Honda Accord: - A classy package, well put together and feels more special than the average family car. It has superb engines and value for money.
2. Subaru Forester: - It is not quite an off roader, much more than the estate with a sporty edge, making it the perfect combination. It has a great all round value.
3. Mazda MX-5: - Blue print for the modern roadster with sweet handling and engines to match. It is extremely easy to live with.
4. Mitsubishi Carisma: - Despite the name, not that interesting to look at or drive, but that's not the point. Here is a no non-sense hatchback that won't let you down.
5. Toyota Yaris: - Superminis don't come better. There are bags of room and perky engines. It is probably the best small car buy.
6. Honda Civic: - Solid build quality and good engines are just part of the appeal. The civic is one of the most spacious small cars around. It has great values.
7. Nissan Almera: - A dull package but that is no reason to dismiss the Almera which is practical and perfect for the small family who need a big boot and utter reliability.
8. 8) Honda CR-V: - Proof that you don't need an XXXL 4X4. Here is a four-wheel drive estate that is flexible, easy to drive and own.
9. Toyota RAV4: - So few four-wheel drives are fun to drive. This car is suitably sporty but very practical. It is an expensive used buy but worth it.
10. Nissan Micra: - It is a driving school favorite. Tough, fairly roomy, but with its light controls, it is easy to steer around town.

The following are certain details on the top ten most dependable cars in the world market, whose names we have already mentioned: -

1. Honda Accord: - The 2011 Honda Accord ranks 7 out of 20 Affordable Midsize Cars. This analysis is based on our analysis of 46 published reviews and test drives of the

Honda Accord and our analysis of reliability and safety data. Among its many awards, it has been named one of Car and Driver's 10 best, an astonishing 24 times. Still, the Accord is beginning to show some signs of early aging. Critics praise its massive interior space. The government actually categorizes it a large car. It has a strong resale value and an impressive long-term reliability. The Honda Accord was updated in 2010. That, however, hasn't stopped Honda from updating it once more. For 2011, Honda has given the Accord a cosmetic feel, improved aerodynamics, added a new trim and increased fuel economy. The 2011 Honda Accord V6 Sedan has a fuel economy of 19 city/ 30 highway miles per gallon, (mpg).

2. Subaru Forester: - You can dress it up in fancy new clothes but there is no way to disguise the familiar boxes engine power train once the key is twisted. Subaru touts the horizontally- supposed layout's inherent balance and low profile, but it still speaks with a gravel throat and jiggles slightly at idle. Growling out 170 horse power in naturally aspirated form, the engine forte is torque, also 170 ft-lbs x T trim level Forester spice it up with a livelier turbocharged engine good for 224 horse powers.

    Fuel economy of 20 city/26 highway mpg isn't horrid for a vehicle spinning a transfer case and differentials at each axle, but we'd snap up Subaru's diesel version of this engine in an instant if we could for its torque and efficiency.

3. Mazda MX-5: - The Mazda MX-5 has won many awards including Wheels Magazine's Car of the Year for 1989 and 2005, Sport's Car International's, "best sports car of the 1990s", and "ten best sports car of all time". 2005-2006 car of the year, Japan, and 2005 Australian Car of the Year, and making Car and Driver magazine annual Ten Best list 7 times. 100% pure sports car, 167 horse powers, 2.0L 4 cylinder engine are some of its features. Incredibly responsive hauling thanks to its light weight and perfect balance. Up to 22 cities/ 28 highways mpg is its fuel economy. Mazda Advanced keyless entry and start system is also one of its features.

4. Mitsubishi Carisma: - The Mitsubishi Carisma is a large family car produced for the European market by Mitsubishi Motors from 1995 to 2004. The model name was derived from a combination of the English Car and the Greek Kharisma, meaning "divine gift". It was co-developed with Volvo, sharing its body with the first generation of Volvo S40, and built at the Ned Car factory in Born, Netherlands, which the two companies co-owned at the time. Over 350,000 were built during its production run.

    Available as a 4-door saloon or a 5-door hatchback, it featured gasoline engines from 1.3 L (introduced later in life) to 1.8 L, a 1.8 L gasoline direct injection engine, and 90 horse powers (67KW) Renault F8Q 1.9 L turbo diesel power plants sourced from Renault, later with the 100 horse powers (70KW), 1.9 DI-D common rail diesel F9Q engine, the same used in both Volvo and Renault cars.

    In spite of its name, the Carisma had a fairly neutral design as a result of being Mitsubishi first attempt to target the traditionally conservative European Company Car market. Even when receiving a mid life facelift in 2001 that characteristic was not improved. The car was placed between the Lancer and Galant, although after production ended, the Lancer took its place in Mitsubishi European range.

    In several markets where the Lancer was not available, the Evolution version was rebadged as a Mitsubishi Carisma GT. The body was also used by Proton to develop the Proton Waja. Economy fuel consumption is 45.6 mpg for Mitsubishi Carisma. For the Mitsubishi Carisma 1.6 car, the fuel economy is 30-33 miles per gallon. For the 2010 Mitsubishi Carisma 1.8 GDI Comfort Plus and 44,000 other cars made since 1900 Fuel Mixed driving 7 liters/100km, (33.6 mpg)

5. Toyota Yaris: - It has a fuel economy of 29 city/ 36 highway miles per gallon. The 2011 Toyota Yaris is offered as a three-door or a five-door hatchback or a four-door sedan. Each comes with a five speed manual or a four- speed automatic transmission and has identical fuel economies of 29 city/ 36 highway mpg. Because the Toyota Yaris hasn't changed

much in the past few years, to save some cash, you might consider buying a 2010 model or a used 2009 model.

The 2011 Toyota Yaris is by no means, the best performer in the class but reviewers say it is fine for city driving. It's light and quick steering mode parking a synch, and the engine is quiet when it isn't pushed too hard. Toyota covered the 2010 model with a basic comprehensive warranty that is good for three years or 36,000 miles.

6. Honda Civic: - The 2010 Honda Civic ranks 2 out of 31 Affordable Small Cars. This ranking is based on our analysis of 76 published reviews and test drives of the Honda Civic and our analysis of reliability and safety data. Its fuel consumption economy is 25 city/ 36 highway mpg.

    As Honda's best known and best loved car drive, the Civic sedan and coupe continue to set the bar in the compact car arena. Long considered the standard by which all other compacts are measured, the Civic is able to lure buyers, thanks to its impressive fuel economy, unrivaled reliability and repair history, and class leading resale values.

7. Nissan Almera: - The Nissan Car Company was established back in the thirties and used the Datsun name in the overseas market until 1983. Nissan's revival began a decade later with the era of super mini and success for the Nissan Micra in the coveted "Car of the Year" award 1993. Later that decade, Nissan signed an agreement with Renault for a Global Alliance – creating the world's fourth largest automobile group. Despite a period of financial difficulty, Nissan is now one of the most profitable car manufacturer's in the world.

    Nissan Almera Range has a fuel consumption [1.8] of (urban) 27.7 mpg; (extra urban) 47.9 mpg. Nissan Almera now justifies itself in terms of price rather better than before and deserves a place on our family hatchback shortlist. It may once have been a car they didn't want you to drive.

8. Honda CR-V: - It has a fuel consumption economy of 21 city/ 28 highway mpg. The 2010 Honda CR-V ranks 1 out of 24 Affordable Compact SUVs. This ranking is based on our analysis of 79 published reviews and test drives of the Honda CR-V, and our analysis of reliability and safety data.

CR-V Performance: - The 2010 Honda CR-V provides a competent and comfortable ride, but its motor has always been an underpowered four cylinder engine. "Although no one is going to call the CR-V fun to drive, it does handle predictably and is nicely responsive with accurate steering and serene ride". Says Car and Driver, the CR-V is the ultimate suburban runabout. Honda has increased the CR-Vs horse power and fuel economy for 2010, which ought to help matters.

9. Toyota RAV4: - The 2010 Toyota RAV4 ranks 4 out of 24 Affordable Compact SUVs. This ranking is based on our analysis of 69 published reviews and test drives of the Toyota RAV4 and our analysis of reliability and safety data.

More than 10 years after it was first introduced, the RAV4 continues to shine for its excellent combination of power, performance, and interior comfort. Later redesigned in 2006, its one of the most well-rounded vehicles in its class. Its fuel economy is 22 city/ 28 highway miles per gallon.

10. 10) Nissan Micra: - Nissan Micra is a super mini produced by Japanese automaker Nissan since 1982. From 1992 until July 2010 over two million Micra cars were built in Europe at the NMUK plant in Sunderland, Tyne and Wear, UK.

Nissan has stated that the model will be built in five countries but only three are confirmed so far. Thailand for the Japanese, South East Asian, and Australian markets, India for Indian, European, Middle Eastern and African markets, and China for the Chinese and Mexican markets. Nissan launched the new Nissan Micra globally on 2nd March.

b) Hot Air Balloons

The concepts of physics that are pertinent to hot air balloons are the Archimedes principle and kinetic theory of gases.

Archimede's Principle: -

Any fluid applies a buoyant force to an object that is partially or completely immersed in it; the magnitude of the buoyant force equals the weight of the fluid that the object displaces:

$\Rightarrow F_B = W_{fluid}$

Note F_B is the magnitude of the buoyant force and W_{fluid} is the weight of the displaced fluid.

Hence buoyant force is an upward force that the fluid exerts on an object which is partially or completely immersed in it. The buoyant force exists because the fluid pressure is larger at greater depths.

Consider a cylinder of height h which is being held under the surface of a liquid. The pressure P_1 on the top face generates the downward force P_1A, where A is the area of the face. Similarly, the pressure P_2 on the bottom face generates the upward force P_2A. Since the pressure is greater at greater depths, the upward force exceeds the downward force.

Hence the liquid applies to the cylinder a net upward force or the buoyant force, whose magnitude F_B is given as follows: -

$$F_B = P_2A - P_1A = (P_2 - P_1) A = \rho ghA$$

In the above equation hA is the volume of the liquid displaced by the submerged cylinder, ρ is the density of the liquid. Hence ρhA is the mass of the liquid displaced, so that the buoyant force equals mg, the weight of the displaced fluid.

Kinetic Theory of Gases:-

A container filled with a gas contains a large number of particles, which are in constant random motion, colliding with each other and the walls of the container. At a given temperature, the atoms and molecules are all moving with different speeds. However it is possible to determine the most probable particle speed for the gas.

As the temperature rises, the most probable particle speed increases. It can be shown, graphically, that the average translational kinetic energy of the particles in a gas is proportional to the temperature of the gas as given below:

Average kinetic energy = $(1/2) mv^2_{(rms)}$ = $(3/2) k T$

Where m is the mass of the individual molecule, k is the Boltzmann's constant with a value of 1.38×10^{-23} J/K, T is the Kelvin temperature, and $v_{(rms)}$ is the root mean square speed of the particle.

If the gas can be treated as an ideal monatomic gas, the internal energy, U, is defined as the total kinetic energy of the N particles that make up the gas as given below:

$$U = N (1/2) mv^2_{(rms)} = N(3/2) k T = (3/2) n RT$$

Note that $N = n N_A$ where n = number of moles of the ideal gas present and N_A is the Avogadro's number whose value is given as N_A =

6.022 x 10^{23} per mol. The density of air is 1.29 kg/m^3 and the density of nitrogen is 1.25kg/m^3.

25)

a) Cryonic Foundation (pros and cons)

A frequent concern of people imagining waking up in the future after decades of being cryonically preserved is that there would be no friends or family. That problem does not exist for those who are able to assist with preserving family members or for families who are mostly in favor of having the whole family preserved. A significant portion of cryonic patients are parents of persons who have made arrangements to be preserved. Many a husband and wife have made arrangements together. As for friends, people who get involved in cryonics and make arrangements to be preserved often make friends of other cryonicists, and these new friendships often involve many mutual interests. On the other hand, there are many people who feel that they cannot live without certain friends and loved ones who have absolutely no interests in cryonics (the vast majority of people have no interests in being preserved). Others feel that there are always new and interesting people to befriend.

Some people imagine that they would be old and sick or that it would be boring to live hundreds or thousands of years. Revival would not happen before all diseases have been cured and people could be rejuvenated to the prime of life. Good health and youth will provide vitality for living. The future is likely to be exciting, just as new technologies make life increasingly interesting today. There will be new forms of entertainment, and space travel will provide new opportunities for exploration. But people bored with current life may not even respond to the opportunities of future life.

Some people fear that they will experience future shock or to be totally unable to a new and strange world. But if technology has advanced to the capability of reviving and rejuvenating cryonic patients, computer-education (virtual realities etc.) will also have advanced, providing for and simplified means for people to learn all sorts of skills. Technology is aimed at making life easier, not harder, and that includes making technology easier to learn how to use. Fear of being unable to be gainfully employed in the future, technology may make it easier for anyone to learn how to become productive. It is likely that the trend will continue toward work shifting more towards human service type occupations.

Concerning overpopulation, with the tiny numbers of people interested in cryonics, it is unlikely that cryonics will be a significant contributer to population. Advanced technologies, like fusion and solar power farms, in space that, microwave energy to earth, could mean, that energy production is far less polluting than it is today. Vast amounts of non-polluting energy could make food production more cheap and easy. There is vast amount of space on earth for more population. Cheap energy could also make space more accessible, and there is enough room in the solar system for trillions upon trillions of people. Cheap non-polluting energy would mean there is nothing to fear from more population. And if each person is a producer rather than a consumer, greater population may mean that there are more people to contribute to the well being of mankind.

b) Boeing 747 Jumbo Jet

The Boeing 747 is a widebody commercial airliner and cargo transport, often referred to by the nickname Jumbo Jet or Queen of the Skies. It is among the world's most recognizable aircrafts, and was the first widebody ever produced. Manufactured by Boeing's Commercial Airplane unit in the United States, the original version of the 747 was two and a half times the size of the Boeing 707, one of the common large commercial aircraft of the 1960s. First flown commercially in 1970, the 747 held the passenger capacity record for 37 years.

The four-engine 747 uses a double deck configuration for part of its length. It is available in passenger, freighter and other versions. Boeing designed the 747's hump-like upper deck to serve as first class lounge or (as is the general rule today) extra seating, and to allow the aircraft to be easily converted to cargo carrier by removing seats and installing a front cargo door. Boeing did so because the company expected supersonic airliner (whose development was announced in the early 1960s) to render the 747 and other subsonic airliners obsolete, while believing that the demand for subsonic cargo aircraft would be robust in the future. The 747 in particular was expected to become obsolete after 400 were sold but it exceeded its critics' expectation with production passing the 1000 mark in 1993. As of June, 2010, 1,418 aircrafts have been built, with 109 more in various configurations remaining in order.

The 747-400, the latest version in service, is among the fastest airliners in service with a high subsonic cruise speed of Mach 0.85-0.855 (up to 570 mph, 420 km/hr). The 747-400 passenger version can accommodate 416 passengers in a typical three-class layout or 524 passengers in a typical two-class layout.

26)

. . . .

a) Cosmology, the Expanding Universe, and Big Bang

Cosmology is the study of the structure and evolution of the universe. In this study both the large as well as the small aspects of the universe are important. Astronomers, for example, study distances that are billions of light years in value where as nuclear scientists study distances as small as 10^{-18} m or smaller. Central to the understanding is the belief that the universe is expanding. The idea that the universe is expanding originated with Hubble (1889-1953). He found that light reaching the Earth from a different galaxy was Doppler shifted towards greater wavelengths, that is, towards the red end of the spectrum. This type of Doppler shift results when the source and the observer are moving away from one another. The speed at which the Earth is receding from a distant galaxy can be measured from Doppler shift in wavelength.

$v = H.d$

Where, "H", is the Hubble's parameter.

$t = d/v = d/Hd = 1/H$

$t = 1/H = 1/ [(0.022xm/s\text{-light years}) (1\text{-light year}/9.46x10^{15}m)]$

$t = 4.3 \times 10^{17}$ seconds or 14 billion years.

The Big Bang Theory postulates that the universe had a definite beginning in a cataclysmic event, sometimes called the Primeval Fireball. Hence the universe is 14 billion years old.

b) Sir Isaac Newton, (1642 – 1727)

Sir Isaac Newton was an English physicist and astronomer. He propounded the basic laws of mechanics and gravitation and applied them to explain the phenomenal solar system for more than two centuries. Although modern physics has modified some of Newton's principles, his discoveries are still considered valid in most of the situations. They form the basis of what is called classical mechanics or Newtonian mechanics.

Isaac Newton was born in Lincolnshire, where his family owned a small estate. His father had died before his birth and his mother soon remarried. Isaac, raised by an aged grandmother, had a lonely and unhappy boyhood.

Young Newton entered Cambridge University in 1661 and received a bachelor's degree in 1665. In mathematics, he formulated the Binomial theorem and invented both the differential and integral calculus.

From Kepler's third law of planetary orbits, Newton quickly came to the hypothesis, later framed in his Law of Gravitation – every particle of matter attracts every other particle with a force proportional to the products of their masses and inversely proportional to the squares of their distances.

Newton resigned his professorship and fellowship in 1701 to reside permanently in London. Newton served as president of the Royal Society from 1703 until his death. He was knighted in 1705. Newton died wealthy and was buried in Westminster Abbey.

27)

. . . .

a) Albert Einstein (1879-1955)

Einstein, Albert (1879-1955) was a German-American physicist and a mathematician. His genius conceived ideas that revolutionized 20th century physics, ushered in the atomic age, and earned a Nobel Prize in physics. Like Copernicus, Newton, and Darwin, Einstein changed the course of science. His major contribution was the theory of relativity. Its two parts viz. the special theory (1905) and the general theory (1913) together with unified field theory (1949) are his explanations of the nature of the universe. The theory of relativity was later confirmed by other scientists, but the unified field theory did not win support.

Almost every concept of modern physics has been influenced, wholly or in part, by Einstein's thinking. His proposals guided other scientists, including Max Planck, Meitner, Lord Rutherford, James Chadwick, Fermi, and Werner Heisenberg, in their study of the basic properties of matter. Such scientific research led to a thorough re-examination of the older laws of science. As a result, many principles were replaced by entirely new concepts of the fundamental nature of matter. Einstein was more concerned with theories than with practical matters. He worked with a paper and a pencil, rather than in a laboratory.

Early Career

Albert Einstein was born in Ulm, Germany, but his boyhood was spent in Munich, Germany. His teachers thought he was stupid. He did not display his talent for mathematics until he was 14, when he taught himself integral calculus and analytical geometry. In 1894 his family moved to Italy and he was sent to Switzerland to study. He attended the Zurich Polytechnic Institute and the University of Zurich, where he earned a doctorate of philosophy in physics. In 1909 he became citizen of Switzerland.

While still at the university, Einstein worked as an inspector in the Swiss Patent Office in Berne. During this period he completed the mathematical computations that led to his 1905 report on the special theory of relativity. The special theory was not well understood because of its complicated mathematical argument, but as more and more scientists learned to comprehend his theory, it became one cornerstone of modern physics.

In other papers of 1905 Einstein contributed to the quantum theory (in explaining the photoelectric effect) and researched atomic motion (in explaining Brownian movement).

Though the quantum theory became a second cornerstone of modern physics, Einstein considered it a mere stop gap, useful until some more general theory was evolved.

Einstein was professor of theoretical physics at the University of Zurich, during 1909-1911, and at the University of Prague, during 1911-1913. In 1913 he was appointed director of the Kaiser Wilhelm Physical Institute in Berlin. Also in 1913 Einstein announced his General theory of relativity, which is an expansion of the Special theory.

Later Career

Einstein became professor of physics at the University of Berlin in 1914. In 1921 he was awarded the Nobel Prize in physics for his research of photoelectric effect (important in electronics). Although the judges must have been more impressed by the theory of relativity, they could not give the Nobel Prize for a theory which had not yet been confirmed by experiment.

As a Jew, Einstein fled Germany when WWII took its toll. The Institute for Advanced Study at Princeton, New Jersey, granted him a lifetime professorship in mathematics in 1933. He became a United States citizen in 1940.

In 1949, after more than 30 year's preparation, Einstein presented his Unified Field Theory. In this theory, which Einstein called an extension of the, Theory of Relativity, he described an apparent relationship between magnetism, electricity, and gravitation. A number of other scientists believe that such a relationship may exist, but they do not regard Einstein's explanations as completely satisfactory.

b) Radio (FM and AM) and Television (TV)

Before we discuss the concepts of Physics that pertain to the performance of radio and television we would like to share the names of the persons who have invented these electronic devices.

These electronic devices, most certainly, have contributed immensely to the enhancement of the entertainment industry, in the present times.

The two names that come to the mind as to the inventors of the radio are Tesla and Marconi. Both of these inventors had struggled very hard during the beginning of the 20th century to become the inventor of the present day wireless radio.

The credit as to who was the inventor of the modern television really comes down to two different people in two different places, both working on the same problem at about the same time: Vladimir K. Zworykin, a Russian born American inventor working for Westinghouse and Philo Taylor Farnsworth, a privately backed farm boy from the state of Utah. These developments took place sometimes in the 1920s.

The A.M radio wave and F.M radio wave imply amplitude modulation and frequency modulation respectively. By amplitude modulation, we mean the amplitude of the radio-wave is being altered or modulated in order to produce sounds broadcast by various A.M. radio stations. By frequency modulation, we mean the frequency is being altered or modulated in the broadcast of radio signals to produce numerous F.M. waves of various frequencies.

In order to understand the meanings of the terms frequency and amplitude we give the equation of a sinusoidal wave or a harmonic wave or a periodic wave.

$$\Rightarrow y(x, t) = A \sin (2\pi ft \pm 2\pi x/\lambda)$$

Note that $y(x, t)$ is the displacement of the wave on the y-axis, "A", is the amplitude of the wave, "f", is the frequency of the wave, "x", is the distance on the x-axis, "λ", is the wavelength of the sinusoidal wave.

Now frequency is defined as number of vibrations per second and has the unit hertz and the angular frequency $w = 2\pi f$, and has the unit radians per second. The phase velocity of the radio wave is given by: v (phase) $= w/k = f \lambda$, and the group velocity of the propagating sound wave is given by: v (group) $= dw/dk$. The wave consists of crests and troughs and the wavelength is defined as the distance between two consecutive crests or two consecutive troughs. A wave performing Simple Harmonic Motion is a sinusoidal wave. The wave equation is a differential equation that describes a harmonic radio wave as follows:-

$$\Rightarrow (1/v^2) d^2u/dt^2 = d^2u/dx^2$$

In three dimensions this becomes,

$$\Rightarrow (1/v^2) d^2u/dt^2 = \Rightarrow^2u$$

Note, v is the velocity of the harmonic radio wave, u is the amplitude of the radio wave, t is the time and the operator del, $\Rightarrow$, is defined as $\Rightarrow^2$ = $[d^2/dx^2 + d^2/dy^2 + d^2/dz^2]$.

In the following equation: -

$\Rightarrow$ v (phase) = f λ

v is the phase velocity, f is the frequency, and λ is the wavelength of the radio wave in phase.

The concept of Physics which pertains to the theory of television is the Photoelectric Effect and for this Albert Einstein was awarded the Nobel Prize in 1921. The Photoelectric effect involves the absorption of a photon of energy E = h v by a metal surface to produce an electron of kinetic energy K.E = $(1/2)$ mv^2.

The value of the plank's constant is h = 6.62606876 x 10^{-34} J-sec.

The equation of photoelectric effect is as follows:-

$\Rightarrow$ E = hv = 1/2 mv^2 + eV

At the threshold frequency when the electrons begin to absorb sufficient energy to be ejected from a metal surface, the kinetic energy of the electrons is zero. In the equation of photoelectric effect, work function of the metal = eV, and may be applied to calculate Plank's constant, h. $\Rightarrow$ e = 1.6x10^{-19} J/ V, and V is the electric potential given by V = k|e|/r. W = eV = k|e||e|/r, and k = 8.99x10^9 Nm^2/C^2 in Coulomb's Law given by: - F = k|q||q|/r^2.

Note |q| is the mod value of the charges and r is their separation.

$\Rightarrow$ E = hv = 0J + eV at threshold frequency

$\Rightarrow$ v = eV/h = threshold frequency ($\because$ K.E = 1/2 mv^2 = 0J)

Hence if eV (work function) and v (threshold frequency) are known, the Plank's constant, h, can be evaluated.

The radio and television are tuned in by the use of resistors, capacitors and inductors. The capacitors store electric energy and the inductors store magnetic energy. The energy can be stored in an electric field as in a capacitor as well as in a magnetic field as in an inductor. In an RCL circuit containing resistor, capacitor, and inductor in series as in a radio, the resonant frequency f_0 at which the radio is tuned in has been discussed as follows: -

At resonance the impedance Z equals the resistance in the expression for impedance as follows: -

$\Rightarrow$ Z = $\sqrt{[R^2 + (X_L - X_C)^2]}$ = Impedance

Now Z = R at resonance, (a condition of minimum impedance).

$\Rightarrow X_L = X_C$

Now $X_L = 2\pi fL$ and $X_C = 1/[2\pi fC]$ where L and C are inductance and capacitance respectively.

The energy stored in a capacitor is given by the following expression:
-

$\Rightarrow E = (1/2) CV^2 =$ Energy stored in a capacitor
Note C is the capacitance and V is the voltage.
The energy stored in an inductor is given by the following expression:
-

$\Rightarrow E = (1/2) LI^2 =$ Energy stored in an inductor
Note L is the inductance and I is the current through the coil.

Now X_L is called the inductive reactance and has the unit of ohm, and X_C is the capacitive reactance and also has the unit of ohm. At resonant frequency f_0 when the frequency is a maximum and the impedance is a minimum, $Z = R$, the inductive reactance equals the capacitive reactance as follows: -

$X_L = X_C$
$\Rightarrow 2\pi f_0 L = 1/[2\pi f_0 C]$

From this last equation it can be verified that the resonant frequency f_0 is given by the following expression: -
$\Rightarrow f_0 = 1/[2\pi\sqrt{(LC)}]$

Hence resonant frequency is the maximum frequency at which the radio is tuned in on the dial. It has the unit of Hertz and the inductance and capacitance have the units of millihenry (mH) and farad (F) respectively. Hence frequency f, inductance L, and capacitance C can be adjusted to attain a maximum resonant frequency f_0 at which the radio is tuned in. Now $1H = 1J/A^2$ and $1F = 1J/V^2$ and $1\Omega = 1V/A$ where H = henry (unit of inductance), F = farad (unit of capacitance), Ω = ohm (unit of resistance), J = joule (unit of energy), V = volt (unit of voltage), and A = ampere (unit of current) respectively. Furthermore X_L = inductive reactance (in units of ohm), and X_C = capacitive reactance (in units of ohm), and R = resistance (in units of ohm). According to Ohm's Law, we have as follows: -
$\Rightarrow V$ (voltage) = I (current) x R (resistance).

28) a) & b) Metropolis or Metropolitan cities: -

A metropolis is defined as the chief city of a country or the capital city. In this discussion we briefly describe three major cities or three metropolitan cities namely New York City, New Delhi, and Bombay; and a hill station called Punchgani Hill Station.

New York City:-

Each of the five boroughs that make up New York City has the same boundaries as the county in which it lies. This is a city of islands, with only one borough, the Bronx, on the mainland. Manhattan and Staten Island are on separate islands and Brooklyn and Queens are on Long Island.

The net land area of New York City is 299.7 square miles. The climate of New York City is not very pleasant. Average temperatures vary from about 33° F (1°C) in January to 76° F (24°C) in July. Average annual precipitation is from 40 to 43 inches which is fairly evenly distributed during the year.

In Upper New York Bay off the tip of Manhattan lie three small islands, each significant in city's history. On Liberty Island stands the Statue of Liberty, a national monument and a symbol of the nation. The other two islands are the Ellis Island and the Governor's Island.

The midtown Manhattan extends from 23rd street to the south boundary of central park at 59th street. The midtown area contains most of the large hotels and many of the points of interests such as the Empire State Building, Rockefeller Center, Madison Square Garden, and the United Nations Building. The J.F.K International Airport is situated in Queens, New York City.

New Delhi:-

New Delhi became the capital of the Independent Republic of India in the year 1947. Since then it has grown rapidly, expanding well beyond the original boundaries. It is situated on the west bank of Yamuna River in the Union territory of Delhi in northern India. The Old City of Delhi is immediately to the north. Government is the primary activity in New Delhi. It is served by excellent roads, and a railway system and an International Airport.

The principle thoroughfare is Rajpath, which is part of a great central mall that extends two miles (3 km) from the main government building to India Gate, a memorial to Indian soldiers who died in WWI. Other major avenues radiate from Connaught Place, the city's chief commercial section.

Among the most prominent buildings are the President's house, the Central Secretariat, Parliament house, and the embassies in the

Diplomatic Enclave. Historic structures in the city include a 16th century fort, an astronomical observatory built in the year 1725 and several elaborate Mogul tombs. New Delhi is a major Indian cultural center, with many outstanding museums and libraries. Especially notable are the National Museum, the National Archives etc. Educational institutions include Jawaharlal Nehru University, University of Delhi Medical College and the National Physical Laboratory which is the city's largest research institution.

Bombay: -

Bombay is one of India's largest cities and capital of the state of Maharashtra. The city is on Bombay and Salsette islands in the Arabian Sea about 10 miles (16 km) off the coast of west central India. The two islands are joined by a causeway. Causeways also join Bombay with mainland. An excellent harbor, one of the world's largest, gives the city the title, "Gateway to India". Bombay is also an important rail and air center. The climate of Bombay is humid for five months, June to October. The rest of the year is very dry. Temperatures average 85^0F (29^0C) in May and 75^0F (24^0C) in January.

Many workers live in slums, but the business section has fine buildings and broad, and clean streets. A beautiful residential section stands along Marine Drive leading to Malabur Hill. The city has many cultural and educational centers, including the University of Bombay, founded in 1857, and the IIT at Bombay, founded in 1958. Bombay's industry is based on petroleum refining, and manufacture of cotton textiles and chemicals. The city also has shipyards, motion picture studios, and an automobile assembly plant.

The first Europeans to take benefit from Bombay as a trade center were the Portuguese. Early in the 16th century they established trading posts. In 1665 Bombay was given to the British as part of the dowry of the infanta of Portugal after her marriage to Charles II. The British controlled the city until India became independent in 1947. The population of Bombay, according to a 1990 United Nation's population estimate for urban agglomeration of Bombay, is 12.2 million, making it the sixth largest city in the world.

Punchgani Hill Station, Maharashtra: -

Points: - Punchgani: - Bhim Chula, Harrison Valley, Parsi Point, and the famous Table Land.

Bhim Chula and Harrison Valley: -

Bhim Chula is an exaggerated name for this place and Harrison Valley both of which are breath taking points in Punchgani.

Parsi Point: -

This is the windiest point in Punchgani. It is near the Dhom dam.

Table Land: -

Table Land is one of the Largest Table Lands in Asia, and many films have been shot here. This point is the most famous of all the points in Punchgani.

29)

. . . .

a) Democracy

Democracy is the government of the people. Democracy is the government by the majority of the people, or majority rule. It differs from monarchy ("rule by one"); aristocracy ("rule by the best or nobles"); and oligarchy ("rule by a few").

Democracy has three different but somewhat similar meanings:

1. A form of government in which those who control the government are elected by the people and are responsible or answerable for their action to the people,
2. A form of society in which there is no privileged class and in which individuals may rise by ability to positions of power and influence, and
3. An ideal or way of life that stresses equality, liberty, individual rights, tolerance, freedom of discussion and compromise.

Most democracies are republics, in which the people elect the head of the state. A monarchy with a hereditary king or queen may also be democratic. Great Britain, for example, is a democracy in the form of limited monarchy. Some countries that call themselves republics are not democracies. A country with a republican constitution may be a dictatorship in which government is under complete control of one person.

b) Forms of Democracy

There are precisely two forms of democracy.

1. Direct or pure Democracy, and
2. Indirect or representative Democracy.

Direct democracy is the oldest form. Under direct democracy all citizens meet in public assemblies to decide on community problems and to choose magistrates. Direct democracy continues to be used in New England town meetings to some extent and also in several of the smaller Swiss cantons. This form is possible only in small area with small population. If the population is too large, public meetings would be too overcrowded to accomplish much business. However two structures of direct democracy, the Initiative and Referendum, have proved practical for areas as large as States.

In large or populous areas the citizens must act indirectly through elected representatives. This system is called representative democracy or representative government. The people elect representatives (aldermen, congressmen, senators, etc.) to act for them. Representatives are answerable to people at frequent elections. In Great Britain, most European countries, and United States in the western hemisphere, there is generally a representative form of government.

The communists call their government a "People's democracy" and they refer to their countries as "Soviet Republics" or "People's Republics". Actually communist governments are dictatorships. Only the communist party is allowed. Elections are held, but the only candidates are those of the communist party. A system such as this, in which authoritarian control is exercised over everything, is often called "Totalitarianism". Communism is similar in its effect to Fascism, another type of Totalitarianism.

Initiative and Referendum:

These are two methods of direct law making by the people. These two devices of direct legislation are sometimes used where the voters have become too numerous or scattered to assemble in one meeting. Initiative and Referendum are separate but are found together. They do not reject the legislation but supplement it. They give the people a voice in lawmaking, when legislation disregards public opinion or bows to political bosses or special interests. Many states and cities in the US and some foreign countries use these methods of direct law making in which petitions are signed before they are adopted by majority vote.

The most famous definition of democracy that I came across in the study of Political Science is as follows: -

"Democracy is the government of the people, by the people, and for the people".

30)

· ·

United States of America (USA)

United States of America (USA) is a country consisting of 50 states, a federal district, and various other units and possessions. Forty-nine of the states and the federal district (the District of Columbia) are in North America. The 50th state, Hawaii, is an island group in the Pacific Ocean. The other units and possessions are in the Pacific Ocean and Caribbean area.

The United States is commonly called America and its people Americans. More properly, however, America applies to the whole of the Western Hemisphere, and Americans to all people who live there.

The United States is one of the largest and most powerful countries in the world. It is exceeded in size only by Russia, Canada, and China. Only China, Russia, and India have larger populations. The United States leads the world in agriculture and industrial production and is one of the world's richest countries in mineral resources.

E. Pluribus Unum (National Motto): -

It is a Latin phrase which means "One out of many". It was proposed as a motto for the United States by Franklin, Jefferson, and Adams on August 20, 1776, and first displayed on the Great Seal (1782). The phrase has continuously displayed on United States coins, though it has never been officially adapted for that purpose. (The official national motto of the United States is "In God We Trust".)

Holiday: - It is a day set apart by law or custom to commemorate an event or to honor a person or group. A holiday was originally a holy day, observed in memory of some sacred event or holy person. In modern usage, religious holidays are usually referred to as festivals or feasts. The world "holiday" usually refers to a legal holiday, established by law and marked by legal restrictions on public (government) business. The extent to which private business is suspended varies for different holidays and, often, in different parts of a country.

The United States has no legal holidays. The federal government establishes legal holidays only for the District of Columbia and for federal employees throughout the nation.

Federal Legal Holidays: -

1. New Year's Day (January 1)
2. Washington's Birthday (third Monday in February)
3. Memorial (or Decoration) Day (last Monday in May)
4. Independence Day (4th of July)
5. Labor Day (first Monday in September)
6. Columbus Day (second Monday in October)
7. Veteran's Day (November 11)
8. Thanksgiving Day (fourth Thursday in November)
9. Christmas Day (December 25)

Each state designates the legal holidays it observes. Most states observe all the federal legal holidays, as well as additional holidays for events or persons the states wish to honor. Certain days such as Arbor Day and Flag Day are legal holidays in only a few states. Some widely observed days, such as St. Valentine's Day and Mother's Day, are not legal holidays.

31)

a) Navigation

The term "navigation" is defined as the art and science of guiding a ship, airplane, spacecraft or land vehicle from one place to another. The term is known from Latin words for "ship" and "to direct". Navigation is commonly associated with travel over large expanses of water, ice or barren land because under these conditions, navigation requires special knowledge and skill. However, some form of navigation is required even on an automobile trip.

The main purpose of navigation is to determine the direction a vehicle should travel to reach a desired destination. Other uses of navigation include determining speed, estimating time of arrival, and detecting the presence of hazards in the path of the vehicle. Positions are usually determined with respect to parallels of latitude and meridians of longitude.

Methods of Navigation

Piloting

This is a method of navigating using earthly landmarks and aids to navigation. Piloting originally referred to the use of visual objects that could be seen on or near land. However in the 21st century, piloting includes the use of radio signals, fathometers and other electronic aids that can be used by aircrafts and ships.

Piloting depends on establishing a line of position from a landmark. This is a line along which the vehicle must be located to be in a given relationship to the landmark. When two intersecting lines of position are established, the vehicle is at the point of intersection of the two lines. A position determined in this way is called a fix.

Lines of position are determined when the direction, called the bearing of a landmark is known or when the distance to a landmark is known. A line of position established from a bearing is a straight line and a line of position established from a direction is a circle. For this fix to be accurate both measurements must be made at approximately the same time.

Electronic aids to navigation can be used to find distance, direction, or both. Radio transmitters that are used as electronic aids to navigation are called radio beacons.

For aircraft, the most common electronic aid to navigation is the Omni station (VHF or very high frequency) radio station that transmits magnetic bearings with relation to the station location.

In some cases, sonar, a system in which sound signals are reflected from obstacles can be used to determine position of a ship from known underwater features viz. trenches in the ocean floor.

Dead reckoning:-

In most cases, a dead reckoning position is determined from the direction steered and the speed through the water or air. The direction of travel is usually determined with a compass. Distance is computed from speed and time. Speed is determined by such devices as a ship's log or the airspeed indicator of an airplane.

The accuracy of dead reckoning can be increased by using electronic devices such as those that make use of inertia and the Doppler Shift. Doppler shift is a change in the wavelength of electromagnetic wave, viz. light or radio waves when emitted or reflected from a moving object.

Celestial Navigation:-

This method is based on the apparent position of various celestial bodies and navigational satellites. The celestial bodies most commonly used are the sun, moon, Venus, Mars, Jupiter, Saturn, and about 25 bright stars.

A point on the earth when a given celestial body is directly overhead or at zenith is called the geographical position of that body. Because the earth is turning, the geographical position of each celestial body varies with time.

Each ship carries Greenwich Mean Time by means of an extremely accurate clock called a chronometer.

Kinds of Navigation:-

Marine Navigation:-

In this kind of navigation, dead reckoning is used between accurate fixes. Except in the vicinity of land where there are frequent hazards, marine navigation is a leisurely process. Sightings of the sun and stars are made many times a day and headings are followed for long periods.

Air Navigation:-

Over much of the world, electronic aids to navigation can be used almost exclusively. This is similar to marine navigation but several factors- including a higher speed and a greater dependence on weather conditions- present special problems to this type of navigation.

Land Navigation:-

In this method or kind of navigation, dead reckoning and celestial navigation are commonly used. When landmarks are available, some form of piloting produces the best and easiest method of navigation.

Underwater Navigation:-

Two methods for increasing the accuracy of underwater dead reckoning include the use of sonar, and an inertial system called SINS (Ship's Inertial Navigation Systems). The atomic submarine USS Nautilus was navigated under the ice cap at the North Pole using SINS.

Space Navigation:-

Within range of earth, position may be known through radio waves. In distance space, dead reckoning or celestial navigation is used. In celestial navigation, lines of position are established by determining the apparent position of the sun, the moon, or a planet against the background of stars.

b) Aviation

Aviation is the science and practice of flying powered, heavier-than-air craft such as airplanes and helicopters. The aviation industry includes the design, manufacturing, sale, and maintenance of heavier-than-air craft as well as flight activities.

The term aerospace industry is collectively used for the aviation industry and the industries concerned with the various aspects of space exploration and missiles and rockets.

Aviation is generally divided into two categories, viz. military aviation and civil aviation. Military aviation is the air force and civil aviation is further sub-divided into air transport industry (or airline) and general, or utility aviation.

The airplanes are classified according to their uses as follows:-

Commercial Airplanes:-

These planes which usually have two, three or four engines are built for service on commercial airlines. Most of these are powered by turbo-pump, turbo-jet, or turbo-fan engines, although piston engine models are still used in some regions for short runs.

Commercial passenger airlines are used in local, transcontinental, and transoceanic travel. The largest United States airlines can carry up to 490 passengers, have kitchen equipment for preparing meals, and can carry large amounts of luggage, freight and mail. Almost all types of passenger planes can be adapted to haul freight.

Military Planes:-

Some military planes are propeller driven, but most combat types are jet-propelled. Propeller-driven planes are still useful in some combat situation, however, such as anti-guerilla operation. Most types of combat planes can carry nuclear weapons.

Private Airplanes:-

The private plane is used by individuals or companies for transportation, work or sport. It is usually a light, single engine plane. Multi-engine planes, commercial type airliner, or converted bombers are sometimes used, especially by large corporations. Although airplanes are rather expensive to operate and maintain, these expenses are often offset by savings in time.

Personal airplanes are used by business-men, hunters and others as a quick means of transportation. Many amateur flying enthusiasts use planes for recreation. Most airports have facilities for storing and servicing personal airplanes. Business air planes are used for fast transportation of personnel or materials over long distances, when the scheduled commercial flights either do not serve the area involved or do not run often enough. Ranchers and farmers use the business air planes for such works as seed planting and crop dusting. Forest ranchers use them to detect fires, and to drop fire fighters by parachute.

On a cold, December morning in 1903, the Wright brothers for the first time in modern history flew 120 feet in 12 seconds. Hence the later developments took place in the beginning of the twentieth century after the year 1903.

In the present times, aviation is a great school, where people are taught the art of flying lighter-than-air craft and it has thousands of useful applications. The world in the present times not only travels on land but it travels on wings as well, that is, the wings of a heavy duty lighter-than-air craft.

The purpose of aviation, which is to cover longest routes in the shortest possible time without any hassle and transport freight as well as people from one place to another place located at the farthest possible corners of the world, is being served with great technology in the present times.

The idea of aviation originated with Wright brothers in the early 1903 when they engineered a project of this type and flew 120 feet in 12 seconds on a cold December morning of that same year.

32)

· ·

United Nations Organization (UNO): -

The United Nations is the international organization founded in 1945 to try to maintain world peace and security. The U.N flag represents more than 150 countries, virtually all the nations of the world. Each member nation retains control over its internal affairs. In its effort to allow nations to solve their disputes by peaceful means, the U.N also tries to do away with political situations that may lead to disputes. It therefore deals with such social and economic problems as poverty, disease, and lack of literacy and skills.

The U.N does its work through six principal organs or branches, which are as follows: -

1. the General Assembly,
2. the Security Council,
3. the Economic and Social Council,
4. the Trusteeship Council,
5. the International Court of Justice, and
6. the Secretariat.

A number of autonomous intergovernmental agencies and bodies cooperate with the U.N. Membership in the U.N is open to all countries that accept the obligations of the U.N Charter, and in the judgment of the U.N, are able and willing to carry out these obligations. Members may be admitted, suspended, or expelled by the General Assembly upon recommendation of the Security Council. The U.N is supported by financial contributions from each member country. Its headquarters are in New York City, on an 18 acre plot of land that is international territory. Other U.N offices are in the principal capitals of the world. The U.N.O's official languages are Arabic, Chinese, English, Russian, French, and Spanish.

Functions and Mottos: -

The United Nations Charter states the following purposes: -

1. To maintain international peace and security...
2. To develop friendly relations among nations...
3. To achieve international cooperation in solving international problems of an economic, social, cultural, or humanitarian character, and in promoting and encouraging respect for human rights and for fundamental freedoms...
4. To be a center for harmonizing the actions of nations in the attainment of these common ends.

Members of the U.N are pledged to settle all international disputes peacefully; to refrain from threats and use of force; to cooperate with all decisions of the U.N; and to assist the U.N when it takes enforcement action against aggression.

The U.N is based on the principle that all its members are sovereign and equal. It does not have the authority to order a member to take a specific action, except in cases of aggression where the Security Council calls for enforcement action.

In all other cases, the U.N has the power to recommend, not require, action. Its authority rests on moral force and the willingness of its members to cooperate.

U.N's Main Branches: -

1. The General Assembly: -

    The General Assembly is the U.N parliament of all member nations. Each nation has one vote but may have as many as five delegates. Regular services are held once a year, usually beginning in September. A special session may be called by vote of the Security Council, or on the request of a majority of the U.N member nations or one member with concurrence of the majority. A president is elected for each session. Important decisions must be approved by two-thirds of the members present and voting; other decisions, by majority.

    The General Assembly may discuss and make recommendations on all matters that come within the scope of the Charter. However, it cannot make recommendations on any question concerning peace and security being considered by the Security Council, unless the council asks it to do so. If the Security Council fails because of the

Assembly veto to act on a threat to the peace, the Assembly can make recommendations to member countries for collective action to maintain or restore peace.

The Assembly has a number of subsidiary bodies, such as the U.N Scientific Advisory Committee and the International Law Commissions. The Assembly approves the U.N's budget and controls the spending of money.

2. The Security Council: -

The Security Council's main responsibility is to maintain peace and security. It consists of 15 members. (The Council's membership was raised from 11 to 15 by amendment of the Charter in 1965) The Charter names five permanent members: the United States, the U.S.S.R (Russia), the United Kingdom (Great Britain and Northern Ireland), France, and China (representation by Nationalist China until 1971, by Communist China thereafter). Ten non-permanent members are elected by the General Assembly for two-year terms-five each year-after which they may not serve again immediately. The Council is organized so that it can work continuously. The chairmanship is rotated among the members monthly.

Each member of the Security Council has one vote. In a case involving the peaceful settlement of a dispute, a country involved in the dispute cannot vote. Decisions require nine affirmative votes. Any resolution, except on a matter of procedure, may be defeated by the negative vote or veto of one of the five permanent members of the Council. The Council is authorized to investigate any dispute that might threaten international peace and security and to make recommendations for its peaceful settlement. If a veto prevents the Council from acting on a territorial issue, the matter may be turned over to the General Assembly where there is no veto.

3. The Economic and Social Council: -

The Economic and Social Council acts under the authority of the General Assembly, to promote international welfare and progress and to advance human rights and fundamental freedoms. The aim is to establish a basis for enduring peace. The Council studies and makes recommendations on international economic, social, cultural, educational, health and related matters. It gives advice to the U.N organs and agencies and to member nations; coordinates technical assistance programs, calls international conferences; and drafts proposed conventions or treaties, for submission to the General Assembly.

The Council has 54 members, 18 of whom are elected each year by the General Assembly for three-year terms. Retiring members may be reelected. Voting is by simple majority. The Council has two regular sessions a year, and may have special sessions.

The Economic and Social Council helps to coordinate the activities of the intergovernmental agencies. The Council has five regional economic commissions- for Europe, Eastern Asia and the Pacific, Western Asia, Latin America, and Africa- and various other commissions, called functional commissions, on special matters such as narcotics, status of women, and human rights.

4. International Court of Justice: -

The International Court of Justice is the principal judicial organ of the United Nations. This court replaced the Permanent Court of International Justice (World Court), which was associated with the League of Nations. The International Court was created by the Charter of the United Nations (1945) but has its own statute or fundamental law. All countries belonging to the United Nations are members also of the court, and other countries may join. The court is in The Hague, the Netherlands. The 15 judges are elected for nine year terms by the U.N Security Council and General Assembly, voting separately, from nominators made by specially appointed national groups. No two judges may be from the same country.

The court hears only those cases that involve countries. As a general rule, it hears only cases, submitted to it by agreement of the two countries. But many countries, by ratifying the Optional Clause of the statute, have agreed to accept the compulsory jurisdiction of the court in certain classes of cases. The court bases its decisions on international conventions, international customs, and general principles of law, judicial decisions of national courts, and the teachings of experts on international law.

The court may give advisory opinions on any legal question submitted to it by the General Assembly or Security Council, or by any U.N organ or specialized agency. The official languages of the International Court are English and French. Decisions are by majority vote.

The court has no means of enforcing its decisions, although they are supposed to be binding. In 1970 for example, the court declared in an advisory opinion that South Africa had no legal authority over South-West Africa (Namibia), but South Africa ignored the opinion and retained its control. In 1972 Iceland extended the limits of its territorial fishing waters despite a court order to refrain from doing so.

5. The Trusteeship Council: -

When the United Nations was formed; the Trusteeship Council was established to oversee the administration by member nations of certain dependent territories called trust territories. Most such territories were formerly League of Nations mandates. By the end of 1949, the General Assembly had approved of 11 trusteeship agreements. Nations with trust territories under their administration were Australia, Belgium, France, Great Britain, Italy, New Zealand, and the United States.

The Trusteeship Council was given responsibility to promote the political, economic, social, and educational development of the inhabitants of the trust territories to prepare them for independence. In the decades that followed, all the trust territories except the Trust Territory of the Pacific Islands (administered by the United States) were granted independence.

6. The Secretariat: -

The Secretariat is the staff of the U.N. It is headed by a secretary general, elected for a five year term by the General Assembly upon the recommendation of the Security Council. The secretary general is the chief administrating officer of the U.N and of its organs. The General Assembly sometimes authorizes him to act as a conciliator in serious disputes between nations.

The Secretariat handles the U.N's day to day administration matters. Its employees, who come from many countries, include secretaries, translators, scientists, guides, writers, and broadcasters. Employees may not seek or receive instructions from any source outside the U.N.

The Establishment of the United Nations: -

The U.N was born during World War II, when the Axis powers viz. Germany, Italy, and Japan, threatened the freedom of the world. In August, 1941, the United States and Great Britain signed the Atlantic Charter, stating broad principles of peace objectives, and human rights. The term "United Nations" first was used on January 1, 1942, when 26 countries at war with the Axis reaffirmed the principles of the Atlantic Charter and signed the Declaration of the United Nations.

In the Moscow Declaration of 1943 the United States, Russia, Great Britain, and China agreed to set up a new international organization to replace the unsuccessful League of Nations that had been formed after World War I. Proposals for the new organization were drafted in meetings held in 1944 at Dumbarton Oaks, Washington D.C., by delegates from four powers. Concerned that the organization would be ineffectual without big-power leadership, the delegates agreed to add a Security Council. Five of the 11 members would be major powers with permanent seats.

At a summit meeting at Yalta in February, 1945, Allied leaders agreed that each of the big powers, to protect its interests, should have the power of veto in the Security Council. The privilege could not be used, however, in procedural matters or in peaceful disputes involving permanent members.

The proposals at Dumbarton oaks and the decisions at Yalta formed the basis for the United Nations Charter. It was drawn up by representatives to the United Nations Conference on International Organization at San Francisco (more commonly known as the San Francisco Conference), April 25 – June 26, 1945. The Charter went into effect on October 24, 1945, which has become known as the United Nations Day.

The General Assembly first met on January 10, 1946, in London with the 51 charter members represented. Trygve Lie of Norway was elected the U.N's first secretary general. The Assembly voted to establish headquarters in or near New York City. John D. Rockefeller, Jr., donated money for land along the East River in New York City and in 1951 the 39 story Secretariat building was completed on the site.

History of the United Nations: -

Diplomatic Difficulties: - The rift between East and West hampered the work of the U.N. Often, when outvoted, Russia used its veto, and many countries charged Russia with abusing the privilege. When Communists gained control of China in 1949, Russia demanded that the Communist government be given China's U.N seat, which was held by the Nationalist China, who occupied Formosa. The demand was rejected and the Russian delegation walked out of the Security Council, staying out a half year.

After a long deadlock over admissions of new members, 16 nations, some communist dominated, were admitted in 1955. Quick expansion followed. In 1960, 17 countries, 16 of them Africans, were admitted. Africa and Asia soon formed a voting bloc and by the end of the decade held a majority of seats in the General Assembly. The decisive majority once held by the United States and its allies was destroyed. Also, all the major powers, including Russia, gradually lost influence and leadership to the small countries, whose interests and concerns were different.

The admission of Communist China to the U.N and the expulsion of Nationalist China in 1971, after 22 years of contention, and over United States opposition – reflected the lessening influence of the United States.

Problems of finance became acute after 1960. Russia, France, and other nations refused to pay assessments for military operations, such as those in the Republic of Congo (now Zaire) and the Middle East that they had not approved.

In 1965, Indonesia became the first nation to withdraw from the U.N. It did so in protest against the seating of Malaysia on the Security Council. In 1966, however, Indonesia resumed its membership.

Supporting Independence: - Since the U.N's beginnings, the organization through its decisions and trusteeship programs has helped bring independence to many nations. During the 1960's and early 1970's the U.N conducted an experiment campaign to bring an end to white minority rule in Africa. Repeatedly the U.N voiced support of armed liberation movements in Portugal's African Colonies. In 1966 the

U.N imposed economic sanctions against Rhodesia, a British Colony whose white supremacist government had declared its independence. (The sanctions ended in 1980 when the nation, renamed Zimbabwe accomplished rule by its black majority)

The U.N in 1966 condemned South African policy of apartheid, racial segregation, and declared that country's mandate over South-West Africa (Namibia) ended. South Africa, however, ignored U.N plans to administer the territory and retained effective control.

Social and Economic Work: - After World War II, the U.N was instrumental in helping to rebuild the war-torn Europe. As many new under-developed nations joined the U.N in the 1960's and 1970's the U.N increasingly concentrated its work on their problems. The inter-governmental agencies of the U.N made far-reaching contributions to the social and economic advancement of the under-developed nations.

Peace-Keeping Efforts: - Throughout its history, the U.N has been useful in resolving differences between the small nations of the world. In 1949 the U.N settled disputes between Indonesia and the Netherlands. Further disagreement between the two countries concerning the possession of West New Guinea led to direct U.N administration of the territory during 1962-63. During 1949, the U.N mediators had also halted fighting between India and Pakistan in Kashmir. When their differences erupted into a full-scale war in 1965 the U.N brought about a cease-fire.

U.N troops helped to maintain order in the Republic of Congo during 1960 – 64. A U.N peace-keeping force that had first gone to Cypress in 1964 helped avert a threatened Greek-Turkish war there in 1967.

The U.N took a major role in peace efforts in the Middle East. U.N intervention helped stop fighting between Arab states and Israel in 1949. British and French forces, which had invaded Egypt's Suez Canal Zone in 1956, withdrew under a U.N-sponsored agreement that also led to the removal of Israeli troops from the Sinai Peninsula.

A U.N Emergency Force, established along the Egyptian-Israeli border to preserve peace, was withdrawn in 1967 at Egypt's request. The six-day Arab-Israeli war that followed ended after a U.N-proposed truce was accepted. In 1973, following a short war between the Arab nations and Israel, the U.N supervised the disengagement of troops and the cease-fire.

33)

· ·

a) Independence Day (India) 15 August, 1947

Independence Day of India is celebrated on 15th August to commemorate its independence from the British rule and its birth as a sovereign nation in 1947. The day is a national holiday in India. All over the country, flag hoisting ceremonies are conducted by the local administration in attendance. The main event takes place in New Delhi, the capital city of India, where the Prime Minister hoists the national flag at the Red Fort and delivers a nationally televised speech from its ramparts. In his speech, he highlights the achievements of his government during the past year, raises important issues and gives a call for further development. The Prime Minister also pays tribute to leaders of the freedom struggle.

History: -

In 1946, the Labour government in Britain, its exchequer exhausted by the recently concluded World War II, and conscious that it had neither the mandate at home, the international support, nor the reliability of native forces for continuing to control an increasingly restless India, decided to end British rule of India, and in early 1947 Britain announced its intention of transferring power no later than June, 1948.

As Independence approached, the violence between Hindus and Muslims in the provinces of Punjab and Bengal continued unabated. With the British army unprepared for the potential for increased violence, the new viceroy, Louis Mountbatten advanced the date for the transfer of power, allowing less than six months for a mutually agreed plan for independence. In June, 1947, the nationalist leaders, including Nehru, Abul Kalam Azad, and Jinnah agreed to a partition of the country along religious lines. The predominantly Hindu and Sikh areas were assigned to the new India and predominantly Muslim areas to the new nation of Pakistan; the plans included a partition of the provinces of Punjab and Bengal.

Many millions of Muslim, Sikh, and Hindu refugees trekked across the newly drawn borders. In Punjab, where the new border lines divided the Sikh region in half, massive bloodshed followed; in Bengal and Bihar, the violence was more limited. In all, anywhere between 250,000 and 500,000 people on both sides of the new borders died in the violence. On 14 August, 1947, the new Dominion of Pakistan came into being, with Muhammad Ali Jinnah sworn in as its first Governor General in Karachi. At the stroke of midnight as India moved into August 15, 1947, Jawaharlal Nehru, read out the famous Tryst with destiny speech proclaiming India's independence. India, now a smaller Union of India, became an independent country with official ceremonies taking place in New Delhi, and with Jawaharlal Nehru assuming the office of the first prime minister, and the viceroy, Louis Mountbatten, staying on as its first Governor General.

Celebration: -

The Independence Day of India is celebrated with the Prime Minister of India hoisting the Indian flag on the historical site, Red Ford, Delhi, on August 15. This is telecast live on the National Channel Doordarshan and many News Channels all over India. Flag hoisting ceremonies and cultural programs take place in all the state capitals. In the cities around the country, the national flag is hoisted by politicians in their constituencies. In various private organizations the flag hoisting is carried out by a senior official of that organization. All over the country, flags are given out to citizens, who wear them proudly to chalk their patriotism towards India. Schools and Colleges around the country organize flag hoisting ceremonies and various cultural events, within their premises, where younger boys and girls in costume do impersonations of their favorite characters of the independence era. They also have a parade. Families and friends get together for lunch or dinner or for an outing. Housing colonies, cultural centers, clubs, and societies hold entertainment programs and competitions, usually based on the Independence Day theme. Most national and regional television channels screen old and new film classics with patriotic themes on Independence Day. Many non-governmental organizations telecast patriotic programs. It is a national festival which is celebrated by every Indian irrespective of religion.

b) Indo-China War of 1962

The Chinese have two major claims on what India deems its own territory. One claim, in the western sector, is on Aksai Chin in the northeastern section of Ladakh District in Jammu and Kashmir. The other claim is in the eastern sector over a region included in the British-designated North-East Frontier Agency, the disputed part of which India renamed Arunachal Pradesh and made a state. In the fight over these areas, the well-trained and well-armed troops of the Chinese People's Liberation Army overpowered the ill-equipped Indian troops who had not been acclimatized to fighting at high altitudes.

After its independence in1947, India not only inherited Britain's occupation of parts of the Chinese territories but also further encroached northward and pushed its borderline to the Mc Mahon Line in 1953, as a result, invaded and occupied 90,000 square kilometers of Chinese territories. At western sector, in 1959, India voiced its claim to the Aksai Chin areas, counted 33,000 square kilometers, of Xinjiang Uygur Autonomous Region of China. In April, 1960, Chinese Premier Zhou Enlai went to New Delhi to hold talks with Indian Prime Minister Nehru; no agreements were reached due to India's insistence on its unreasonable stand. The ensuing meetings between the officials of the two countries also produced no results.

Unable to reach political accommodation on disputed territory along the 3,225 kilometer-long Himalayan border, the Chinese attacked India on October 20, 1962. At that time nine divisions from the eastern and western commands were deployed along the Himalayan border with China. None of these divisions was up to its full troop strength, and all were short of artillery, tanks, equipment, and even adequate articles of clothing.

Indian decisions taken at that time were not grounded in adequate, up-to-date, knowledge of what was transpiring within China or the motivations of China's then key decision-makers. Stated briefly, New Delhi failed to decipher the "Chinese calculus of deterrence" and India suffered disproportionately.

In Ladakh, the Chinese attacked south of the Karakorum Pass at the northwest end of the Aksai Chin Plateau and in the Pan gong Lake area about 160 kilometers to the southeast. The defending Indian forces were easily ejected from their posts in the area of the Karakorum Pass and from most posts near Pan gong Lake. However, they put up spirited resistance at the key posts of Daulat Beg Oldi (near the entrance to the pass) and Chushul (located immediately south of Pan gong Lake and at the head of the vital supply road to Leh, a major town and location of an air force base in Ladakh). Other Chinese forces attacked near Demchok (about 160 kilometers southeast of Chushul) and rapidly overran the Demchok and Jara La posts.

In the eastern sector, in Assam, the Chinese forces advanced easily despite Indian efforts at resistance. On the first day of the fighting, Indian forces stationed at the Tsang Le post on the northern side of the Namka Chu, the Khinzemane post, and near Dhola were overrun. On the western side of the North-East Frontier Agency, Tsang Dar fell on October 22, Bum La on October 23, and Tawang, the headquarters of the Seventh Infantry Brigade, on October 24. The Chinese made an offer to negotiate on October 24. The Indian government promptly rejected this offer.

With a lull in the fighting, the Indian military desperately sought to regroup its forces. Specifically, the army attempted to strengthen its defensive positions in the North-East Frontier Agency, and Ladakh and to prepare against possible Chinese attacks through Sikkim and Bhutan. Army units were moved from Calcutta, Bihar, Nagaland, and Punjab to guard the northern frontiers of West Bengal and Assam. Three brigades were hastily positioned in the western part of North-East Frontier Agency, and two other brigades were moved into Sikkim and near the West Bengal border with Bhutan to face the Chinese. Light staurt tanks were drawn from the Eastern Command headquarters at Calcutta to bolster these deployments.

In the western sector, a divisional organization was established in Leh, several battalions of infantry, a battery of twenty-five pounder guns, and two troops of AMX light tanks were airlifted into the Chushul area from Punjab. On November 4, the Indian military decided that the post at Daulat Beg Oldi was untenable, and its defenders were withdrawn over the 5,300 meter-high Sasar Brangsa Pass to a more defensible position.

The reinforcements and redeployments in Ladakh proved sufficient to defend the Chushul perimeter despite repeated Chinese attacks. However, the more remote posts at Rezang La and Gurung Hill and the four posts at Spanggur Lake areas fell to the Chinese.

In the North-East Frontier Agency, the situation proved to be quite different. Indian forces counter-attacked on November 13, and captured a hill northwest of the town, Walong. Concerted Chinese attacks dislodged them from this hard won position, and the nearby garrison had to retreat down the Lohit Valley.

In another important section of the eastern sector, the Kameng Frontier Division, six Chinese brigades attacked across the Tawang Chu near Jang and advanced some sixteen kilometers to the southeast to attack Indian position at Nurang, near Se La, on November 17.

Despite the Indian attempt to regroup their forces at Se La, the Chinese continued their onslaught, wiping out virtually all Indian resistance in Kameng. By November 18, the Chinese had penetrated close to the outskirts of Tezpur, Assam, a major frontier town nearly fifty kilometers from the Assam-North-East Frontier Agency border.

The Chinese did not advance farther and on November 21 declared a unilateral cease-fire. They had accomplished all their territorial objectives, and any attempt to press farther into the plains of Assam would have stretched their logistical capabilities and their lines of communication to a breaking point. By the time the fighting stopped, each side had lost 500 troops.

After administering a blistering defeat in 1962, the Chinese forces withdrew 20 kms behind Mc Mahon Line, which China called "the 1959 line of actual control" in the Eastern Sector, and 20 kms behind the line of its latest position in Ladakh, which was further identified with "the 1959 line of actual control" in the Western Sector.

c) Indo-Pakistan War of 1965

The second Indo-Pakistani Conflict (1965) was also fought over Kashmir and started without a formal declaration of war. The war began in August 5, 1965 and was ended September 22, 1965.

The war was initiated by Pakistan who, since the defeat of India by China in 1962, had come to believe that Indian military would be unable or unwilling to defend against a quick military campaign in Kashmir and because the Pakistani government was becoming increasingly alarmed by Indian efforts to integrate Kashmir within India. There was also a perception that there was widespread support within for Pakistani rule and that the Kashmiri people were dissatisfied with Indian rule.

After Pakistan was successful in the Rann of Kutch earlier in 1965, Ayub Khan (by nature a cautious person) was pressured by the hawks in the cabinet (led by Z. A. Bhuttu) and the army to infiltrate the cease-fire line in Kashmir. The action was based on the incorrect premise that indigenous resistance could be ignited by a few saboteurs. Ayub resisted the idea as he foresaw India crossing the international frontier in retaliation at a point of its choosing. The Bhuttu faction, which included some prominent generals, put out the canard that Ayub's cowardice stemmed from his desire to protect his newly acquired wealth. It was boasted at the time that one Pakistani soldier was equal to four Indian soldiers and so on.

On August 5, 1965 between 26,000 and 33,000 Pakistani soldiers crossed the Line of Control dressed as Kashmiri locals headed for various areas within Kashmir. Indian forces, tipped off by the local populace, crossed the cease-fire line on August 15.

The initial battles between India and Pakistan were contained within Kashmir involving both infantry and armor units with each country's air force playing major roles. It was not until September when Pakistani forces attacked Ackhnur that the Indians escalated the conflict by attacking targets within Pakistan itself, forcing the Pakistani forces to disengage from Ackhnur to counter Indian attacks.

The largest engagement of the war occurred in the Sialkot region where some 400 to 600 tanks squared off. Unfortunately the battle was indecisive.

By September 22 both sides had agreed to a UN mandated cease-fire ending the war that had by that point reached a stalemate.

Overall, the war was militarily inconclusive, each side held prisoners and some territory belonging to the other. Losses were relatively heavy on Pakistani side, twenty aircrafts, 200 tanks, and 3,800 troops. Pakistan's army had been able to withstand Indian pressure, but a continuation of the fighting would only have led to further losses and ultimate defeat of Pakistan. Most Pakistanis, schooled in the belief of their own martial prowess, refused to accept the possibility of their country's military defeat by "Hindu-India" and were, instead, quick to blame their failure to attain their military aims on what they considered to be the ineptitude of Ayub Khan and his government.

Pakistan was rudely shocked by the reaction of the United States to the war. Deciding the matter to be largely Pakistan's fault, the United States not only refused to come to Pakistan's aid under the terms of the Agreement of Cooperation, but issued a statement declaring its neutrality while also cutting off military supplies. The Pakistani's were embittered at what they considered a friend's betrayal and the experience taught them to avoid relying on any single source of support. For its part, the United States was disillusioned by a war in which both sides used United States- supplied equipment. The war brought other changes in the security relationship. The United States withdrew its military assistance advisory group in July, 1967. In response to these events, Pakistan declined to renew the lease on the Peshawar military facility, which ended in 1969.

Eventually, United States-Pakistan relations grew measurably weaker as the United States became more deeply involved in Vietnam and as its broader interest in the security of South Asia waned.

Iran, Indonesia, and especially China gave political support to Pakistan during the war, thus suggesting new direction in Pakistan that might translate into support for its security concerns. Most striking was the attitude of the Soviet Union. The Soviet Union had a neutral position and ultimately provided the good offices at Tashkent, which led to the January 1966 Tashkent Declaration that restored the status quo ante.

The aftermath of the 1965 war saw a dramatic shift in Pakistan's security environment. Instead of a single alignment with United States against China and Soviet Union, Pakistan found itself cut off from United States military support, on increasingly warm terms with China, and treated equitably by the Soviet Union.

Unchanged was the enmity with which India and Pakistan regarded each other over Kashmir. The result was the elaboration of a new security approach, called by Ayub Khan the "triangular tightrope"- a tricky endeavor to maintain good ties with the United States while cultivating China and Soviet Union. Support from other developing nations was also welcome. None of the new relationships carried the weight of previous ties with the United States, but taken together, they at least provided Pakistan with a political counterbalance to India.

d) Indo-Pakistan War of 1971 and Independence of Bangladesh

Indo-Pakistan war of 1971 was a military conflict between India and Pakistan. The war is closely associated with the Bangladesh Liberation War (sometimes also referred to as the Pakistan Civil War). Hostilities began on 3December, 1971 and ended on 16 December, 1971. This period is called Indo-Pakistan War by the Bangladeshi and Indian armies both, while Pakistan considers it a larger part of the East Pakistan Rebellion.

The Indo-Pakistan conflict was sparked by the Bangladesh Liberation War, a conflict between the traditionally dominant West Pakistanis and the majority East Pakistanis. The Bangladesh Liberation War was instigated after the1970 Pakistan election in which East Pakistani Awami League won 167 of 169 seats in East Pakistan and secured a simple majority in the 313 seat Lower House of the Majlis-e-Shoora (Parliament of Pakistan). Awami League leader Sheikh Mujibur Rahman presented the six points to the president of Pakistan and claimed the right to form the government. After the leader of the Pakistan People's Party, Zulfiqar Ali Bhuttu refused to yield the premiership of Pakistan to Mujibur Rahman, President Yahya Khan called the military, dominated by West Pakistanis, to suppress dissent.

Mass arrests of dissidents began, and attempts were made to disarm East Pakistani soldiers and police. After several days of strikes and non-cooperation movements, the Pakistani military cracked down on Dhaka on the night of March 25, 1971. The Awami League was banished and many members fled into exile in India. Mujibur Rahman was arrested on the night of 25-26 March, 1971 at about 1:30 A.M (as per Radio Pakistan News on 29 March, 1971) and taken to West Pakistan.

On 27 March, 1971, Ziaur-Rahman, a rebellious major in the Pakistani army, declared the Independence of Bangladesh on behalf of Mujibur Rahman. In April, exiled Awami League leaders formed a government in exile in Baidyanathtala of Meherpur. The East Pakistan Rifles, a paramilitary force defected to the rebellion. A guerrilla troop of civilians, the Mukti Bahini was formed to help the Bangladesh army. This war had caused a refugee accommodation crisis on the eastern frontier, an extreme dearth of food supplies, medicines, and equipmen, and a prisoner of war (POW) issue, also in the eastern hemisphere.

Instrument of Surrender:-

The instrument of surrender was signed at Ramna Race Course in Dhaka at 16:31 IST on 16 December, 1971 by Lieutenant General Jagjit Singh Aurora, General Officer Commanding-in-Chief of the eastern command of the Indian army and Lieutenant General A. A. K. Niazi, commander of Pakistani forces in Bangladesh. Aurora accepted the surrender without a word, while the crowd on the race course started shouting anti-Niazi and anti-Pakistani slogans and abuses.

Niazi along with over 90,000 of Pakistani soldiers unconditionally surrendered to the Indian forces making it the largest surrender since World War II.

The war ended with the surrender of the Pakistani military to the allied forces of India and Bangladesh, jointly known as the Mitro-Bahini. Bangladesh became an independent nation, the world's third most populous Muslim state. The loss of East Pakistan demoralized the Pakistani military. President Yahya Khan resigned to be replaced by Zulfiqar Ali Bhutto. Mujibur Rahman was released from a West Pakistani prison, returning to Dhaka on January 10, 1972.

In 1972 the Simla Agreement was signed between India and Pakistan, the treaty ensured that Pakistan recognized the independence of Bangladesh in exchange for the return of the Pakistani P.O.W.s. India treated all the P.O.W.s in strict accordance with the Geneva Convention Rule 1925.

It released more than 90,000 Pakistani P.O.W.s in five months. Further as a gesture of goodwill nearly 200 soldiers who were sought for war crimes by Bengalis were also pardoned by India.

The accord also gave the seized Pakistani land by the Indian army back to Pakistan to have a lasting peace in the Indo-Pakistan-Bangladesh sub-continent.

34)

· ·

a) Population Explosion:-

Population is defined as the total number of persons living in a political or geographical area at a particular time. Population statistics include total population figures, data on population density, age, sex, and racial groupings within the population, and many other features.

Population statistics reflect the state of an area's population at the time in history during which the statistics were accumulated. For example, the 1980 census of the USA reports the number of persons living in this country on April 1, 1980, the census date. Because changes occur continuously in any population, the census figures are considered accurate for April 1 but not for any other day. (Actually, they are not even accurate for that day due to numerous errors and cancellations). To record those events that cause these variations, continuous records are needed. Such records are generally totaled, usually by the month and year and are termed vital statistics and migration statistics.

Vital statistics are records of live births, deaths, fetal deaths, marriages, divorces, adoptions, annulments, and related occurrences. Migration statistics are records of emigrations or permanent departures by an area's inhabitants and of immigration or arrivals of new permanent residents from other areas.

Importance of Population Statistics:-

Population statistics have many uses. In the USA the census is used as the basis for apportioning seats in the House of Representatives among the states according to their populations. Many other countries also determine representatives in governing bodies by the use of population statistics.

Population statistics are a fundamental tool of the science of demography, the statistical analysis and study of population. Accurate population statistics are necessary in planning immigration policies, public health programs, advertising and marketing campaigns and many other public and private activities.

Sources of Population Statistics:-

A census of a population is the process of counting the inhabitants of a fixed area, compiling the figures, and transforming the figures into useful facts, statistics and maps. Most of the world's nations take a census of population at regular or approximately regular intervals.

In some countries, especially the countries of Europe, local authorities maintain a continuous vital statistics record of all new residents, births, deaths, and permanent departures. Such records called, population registers, can be used to establish population statistics for any particular day. They are extremely detailed and mostly used to double check census results.

Population estimates are calculated by most countries that do not take censuses, by census taking countries between censuses, by international organization such as the United Nations, and by other public and private bodies. Enumerations vary widely in reliability.

The most reliable are generally based on most recent complete censuses or registrations. Less reliable are those based on sample or partial census, registration, or surveys, or on old population records. The least reliable are based on no statistical records but on guesses and inferred estimates. Estimates of tribal population in remote areas of the world are usually of this type.

Causes of Population Variations

Variation in the total population of the earth is based primarily on the relation between the birth rate and the death (or mortality) rate. An excess of births over deaths, called birth increase, results in long term population growth.

The rate of natural increase is expressed as the number of births minus deaths per thousand persons per year, or as a percentage. An average birth rate averaging 35 per 1,000 and a death rate averaging 20 per 1,000 add up to an annual average rate of natural increase of 15 per 1,000. This result is equivalent to 1.5 per 100, or 1.5 per cent.

Population statistics are also affected by larger longevity or the average length of life of individuals. Within any given area of the world, such as a nation, migration is also an important factor in population variations.

Population Growth:-

Well understood statistics on population are available for only the most recent few centuries. Partial and approximate information is available for a much longer period and some enumerations of a general character have been made regarding ancient and preliterate man. These facts and figures indicate a continuous but uneven growth in man's numbers.

Growth to the 17th century: Until man began to cultivate land and domesticate animals, about 11,000 years ago, the number of human beings on earth at any one time never exceeded a few million. The average life span was only about 25 years and the rate of natural increase was measurable only in small fractions of one per cent and may have been zero or negative for considerable periods.

The cause of early man's low rate of population growth was his way of life. As a hunter and gatherer of food, man had to wander over large territory to find enough to eat. Under such circumstances large families were undesirable. The sick, injured, and aged were, in many cases, either killed or abandoned so as not to disturb the main course. Excess children were killed, a practice called infanticide, or left to die.

By 7000 B.C communities with well developed social and economic systems had come into existence in the Middle East. Between 7000 B.C to about 4000 B.C the earth's population multiplied 15 to 20 times.

The rise in the rate of natural increase was due essentially to children who survived to reproduce. Farming made large families desirable. Many hands were needed to till the soil, harvest the crops, and care for livestock. Children and older members of the community could help in this work and therefore became valued members of society, instead of liabilities.

Agriculture was a much more efficient source of food than hunting and gathering, and persons living in communities were safer from natural or human enemies than those living in isolation. At the same time, however, man was subject to natural disasters such as draught, and flood, and to more organized and deadly warfare than had existed previously. Furthermore crowded living conditions brought a great increase in deadly, quick spreading diseases. These factors kept longevity low and death rates high.

During the next 4,000 years, the rate of natural increase dropped drastically in many places. The dangers inherent in urban life, epidemic diseases in particular, began to offset the benefits. Natural disasters and man-made disasters such as erosion tended to balance the advantages of farming. By the beginning of the first century A.D the earth's population was about 130,000,000 less than double that of 4,000 years before.

A slight upward trend in natural increase took place during the next 17 centuries. But widespread epidemics, famine, and war prevented any advance in longevity or lowering of death rate. By 1650 the earth's population was about 545,000,000. The average annual rate of natural increase was about 0.3 per cent or 3 per 1,000 and the average life span was less than 40 years.

From 1650 to World War II: Circumstances affecting population growth began to change in northwestern Europe during the 17th century. While birth rates remained stable, death rates dropped, slowly at first, but rapidly beginning in the late 18th century. Advances in medicine, sanitation, and public health lowered the mortality rates. The decrease was especially significant among children.

During the 18th and 19th centuries this trend spread to North America and other parts of the world, principally those inhabited by emigrants from Europe. The result was a rise in the earth's rate of natural increase. Between 1650 and 1850 the rate doubled and between 1850 and 1940 it doubled again.

Northwestern Europe was the first area of the earth to experience significant population growth due to a reduction in mortality rate. It was the first area to experience population-limiting trend that are typical of advanced industrial nations of today.

The countries of northwestern Europe were culturally and economically, the most advanced in the world when their population began to increase quickly. This was the period of Industrial Revolution. People who wanted to enjoy the social, economic, and educational advantages of this period avoided having large families at an early age. They began to limit family size by such means as late marriage, contraceptives (preventing pregnancy), and abortion. Even in rural areas the pattern of early marriage and large families began to change as new land became insufficient and farming more complicated.

Perhaps the most essential population control in Europe during this period was emigration. Many millions of emigrants left Europe to settle in other lands.

In North and South America, Africa, and Australia they found land and opportunity and in these lands continued the pattern of early marriage and large families. With prosperity and industrialization, however, most of their descendents now follow example of northwestern Europe.

While population growth paralleled industrial development in advanced nations, and longevity rose to a 60 years level in these nations, the less advanced areas of the earth made little progress. In most of Asia and Africa, and in many parts of Latin America, disease and famine continued to limit population growth and keep the life span below 40 years.

After World War II: A drastic and still continuing change in world population growth occurred after World War II. Widespread public health program were begun for the first time in countries of Asia, Africa, and Latin America. Diseases such as malarial fever, which yearly claimed millions of lives, were brought under control.

Death rates dropped quickly. Longevity increased. The world's annual rate of natural increase has risen to about 2 per cent, almost double the pre-war rate, causing what has been called a "population explosion".

Most of the rapid increases in population are occurring in developing countries, a fact that has created tremendous problems. Most of the countries are attempting to industrialize and raise their living standards. In most of them, however, the population is increasing at a rate that equals or exceeds their economic growth rate, hence preventing rise in living standards.

Most of the nations of the world are trying to reduce their population growth but some countries like Canada, France, and Australia are among those trying to encourage it. Controlling natural increase has become one of the most important and universal problems of our time. Beginning in the 1960s many world governments, international organizations, scientific groups, and leading economic and scientific thinkers attempted to find solution to the population problem. In the 1970s the problem of rapidly expanding population in developing countries became critical. In the USA some scientists advocated zero population growth – through which the birth rate would equal the death rate.

World Population:-

The term world population commonly refers to the total number of living human beings on earth at a given time. As of October 28, 2009, the earth's population is estimated by the United States Census Bureau to be 6.793 billion. The world population has been growing continuously since the end of the Black Death around 1400 A.D. There were also short term falls at other times due to plague, for example in the mid 17th century. The fastest rates of world's population growth (above 1.8%) were seen briefly during the 1950s, then for a longer period during the 1960s and 1970s. According to population projections, world population will continue to grow until around 2050. The 2008 rate of growth has almost halved since its peak of 2.2% per year, which was reached in 1963.

World births have leveled off at about 134 million per year, since their peak of 163 million in the late 1990s and are expected to remain constant. However, deaths are only around 57 million per year, and are expected to increase to 90 million by the year 2050. Because births outnumber deaths, the world's population is expected to reach about 9 billion by the year 2040.

Population density is the total number of persons living per square mile or per square kilometer per year. Asia accounts for over 60% of the world population with almost 3.8 billion people. The People's Republic of China and India alone comprise 20% and 17% respectively. Africa follows with 840 million people, 12% of the world's population. Europe's 710 million people make up 11% of the world's population. North America is house to 514 million (8%), South America to 371 million (5.3%) and Australia to 21 million (0.3%). As of 1 July, 2008 est. the population of China is 1,322,044,605; the population of Japan is 127,288,628; the population of India is 1,147,995,226; the population of Pakistan is 167,762,049; and the population of Bangladesh is 153,546,901. The world population as of October, 2010 is 6,877,537,367 and the population of the U.S.A as of October, 2010 is 310,567,515.

b) The Atmosphere: -

The atmosphere is a layer of gases surrounding a celestial object. Atmospheres are known to surround all of the solar system's planets except Pluto. At least one natural satellite – Saturn's Titan – has an atmosphere. Stars, such as the sun, also have atmospheres. The atmosphere of the earth and, possibly, some of the other planets contain liquid and solid particles, (for example, water droplets and dust) in suspension, that is, dispersed within the gases.

An atmosphere is held in place by the gravitational attraction of the celestial object it surrounds. Although the term atmosphere means, "sphere of air", only the atmosphere of the earth is known to contain the particle combination of gases known as air. Other planets have atmospheres of different gases. Jupiter's atmosphere, for example, appears to consist primarily of hydrogen and helium, together with small amounts of methane and ammonia. The atmospheres of stars contain large quantities of hydrogen and helium.

There are several theories about the origin of planetary atmospheres. One theory is that most of the planets at one time had atmosphere similar to the present atmosphere of Jupiter and Saturn. However, low gravitational attraction and intense solar radiation changed the conditions on the planets. Closest to the sun, most of planet Mercury's atmosphere was driven off. Venus, Earth, and Mars lost large portions of their atmospheres, particularly the lighter elements and compounds, leaving atmospheres with heavier gases predominating.

An atmosphere is densest near the surface of the celestial object it surrounds. As the distance from the celestial object increases, the atmosphere becomes less and less dense until it cannot be distinguished from the vacuum of space. The atmosphere that surrounds the Earth is essential to life. The lower portion of the atmosphere contains the oxygen required by all land animals and many land plants. The atmosphere acts as an insulator that prevents extreme temperature changes between day and night, such as those that take place on the moon. The atmosphere also absorbs some radiation, such as most ultraviolet rays, that would be harmful to living organisms if it reached the Earth's surface.

The Atmosphere of the Earth:-

The Earth's atmosphere is made up of a series of layers, each of which has a different set of characteristics.

I) The Troposphere: The troposphere ("sphere of change") is the atmospheric layer closest to the earth. It extends from the earth's surface to an average altitude of about 7 miles. The upper limit of the troposphere is lower at the poles and higher near the equator. About

75% of the total mass of the atmosphere is within the troposphere. Most climatic variations occur within this layer. In the upper troposphere are high speed currents of winds called jet streams. The temperature of the air in the troposphere decreases as the altitude increases.

II) The Stratosphere: The stratosphere extends from the upper boundary of troposphere to an altitude of about 30 miles above the earth's surface. The stratosphere contains the ozone layer, which extends from about 12 miles to about 30 miles. Ozone is a form of oxygen in which each molecule contains three atoms of oxygen instead of two atoms found in ordinary oxygen.

The ozone layer absorbs most of the ultraviolet radiation from the sun and prevents it from reaching the surface of the earth. In the stratosphere the temperature increases slowly with increasing altitude until the bottom of the ozone layer is reached; the temperature then increases rapidly through the ozone layer.

The air within the stratosphere is dry. Clouds occur only rarely. High speed aircrafts usually fly in the lower stratosphere because of lack of clouds and storms and because of the low air resistance. Planes that fly in the stratosphere must have pressurized cabins and a supply of oxygen because the air is too thin for breathing.

III) The Mesosphere: The mesosphere extends from the upper boundary of stratosphere to an altitude of about 50 miles. The temperatures in this layer decrease with increasing altitude up to the upper boundary of mesosphere.

IV) The Thermosphere: The thermosphere extends from about 50 miles to about 300 miles above the earth. The temperatures in the thermosphere increase as the altitude increases. Within the thermosphere lies most of a layer called the ionosphere, which begins 30 to 40 miles above the earth and extends outward to about 300 miles. In the ionosphere, most of the atoms and molecules of gas have lost one or more electrons and have become electrically charged particles called ions. The ionosphere reflects radio waves of certain frequencies and therefore permits radio broadcasting around the curvature of the earth. The luminous phenomena called, "auroras" also occur within the ionosphere. Aurora Borealis is also called northern lights and is a glow in the night sky in the region near the north magnetic pole. A similar glow occurs in the area of the south magnetic pole at the same time. It is called southern lights.

V) The Magnetosphere or Exosphere: The magnetosphere or exosphere begins at an altitude of about 300 miles. Cosmic rays and other high energy particles are trapped in the magnetosphere. These trapped particles occur in greatest concentration in a region within the magnetosphere known as, the "Van Allen Radiation Belt".

The motion of these particles is strongly influenced by the earth's magnetic field. The magnetosphere has the general shape of an elongated tear drop, extending a tail tens of thousands of miles into space in the direction away from the sun.

The great calamitous atmospheric disturbances which have caused a great devastation on Earth and have claimed hundereds of thousands of lives at a time are known by such names as hurricanes, cyclones, tornadoes, and typhoons, which are all types of storms in the atmosphere.

The Deadliest Atmospheric Disturbances:-

In the discussion that follows, we have attempted to describe some of the worst historical atmospheric disturbances that have occurred on earth.

Typhoons: - Typhoon is a violent hurricane in East Asia.

Typhoon Saomai was the biggest typhoon that ever occurred in Japan. It is sometimes called Super Typhoon Saomai. This typhoon brought heavy rain and wind to areas of the Mariana Islands; the Philippines, Taiwan, and the east coast of China. It is responsible for 458 deaths and $ 2.5 billion (USD 2006) in damage. China Meteorologist Administration reported that Saomai was the strongest typhoon that ever occurred over China's offshore region as well as the most powerful typhoon ever to make landfall over mainland China.

Hurricanes: - Hurricane is also called a typhoon, whirlwind, gale, etc. Hurricane is a storm with a violent wind, especially, a cyclone in the West Atlantic. Hurricane Carla was one of the most powerful storms to ever strike the United States, in 1961 Atlantic Hurricane Season. Except for the Great Galveston Hurricane of 1900, Hurricane Carla was the strongest storm to ever strike the Texas coast. The storm caused 2 billion dollars (USD 2005) in damage, but due to the evacuation of over 500,000 residents, the death toll was only 43.

Cyclone: - A cyclone is a violent, low pressure hurricane of limited diameter. A cyclone is also called a hurricane.

Of the 13 deadliest cyclones recorded, nine occurred in the Bay of Bengal. The biggest cyclone to hit Bangladesh was in 1991. The 30 foot storm surge near the coast of Chittagong killed 143,000 people but the biggest killer to hit Bangladesh occurred in1970, when more than 500,000 people died. Bangladesh has a population of 142 million and 10 million Bangladeshis live along the southern coast. Bangladesh is one of the most densely populated areas of the world. Cyclone Sidr also hit India's state of Western Bengal including Kolkata, with high winds and rain and also hit Myanmar.

Tornado: - A tornado is a violent, usually localized storm with whirling wind in a funnel-shaped cloud.

The deadliest tornado in US history occurred in the Tri-state Tornado Area. On 18th of March, 1925 it travelled over 125 MPH in about 3 hours. A tornado is a violently rotating column of air, pendant from a cumuliform cloud, and often (but not always) visible as a funnel cloud. Literally, in order for a vortex to be classified as a tornado, it must be in contact with the ground and the cloud base. The Tri-state tornado of 18th of March, 1925 killed 695 people as it raced along at 60-73 MPH in a 219 mile long track across the states of Missouri, Illinois, and Indiana. This event also holds the known record for most tornado fatalities in a single city or town, at least 234 at Murphysboro, Illinois.

35)

· ·

a) Ganges and Jumna (or Yamuna) Rivers

Ganges River: - Ganges river is a major river of India and Bangladesh and one of the great rivers of the world. It is formed by the junction of the Bhagirathi and Alaknanda rivers in the foothills of the Himalayas in northern India. The Ganges flows mostly southeastward, in a 1,550 miles (2,494 km) course to the Bay of Bengal. Generally the river's course is across the Ganges Plain, a flat and fertile land lying between the snow-clad Himalayas and the plateau and hills of central India.

The Ganges has numerous tributaries, including the Yamuna (Jumna), Ghaghara, Gandak, and Son. In Bangladesh, the Ganges divides into a number of branches, or distributaries, which merge with those of the Brahmaputra (called Jumna in this area). Many distributaries carry the combined waters through the Ganges-Brahmaputra delta into the Bay of Bengal. The chief branch is the Padma River on the east side of the delta. It becomes the Meghna River near the coast. The Hooghly River, on which Calcutta is situated, is the main distributary on the west side of the delta. Between the Hooghly and Meghna lies a swamp, stretching 200 miles (320 km) along the coast, called the Sundarbans.

Floods occur frequently, especially on the delta. They come mainly during summer (June through September), when the south-west monsoon brings heavy rain. Tropical cyclones and melting Himalayan snows add to the dangers of flooding. During the rest of the year the basin is relatively dry, and the river flows at low level.

Importance of Ganges River and its Plain: - To Hindus the Ganges is a sacred river, one strongly devoted to their religious beliefs. Its waters are believed to be holy and capable of washing away sins. The river's banks are aligned with temples of cities. The holiest of the cities is Varanasi (Banaras). The Ganges Plain, with its deep, rich soils, is one of the most productive agricultural regions in Asia. Grains (especially rice and wheat), sugar cane, cotton, jute, and oilseeds are the main crops. During the dry season the river provides irrigation water, chiefly through the Upper and Lower Ganges canals, both of which are in the west.

The plain is also one of the world's most densely populated regions. On or near the Ganges and its tributaries stand many of India's principal cities.

Jumna or Yamuna River: - It is a river of northern India. It is the longest tributary of the Ganges River, having a length of about 860 miles. The source of Jumna is in the western Himalayas. It first flows south and then southeast, running parallel to and just west of the Ganges. It passes by Delhi and Agra, and empties into the Ganges at Allahabad. Hindus consider the point where the rivers meet to be one of holiest places in India.

The Jumna River is navigable for small boats and barges. During the hot season the river dwindles to a small stream, partly due to evaporation, and partly because water is drawn off by irrigation canals.

b) Prime Meridian:-

The angular distance on the earth's surface measured in degrees from a certain meridian is called a longitude.

A meridian is an imaginary line extending from the North Pole to the South Pole at right angles to the Equator. Usually the meridian that passes through Greenwich (a part of London, England) is used in determining longitude. This meridian is called the "Prime Meridian". The longitude of a place reveals how far east or west it is, in degrees of the prime meridian. The corresponding North-South measure is called latitude.

The prime meridian marks 0° longitude. Half way around the earth is 180° longitude. Hence the earth is longitudinally divided into two hemispheres of 180° apiece, the eastern hemisphere, east of Greenwich and the western hemisphere, west of Greenwich.

Meridians are spaced farthest apart at the equator and converge at the poles. At the equator, 1° of longitude spans about 69 miles (111 km), at 30° north and south, about 60 miles (97 km), at 60° north and south, about 35 miles (56 km), and at the poles 0 miles.

The longitude of a place is generally expressed in whole degrees. New York City's longitude, for example, is 74° west, the 74th meridian west of Greenwich. More exact longitudes are expressed in degrees, minutes (60 minutes in a degree) and seconds (60 seconds in a minute). The longitude of Central Manhattan, for example, is 74°, 0', 23" west.

Longitude is also an important factor in determining time – hours, minutes, seconds, in all parts of the world. The earth makes one complete rotation on its axis every 24 hours. Therefore it turns 15° in one hour (15° of longitude). Thus New York City's time is 4 hours and 56 minutes earlier than that of Greenwich.

36)

· ·

a) The Tropics

The Tropics is the region circling the earth between the Tropic of Cancer (23° 27' N), and the Tropic of Capricorn (23° 27' S). These two parallels, or imaginary lines of latitude, mark the farthest points reached by the sun's vertical rays. At all other points between the two parallels, the sun passes directly overhead twice during the year. Because the sun remains high in the sky all year, average annual temperatures in the Tropics are greater than those found elsewhere in the world. However, daily highs rarely equal the summer temperatures in the interior of Eurasia or North America – in the so-called temperature zones.

The usual four seasons of the world's temperature areas do not occur in the Tropics. Instead, several changes take place primarily of rainy and dry periods that vary with distance from the Equator. Near the Equator, even this distinction is missing, since rainfall is evenly distributed throughout the year and there is no dry period.

Equatorial areas frequently receive 100 inches or more of rain annually. In this warm, humid climate grow the tropical rain forests, a dense stand of tall, broad leaved evergreen trees and undergrowth. A few degrees of latitude away from the equator, when alternate rainy and dry periods begin, the rain forest gives way gradually to more open wooded areas. Rain fall decreases steadily and grasslands become the dominant vegetation, as distance from the Equator lengthens. Near the margins of the Tropics are the semiarid steppes and, finally, the desert. Most of the world's great deserts are crossed by either the Tropic of Cancer or the Tropic of Capricorn.

In the Tropics, as in much of the rest of the world, great changes in climate and vegetation are caused by winds, elevation, being close to the coast, ocean's currents, and the location of large mountain ranges. East Africa, for example, although crossed by the Equator, has a relatively dry, cool climate because of its high elevation.

b) The Equator

In Geography, an imaginary line circling the earth midway between the north and south poles is called the Equator. This great circle, 24,902 miles (40,076 km) in circumference and 7,927 miles (12,757 km) in diameter, divides the earth into the northern and southern hemispheres. It lies 6,215 miles (10,002 km), or 90° of latitude for each pole. Beginning at the Equator, north and south distances are measured in degrees of latitude. Degrees of longitude are about 69 miles (111 km) long at the Equator and gradually become smaller, diminishing to zero at the poles.

The rays of the sun strike vertically on the Equator twice each year – usually march 2 and September 23. These dates are called the Equinoxes. During the rest of the year, the sun's rays strike vertically in either the Northern hemisphere or the Southern hemisphere. Equatorial climates are often assumed to be the hottest in the world, but this is incorrect.

The hottest climates are found in the interior of the large land masses to the North, in such lands as the Sahara Desert, Saudi Arabia, Iran, and India. Most of the area close to the equator is water and does not heat quickly. Some portion of the land on the Equator is on a higher platform, which moderates the climate.

The Celestial Equator is an imaginary line that circles the celestial sphere or the visible universe, in the same way that the Geographic or Terrestrial Equator circles the earth. The Celestial Equator divides the sky equally into Northern and Southern hemisphere. It is used to locate heavenly bodies.

Magnetic Equator is an imaginary, irregular line circling the earth's surface. Its shape and position vary from year to year, but it is always near the Geographical Equator. The attraction of the North and South Magnetic Poles is equal at all points on this line. For this reason a dipping needle has no inclination, or dip on this line but lies horizontal.

37)

······································

a) National Aeronautics and Space Administration, (NASA)

NASA is an independent organization of the US government, in charge of space research programs. The main purpose of NASA is to explore space with unmanned and manned space vehicles. NASA develops some of the equipment needed to explore space, the rest being developed by private companies under contract with NASA.

NASA was created by the National Aeronautics and Space Act of 1958. NASA merged with the National Advisory Committee for Aeronautics (NACA) and took over the non-military space research projects of the Army, Navy, Air Force, and Department of Defense. The head of NASA is an administrator appointed by the President with approval of the Senate. NASA headquarters are in Washington D.C.

The National Aeronautics and Space Administration (NASA) is an Executive Branch agency of the United States government, responsible for the nation's civilian space programs and aeronautics and aerospace research. Since February 2006, NASA's self-described mission statement is to pioneer the future in space exploration, scientific discovery, and aeronautics research.

NASA was established by the National Aeronautics and Space Act on July 29, 1958, replacing its predecessor, the National Advisory Committee for Aeronautics, (NACA). The agency became operative on October 1, 1958. NASA has led U.S efforts for space exploration since, including the Apollo moon-landing missions, the Skylab space station, and later the Space Shuttle. Currently, NASA is supporting the International Space Station and has been developing the manned Orion spacecraft.

NASA science is focused on better understanding Earth through the Earth Observing System, advancing heliophysics through the efforts of the Science Mission Directorate's Heliophysics Research, exploring bodies throughout the solar system with advanced robotic missions such as New Horizons, and researching astrophysics topics such as the Big Bang, through the Great Observatories and associated programs. NASA shares data with various national and international organizations such as from the Great Observing Satellites.

History: -

After the Soviet Space program's launch of the world's first artificial satellite (Sputnik 1) on October 4, 1957, the attention of the United States turned towards its own fledgling space efforts. The U.S Congress, alarmed by the perceived threat to national security and technological leadership (known as the "Sputnik Crisis"), urged immediate and swift action; President Dwight D. Eisenhower and his advisers counseled more deliberate measures. Several months of debate produced an agreement that a new federal agency was needed to conduct all non-military activity in space. The Advanced Research Projects Agency (ARPA) was also created at this time to develop space technology for military applications.

National Advisory committee for Aeronautics (NACA): -

From late 1957 to early 1958, the National Advisory Committee for Aeronautics (NACA) began studying what a new non-military space agency would entail, as well as what its role might be, and assigned several committees to review the concept. On January 12, 1958, NACA organized a "Special Committee on Space Technology" headed by Guyford Stever. Stever's committee included consultation from the Army Ballistic Missile Agency's largest booster program referred to as the Working Group on vehicular program, headed by Wernher Von Braun, a German scientist who became a naturalized US citizen after World War II.

On January 14, 1958, NACA Director Hugh Dryden published "A National Research Program for Space Technology" stating "It is of great urgency and importance to our country both from consideration of our prestige as a nation as well as military necessity that this challenge (Sputnik) be met by an energetic program of research and development for the conquest of space… It is accordingly proposed that the scientific research be the responsibility of a national civilian agency… NACA is capable, by rapid extension and expansion of its efforts, of providing leadership in Space Technology.

Launched on January 31, 1958, Explorer 1, officially satellite 1958 Alpha, became the U.S's first earth satellite. The Explorer 1 payload consisted of the Iowa Cosmic Ray Instrument without a data recorder which was not modified in time to make it onto the satellite. On March 5, PSAC Chairman James Killian wrote a memorandum to President Eisenhower, entitled, "Organization for Civil Space Program", encouraging the creation of a Civil Space program based upon a "strengthened and redesigned" "NACA which could expand it research programs" with a minimum of delay". In late March, a NACA report entitled, "Suggestion for a Space Program" included recommendations for subsequently developing a hydrogen fluorine fueled rocket of 4,450,000 newton (1000000 lbs) thrust designed with second and third stages.

In April, 1958, Eisenhower delivered to the U.S Congress an executive address favoring a national civilian space agency and submitted a bill to create a "National Aeronautical and Space Agency". NACA's former role of research alone would change to include large-scale development, management, and operations. The U.S Congress passed the bill, somewhat reworded, as the National Aeronautics and Space Act of 1958, on July 16. Only two days later von Braun's Working Group submitted a preliminary report severely criticizing the duplication of efforts and lack of coordination among various organizations assigned to the United States Space Programs. Stever's Committee on Space Technology concerned with the Criticism of the von Braun Group, (a final draft was published several months later in October.)

On July 29, 1958, Eisenhower signed the National Aeronautics and Space Act, establishing NASA. When it began operations on October 1, 1958, NASA absorbed the 46 year old NACA intact; it's 8,000 employees, an annual budget of US $100 million, the major research laboratories (Langley Aeronautical Laboratory, Ames Aeronautical Laboratory, and Lewis Flight Propulsion Laboratory) and two small test facilities.

Elements of the Army Ballistic Missile Agency of which von Braun's team was a part, and the Naval Research Laboratory were incorporated into NASA. A significant contributor to NASA's entry into the Space Race with Soviet Union was the technology from the German rocket program (led by von Braun) which in turn incorporated the technology of Robert Goddard's earlier works. Earlier research efforts within the U.S Air Force and many ARPA's early space programs were also transferred to NASA. In December, 1958, NASA gained control of the

Jet Propulsion Laboratory, a contractor facility operated by California Institute of Technology.

NASA PROGRAMS: -
Manned Programs: -
Project Mercury: -

Conducted under the pressure of the competition between the U.S and Soviet Union that existed during the Cold War, Project Mercury was initiated in 1958 and started NASA down the path of human space exploration with missions designed to discover if man could survive in space. Representatives from the U.S Army, Navy, and Air Force were selected to provide assistance to NASA. Pilot selections were facilitated through coordination with U.S defense research, contracting, and military test pilot programs.

On May 5, 1961, astronaut Alan Sheppard became the first American in Space when he piloted Freedom 7 on a 15 minute sub-orbital flight. John Glen became the first American to orbit the Earth on February 20, 1962 during the flight of Freedom 7. There were more orbital flights followed.

Project Gemini: -

Project Gemini focused on conducting experiments and developing and practicing techniques required for lunar missions. The first Gemini flight with astronauts on board, Gemini 3 was flown by Gus Grissom and John Young on March 23, 1965. Nine missions followed, showing that long-duration human space flight and rendezvous and docking with another vehicle in space were possible, and gathering mechanical data on the effects of weightlessness on humans. Gemini missions included the first American Spacewalks, and new orbital maneuvers including rendezvous and docking.

Apollo Program: -

The Apollo programs landed the first humans on Earth's moon. Apollo 11 landed on the moon July 20, 1969 with astronauts Niel Armstrong and Buzz Aldrin while Michael Collins orbited above. Five subsequent Apollo missions also landed astronauts on the Moon, the last in December, 1972. In the six Apollo space flights, twelve men walked on the Moon.

These missions returned a wealth of scientific data and 381.7 kg (842 lbs) of lunar samples. Experiments included soil mechanics, meteorite, seismic, heat flow, lunar ranging, magnetic fields, and solar wind experiments.

Apollo set major milestone in human space flights. It stands alone in sending manned missions beyond low Earth orbit, and landing humans on another Celestial body. Apollo 8 was the first manned spacecraft to orbit another celestial body, while Apollo 17 marked the last moonwalk and the last manned mission beyond low Earth orbit. The program spurned advances in many areas of technology peripheral to rocketry and manned space flights, including avionics, telecommunications, and computers. Apollo sparked interest in many fields of engineering and left many physical facilities and machines developed for the program as landmarks. Many objects and artifacts for the program are on display at various locations throughout the world, notably at the Smithsonian Air and Space Museums.

Skylab: -

Skylab was the first space station the United States launched into orbit. The 100 short tons (91 t) station was in Earth orbit from 1973 to 1979, and was visited by crews three times, in 1973, and 1974. It included a laboratory for studying the effects of microgravity and a solar observatory. A Space Shuttle was planned to dock with and elevate Skylab to a higher safe-altitude, but Skylab re-entered the atmosphere and was destroyed in 1979 before the first Shuttle could be launched.

Apollo-Soyuz Test Project, (ASTP): -

The Apollo-Soyuz Test Project (ASTP) was the first joint flight of the U.S and Soviet Space program. The mission took place in July, 1975. For the United States, it was the last Apollo flight as well as the last manned space launch until the flight of the first Space Shuttle in April, 1981.

Space Shuttle Programs: -

The Space Shuttle became the major focus of NASA in the late 1970s and the 1980s. Planned as a frequently launch able and most reusable vehicle, four space shuttle orbiters were built by 1985. The first to launch was Columbia on April 12, 1981.

In 1995 Russian-American interaction resumed with the Shuttle-Mir mission. Once more an American vehicle was docked with a Russian craft, this time a full-fledged space station. This cooperation continues today with Russian and American, the two biggest partners, in the largest space station ever built, namely, the International Space Station, (ISS). The strength of this cooperation on this project was even more evident when NASA began relying on Russian launch vehicles to service the ISS during the two-year grounding of the Shuttle fleet following the 2003 Space Shuttle Columbia disaster.

The Shuttle fleet lost two orbiters and 14 astronauts in two disasters: Challenger 1986, and Columbia 2003. While the 1986 loss was mitigated by building the Space Shuttle Endeavor from the replacement parts, NASA did not build another orbiter to replace the second loss. NASA's Shuttle program has made 132 successful launches as of May, 2010.

International Space Station, (ISS): -

The International Space Station (ISS) is an internationally developed research facility currently being assembled in Low Earth Orbit. On-orbit construction of the Station began in 1998 and is scheduled to be completed by 2011, with operations continuing until at least 2015. The Station can be seen from the Earth with the naked eye, and as of 2009, is the largest artificial satellite in the Earth's orbit, with a mass larger than that of any previous space station.

The ISS is operated as a joint project among NASA, the Russian Federal Space Agency, the Japan Aerospace Exploration Agency, the Canadian Space Agency, and the European Space Agency (ESA). Ownership and utilization of the Space Station is set out via several intergovernmental treaties and agreements, with the Russian Federation retaining full ownership of its own modules, and the rest of the Station being allocated among the other international partners. The International Space Station relied on the Shuttle fleet for all major construction shipments.

The cost of the Station project has been estimated by ESA as $100 billion over a course of 30 years, although cost estimates vary between 35 billion dollars and 160 billion dollars, making the ISS the most expensive object ever constructed.

Unmanned Probes: -

1. Mariner Program: -

The Mariner program conducted by NASA launched a series of robotic interplanetary probes designed to investigate Mars, Venus, and Mercury. The program included a number of firsts, including the first planetary flyby, the first picture from another planet, the first planetary orbiter and the first gravity assist maneuver. Of the ten vehicles in the Mariner series, seven were successful and three were lost. The planned Mariner 11 and Mariner 12 vehicles evolved into Voyager 1 and Voyager 2 of the Voyager program, while Viking 1 and Viking 2 Mars orbiter were enlarged versions of Mariner 9 spacecraft. Other Mariner-based spacecraft, launched since Voyager, included the Magellan probe to Venus and Galileo probe to Jupiter. A second generation Mariner spacecraft, called the Mariner Mask 11 series, eventually evolved into the Cassini-Huygens probe, now in orbit around Saturn.

All Mariner spacecrafts were based on a hexagonal or Octagonal "bus", which housed all the electronics, and to which all components were attached, such as antenna, cameras, propulsion, and power sources. All probes except Mariner 1, Mariner 2, and Mariner 5 had T.V cameras. The first five Mariners were launched on Atlas-Agua rockets; while the last five used the Atlas Centaur. All Mariner-based probes after Mariner 10 used Titan III E, Titan IV unmanned rockets or the space shuttle with a solid fueled Inertial Upper Stage and multiple planetary flybys.

2. Poineer Program: -

The Poineer program is a series of NASA unmanned space missions that was designed for planetary exploration. There were a number of such missions in the program but the most notable were Poineer 10 and Poineer 11, which explored the outer planets and left the solar system. Both carry a golden plaque, depicting a man and a woman and information about the origin and the creation of the probe, should any extra terrestrial find them someday.

Additionally, the Poineer missions to Venus consisted of two components, launched separately. Poineer Venus 1 or Poineer Venus Orbiter was launched in 1978 and studied the planet for more than a decade after orbital insertion in

1978. Poineer Venus 2 or Poineer Venus Multi-probe sent four small probes into the Venusian atmosphere.

3. Voyager Program: -

The Voyager program is a series of NASA unmanned space missions that consists of a pair of unmanned scientific probes, Voyager 1 and Voyager 2. They were launched in 1977 to take advantage of a favorable planetary alignment of the late 1970s. Although they were officially designated to study just Jupiter and Saturn, the two probes were able to continue their mission into the outer solar system. Both probes have achieved escape velocity from the solar system and will never return. Both missions have gathered large amounts of data about the gas giants of the solar system of which little was previously known.

Voyager 1 is currently the farthest human-made object from Earth at about 110.94AU (16.596 billion kms or 10.312 billion miles) travelling away from both the earth and the sun at a speed of 17 km (11 miles)/sec., which corresponds to a greater specific orbital energy than any other probe.

4. Viking Program: -

The Viking program consisted of a pair of space probes sent to Mars-Viking 1 and Viking 2. Each vehicle was composed of two main parts, an orbiter designed to photograph the surface of Mars from orbit, and a Lander designed to study the planet from the surface. The orbiters also served as communication relays for the Landers once they touched down.

Viking 1 was launched on August 20, 1975, and the second craft Viking 2 was launched on September 9, 1975, both riding atop Titan III E rockets with Centaur upper stages. By discovering many geological forms that are typically formed from large amounts of water, the Viking program caused a revolution in scientific ideas about water on Mars.

The primary objective of the Viking orbiter was to transport the Lander to Mars, perform reconnaissance to locate and certify landing sites, act as a communication relays for the Landers, and to perform their own scientific investigations. The orbiter, based on earlier Mariner 9 spacecraft, was an octagon approximately 2.5 m across. The total launch mass was 2,328 kg (5,130 lb), of which 1,445 kg (3,190 lb) were propellant and altitude control gas.

5. Helios Probes: -

The Helios I and Helios II space probes, also known as Helios A and Helios B, were a pair of probes, launched into heliocentric orbit for the purpose of studying the solar processes. A joint venture of the Federal Republic of Germany (West Germany) and NASA, the probes were launched from Cape Canaveral Air Force Station, Florida, on December 10, 1974, and January 15, 1976, respectively.

The probes were notable for setting a maximum speed record among spacecrafts at 257,792 km (157,078 miles)/hr. The Helios space probes completed their primary mission by the early 1980, but they continued to send data up to 1985. The probes are no longer functional but still remain in the elliptical orbit around the sun.

6. Hubble Space Telescope: -

The Hubble Space Telescope (HST) is a space telescope that was carried into orbit by a space shuttle in April, 1990. It is named after American astronomer Edwin Hubble. Although not the first space telescope, Hubble is one of the largest and most versatile, and is well-known as both a vital research tool and a public relations boon for astronomy. The HST is collaboration between NASA and the European Space Agency and is one of NASA's Great Observatories, along with the Compton Gamma Ray Observatory and the Spitzer Space Telescope. The HST's success has paved the way for greater collaboration between the agencies.

The HST was created with a relatively small budget of $2 billion and has continued operation since 1990, delighting both scientists and the public. Some of its images, such as the ground breaking Hubble Deep Field, have become famous.

7. Magellan probe: -

The Magellan spacecraft was a space probe sent to the planet Venus, the first unmanned interplanetary spacecraft to be launched by NASA since its successful Poineer Orbiter, also to Venus in 1978. It was also the first of three deep-space probes to be launched on the space shuttle, and the first spacecraft to employ aero-braking techniques to lower its orbit.

Magellan created the first (and currently the best) high resolution mapping of the planet's surface features. Prior Venus missions had created low resolution radar globes of general, continent-sized formation. Magellan, performed detailed imaging and analysis of craters, hills, ridges, and other geologic formations, to a degree comparable to the visible-light photographic mapping of other planets.

8. Galileo probe: -

Galileo was an unmanned spacecraft sent by NASA to study the planet Jupiter and its moons. It was launched on October 18, 1989, by the space shuttle Atlantis on the STS-34 mission. It arrived at Jupiter on December 7, 1995, a little more than six years later via gravitational assist flybys of Venus and Earth.

Despite antenna problems, Galileo conducted the first asteroid flyby, discovered the first asteroid moon, was the first spacecraft to orbit Jupiter, and launched the first probe into Jupiter atmosphere. Galileo's prime mission was a two-year study of the Jovian system. The spacecraft travelled around Jupiter in elongated ellipses, each orbit lasting about two months. The differing distances from Jupiter afforded by these orbits allowed Galileo to sample different parts of the planet's extensive magnetosphere. The orbits were designed for close up flybys of Jupiter's largest moons. Once Galileo's prime mission was concluded, an extended mission followed starting on December 7, 1997; the spacecraft made a number of daring close flybys of Jupiter's moons Europa, and Io. The closest approach was 180 km (110 miles – 112 miles) on October 15, 2001.

On September 21, 2003, after 14 years in space and eight years of service – to Jovian system, Galileo's mission was terminated by sending the orbiter into Jupiter's atmosphere at a speed of nearly (50 km/second) to avoid any chance of it contaminating local moons with bacteria from Earth. Of particular interest was the ice crusted moon Europa, which, thanks to Galileo, scientists now suspect harbors a salt water ocean beneath its surface.

9. Mars Global Surveyor: -

The Mars Global Surveyor (MGS) was developed by NASA's Jet Propulsion Laboratory and launched November, 1996. It began the United State's return to Mars after a 10-year absence.

It completed its primary mission in January, 2001 and was in its third extended mission phase when, on November2, 2006, the spacecraft failed to respond to commands. In January, 2007, NASA officially ended the mission.

The Surveyor spacecraft used a series of high – resolution cameras to explore the surface of Mars returning more than 240,000 images spanning portion of 4.8 Martian years, from September, 1997 to November, 2006. The Surveyor's cameras utilized 3 instruments, a narrow angle camera that took (black and white) high resolution images (usually 1.5 to 12 m per pixel) red and blue wide angle pictures for context (240 m per pixel) and daily global imaging (7.5 km or 4.7 miles per pixel).

10. Mars Pathfinder: -

The Mars Pathfinder (MESUR Pathfinder) later renamed the Carl Sagal Memorial Station, was launched on December 4, 1996, just a month after the Mars Global Surveyor was launched. On board the Lander was a small rover called Sojoumer that would execute many experiments on the Martian surface. It was the second project from NASA's Discovery Program, which promotes the use of low – cost spacecraft and frequent launches under the motto, "cheaper, faster, and better" promoted by the administrator, Daniel Goldin. The mission was directed by the Jet Propulsion Laboratory, a division of the California Institute of Technology, responsible for NASA's Mars Exploration Program.

This mission, besides being the first of a series of missions to Mars that included rovers (robotic exploration vehicles) was the most important since the Viking landed on the red planet in 1976, and also was the first successful mission to send a rover to a planet. In addition to scientific objectives, the Mars Pathfinder mission was also a "proof-of-concept" for various technologies, such as airbag mediated touch-down and automated obstacle avoidance, both later exploited by the Mars Exploration Rovers. The Mars Pathfinder was also remarkable for its extremely low price, relative to other unmanned missions to Mars.

11. Mars Exploration Rovers: -

NASA's Mars Exploration Rover Missions (MER), is an ongoing robotic space mission involving two rovers exploring the planet Mars. The mission is managed for NASA by the Jet Propulsion Laboratory, which designed, built, and is operating the rovers.

The mission began in 2003 with the sending of the two rovers – MER-A Spirit and MER-B Opportunity – to explore the Martian surface and geology. The mission's scientific objective is to search for and characterize a wide range of rocks and soils that hold clues to past water activity on Mars. The mission is part of NASA's Mars Exploration Programs, which includes three previous successful landers the two Viking programs 1976 and Mars Pathfinder probe in 1997.

The total cost of building, launching, and operating the rovers on the surface for the initial 90 Martian – day (sol) primary mission was US $820 million. Since the rovers have continued to function far beyond their initial 90 sol primary mission (to date both rovers have been functioning on the Martian surface for nearly seven years), they have each received multiple missions extensions.

In recognition of the vast amount of scientific information amassed by both rovers, two asteroids have been named in their honor: 37452 Spirit and 39382 Opportunity.

12. New Horizon Probe: -

New Horizons is a NASA robotic spacecraft missions currently en route to the dwarf planet Pluto. It is expected to be the first spacecraft to fly by and study Pluto and its moons, Charon, Nix, and Hydra. Once New Horizon leaves the solar system, NASA also approves flybys of one or more other Kuper Belt Objects.

New Horizons was launched on January 19, 2006 directly into an Earth-and-solar-escape trajectory. It had an Earth relative velocity of about 16.26 km (10.0 miles)/ second after its last engine shut down. Thus, it left Earth at the fastest launch speed ever recorded for a man-made object (although its specific orbital energy is less than that of Voyager 1, and the Helios Probes retain the maximum speed record for a spacecraft). New Horizons flew by Jupiter on February 28, 2007 and Saturn's orbit on June 8, 2008. It will arrive at Pluto on July 14, 2015, and then continue into the Kuper Belt.

NASA's Future: -

During much of 1990s, NASA was faced with shrinking annual budgets due to Congressional belt tightening. In response, NASA's ninth administrator, Daniel Goldin, pioneered the "faster, better, cheaper" approach that enabled NASA to cut costs while still delivering a wide variety of aerospace programs (Discovery Program). That method was criticized and re-evaluated following the twin losses of Mars Climate Orbiter and Mars Polar Lander in 1999. It is the current space policy of the United States that NASA "execute a sustained and affordable human and robotic program of space exploration and develop, acquire, and use civil space system to advance fundamental scientific knowledge of an Earth system, solar system, and the universe. NASA's ongoing investigations include in-depth surveys of Mars and Saturn and studies of the Earth and the Sun. Other NASA spacecrafts are presently en-route to Mercury, Pluto, and the asteroid belt.

With missions to Jupiter in planning stages, NASA's itinerary covers over half the solar system. An improved and larger planetary rover, Mars Science Laboratory, is under construction and slated to launch in 2011, after a slight delay caused by hardware challenges, which has bumped it back from the October, 2009 scheduled launch. The New Horizon's mission to Pluto was launched in 2006 and will fly by Pluto in 2015. The probe received a gravity assist from Jupiter in February, 2007, examining some of Jupiter's inner moons and testing on-board instruments during the fly-by. On the horizon of NASA's plans the MAVEN spacecraft as part of the Mars Scout Program to study the atmosphere of Mars.

b) Motion of the Planets: -Kepler's Laws of Planetary Motion

Kepler discovered three empirical laws that accurately describe the motion of the planets, and these are given as follows: -
1. 1) Each planet moves in an elliptical orbit, with the sun at one focus of the ellipse.
2. 2) A line from the sun to a given planet sweeps out equal areas in equal times.
3. 3) The periods of the planets are proportional to the 3/2 powers of the major axis lengths of their orbits.

$T_1/T_2 = (R_1)^{3/2} / (R_2)^{3/2}$

This equation which is Kepler's Third Law of Planetary Motion can be derived from Newton's Law of Universal Gravitation as follows: -

According to Newton's Law of Universal Gravitation we have the following expression: -

$F = GMm/R_1^2$

For the sake of argument let us assume that the planet's trajectories are circular, then we have as follows: -

$F = GMm/R_1^2 = mv^2/R_1$

Note that v is the velocity of the planet we are considering for our argument and v^2/R_1 is the acceleration due to gravity of the planet.

$v^2 = GM/R_1$

If the period is T_1, then for the velocity v we have as follows: -

$v = 2\pi R_1/T_1$

OR

$v^2 = 4\pi^2 R_1^2/T_1^2$
$v^2 = 4\pi^2 R_1^2/T_1^2 = GM/R_1$
$T_1^2/R_1^3 = 4\pi^2/GM$

Similarly we may have through a same argument, with a period T_2 and major axis R_2, the following expression: -

$T_2^2/R_2^3 = 4\pi^2/GM$
$T_1^2/R_1^3 = T_2^2/R_2^3 = 4\pi^2/GM$
$T_1/T_2 = (R_1)^{3/2}/(R_2)^{3/2}$

The last expression is the Kepler's Third Law of Planetary Motion which we have derived from Newton's Law of Universal Gravitation.

38)

．．

a) The Moon Exploration:-

Space exploration is the investigation of the regions beyond the earth's atmosphere with the aid of manned and unmanned space vehicles.

For as long as man has been able to think and reason intelligently, he has dreamed of going beyond the earth's atmosphere to explore space. Not until the second half of the 20th century, when the science of astronautics was born, was that possible. Dealing with the building and flying of space vehicles, the new science began as a theoretical field. By the 1960's it had developed into a major scientific and industrial activity, involving the efforts of thousands of scientists, engineers, and technicians. Less than a dozen years after a rocket lifted the first small satellite into orbit around the earth in 1957, man had walked on the moon and began sending unmanned spacecrafts to distant parts of the solar system.

Space men-called astronauts in the United States and Cosmonauts in Russia- were national heroes.

Reasons for exploring space are many and diverse. The major goals, some of which have already been accomplished, are to establish scientific laboratories in space and to send men to the moon, the planets, and perhaps beyond. Already, much new information has been gathered about matter, radiation, and magnetism in the regions of space around the earth and the moon. Studies of lunar rocks and experiments conducted on the moon's surface may enable scientists to unlock secrets of the origin of moon and earth. From telescopes in space stations orbiting the earth, many types of studies of the sun, stars, and planets can be made that are difficult or impossible from earth-bound observatories.

Perhaps the most compelling reason for exploring space, however, is not scientific in origin. Like the unclimbed mountains or the impenetrable ocean deep, space challenges the imagination and abilities of man and never has man been able to resist such a challenge.

The Space Environment:-

What is space? In the broadest sense, it is the region beyond the earth's atmosphere. Because the earth's atmosphere thins out gradually over many miles of altitude, no definite boundary can be established between earth and space. For most purposes, an altitude of 50 miles to 100 miles above sea level is considered by many scientists to mark the beginning of space. There is no known outer limit, since space is considered to include the entire universe.

The portion of space, in which present exploration takes place, is within our own solar system, since existing rockets and space-crafts are not suited for travel to distant regions. Although extremely small in comparison with the entire universe, the solar system is huge when measured by earth standards. It consists of nine planets that revolve around a medium sized star called the sun. The four planets close to the sun-Mercury, Venus, Earth, and Mars- are relatively small and dense.

The next four-Jupiter, Saturn, Uranus, and Neptune – are much larger than the first four. They consist largely of gases and liquids, surrounding cores of unknown sizes beneath their thick atmospheres. Little is known about Pluto, the ninth planet. Several of the planets, including the earth, have natural satellites or moons.

The earth's closest neighbor in space is its moon, a dry, airless sphere that has become the focal point of many space exploration efforts. Its cratered and boulder-strewn face has changed little during the billions of years the moon and earth have travelled around the sun together. Of the planets, Venus and Mars – Earth's closest planetary neighbors – have received the most attention through space exploration. Unmanned space probes have already provided information that has changed considerably man's idea of these two planets.

Space Vehicles:-

The term space vehicle generally refers to the entire combination of rockets, space exploration craft, and associated systems needed to carry out a complete mission in space.

The various parts of the space vehicle make up two basic sections, the launch vehicle and the space craft.

Launch Vehicles: - Rockets are used to propel launch vehicles because rockets are the only type of engines that are able to operate in both the earth's atmosphere and the vacuum of space. Moreover, rockets are the only propulsion system that can develop the tremendous power needed to lift heavy payloads into space.

Most launch vehicles are of the multi-stage type, consisting of two or three separate rockets stacked together. At launching only the lowest, which is the first stage, is in operation.

When its propellant is used up, the first stage is discarded in flight and the second stage engine begins to fire. In this way high speeds can be reached, since the launch speed of the succeeding stage is equal to the speed developed by the previous stage. The first stage, which is the most powerful stage, produces 7.5 million pounds of thrust or pushing force.

The rockets used in launch vehicles are mainly of three types as follows:-

1. Chemical Rockets: - All rockets presently in use for space exploration are of chemical type. Their propellant, whether liquid or solid are composed of various chemicals that react (by burning) to produce the engine's thrust.
2. Nuclear Rockets: - Nuclear fission reactors produce heat energy that can provide rocket thrust. A small reactor can be used to heat a "working fluid" such as helium, hydrogen, and ammonia. The heated fluid is then ejected from a nozzle at the rear of the rocket to produce thrust.
3. Ion Rockets: - Ions are electrically charged atoms or groups of atoms. They can be accelerated by a magnetic field to form a high speed stream that is ejected from the engine. It does not produce enough thrust. Its thrust is low but continuous. Its most probable use would be in propelling space-crafts on long interplanetary flights.

Space-crafts: - Every space craft is designed to carry out a specific mission in space. For this reason, there are many different types and sizes of crafts in use, ranging from small, unmanned earth satellites to large, highly complex manned craft capable of carrying several crew members.

Man in Space:-

Debate has raged since the beginning of space age as to whether manned space-craft should be used for space exploration. It is argued that men must go into space if full advantage is to be taken of the time and money spent on space program.

Weightlessness: - A coasting space craft is in a condition known as free fall. Free fall can be in any direction, not necessarily toward the earth or any other body. In this condition the craft and everything in it are without apparent weight.

Weightless periods of a few weeks or less appear to have little or no harmful effects on human beings. However certain changes occur as the body apparently attempts to adapt to the new environment. Among these changes are a significant loss of body fluids, lowering of the calcium level in the bones, weakening of muscles, and accumulation of blood in the legs. Changes in heart beat rate and blood pressure have also occurred. Special medication and regular exercise during space flights are used to overcome some of these problems. Future flights lasting many weeks or months may use artificial gravity to prevent possible serious effects of prolonged weightlessness.

Acceleration: - During launch and entry, spacemen and the craft are subjected to stress caused by acceleration. Acceleration refers to both increase and decrease in velocity. The effect of acceleration is to increase the weight of the space craft and its occupants.

Escape Velocity: - The escape velocity, in this context, implies that magnitude of the velocity required by a rocket to escape the gravitational pull of the earth. We now calculate the escape velocity of a space probe leaving earth. Let m be the mass of the space probe and the astronauts inside the space probe, m_E be the mass of the planet earth, R_E be the radius of the earth, G be the Universal Gravitational Constant (G = 6.673×10^{-11} N-m^2/kg^2), and the escape velocity v of the space probe will be determined as follows:-

$(1/2)\, mv^2 = Gm_E m/R_E$

$v = \sqrt{[2Gm_E/R_E]}$

$v = \sqrt{[2 \times 6.673 \times 10^{-11} \text{N-m}^2/\text{kg}^2 \times 5.98 \times 10^{24} \text{kg}/6.38 \times 10^6 \text{m}]}$

$v = 1.11844804 \times 10^4$ m/s = 11.18 km/s

$v = 40,200$ km/h = 25,000 mi/h

Hence v = 25,000 mi/h is the escape speed of the space probe trying to break away from the gravitational pull of the earth.

Natural Hazards: - Radiation in space can produce harmful effects in space travelers. Among the types of radiations that may be encountered are those within the earth's magnetic field, specially the Van Allen Radiation Belt, cosmic rays, and solar flare radiation.

Prolonged exposure to Van Allen Radiation Belt would be highly dangerous without having shielding. Cosmic rays which are highly charged atomic particles found in space are potentially harmful to man but lightweight shielding is usually adequate for protection.

Perhaps the most hazardous radiation source in space is the solar flare, wich releases huge amounts of deadly particles. The service module, however, may be allowed to act as a radiation shield.

First Moon Landing:-

On July 16, 1969, astronauts Niel A. Armstrong, Edwin E. Aldrin (Jr.), and Michael Collins rocketed into earth orbit aboard Apollo 11. The 363 foot long Saturn V rocket with the attached moon ship was the heaviest object (6,500,000 pounds) ever launched. During the second orbit; Saturn's third stage engine was fired and Apollo 11 sped along its planned trajectory toward the moon.

On July 19, the space craft entered the moon's gravitational field and went into orbit. During the 13th orbit, on July 20, Niel A. Armstrong and Edwin E. Aldrin (Jr.) transferred to the lunar module Eagle while Collins remained in the command module Columbia. The two sections were separated – Columbia to continue in lunar orbit, Eagle to begin man's first landing on the surface of another celestial body. During the following orbit, the lunar module descended toward the sea of tranquility. Niel A. Armstrong, commander of the mission, piloted Eagle to touch down at 4:17 P.M (EDT) Sunday, July 20, 1969.

At 10:56 PM (EDT), as millions throughout the world watched on television, Armstrong stepped on the powdery lunar soil and said, "That's one small step for (a) man, one giant leap for mankind". Soon after, Niel A. Armstrong was joined by Edwin E. Aldrin (Jr.). They unveiled a plaque that read, "Here men from the planet earth first set foot on the moon, July, 1969 A.D. We came in peace for all mankind".

The astronauts erected an American flag, collected lunar soil and rock samples, conducted scientific experiments, and took photographs during their approximately two hour moonwalk.

After a 22 hour stay, Eagle lifted off the moon, and rendezvoused with the orbiting Columbia. The triumphant voyage ended on July 24, when the astronauts safely splashed down in the Pacific Ocean and were picked up by the U.S Navy.

b) The Solar Interplanetary System

The solar system consists of the sun and those heavenly bodies bound to it by gravity, all of which formed from the collapse of a giant molecular cloud approximately 4.6 billion years ago. The four smaller, inner planets, Mercury, Venus, earth, and Mars, also called the terrestrial planets are primarily composed of rocks and metals. The four outer most planets also called the gas giants are composed largely of hydrogen and helium, and are far more massive than the terrestrial. Pluto is termed the dwarf planet.

The principle component of the solar system is the sun which contains 99.86% of the system's known mass. Jupiter and Saturn, the sun's two largest orbiting bodies account for more than 90% of the remaining mass.

The planets are known to revolve around the sun in elliptical orbits according to laws of planetary motion demonstrated by Newton's Universal law of Gravitation.

A planet's closest approach to the sun is called its perihelion while its most distant point from the sun is called its aphelion. Each heavenly body moves fastest at its perihelion and slowest at its aphelion.

The sun has a mass 332,900 times the mass of the earth. The sun is growing brighter. Early in its history it was only 70% brighter as it is today.

The mass of the sun is 1.99×10^{30} kg and its radius is 6.96×10^8 m. The mass of the earth is 5.98×10^{24} kg and its radius is 6.38×10^6 m. Its mean distance from the sun is 1.5×10^{11} m.

The moon has a mass of 7.35×10^{22} kg and its radius is 1.74×10^6 m and its mean distance from the earth is 3.85×10^8 m.

The density of atmospheric air is 1.29 kg/m^3 at standard temperature and pressure. The atmospheric pressure at sea level is 1.013×10^5 Pa. The acceleration due to gravity is 9.8 m/sec^2, on the surface of planet Earth, which is a general constant value.

The speed of sound in air at 20°C is 343 m/sec. The value of the Universal Gravitational Constant is $G = 6.673 \times 10^{-11}$ N-m^2/kg^2. The value of the velocity of light in vacuum is constant and is given by: $c = 2.99792458 \times 10^8$ m/sec.

The force of gravitation of the planet earth and the sun, which is a force of attraction, is given by the following equation:-

$$F = G (Mm/R^2) = mg = mv^2/R$$

Note M and m are the masses of the sun and the earth and R is the mean distance of the sun from the earth.

Assuming the orbit of the earth around the sun is circular, the speed of the earth around the sun is given by:-

$v = \sqrt{(GM/R)}$

$= \sqrt{[6.673 \times 10^{-11}N\text{-}m^2/kg^2 \times 1.99 \times 10^{30}kg/1.5070238 \times 10^{11}m]}$

$v = 2.968431593 \times 10^4$ m/sec. $= 29.7$ km/sec.

Hence the speed of planet Earth around the sun is approximately 86.5 times greater than the speed of sound in air at 20^0C. In the above calculations, M is the mass of the sun and R is the mean distance of the center of the earth from the center of the sun.

The sun and the celestial bodies that travel through space in closed orbits (paths) under the sun's gravitational influence are called the solar system. In addition to the sun, the solar system consists of nine major planets, thousands of minor planets called asteroids, natural satellites such as the moon, which travel around planets, comets, meteorites, dust, and gases. The name of the system comes from sol, the Latin word for, sun.

The sun, a star, is the largest and most massive body in the solar system. Its great mass is the basis for the gravitational attraction that holds all of the other bodies in the solar system in their orbits.

The nine major planets,- Mercury, Venus, Earth, Mars, Jupiter, Saturn, Uranus, Neptune, and Pluto – travel around the sun in nearly the same plane at varying distances from the sun. Seven of the planets, in turn, have natural satellites that travel around them.

Earth has one natural satellite, Mars has two known natural satellites, Jupiter has 13 natural satellites, Saturn has 10 natural satellites, Uranus has 5 natural satellites, Neptune has 2 natural satellites, and Pluto has one.

A number of additional satellites for Jupiter and Saturn have been tentatively identified.

Asteroids are small and irregularly shaped. Most have orbits that lie between the orbits of Mars and Jupiter. There is evidence that indicates that some asteroids also have moons.

The comets travel out from the sun farther than any other bodies in the solar system. Near the sun, comets have glowing heads and long gaseous tails. Away from the sun, where little radiation strikes them, they are dark and have no tails.

Meteorites are pieces of rock and metal that travel through space. When they intercept the earth's atmosphere they are called meteors. No count is possible of the number of meteorites in the solar system.

The outer most major planet, Pluto, is on the average 3,666,100,000 miles (5,900,000,000 km) from the sun, but other objects far beyond Pluto remain within control of the sun's gravitation. This is true, for example, of many comets.

A quantum unit of gravitational force field, called the graviton, has not yet been discovered.

Planet Mercury: -

The planet Mercury is the planet closest to the sun. It is the solar system's one of the smallest major planets, where only Pluto is smaller. It is difficult to observe Mercury from Earth. It never appears very far from the sun and is usually hidden in the brightness of morning or evening twilight. Mercury, however, can be seen easily with the naked eye, looking like a bright reddish object low in the sky as morning twilight begins or evening twilight ends.

Mercury travels swiftly in its orbit and completes a complete revolution around the sun once every 88 days. The plane of Mercury's orbit is inclined 7^0 to that of the Earth's plane of orbit.

Astronomers for many years believed that Mercury rotates around its axis only once for every revolution around the sun. Radio telescope studies, however, indicate that the true rotation period is 59 days, or almost exactly 2/3 of the length of the planet's year.

Photos from space probes show the surface of Mercury to be heavily cratered, much like the Earth's natural satellite, which is the moon. The photos show cliffs and groove like hills, but no mountain ranges. The planet has a weak magnetic field and extends their atmosphere that consists mostly of helium and argon. Because Mercury's density is comparable to the Earth's density, scientists theorize that Mercury must have a large core of iron or some other dense material. Closeness to the sun and slow rotation causes surface, day-light temperatures to reach 400^0F (205^0C) or higher and at night the surface cools rapidly to as low as -280^0F (-173^0C)

The diameter of Mercury is 3,032 miles or (4,880km). The Earth's diameter is 2.5 times as large.

Its mean distance from the sun is 36,000,000 miles or (58,000,000km).

Length of Mercury's day = 59 Earth's days.
Length of Mercury's year = 88 Earth's days.
Density – 5.4 times that of water, compared at 5.522 for the Earth.

Planet Venus: -

The planet Venus, in astronomy, is the second planet outward from the sun. Except for the sun and the moon, Venus is the brightest object in the sky, displaying a brilliant white star like looks. The orbit of Venus lies about midway between those of Mercury and Earth, and it is inclined about 3.5^0 to Earth's orbit. When Venus is at inferior conjunction (the position exactly between the sun and Earth), it comes closer to the Earth than any other planet. Observed telescopically, Venus is seen to pass through phases much like those of the Earth's moon.

In most general terms, Venus seems to resemble the Earth quite closely. Both planets are similar in size, mass, and density, and both have appreciable atmospheres. But while Earth's atmosphere is relatively transparent, that of Venus is completely and permanently choked in a thick blanket of clouds. Because the planet itself is never visible, little is known of its surface features. Radar studies from Earth have detected low mountains and numerous large and low pitched craters. Because of the planet's high density, astronomers believe that Venus has a large heavy core, and an interior shape similar to Earth.

Venus rotates very slowly about its axis, completing a full turn in slightly more than one Venusians year. The direction is east to west, opposite that of other planets.

Although Venus atmosphere, which consists of carbon dioxide, is featureless when seen in ordinary sunlight, it displays considerable detail if viewed in ultraviolet light. Photos from unmanned probes have provided a pattern of atmospheric cloud formation somewhat like that of Earth, but moving many times faster. Some scientists estimate that clouds near the equator are moving at 200 miles per hour (320 km/ hour) and that the speeds near the poles are even higher. On the surface of Venus, temperatures probably are as high as 900^0F (500^0C) and the atmospheric pressure is 90 times that at sea-level on Earth.

The diameter of Venus is 7,521 miles or (12,104 km).

The average distance from the sun is 67,200,000 miles or (108,124,800 km).

The length of one day on Venus = 243 Earth's days.

The length of one year on Venus = 224.7 Earth's days.
The density is 5.2 times that of water, or 95% that of the Earth.

Planet Earth: -

Earth is the planet on which we live. The Earth is part of the solar system, a group of nine planets that revolve around a star we call the sun. Revolving around the Earth is its one natural satellite, the moon. Sun, Earth, and all other planets form only a small part of the Milky Way, which itself is only one of the many large groups, or galaxies, of stars that make up the universe.

The Earth is the third planet from the sun, (Mercury and Venus are nearer) and the fifth largest planet of the solar system, (Jupiter, Saturn, Uranus, and Neptune are larger). The Earth is the only known planet suited to human life. It might be the only planet in the solar system that is suited to life of any kind.

The Earth is usually thought of as being shaped like a ball, but slight bulges and flattened areas give it a slightly irregular shape. The planet is surrounded by a thick blanket of air, known as the atmosphere. Oceans make up approximately three-fourth of the Earth's surface. The land area consists of four larger masses divided into seven continents plus thousands of smaller masses or islands.

The "top and bottom" of the Earth are the two poles; they are the points about which the Earth turns in its daily rotation. For convenience, the North Pole is considered the top and the South Pole the bottom. The Equator, an imaginary line circling the earth midway between the poles, divides the Earth into the northern and southern hemispheres. North, South, and Central America are in the Western hemisphere; and Europe, Asia, Africa, and Australia are in the Eastern hemisphere.

Statistics of the Earth: -

The Radius: - The average radius of the Earth is 6.38×10^6m.

The Density: - The density of the Earth is 5.522 times that of water.

The Mass of the Earth: - The mass of the Earth is 5.98×10^{24}kg.

The Mean Distance from the Sun: - The mean distance from the sun is 1.5×10^{11}m

Acceleration due to Earth's gravity is generally 9.8m/sec^2

Atmospheric pressure at sea level is one atmosphere which is equal to 1.013×10^5Pascals or Newton per square meter.

Planet Mars: -

In astronomy, planet Mars is the fourth planet from the sun and the next planet outward from the Earth in the solar system. Often called the red planet, Mars looks like a bright star with a distinct reddish color in the night sky.

For centuries Mars has been a subject of fascination and observation, ranking second only to the moon among the heavenly bodies in space. From the earliest times, its remarkable color and its unusual movement against the background of stars aroused great interests among scientists. With the invention of the telescope, surface details on Mars became visible and the planet was soon being compared to Earth. The possibility of the existence of life on Mars, chiefly intelligent life, quickly became a popular topic among astronomers and public. "Canals" seen by some observers were considered as essential proof of a Martian civilization. In the 1970's unmanned probes from Earth provided the first close look at the planet and revealed that the canals had been an illusion. Unmanned probes were sent to the planet's surface in an attempt to discover whether life exists or had ever existed on planet Mars.

Characteristics and Appearance: -

Mars is a relatively small planet and its diameter is about half that of earth. It travels around the sun every 687 earth days in an orbit, which is an elliptical orbit like other planets. Its distance from the sun and the earth varies considerably during the Martian year. Once every 2.1 earth years, Mars reaches opposition, the point at which it is closest to the earth and can be easily studied by the astronomers.

Mars seems to resemble earth in many ways. The Martian day, for example, is only slightly larger than an earth day. Seasonal patterns resemble those of the earth, since the tilt of Mars's axis (about 25^0) is about the same as that of the earth (23.5^0). Because of the length of the Martian year, however, each season is about twice as long as its counterpart on earth. Mars like earth is flattened at its poles and bulges somewhat at the equator.

Mars has pinkish tan color with scattered dark patches of gray or grayish green. The patches tend to vary the brightness from time to time, due to changes in surface material by strong winds. Brilliant white polar caps are conspicuous during much of the Martian year, advancing and retreating seasonally.

Surface Features: -

The surface of Mars is a dynamic, geologically varying world with volcanic mountains, extensive lava flows, and indications of crustal faults, (cracks in the outer layer of the planet, associated with internal disturbances). Water now trapped in the polar ice caps, and possibly elsewhere, as thick layers of underground ice – apparently once flowed over large areas of the planet's surface.

Much of Mars's northern hemisphere is a comparatively smooth plain dotted with the wind eroded remains of ancient craters. Some of the craters are of volcanic origin; but others were most probably formed by meteorite impacts. The southern hemisphere is somewhat more rugged, with younger craters and considerable changes in elevation from place to place.

In 1976, two unmanned Viking launchers, launched by the US, reached the surface of Mars's northern hemisphere. Pictures relayed to earth by Viking show the soil and many rocks as bright orange. The sky is not a deep blue, as had been expected, but a pinkish orange, apparently due to the concentration of dust particles in the atmosphere. As expected, silicon and iron are the essential soil components with lesser amounts of calcium, aluminum, phosphorous and some other elements also present. Martian rocks seem to be of a different composition than those of the earth or the moon.

Atmosphere and Climate: -

The atmosphere of Mars is extremely thin with ground level pressure equal to that found 20 miles above sea level on earth. The main component is CO_2; there are also small amounts of nitrogen, argon, oxygen, water vapor, krypton, and xenon. Cirrus like clouds of frozen water vapor often form near higher mountains, or shift across the planet at high altitudes. Fog like vapor also occurs occasionally in craters and other low lying areas.

Because of Mars's greater distance from the sun, daytime temperatures are generally lower than those on earth. At midday in equatorial regions, the temperatures rarely rise above 70°F. Overnight, the temperature plunges as much as 150 degrees because the thin air retains little of sun's heat. At the poles, the year round temperature remains near -180°F.

Strong winds, caused by the rapid and wide temperature variations, are common on Mars. The most drastic winds occur when the planet is closest to the sun and is undergoing maximum heating. During this period, winds of up to 200 miles per hour whip surface dust into gigantic dust storms that may cover large areas of the planet for weeks at a time. Lesser dust storms occur throughout the Martian year.

Natural Satellites: -

Mars has two moons viz. Phobos and Deimos, which in English mean (Fear and Terror), respectively.

Both are very small, shaped somewhat like potatoes, and scarred by numerous meteorite craters. Phobos is the larger of the two moons, measuring 12 miles along one axis and 17 miles along the other. It orbits only 3,700 miles above Mars, circling the planet once every 15/2 hours, rising and setting twice each Martian day. Deimos, the smaller moon, measures 6 by 10 miles. It orbits 12,500 miles above Mars and makes a full revolution every 121/4 hours.

The Diameter of Planet Mars: - The equatorial diameter of planet Mars is about 4,217 miles and the polar diameter is about 4,170 miles.

The Distance of Planet Mars from The sun: - The mean distance of planet Mars from the sun is 141,600,000 miles, the maximum distance is 154,900,000 miles, and the minimum distance is 128,400,000 miles.

The Length of Martian Day: - 24 hours, 37 minutes.

The Length of Martian Year: - 687 earth days.

The Surface Gravity: - 0.38g (38% that of earth's acceleration due to gravity)

The Density: - 3.90 times that of water, compared to 5.522 for earth.

Planet Jupiter: -

Jupiter is the fifth planet from the sun and is the largest of the solar system's nine major planets with a diameter 11 times that of earth and a mass more than twice that of other eight planets combined. Seen in the night sky, Jupiter looks like a bright star like object.

Information relayed to earth from unmanned space probes indicates that Jupiter consists chiefly of hot liquid hydrogen and helium. Very little of this large planet is solid; at most, there is a solid core about the size of the earth. Jupiter is mostly liquid and turns very rapidly on its axis, and it bulges noticeably at the equator. This planet radiates two to three times the amount of heat it receives from the sun and this is an evidence of the great heat in the interior, which may range as high as 54,000°F (30,000°C). Despite the very high temperature, the liquid does not boil away because it is under tremendous pressure from the weight of the atmosphere above it.

The layer surrounding the core is about 40,000 miles (64,000km) thick and consists mostly of liquid hydrogen. So great is the pressure in the lower part of this layer that the hydrogen assumes metallic properties, including the ability to conduct electricity.

Near the outer limits of the liquid layer, there is a gradual merging of liquid hydrogen with the gases of the atmosphere.

Jupiter's atmosphere is a thick layer of turbulent clouds that completely hides the rest of the planet from view. The atmosphere consists chiefly of hydrogen and helium, with traces of water (in both droplet and ice crystal form), ammonia, and ammonium hydrosulphide. The outermost portion of the atmosphere displays a distinctive series of light and dark cloud bands running parallel to the equator. These bands, which are apparently caused by currents of rising and falling gases, change in color from time to time and occasionally display spots and other markings.

The most outstanding feature of Jupiter's atmosphere is the Great Red Spot, a vast oval object in the southern hemisphere. The spot remains approximately constant in size and structure, but changes in color and brightness. Some scientists believe that the spot is the top of a giant hurricane like storm. Such a storm could last many centuries because apparently all the energy needed to keep it in motion comes from Jupiter's interior in a steady flow, night and day.

By contrast, the energy that creates earth's weather is provided by heat from the sun, which changes widely depending on the season, latitude, and time of day.

Other observations made by space probes have verified that Jupiter has a magnetic field similar to earth's magnetic field but much stronger. The magnetic field traps high energy particles from the sun and forms an immense magnetosphere. The trapped particles are a source of radio-wave emissions. Space probe photographs have revealed that Jupiter is encircled by a faint ring, which is probably composed of dust particles. Space probes also have detected auroras in Jupiter's Polar Regions and powerful lightning flashes at the tops of Jupiter's clouds.

The Satellites of Jupiter: -

Jupiter has 16 known satellites. All of these satellites except for four are very small and many of them may be captured asteroids.

Four of the smaller satellites revolve around Jupiter in a direction opposite to that of the rest. The large satellites viz. Ganymede, Callisto, Io, and Europa are known as Galilean satellites. Ganymede is larger than planet Mercury, Callisto is slightly smaller. Io and Europa are nearly the same size as the earth's moon.

Most of the information about the Galilean satellites was obtained by the Voyager space probes that flew past Jupiter in 1979. Each Galilean satellite was found to have distinctive surface features. Io, the closest of the four to Jupiter, has a yellow to orange surface which is probably composed of sulphur and compounds of sulphur. A major discovery was that there are several active volcanoes on Io. The volcanoes are much more violent than those on earth. Europa, the Galilean satellite second closest to Jupiter, has a very smooth surface crisscrossed by long streaks. The streaks may be cracks in a thin crust of ice. Ganymede presents a variety of features: dark, heavily cratered areas; grooved terrain; systems of faults. Callisto, the most distant from Jupiter of the four satellites, has a surface almost entirely covered with craters. There are also several small basins surrounded by ridges forming concentric rings. Ganymede and Callisto are both thought to be covered by a thick layer of ice.

Diameter of Jupiter: - Equatorial diameter = 88,700 miles or (142,700km);

Polar diameter = 82,900 miles or (133,400km).

Average Distance of Jupiter from the Sun: - 483,600,000 miles or (778,300,000km).

Length of Day on planet Jupiter: - At equator 9 hours, 50 minutes; near poles 9 hours, 55 minutes.

Length of Year on planet Jupiter: - 11.86 earth years.

Density of Jupiter: - 1.3 times that of water, compared to 5.522 for earth.

Planet Saturn: -

The planet Saturn is the sixth planet from the sun. It is the second largest planet in the solar system (Jupiter being the largest), and the most distant to be easily visible with the naked eye (Uranus is just barely visible). Saturn is noted specially for the brilliant rings that circle it.

Saturn is made up largely of liquid hydrogen and helium. At its center may be a rocky core somewhat larger than the Earth. The outer margin of immersed liquid layer blends gradually into a dense atmosphere of hydrogen gas with lesser amounts of helium, ammonia, methane, and other gases. Saturn's atmosphere is the only visible portion of the planet. It is yellowish in color and has numerous bands paralleling the equator.

The rings of Saturn were first observed in 1610 by Galileo Galilee, who misunderstood them for moons. Some fifty years later, the Dutch astronomer Christian Huygens reported that Saturn was being encircled by what he thought was one ring. It is now known that there are many rings. The rings are thin and composed of countless small particles. From the photographs taken of Saturn there are two rings visible.

The wider ring is called ring A and the other is called ring B. The dark space that separates the two rings is called Cassini's division. Images obtained from spacecrafts sent past Saturn have revealed that these rings consist of hundreds of narrow concentric rings.

Because these rings are tilted with respect to the plane of Saturn's orbit, they show changes in position, as seen from Earth, during the planet's year (about 30 earth years). The rings can be seen edge on every 15 years.

Saturn is known to have 10 moons, and additional moons have been sighted by spacecrafts but not yet confirmed. Saturn's largest moon, the Titan, has an atmosphere and is larger than planet Mercury.

Diameter of Saturn: - Equatorial diameter = 74,600 miles or (120,100km); Polar diameter = 67,500 miles or (108,630km).

Average Distance of Saturn from the Sun: - It is 886,700,000 miles or (1,427,000,000km).

Length of Day: - Saturn's day is 10 hours and 39 minutes.

Length of Year: - Saturn's year = 29.46 earth years.

Density: - Saturn's density is 0.7 times that of water, compared to 5.522 for the earth.

Planet Uranus: -

Planet Uranus is the seventh planet from the sun. Uranus was the first planet to be discovered telescopically, the five bright planets from Mercury to Saturn being readily visible to the naked eye. When Sir William Herschel discovered Uranus in 1781, he at first misunderstood it for a comet. It is just visible to a person of keen eye sight who knows where to look.

Uranus has greenish color, probably due to the presence of large amounts of methane gas in its atmosphere. The planet's axis of rotation is extremely tilted. It is almost level with the planet's orbit. Uranus has five known moons. With the orbits of the moons, a series of nine narrow rings encircle the planet. Unlike the rings of Saturn, these rings are fairly dark and are probably composed of particles of rock. The rings of Uranus were first discovered in 1977.

The Diameter of Uranus: - The diameter of Uranus is 32,200 miles or (51,800km), which is about four times that of earth.

Average Distance from Sun: - The average distance of Uranus from the sun is 1,783,100,000 miles or (2,869,600,000km).

Length of Day on Uranus: - The length of day is 10.8 hours.

Length of Year on Uranus: - 84.01 earth years.

Density: - It is 1.2 times that of water, compared to 5.52 for Earth.

Planet Neptune: -

Neptune is the eighth planet from the sun in the solar system. By telescope, Neptune looks like a small greenish disc, but is not visible with the unaided eye. It is one of the giants, or Jovian planets. Uranus, the seventh planet and Neptune, the eighth planet are similar in size and telescopic appearance and are often referred to as the twin planets.

Neptune is surrounded by a thick atmosphere containing large amounts of methane. No markings are visible on its surface. The theoretical average temperature of Neptune is about -380°F or (-229°C), but its temperature has not been accurately determined.

Neptune was discovered in 1846 through its effects on Uranus. Uranus had been observed sometimes ahead of and sometimes behind the position it could have had, bearing on the effects of the sun and the known planets. In 1845 and 1846 two men John C. Adams in England and Urbain Levenier in France independently captured the orbit of an unknown planet that would account for the observed behavior of Uranus. Levenier's calculations were first tested and Neptune was immediately found in the predicted position by Johann Galle of Berlin Observatory.

Neptune has two satellites viz. Triton and Nereid. Triton, which is closest to Neptune is larger than the Earth's moon and may have an atmosphere. Nereid is much smaller than Triton. Nereid revolves around

Neptune in the same direction that the planet rotates. Triton revolves in the opposite direction.

Diameter of Neptune: - The diameter of Neptune is about 30,800 miles or (49,600km), which is more than three times the earth's diameter.

Average Distance of Neptune from the Sun: - The average distance of Neptune from the sun is 2,794,100,000 miles or (4,496,600,000km), which is more than 30 times the earth's average distance from the sun.

Length of Day on Neptune: - The length of day on Neptune is 16 earth's hours.

Length of year on Neptune: - The length of year on Neptune is 164.8 earth's years.

Density: - The density of Neptune is about 1.7 times that of water, compared to 5.52 for earth.

Planet Pluto: -

Planet Pluto is the ninth planet from the sun. Its average distance from the sun is greater than that for any other planet. However, because of the structure of its orbit (path), a flattened ellipse, Pluto is not always the most distant planet. At its perihelion (the point on its orbit closest to the sun), Pluto is 35,000,000 miles or (56,327,000km) closer to the sun than is the orbit of Neptune. Pluto has reached this point, for the first time since it was discovered, in 1989.

Because of its great distance from the sun, Pluto must be extremely cold. The planet is so small and far away, however, that very little reliable data about it has been made available. Its surface seems to be frozen methane. Some astronomers believe that Pluto is an escaped moon of Neptune.

Pluto was discovered in 1930 at Lowell Observatory, Arizona; by Clyde W. Tombaugh. His search was based on the prediction of the existence of the planet made by Percival Lowell in the early 20th century. The name Pluto was selected because it begins with Lowell's initials. In 1978, it was discovered that Pluto has a moon.

The Diameter of Pluto: - The diameter of Pluto is estimated at about 1,900 miles or (3,000km).

Average Distance of Pluto from the Sun: - The average distance of Pluto from the sun is about 3,666,100,000 miles or (5,900,000,000km), which is about 39.5 times that of earth from the sun.

Length of Day on Pluto: - It is 6 days and 9 hours on earth.

Length of Year on Pluto: - The length of Pluto's year is equal to 247.7 earth's years approximately.

Density: - The density of Pluto is about the same as the density of water, compared to 5.522 times that of water for earth.

39)

· ·

a) The Milky Way Galaxy

The Milky Way Galaxy, that is, our own galaxy is 100,000 light years (9.5 x 10^{17} km) in diameter and is about 1000 light years (9.5 x 10^{15} km) thick. It is estimated to contain at least 200 billion stars and possibly up to 400 billion stars, the exact figure depending on the number of very low-mass stars which is highly uncertain. Recent observations indicate that the gaseous disk of the Milky Way Galaxy has a thickness of around 12,000 light years (1.1 x 10^{17} km) twice the previously accepted value. As a guide to the relative physical scale of the Milky Way, if it were reduced to 100 m in diameter, the solar system, including the Oort Cloud, would be no more than 1 mm in width. The size of our galaxy is now considered to be roughly similar to that of our largest local neighbor, the Andromeda Galaxy.

The Milky Way Galaxy's rotational speed around the galactic center puts the figure at about 254 km/sec., significantly higher than the widely accepted value of 200 km/sec.

This implies that the Milky Way has a total mass equivalent to around 3 trillion suns, about 50% more massive than previously thought.

It is extremely difficult to define the age at which the Milky Way formed, but the age of the oldest star in the galaxy yet discovered H E 1523-0901, is estimated to be about 13.2 billion years, nearly as old as the universe itself. The universe is 14 billion years old, according to the Big Bang Theory.

The Milky Way Galaxy's mass is thought to be about 5.8 x 10^{11} solar masses, comprising 200 to 400 billion stars. The distance from the sun to the galactic center is now estimated at 26,000 ±1400 light years while older estimates could put the sun as far as 35,000 light years from the central bulge. Most galaxies are believed to have a super-massive Black Hole at their center. The galactic center of the Milky Way Galaxy is also a super-massive Black Hole. It is called Sagittarius A*, thought to mark the center of the Milky Way Galaxy Box. It is thought to be about 27,000 light years long, running through it, centers at a 44±10 degree angle to the line between the sun and the center of galaxy.

It is composed primarily of red stars, believed to be ancient (Red Dwarf, Red Giant). The box is surrounded by 5 kpc ring that contains large portions of hydrogen present in the galaxy as well as the Milky Way star formation activity, viewed from the Andromeda Galaxy; it would be the brightest feature of our own galaxy.

b) The Andromeda Galaxy:-

Galaxy: Galaxy is a collection of stars, star clusters, nebulae, and inter-s-teller matter. Star clusters are of two types viz. (1) Open, consisting of up to a few hundred stars, and (2) Globular, consisting of 20,000 to 200,000 stars. Nebulae are cloud-like masses of gaseous or finely divided matter. Inter-s-teller matter consists of dust and gas, chiefly hydrogen and atoms of various other elements.

The most familiar galaxy is the Milky Way, often called simply galaxy, of which the sun and the solar system are a part. The Milky Way galaxy is a broad luminous band stretching across the sky from horizon to horizon. Galaxies beyond the Milky Way galaxy, called exterior galaxies, number into the millions. The most distant galaxy visible to the unaided eye is that of the constellation Andromeda, estimated to be more than 2 million light years from the earth.

Types of Galaxies: - Galaxies are classified as elliptical, spiral, and irregular.

Elliptical Galaxies: - Elliptical galaxies vary in shape from spherical to somewhat elongated. They have bright nuclei (center), fading out toward the edges. They are believed to be the oldest galaxies, star formation having ceased in them.

Spiral Galaxies: - Spiral galaxies, such as the Milky Way galaxy, are circular in appearance. Their bright nuclei fade into definite or barely visible arms at the edges. In the barred spiral galaxy, a bright band across the nucleus usually terminates in two distant arms.

Irregular Galaxies: - Irregular galaxies are much less common than the other types, lack well defined nuclei and have no definite shapes or structure. They are the youngest galaxies and are thought to be forerunner of the spiral type.

The Andromeda Galaxy: - The Andromeda galaxy is a spiral galaxy that is larger than the Milky Way (The galaxy to which earth belongs) but similar to it in structure. (A galaxy is a large concentration of stars, dust, gas, and other material). The Andromeda galaxy is the only galaxy beyond the Milky Way that can be seen with the unaided eye from the middle latitudes of the northern hemisphere. It appears as a hazy spot in the constellation Andromeda.

The Andromeda galaxy is about 2.2 million light years from earth, (A light year is the distance light travels in one year at the rate of 186,282 miles per second). It is estimated to be about 92,000 light years long and about 23,000 light years wide. The galaxy is actually wheel-shaped, but the view from earth is nearly edge on, making it appear to be elongated because of the similarities between it and what astronomers have been able to map of the Milky Way. Information obtained on the Andromeda galaxy helps man understand the structure of his own galaxy.

After the invention of the telescope in the 17th century, Andromeda galaxy was called the great nebulae of Andromeda, (A name that is still sometimes used) and was thought to be a cloud of dust within the Milky Way. In the 19th century, some astronomers theorized that the Andromeda galaxy was not a dust cloud, but a large group of stars, so far away that the telescope of the time could not separate the individual stars. This theory was upheld in 1923 when Edwin Hubble, an American astronomer, discovered some variable stars in the edges of the Andromeda galaxy. In 1944 Walter Baade, a German-American astronomer, was able to identify individual stars in the nucleus or central portion of the galaxy.

40)
· ·

a) Ursa Minor and Ursa Major:-

Ursa Minor:-

The Ursa Minor Dwarf is a dwarf elliptical galaxy and it was discovered by A.G. Wilson of the Lowell Observatory in 1954. It is part of the Ursa Minor constellation, and a satellite galaxy to the Milky Way. The galaxy consists mainly of older stars and there appears to be little to no ongoing star formation in the Ursa Minor Dwarf Galaxy.

Evolutionary History:- In 1999, Mighell & Burke used the Hubble Space Telescope to confirm that the UMi system had a straight forward evolutionary history with a single ~2 Gyr long burst of star formation around 14 Gyr ago.

Ursa Major:-

Ursa Major II Dwarf is a dwarf galaxy orbiting the Milky Way galaxy. The discovery by D.B. Zucker et al. was announced in 2006.

It is a small dwarf galaxy with projected size of 250 x 125 pc. The absolute magnitude of the object is only ~3.8, meaning that it is less luminous than some stars, like Canopus in the Milky Way. It is comparable in luminosity to Bellatrix in Orion.

It is located at a distance of about 97,800 light-years from the Earth. There is another object called Ursa Major I Dwarf, discovered by Beth Willman in 2005.

Coordinates: $15^h 09^m 08.5^s$, $+67° 13' 21"$

Ursa Minor Dwarf:-

Observation data (J2000 epoch)

Constellation Ursa Minor Constellation

Right ascension $15^h 09^m 08.5^{s[1]}$

Declination $+67° 13' 21"^{[1]}$

Red shift -247 ± 1 km/s[1]

Distance 200 ± 30 kly (60 ±10 kpc)

Type E[1]
Apparent 30'.2 x 19'.1[1]
Dimensions (V)
Apparent 11.9[1]
Magnitude (V)
Notable features satellite galaxy of Milky Way
Coordinates: 08ʰ 51ᵐ 30ˢ, +63° 07' 48"
Ursa Major II Dwarf
Observation data (J2000 epoch)
Constellation Ursa Major
Right ascension 08ʰ 51ᵐ 30.0ˢ[1]
Declination +63° 07' 48"[1]
Distance 98 kly (30 kpc)
Type dSph-Irr
Apparent magnitude (V) 14.3
Other designations
UMa II dwarf,[1] Ursa Major II dSph[1]

b) Nova and Supernova, (General Astronomy)

Nova is a star that rapidly increases in brightness and then fades again. The term comes from Latin for "new". Before the invention of the telescope such stars were thought to be new because they suddenly appeared where no star had been seen before. It was later found that becoming novae, most of these stars were too dim to be seen with the naked eye. There are probably as many as 30 novae per year in the Milky Way, but generally only one or two are visible from the earth. A few novae briefly appear as bright as the brightest stars in the sky, but most can be observed only with a telescope.

A typical nova increases in brightness by 10,000 to 1,000,000 times within a few days. It then gradually declines to its original brightness over a period of several months or years. After several decades some novae flare up again; they are called recurring novae.

A nova is usually a relatively old star and a member of a binary system (or a double star). A nova's sudden brightness is caused by an explosion near the star's surface, which causes a thin shell of gas to be expelled from the star. According to one theory, the explosion occurs when the star draws towards itself a large amount of matter from its binary companion.

A supernova reaches its maximum brightness much greater than that of a nova; it can increase in brightness by as much as a billion times. A supernova recorded by the Chinese in 1054 A.D could be seen in full daylight for many weeks. The last known supernova in the Milky Way was observed in 1604. However, astronomers have discovered and studied supernovae in many other galaxies since then. A supernova results from the collapse of an old dying star. The collapse generates a neutron star.

c) Black Holes and Alpha Centauri: -(General Astronomy)

There are countless billions of solar systems and interplanetary systems like our own solar system and interplanetary system which comprise countless billions of galaxies like our own Milky Way galaxy.

These countless billions of galaxies together form countless billions of Super Clusters comprising the whole universe.

Besides planets, asteroids, comets, and meteorites, there are like countless billions of natural satellites bound to the gravitational attractions of countless billions of planets like the earth and the moon.

Recent studies have revealed the existence of "Black Holes".

The mass of a "Black Hole" is countless billions of times greater than any star known in the universe.

The Black Holes are like areas of space-time with a gravitational field so intense that nothing can escape, not even light.

Hence this implicates super-massive black holes in this seemingly benign system. The super-massive black holes have a mass that is countless billions of times greater than our sun.

In the constellation Cygnus is a binary (two-star) system consisting of a large visible star and a tiny invisible object that may be a black hole. The area around the invisible member of the system is a strong source of X- rays, possibly the result of vast quantities of energy released by gases drawn into the black hole from the visible star.

Black Holes are usually located at the galactic centers of a Super Cluster. Sagittarius A* is the galactic center of the Super Cluster in which Milky Way Galaxy revolves. Sagittarius A* is a "Black Hole" as well as our "galactic center".

Alpha Centauri: -

Alpha Centauri is a system of three stars, one of whose members; namely, Proxima Centauri is the star nearest the sun. Proxima can be seen only with a telescope. The other two stars are visible as a single bright star to the naked eye. Alpha Centauri is a little more than four light-years from the sun. Alpha Centauri is in the constellation called, Centaurus.

41)

. . . .

a) The Hydro-electric Power Generating Plants:-

Flowing or falling water is an important source of energy. Unlike most other sources of energy, it does not require some part of earth's raw material as fuel, and it does not produce pollution. Water power is often considered the least costly source of energy, since it is constantly produced by the forces of nature. However, the dams and the machinery required to make use of water power are often very costly to build and to maintain.

Heat from the sun evaporates water from the oceans, lifting it up into the atmosphere to form clouds. Wind carries these clouds over land, where the water falls again as rain or snow. Ultimately it finds its way back to the ocean through streams and rivers. Along the way it can be made to do work, turning water wheels or turbines in hydroelectric power plants. The generation of electric power is the chief use of water power today.

The power available at a dam or waterfall depends on the amount of water that passes it (the flow) and the height from which it falls (the head).

The installed capacity (the maximum generating capacity of the hydroelectric power plant) is measured in kilowatts.

How falling water generates electricity:-

Water from the reservoir flows down the penstock and turns the turbine. The turbine operates the generator, which produces electricity. The voltage is brought to the proper level by the transformer and the electricity is sent out to the consumers through the power lines.

History of Water Power:-

The first hydroelectric power plant was constructed at Appleton, Wisconsin, in 1882. Since then, hydroelectric power has been developed on a larger scale, particularly in the United States, Canada, and other countries like Russia, Japan, France, Brazil, Italy, Norway, Sweden, and Spain.

Hydro-mechanics: -

Hydro-mechanics is that branch of physics that deals with forces acting upon and within fluids. Hydro-mechanics is divided into hydrostatics, the study of fluids at rest; and hydrodynamics, the study of fluids in motion.

Principles of the hydro-mechanics of fluids are applied in hydraulics, which deals with water or other fluids at rest or in motion; in aerodynamics, which deals with the motion of air and with relative motion between air and objects in the air; in fluidics, which deals with automated sensing and controlling devices that use the movements of the fluids to operate; and in pneumatic devices, which deals with the mechanical properties of gases.

Hydrodynamics: -

A liquid or gas flows from regions of high pressure to regions of low pressure. This happens, for example, when water is squeezed from a sponge or squirted from a hose. The flow of fluids is influenced by viscosity, the resistance that opposes the motion of a fluid. Some liquids flow by capillary action, which depends largely on adhesion and surface tension.

Viscosity: - Viscosity is the resistance fluids have to flowing. The viscosity of such fluids as water and kerosene (and gases) is relatively low; that of such fluids as molasses and glycerin is relatively high. A slow flowing fluid, that is, one with a high viscosity, is often said to be viscous. The viscosity of liquids generally decreases with increasing temperatures. Molasses, for example, is more easily poured when heated than when cold. With gases, however, the viscosity generally increases with increasing temperatures.

The viscosity of the air causes sounds to die away and the winds to drop. The viscosity of water causes waves to subside. Viscosity has an important role to play, on the speed of airplanes, automobiles, and boats; on the efficiency of lubricating oils; and on the flow of materials through a pipeline. The unit of viscosity is Pascal-second, whereas the unit of pressure is Pascal which is Newton per meter square.

Surface Tension: - This is the tendency for the surface of a liquid to behave like a stretched elastic membrane. Cohesion is the force that holds molecules together. Surface molecules are not subject to cohesive force from the top. As a result of this unequal attraction, which attempts to pull the surface inward; the entire surface acts as if it were under tension.

Small drops of liquid tend to take on a spherical shape because the surface tension acts to make each drop as small as possible. Capillary action, the tendency of liquids to rise within small-diameter tubes, is due in part to surface tension.

Water has a higher surface tension than most liquids. It is possible to float a steel needle or razor blade on water if the surface is not penetrated. The very high surface tension of mercury, which is six times that of water, is the main reason why this liquid metal tends to form "beads", which do not wet most surfaces. The surface tension of water at 0°C, 20°C, and 100°C is 0.076 N/m, 0.072 N/m, and 0.059 N/m, respectively. The surface tension of mercury at 20°C is 0.44 N/m.

The flow of a liquid or gas can be laminar (smooth) or turbulent (rough and eddying). The nature of the flow depends on the viscosity and density of the fluid, on the speed at which the fluid is moving, and on the surface and shape of objects in contact with the fluid. An object whose shape offers little resistance to the smooth flow of a fluid is said to be streamlined.

Bernoulli's Principle: - This principle states that the pressure exerted by a flowing fluid on the walls of a tube (for example, a hose or a pipe) decreases where as the speed of a fluid increases (as at the exit of a nozzle). Bernoulli's principle explains the lift obtained by hydrofoil boats and by aircraft with wings or rotors. This principle also explains the reduced pressure in a venture throat, which is a constricted portion of the tube. This principle is used, for example, in the air intake passes of a carburetor of a car.

Torricelli's Theorems: - This is an application of the law of falling bodies in liquids. It states that a liquid flowing from an outlet of a tank has the same speed as an object falling freely from the level of the liquid surface to the level of the outlet. This theorem also states that a jet of water rises to the level of the source, unless opposed by friction.

Hydrostatics: -

This is the study of fluids at rest. Under this heading we discuss Archimedes' principle and Pascal's law as follows:-

Archimedes' Principle: - According to Archimedes' principle a fluid exerts a buoyant (lifting) force on an object placed in the fluid. The force is equal to the weight of the fluid displaced by the object. This principle explains why ships and balloons float in water and air, respectively.

Pascal's Law: - This law was formulated by Pascal (1623-1662) and it applies to any fluid in a container. The law states that pressure upon the fluid at any point will be transmitted uniformly throughout the fluid. Pascal's Law explains the action of a hydraulic press and similar devices.

b) The Largest Hydropower Project in the World

The Three Gorges Dam is the world's largest hydropower project and most notorious dam. The massive project sets records for the number of people displaced (more than 1.2 million), the number of cities and towns flooded (13 cities, 140 towns, 1,350 villages), and length of reservoir (more than 600 kilometers). The project has been plagued by corruption, spiraling costs, technological problems, human rights violations, and resettlement difficulties.

The environment impacts of the project are profound, and are likely to worsen as the time goes on. The submergence of hundreds of factories, mines and waste dumps, and the presence of massive industrial centers upstream are creating a festering bog of effluent, silt, industrial pollutants and rubbish in the reservoir. Erosion of the reservoir and downstream riverbanks is causing landslides, and threatening one of the world's biggest fisheries in the East China Sea. The weight of the reservoir's water has many scientists concerned over reservoir-induced seismicity. Since 2007, Chinese scientists and government officials have become increasingly concerned about the environmental and social impacts of the project.

The Three Gorges Dam is a model for disaster, yet the Chinese government is replicating this model both domestically and internationally. Within China, huge hydropower cascades have been proposed and are being constructed in some of China's most pristine and biologically and culturally diverse river basins- the Lancang (Upper Mekong) River, Nu (Salween) River and upstream of Three Gorges Dam on the Yangtze River and tributaries.

Government and Companies from around the world have helped fund and build the Three Gorges Dam. Yet through this project, China has acquired the know-how to build large hydropower schemes and is now exporting similar projects around the world. While Three Gorges is the world's biggest hydro-project, the problems at Three Gorges are not unique. Around the world, large dams are causing social and environmental devastation while better alternatives are being ignored.

International Rivers protects rivers and defends the rights of the communities which depend on them. They monitor the social and environmental problems of the Three Gorges Dam, and work to ensure that the right decisions are made for energy and water projects in China and around the world.

c) The World's Largest Hydroelectric Power Plant

The Itaipu hydroelectric power plant is the largest development of its kind in operation in the world. Built from 1975 to 1991, in a joint development on the Parana River, Itaipu represents the efforts and accomplishments of two neighboring countries, Brazil and Paraguay. The power plant's 20 generating units add up to a total production capacity of 14,000 MW (megawatts). In 2000, the power plant generated 93,428 GWh (gigawatthours) of electricity, a world record for hydroelectricity generation.

The magnitude of the project also can be demonstrated by the fact that in 2000 Itaipu alone provided 20% of the energy supply in Brazil and 94% in Paraguay. The Spillway is located on the right bank, and it has 14 segmented sluice gates with a total potential discharge rate of 62,200 cubic meters per second (twice that of the highest flood-level on record). The Itaipu dam is 7,919 meters long (counting the Hernandarias dike) with a maximum height of 196 meters, equivalent to a 65-story building. It consumed 12.3 million cubic meters of concrete, while the iron and steel employed would permit the construction of 380 Eiffel Towers: diversion that transformed the power plant into a reference with respect to concrete studies and dam safety.

42)

· ·

a) The Pollution Crisis

Pollution is the presence of impurities in the environment. The impurities, called pollutants, may be of man-made or natural origin. Natural pollutants include pollen and dust. The most serious and persistent types of contamination result from man's activities, particularly in technologically advanced and heavily populated areas.

Water in wells, lakes, rivers, and oceans may be polluted with untreated sewage, garbage, factory wastes, laundry detergents, pesticide residues, and oil spillage. The air of most cities is laden with automobile exhaust fumes, coal and fuel oil smoke, and chemicals from factories. The land is polluted with litter, junk, pesticides, and radioactive wastes.

It was in the late 1960s that public awareness grew for the need to preserve and improve the quality of the environment. People became conscious that the resources of the earth, viz. land, air, and water, that are needed to sustain life, are being threatened by pollution. Scientists warned that the biosphere, the part of the earth that sustains life, can absorb only a limited quantity of contaminants before becoming unfit for living organisms.

Some experts say that to maintain a good quality environment it is necessary to limit the growth of the world's population.

Others blame pollution not on the growth of the world's population essentially but on the economic growth of technologically advanced countries in which the consumption of manufactured products is high.

Although the wastes created by animals can be objectionable, these do not accumulate because such wastes are reintegrated into nature by the action of microbes and by other natural processes. There is no natural process that can reintegrate into nature the waste of modern technology, such as discarded automobiles, television sets, plastic bags and beer cans; and the chemical components of exhaust fumes and most pesticides. Worldwide efforts to curb environmental pollution exist, but effective international controls are largely lacking. It is difficult to achieve cooperation for pollution controls with developing countries whose essential concern is to provide such basic needs as food, shelter, and employment for their people. Furthermore, industries in some countries fear that the expenses of pollution controls might make it difficult to compete in exporting with rival nations whose pollution controls may be less expensive.

Experts agree that effective pollution controls at local, national, and international levels require massive efforts by individual consumers, industry, and government.

In the United States of America, the Environment Protection Agency was established in 1970 to attack on the federal level the problems of air and water pollution, solid waste management, pesticides, radiation, and noise.

b) Air Pollution

Each year about 200 tons of man-made waste products are released into the air in the United States of America. About half of this comes from transportation facilities, specially the automobile. Smog is a special type of air pollution that is a serious problem in many cities. Air pollution is supposed to contribute significantly to bronchitis, asthma, emphysema, and lung cancer. Many types of plant damage have also been attributed to air pollution. In addition, there is concern that air pollution, primarily increased amounts of carbon dioxide and smoke, may have long range effects on weather and climate. Hence air pollution is the contamination of the atmosphere by the addition of impurities called pollutants.

Types of Air Pollutants: - The most significant man-made pollutants include oxides of carbon, sulfur, and nitrogen; hydrocarbons; particulate matter; and various photochemical substances that are among the principle ingredients in the irritating mixture known as smog.

Oxides of carbon make up the largest single group of pollutants. Automobiles and other vehicles are probably the largest source of carbon monoxide, a colorless and odorless poison, which is a gas produced when fuel is incompletely burned in engines and furnaces. Although carbon dioxide is not a serious pollutant in itself but it is believed that a long-term build of this gas in the atmosphere could reduce the flow of heat from the earth back into space causing a dangerous warming of the earth.

Oxides of sulfur specially sulfur dioxide, are among the most dangerous and irritating of all air pollutants. Factories and electric power plants are the chief producers of sulfur dioxide since their fuels are often sulfur containing coal or oil. In the air some sulfur dioxide is converted into sulfuric acid and other corrosive compounds. Oxides of nitrogen are the products of automobile engines and other sources where combustion takes place at high temperatures. When exposed to sunlight, these oxides are the main contributors to smog.

Hydrocarbon pollutants are the products of unburned fuel, and are mainly emitted by gasoline powered vehicles. Like oxides of nitrogen, hydrocarbons also contribute to smog.

Particulate matter refers to tiny liquid or solid particles in the air. These include smoke, dust, black powdery deposit from smoke, and toxic substances like lead and fluorides. Steel mills and oil refineries are the major producers of particulate matter.

Photochemical substances, one of which is ozone, are formed when certain other pollutants go through complex chemical reactions upon exposure to the ultraviolet portion of sunlight. These substances, together with fog and smoke, form smog.

Reducing Air Pollution: - Although most of the world's cities and industrial regions have been plagued with air pollution for centuries, there was little organized effort to combat the problem until the mid-20th century.

The Clean Air Act of the Environmental Protection Agency (EPA) provides for financial assistance to state pollution control agencies and sets strict standards for automotive emissions. The (EPA) also sets general standards for air quality and operates an air monitoring network.

Many devices and systems have been developed to reduce or prevent industrial air pollution. Electrostatic precipitators, for example, remove pollutant particles by ionizing them (charging them electrically) and collecting them on electrodes that are oppositely charged.

Cyclone separators rotate impure air with a force that hurls particles against the side walls of the separators. In scrubbers, air is passed through water sprays that remove impurities.

Federal regulations for restricting automotive air pollution require the installation of various antipollution devices on cars and trucks at the time of manufacture. The most common of these is the catalytic converter.

Air Pollution Control Act: - The Air Pollution Control Act of 1955 was the first United States Clean Air Act enacted by Congress to address the national environmental problem of air pollution on July 14, 1955. This was "an act to provide research and technical assistance relating to air pollution control". The act "left states principally in charge of prevention and control of air pollution at the source. The act declared that air pollution was a danger to public health and welfare, but preserved the "primary responsibilities and rights of the states and local governments in controlling air pollution. The act put the federal government in a purely informational role, authorizing the United States Surgeon General to conduct research, investigate, and pass out information "relating to air pollution and the prevention and abatement thereof. Therefore The Air Pollution Control Act contained no provisions for the federal government to actively combat air pollution by punishing polluters. The next Congressional statement on air pollution would come with the Clean Air Act of 1963. California was the first state to act against air pollution when the metropolis of Los Angeles began to notice deteriorating air quality. The location of Los Angeles furthered the problem as several geographical and meteorological problems unique to the area exacerbated the air pollution problem.

c) Water Pollution:-

Sewage and other objectionable organic matter in water are normally broken down and rendered harmless by beneficial bacteria and other microorganism living there. When contaminants in enormous amounts are added to a body of water, however, the water's free oxygen supply is reduced in quantity, killing off the beneficial organisms. The water is no longer self-cleansing, other forms of life die out, and it gradually becomes biologically dead.

Certain pollutants are non-biodegradable, that is, they cannot be broken down by natural biological processes. Examples are certain pesticides, agricultural fertilizers, radio-active material, oil discharges from ships and boats, and various chemicals.

Dettol: - Dettol is an ANTISEPTIC GERMICIDAL and provides effective protection. For First Aid Medical and Personal Hygiene Use Diluted. It is recommended by the "Indian Medical Association". One affected by pollutants, may use a drop of dettol in the bathtub, to take a complete hygienic and medicated bath.

Some contaminants, such as phosphates, provide an excess of plant nutrients, stimulate excessive growth of water plants, and disturb the ecological balance of the waters. Heated water, discharged mainly by the electric power industry, causes thermal pollution. This occurs when water used for industrial cooling is returned to lakes and streams at high temperatures. Not only are many water plants and animals extremely sensitive to even a slight variation in temperature, but at high temperatures water cannot hold enough free oxygen either.

Efforts to stop water pollution focus chiefly on the construction of improved sewage treatment plants and the prohibition of the discharge of industrial wastes, municipal wastes, and heated water.

42) d) Solid Waste Management:-

With only 7% of the world's total population, the United States of America consumes approximately half of the earth's industrial raw materials. The amount of solid wastes it produces is enormous, almost 4.5 billion tons a year. Present waste disposal methods pollute land, air, and water.

Open dumps take up space and wreck the countryside. Incinerators (which burn to ashes) pollute the air; dumping into the sea contaminates the water.

Modern packaging stresses attractiveness, convenience, and durability but tends to squander natural resources and creates mountains of such non-biodegradable wastes as aluminum cans, one-way bottles, and plastic wrappings. Efforts to recycle (that is, gather and reuse) such solid wastes as glass, paper, and metal are being made as part of the answer of getting rid of waste.

42) e) Pesticides, Radiation, and Noise:-

Pesticides: The use of pesticides has increased world food production and has controlled such human diseases as malarial fever. However, their widespread and often indiscriminate use has not only killed many harmless or beneficial organisms but also has produced a special kind of pollution. It is known that some of the more persistent pesticides, such as DDT, accumulate in the tissues of birds, fish, other wild life, and man. There is evidence that in certain animals these pesticide residues have adverse effects on the ability to reproduce and on other body processes. What, if any, harmful effects they may have in man is not known.

Radiation: Radiation occurs naturally but can also be released as a result of man's activities. Certain amounts of radiation are released from nuclear reactors that produce electricity and power fuels. Testing of nuclear weapons also adds to man-made radiation. Another danger lies in a possible accidental leakage from radioactive wastes that have been disposed of. Health hazards from excessive radiation include cancer, eye damage, and damage to reproductive cells.

Radiation and the Human Body: Light, heat, and ultraviolet radiation are essential to life, but excessive amounts are harmful. Gamma rays, X- rays, and beta radiation are injurious even in small amounts. They can destroy tissues and cause cancer, leukemia, and cataracts. They can injure the reproductive glands, cause premature aging, and do damage that always results in death.

Background Radiation: A certain amount of injurious radiation is inescapable. This background radiation forms part of our natural environment. It comes from secondary cosmic rays, which are constantly piercing every living thing; radioactive particles and gases in the air; and radioactive substances in the earth and foods. Small quantities of carbon 14, radium, thorium, and other radioactive elements and isotopes are contained in every human body.

Fallout: The danger of radiation injury has been greatly increased by fallout, the radioactive debris of atomic bombs. The danger of fallout injury is greatest near bomb testing sites, but there is not a place on earth where winds have not carried fallout.

A number of radioactive substances are involved in fallout. Among these strontium 90 is particularly dangerous because it replaces essential calcium in living things. Many scientists believe that radioactive substances in fallout have increased such diseases as leukemia, which is a malignant disease in which too many leukocytes (white blood cells) are produced.

Radiation Sickness: Radiation injures the body by destroying cells and part of cells. It hinders cells from dividing, and often brings about the production of cells that cannot divide. Radiation can therefore destroy unborn children or convert them into congenital monsters.

Sex cells are particularly subject to radiation damage. They may be rendered infertile, and the heredity factors they contain may be altered. Alterations of the heredity factors cause changes called mutations in offspring.

Radiation also destroys blood cells and hinders or prevents their production. The destruction of white blood cells reduces the ability of the body to fight infection.

Destruction of red blood cells results in anemia which is a deficiency of red cells and their hemoglobin. Destruction of platelets (blood cells essential to the clotting of blood) causes hemorrhage.

Beta radiation causes skin burns and sores that are slow to heal. It also causes temporary or permanent baldness. More severe radiation, particularly by gamma rays, causes cancers and cataracts.

In acute radiation sickness, the first symptoms are vomiting, nausea, and listlessness, which means tired, lifeless, and drained. In cases of massive radiation, death can follow within a few hours or a few days. Commonly, the patient apparently recovers for a few days or a few weeks. Then it is followed by fever, loss of appetite, loss of weight, hemorrhage, and complete exhaustion.

The patient may die within two to four weeks or slowly recover over a period of months. Recovery from radiation sickness is likely to be accompanied by general ill-health, permanent damage to the sex glands, anemia, premature aging, and cancer or cataracts.

Protection from Radiation: - Special precautions must be taken by employees of the atomic energy plants, workers using radioactive substances, X-ray technicians, uranium miners, and others who might be exposed to dangerous amounts of radiation.

Badges, bracelets, and rings containing photographic film are worn by workers. The films measure the amounts of radiation the workers receive. The films are developed weekly or when overexposure is suspected.

For daily checking, ionization chambers are used. The ionization chamber, about the size and shape of a fountain pen, is charged with an electrical voltage. Ionization of the air or gas within the chamber causes the chamber to discharge. The voltage remaining at the end of the day indicates how much radiation a worker has received.

Workers wear rubber gloves, overshoes, respirators, and other protective clothing when necessary. Geiger-Muller counters and other devices sound an alarm when a worker is in danger of exposure to radiation. Doorways are guarded by Geiger-Muller counters that sound an alarm when a polluted worker passes through.

The extremely dangerous materials are handled in concrete cells, or caves, with walls at least two feet thick. Workers are shielded from radioactive substances by walls of lead or other materials, and all work is done with remote-control devices. Less dangerous substances are handled in a glove box, a glass topped box having a pair of rubber gloves sealed to its front.

Noise: Noise, specially the noise produced by machines, has always been regarded as an irritation. It has also been known for some time that persons in certain occupations can suffer noise-induced hearing loss. It has also been experimentally found, that the public is suffering from some type of a hearing loss because of increased mechanical noise in the environment. There is also an indication that excessive noise may have bad psychological effects on mankind.

f) Biological Effects of Ionizing Radiation: -

Ionizing radiation consists of photons and/or moving particles that have enough energy to ionize an atom or molecule. Exposure is a measure of the ionization produced in air by X-rays or γ-rays. When a beam of X-rays or γ-rays is sent through a mass m of dry air (0^0C, 1 atmosphere) and produces positive ions whose total charge is q, the exposure in coulombs per kilogram (C/kg) is given by: -

Exposure (in Coulomb/kg) = q/m

With q in coulombs (C) and m in kilogram (kg), the exposure in roentgen is given by: -

Exposure (in roentgen) = $[1/(2.58 \times 10^{-4})]$q/m

The absorbed doze is the amount of energy absorbed from the radiation per unit mass of the absorbing material.

Absorbed doze = Energy Absorbed/ Mass of Absorbing material

The SI unit of absorbed doze is the gray (Gy); 1 Gy = 1J/kg. However the rad (rad) is another unit that is often used: -

1 rad = 0.01 Gy

The amount of biological damage produced by ionizing radiation is different for different types of radiations.

The relative biological effectiveness (RBE) is the absorbed dose of 200 keV X-rays required to produce a certain biological effect divided by the dose of a given type of radiation that produces the same biological effect.

R.B.E = The dose of a 200keV of X-rays that produce a certain Biological effect / The dose of radiation that produces the same Biological effect The biologically equivalent dose (in rems) is the product of the absorbed dose (in rads) and the R.B.E.

Biologically Equivalent Dose (in rems)

= Absorbed Dose (in rads) x R.B.E

Relative Biological Effectiveness (R.B.E) for Various Types of Radiation: -

Type of Radiation R.B.E

1. 200keV X-rays 1
2. γ-rays 1
3. β⁻ particle (electrons) 1
4. Proton 10
5. α- particle 10-20
6. Slow Neutrons 2
7. Fast Neutrons 10

Average Biologically Equivalent Doses of Radiation Received by a US Resident: -

Sources of Radiation: - Biological Equivalent Doses: -

Natural Background Radiation: - (mrem / year)

1. Cosmic Rays 28
2. Radioactive Earth and Air 28
3. Internal Radioactive Nuclei 39
4. Inhaled Radon ~ 200

    Man-made Radiation: -

5. Consumer products 10
6. Medical/dental diagnostics 39
7. Nuclear medicine 14

_____

Total = 360 mrem/year

Note that the unit "rem" stands for "Roentgen Equivalent, Man" and 1 mrem = 10^{-3} rem.

A dose less than 50 rem causes no short-term ill effects. A dose between 50 and 300 rem brings on radiation sickness, the severity increasing with increasing dosage. A whole body dose in the range of 400 – 500 rem is classified as an LD_{50} dose, meaning that it is a lethal dose (LD) for about 50 % of the people so exposed; death occurs within a few months. Whole body doses greater than 600 rem results in death for almost all individuals. For more information on the harmful effects of radiation, consult the preceding discussion on Pollution. Biological Effects of Ionizing Radiation: -

Numerical Problems: -

1. An 80 kg person is exposed to 50 mrem of α-particles (R.B.E = 15). How much energy has this person absorbed?

    Solution: -

    1 rad = .01 Gray

    Biological equivalent dose (in rem i.e. roentgen equivalent, man)

    = Absorbed Dose (in rad) x R.B.E.

    R.B.E = Relative Biological Effectiveness

    Absorbed Dose = Biologically Equivalent Dose (in rem)/ R.B.E

    Absorbed Dose = 50×10^{-3} rem / 15 (R.B.E) = 3.33×10^{-3} rad

    = 0.0333×10^{-3} Gray

    Energy = 0.0333×10^{-3} Gray x 80 kg = 2.66×10^{-3} Joules

    Hence this person has absorbed 2.66×10^{-3} J of energy.

2. A film badge worn by a radiologist indicates that she has received an absorbed dose of 3×10^{-4} Gy. The mass of the radiologist is 90 kg. How much energy has she absorbed?

    Solution: -

    Absorbed Dose = Energy / Mass

    Energy = Mass x Absorbed Dose

    Energy = 90 kg x 3×10^{-4} Gy = 2.7×10^{-2} J

    Hence the radiologist has absorbed 2.7×10^{-2} J of energy.

3. A beam of γ-rays passes through 6×10^{-2} kg of dry air and generates 2×10^{13} ions, each with a charge of +e. What is the exposure in (roentgen)?

    Solution: -

    Exposure (in roentgen) = $[1/ (2.58 \times 10^{-4})]$ q/m

    q = 2×10^{13} ions x 1.6×10^{-19} J/eV

    q = 3.2×10^{-6} C

    mass = 6×10^{-2} kg

    Exposure = $[1/(2.58 \times 10^{-4})]$ x $[3.2 \times 10^{-6}$ C/ 6×10^{-2} kg]

    Exposure = 0.2067 roentgen

    Hence the exposure is 0.2067 roentgen.

4. A 3 kg tumor is being irradiated by a radioactive source. The tumor receives an absorbed dose of 10 Gy in a time of

900 seconds. Each disintegration of the radioactive source produces a particle that enters the tumor and delivers an amount of energy of 0.3 MeV. What is the activity $\Delta N / \Delta t$ of the radioactive source?

Solution: -

Activity $= \Delta N / \Delta t = \lambda N_0$

Absorbed Dose $=$ Energy Absorbed/ Mass of Absorbing Material

Energy Absorbed $=$ Absorbed Dose x Mass of Absorbing Material

Energy Absorbed $= 10$ Gy x 3 kg $= 30$ J

$E = 30$ J/1.6×10^{-19} J/eV $= 18.75 \times 10^{19}$ eV $= 18.75 \times 10^{13}$ MeV

$N = 18.75 \times 10^{13}$ MeV/0.3 MeV $= 6.25 \times 10^{14}$

$N = 6.25 \times 10^{14}$

Activity $= \Delta N / \Delta t = 6.25 \times 10^{14} / 900$s

$= 6.944 \times 10^{11}$ s^{-1}

Activity $= 6.944 \times 10^{11}$ second^{-1}

Hence the activity $\Delta N / \Delta t$ of the radioactive source is 6.94×10^{11} sec^{-1}.

5. What absorbed dose (in rad) of γ-rays is required to change a 2 kg block of ice at 0^0C into steam at 100^0C?

Solution: -

$E = mL_F + mc\Delta t + mL_V$

$E = m [L_F + c\Delta t + L_V]$

$E = m [33.5 \times 10^4 + 4186 \times 100 + 22.6 \times 10^5]$

$E = m [3.0136 \times 10^6]$J

$E = 2$ kg (3.0136×10^6)J / 0.01 Gy/rad

$E = 6.026 \times 10^8$ rad

Hence the absorbed dose (in rad) of γ-rays required to change a 2 kg block of ice at 0^0C into steam at 100^0C comes out to be $E = 6.026 \times 10^8$ rad.

6. A beam of X-rays passes through 8×10^{-3} kg of dry air and generates 1×10^{14} singly charged ions. What is the exposure in roentgen?

Solution: -

Exposure $= [1/ (2.58 \times 10^{-4})] \times [q/ m]$

Exposure $= [1/(2.58 \times 10^{-4})] \times [(1 \times 10^{14} \times 1.6 \times 10^{-19})/ 8 \times 10^{-3}$ kg]

Exposure = $[1/(2.58 \times 10^{-4})][0.2 \times 10^{-2}]$
Exposure = 7.751938 roentgen
Hence the exposure is 7.75 roentgen.

7. A person stands near a radioactive source and receives doses of the following radiations; β^- particle (40 mrad, R.B.E = 1), proton (8 mrad, R.B.E. = 10), and α-particles (2 mrad, R.B.E = 12). What is the total biologically equivalent dose?

   Solution: -

   β^-: - 40×10^{-3} rad x 1 R.B.E = 40 mrem

   proton: - 8×10^{-3} rad x 10 R.B.E = 80 mrem

   α-particle: - 2×10^{-3} rad x 12 R.B.E = 24 mrem

   _____

   Total Biologically Equivalent Dose = 144 mrem

   BED = 144 mrem

   Hence the total Biologically Equivalent Dose is 144 mrem.

8. During an X-ray examination, a person is exposed to radiations at a rate of 220 milligrays per hour. The exposure time is 0.2 seconds, and the mass of the exposed tissue is 2 kg. Determine the energy absorbed.

   Solution: -

   Absorbed Dose = 220×10^{-3} Gy x 0.2 sec/ 3600sec

   Absorbed Dose = 1.222×10^{-5} Gy/sec.

   Energy Absorbed = Absorbed Dose xMass of Absorbing Material

   Energy Absorbed = 1.222×10^{-5} Gy x 2kg = 2.444×10^{-5} J

   Hence the energy absorbed is 2.44×10^{-5} Joule.

g) Pollution crisis in Calcutta

A high court-appointed committee in June 2000 recommended a ban on commercial vehicles more than 15 years old, which hasn't been implemented.

Calcutta crisis: About 55,000 autos, including those banned in other cities for pollution, ply in this city. About 24,000 are registered.

Natural Gas Program: Delhi now has 154 CNG stations that fuel over 12,000 buses, 72,000 three wheelers, and 50,000 private cars.

Calcutta crisis: Calcutta does not have access to CNG. Hardly 5000 vehicles, including 2,500 autos, run legally on liquefied petroleum gas

LPG. Thousands of vehicles illegally use domestic LPG which is cheaper. In 2004, the transport department recommended setting up of 72 LPG stations urgently. Four years on, there are only 12 LPG stations.

Fuel Adulteration: A fuel testing laboratory was set up in Delhi on the basis of the Supreme Court's July 1998 order. The court's directive led to a study by the government into fuel adulteration that paved the way for a 2002 order to introduce non-adulterated fuel like CNG and LPG in polluted cities.

Status: Import of Kerosene by private agencies, a major source of adulteration has been banned. Calcutta crisis: Auto rickshaws mostly run on adulterated fuel.

h) Pollution crisis in Bombay

Conditions such as famine in the countryside and epidemics in the city have created an unbalanced demographic profile throughout the city's history. The 1990 United Nations population estimate for the urban agglomeration of Bombay was 12.2 million, making it the sixth largest city in the world.

The water supply situation in Bombay is critical, with the level of supply so much below the demand that water use is restricted and reaches emergency proportions when the monsoon fails. Bombay is also one of the noisiest cities in the world and suffers from serious air pollution, both from noxious industries and automobile emissions. Despite a substantial public transport system, congestion in the metropolitan area continues.

More than 2 million Bombay residents have no sanitary facilities, and most sewage collected in Bombay is discharged untreated or partially treated into creeks or coastal waters. Attempts have been made to relocate industries outside the island city, but industrial pollution remains a serious problem.

i) Pakistan faces Pollution crisis:-

Air pollution in Pakistan's major cities is among the highest in the world, economic planners have warned. Dust and smoke particles are "generally the twice the world average" and 5 times higher than the developed world, the Pakistani Economic Survey found.

The pollution crisis is compounded by severe water scarcity, the report says. The number of vehicles has increased five times in the past 20 years. The biggest increase in the automobile sector is seen in the two storied vehicles and diesel-powered goods wagons, which are among the most polluting in the world. Besides, more people are using cheap, inefficient and highly polluting fuels to meet their energy demands. The government has been encouraging the use of vehicles powered by the less polluting, compressed natural gas (CNG).

At present, CNG vehicles in Pakistan are estimated at approximately one million, making Pakistan CNG fleet the third largest in the world after Argentina and Brazil. According to the survey, the annual per capita water availability dropped to 1,105 cubic meters – just above the 1000 cubic meters threshold level. With the present population growth rate and low rainfall, the scarcity threshold of 1000 cubic meters is expected to be reached by the year 2010. Pakistani government has proposed meeting water shortages by building hundreds of local water purification plants. The government plans to build more than 6,500 water purification plants across the country over the next few years.

Karachi's Polluted Coastline

The Karachi coastline, which stretches over 135 km, is facing severe pollution due to a combination of industrial, port, municipal, and transportation activities in the area. The coastline is being overwhelmed with water- borne pollution which is being discharged in the shipping process in the marine environment.

A recent study found that some of the marine life was contaminated with lead, which is consumed by human beings as sea food, and this has been linked to anemia, kidney failure, and brain damage.

The mangrove forests that protect the feeder creeks from sea erosions and which are also a sustenance for the fisherman are being threatened by pollution. Pakistan is heavily dependent on these mangrove forests to maintain the ecological balance. The shipping industry, through its discharges, water pollution, and possible leakage and spills impacts on this environment.

j) Pollution independent Pittsburgh

Pittsburgh is the second largest city in the US Commonwealth of Pennsylvania and the county seat of Allegheny County. Regionally, it anchors the largest urban area of Appalachian and the Ohio River Valley, and nationally it is the 22nd largest urban area in the United States. The population of the city in 2010 was 305,704, while that of the seven county metropolitan areas stood at 2,356,283. Downtown Pittsburgh retains substantial economic influence, ranking at 25th in the nation for jobs within the urban core and 6th in job density. The characteristic shape of Pittsburgh central business district is a triangular tract carved by the confluence of the Allegheny and Monongahela rivers, which form Ohio River. The city features 151 high rise buildings, 446 bridges, two inclined railways, and a prerevolutionary fortification. Pittsburgh is known colloquially as "The City of Bridges" and "The Steel City" for its many bridges and former steel manufacturing base.

The city is headquarters to major global financial institutions, PNC Financial Services (the nation's sixth largest bank), Federated Investors and the regional headquarters of BNY Mellon, descended from Mellon Fiancial and the Mellon Family. Major publication often note Pittsburgh high livability compared to other American cities, with the city claiming the top overall spot in the United States in recent "most livable city" lists by Rand Mc Nally (2007), Forbes (2010) and The Economist (2011).

43)

······································

a) The Beautiful Kashmir Valley

The Kashmir Valley, often known as Paradise on Earth, is famous for its beautiful mountainous landscape.

The Kashmir Valley is 100 km (62 miles) wide and 15,520.3 km² (5,992.4 square miles) in area. This densely settled and beautiful valley has an average height of 1,850 m (6,100 feet) above sea level. The Jhelum River is the only major Himalayan River which flows through Kashmir Valley.

Islam is practiced by 97% of the population of the Kashmir Valley. The principal language of Kashmir is Urdu. Tourism in the Kashmir Valley has rebounded in recent years and in 2009, the state became one of the top tourist destinations of India. Gulmarg, one of the most popular ski resort destinations in India, is also home to the world's highest green golf course.

The Dumhal is a famous dance in the Kashmir Valley, performed by men of the Wattal region. The women perform the Rouf, another traditional folk dance. Kashmir has been noted for its fine arts for centuries, including poetry and handicrafts.

Shikara, a traditional small wooden boat, and houseboats are a common feature in various lakes and rivers across the valley. The constitution of India does not allow the people, other than those from Kashmir, to purchase land in the valley. As a result, houseboats are becoming popular among those who are unable to purchase land in Kashmir. Most of the buildings in Kashmir Valley are made from soft wood and are influenced by Indian, Tibetan, and Islamic cultures.

Notable higher education or research institutions in Kashmir include National Institute of Technology, Srinagar, University of Kashmir, Sher-e-Kashmir, University of Agricultural sciences and Technology of Kashmir, Islamic University of Science and Technology, Baba Ghulam Shah Badhshah University etc. As of 5 January, 2009 until the present, the chief minister of Jammu and Kashmir or the Princely State of

Jammu and Kashmir has been Mr. Omar Abdullah and he belongs to the National Conference.

b) The Observatories

An Observatory is a building that houses a huge telescope of various types to study the heavens. An orbiting observatory is an assembly of astronomical instruments installed in an earth's artificial satellite. Hence an observatory is an astronomer's laboratory.

There are two basic types of ground observatories viz. optical observatory and radio observatory.

Optical Observatory: -

The main telescope in an optical observatory is either a reflector or refractor and that is, it is either a reflecting telescope or a refracting telescope. An ideal location for an optical observatory is on a mountaintop in an area where rain and cloudiness are relatively infrequent. The air through which observations are made is usually clear and still. Mountaintop cites are usually far from cities so that lights and haze do not block viewing.

Most optical observatories also have smaller telescope in addition to the main telescope. Among the common telescopic attachments are plate holders, for photography; and such instruments as interferometers, photometers, and spectrographs.

The telescope is housed in a metal dome, which is on top of a building. The dome has a slit extending from the base to the top along one side, covered by movable metal doors. The entire dome can be rotated, turned mechanically or by hand.

A telescope mounting must bear the entire weight of the telescope, while allowing the instrument to move easily. The most common type of mounting for an optical telescope is equatorial mounting, where the telescope can turn on two axes. One axis, called the polar axis is aligned with the earth's axis of rotation. The other axis is at right angle to the polar axis.

Once the telescope is aimed, a driving mechanism turns the telescope slowly on the polar axis to counteract the rotation of the earth, and keep the object in the field of view.

Telescope: -

The telescope in its simplest form consists of a tube with a larger lens, (the objective) on one end, and a smaller lens or lenses, (the eye piece) on the other end of the tube. The three main features of a telescope are (a) the light-gathering power, (the larger the objective, the more light-gathering power); (b) resolving power, (the larger the objective, the more the resolving power); (c) magnifying power, which is the ratio of the focal length of the objective to the focal length of the eye piece. Hence a flat objective forms a larger image than an objective with a larger curvature. This implies D (in diopters) = 1/f (in meters), where diopters is a unit of power of a lens.

Types of Telescopes

There are two ways of classifying telescopes. These are classified by use and also by performance.

When these are classified by use, the two basic types are (a) the terrestrial telescopes, and (b) the astronomical telescopes. The terrestrial telescopes are used to observe objects on land, sea, or in the atmosphere, and astronomical telescopes are used for observing celestial objects.

The astronomical telescopes are further classified as (a) astronomic telescopes, for detecting the position and motion of stars, (b) transits, for observing passages of stars and other celestial objects across the observer's meridian (an imaginary line running north and south and passing directly overhead), and (c) solar telescopes, for observing the sun.

The telescopes are also classified by performance and there are three basic types, viz. (a) refracting telescopes or refractors, which use a lens or combination of lenses as an objective, (b) reflecting telescopes or reflectors, which use a mirror as the objective, and (c) refracting-reflecting telescopes.

The size of a telescope is specified by the diameter of the objective. Refractors, which are used for both terrestrial and astronomical observations, range in size from less than one inch in the smallest glasses to 40 inches in telescope installed in Yerkes observatory, Williams Bay, Wisconsin. Reflectors are used mostly for astronomical observatories and range in size from 3 inches in telescopes used by amateur astronomers to 236 inches in the giant Russian telescope in the Caucus Mountains.

Refracting telescopes

Refracting telescopes or refractors are subject to chromatic aberrations and spherical aberrations. In chromatic aberration, the image is surrounded by blurred and colored fringes, and in spherical aberration, the image of a point object appears as a disc.

Chromatic aberration can be reduced but not eliminated by using an achromatic lens as an objective. An achromatic lens consists of two or more thin lenses cemented together. Spherical aberrations can be overcome by using lenses of different shapes in combination.

Reflecting telescopes

Curved mirrors can be used to form images by reflection. With mirrors no chromatic aberration occurs. In reflecting telescopes, the objective is called a primary, which is a concave mirror, and there is a secondary mirror, and finally an eye piece through which observations are made.

Radio Observatory

A radio observatory is equipped to study the heavens with radio waves, either emitted by the objects being studied or transmitted from earth and reflected from the moon or the planet.

Radio telescopes are much larger than the optical telescopes. The greater size is needed because radio waves are much longer than the light waves. Some radio telescopes are circular and movable and others have various shapes such as an X and there are others that cannot be moved.

Radio telescopes are generally not housed inside special structures. Small ones are sometimes built on roof tops and the larger ones are built in open fields.

Radio observatories are located in big valleys surrounded by mountains. Light, clouds, and turbulent air have no effect on radio waves telescope. Radio waves are not visible and the immediate knowledge comes from radio receivers that print an amplified view of the observation. Radio observations can be made 24 hours a day in all types of weather. Radio equipment must be tuned to one wavelength or band of wavelengths at a time. Tuning can be done at high speed to gain a composite result in second wavelength.

c) The Top 10 Universities of the World

The following is a list and a brief discussion on the top 10 universities in the world for the year 2010. The rankings given to universities differ with different sources. The different sources use a wide range of parameters in order to evaluate the rank of a particular university.

1. Massachusetts Institute of Technology (MIT)
    Located in Cambridge, Massachusetts, the MIT is ranked No.1 University for the year 2010. The 68 ha Campus of MIT houses a college and 5 schools which altogether have 32 departments. For the 2009-2010 fall terms, 4,232 undergraduates, and 6,152 graduates took admissions for different courses in MIT. The University has produced 75 Nobel laureates till date; 31 'Mac Arthur Fellows' and 47 recipients of 'National Medal of Science' are also from the MIT.

2. Stanford
    This private university was established in 1891; the university is actually named as Leland Stanford Junior University and enrolls 8,300 graduates and 6,800 undergraduates every year. Students from the university are placed in reputed companies like Google, Sun Microsystems, Cisco Systems and Hewlett-Packard to name a few. Different schools included in the university are 'Stanford School of Medicine', 'Stanford Law School', 'Stanford School of Engineering' and 'Stanford Graduate School of Business'.

3. Harvard
    Established in 1636, Harvard University is one of the members of Ivy League. Every year, 7,181 students take admissions for graduate program and 14,044 other for postgraduate programs in Harvard University. Harvard is the oldest institution in the USA for higher studies. The university's financial endowment is higher than any other university in the world. The September, 2009 figure for the financial endowment were USD 26 billion.

4. Universidad Nacional Autonoma de Moxico, (National Autonomous University of Mexico)

    Based in Mexico City, the Universidad Nacional Autonoma de Moxico or National Autonomous University of Mexico is the largest university in America in terms of student population. For the academic year 2008-2009, 305,969 students took admissions for various courses in the university. Justo Sierra founded this university on 22nd September, 1910. The campus of this university is declared as a World Heritage Site.

5. University of California, Berkeley

    The University of California offers 300 graduate and undergraduate programs. Set in a huge campus of 2,692ha, the university enrolls 25,530 and 10,313 students for graduate and postgraduate programs respectively. As per the Academic Ranking of World Universities, this institution is ranked 3rd in the world.

    The University of California, Berkeley has produced 65 Nobel laureates and prominent leaders placed in companies like Google, Apple Inc., Sun Microsystems and many more.

6. Peking University

    Founded as the 'Imperial Capital University' in the year 1898, Peking University is located in Beijing. It is the first university to be formally established in China. The university is credited with producing prominent thinkers who laid the foundation of modern China. The students enrolled in this university for graduate and postgraduate programs are 25,128 and 15,039 respectively.

7. University of Pennsylvania

    In terms of higher education, the University of Pennsylvania is the 4th oldest in the US. Member of the Ivy League, this university was founded by Benjamin Franklin in 1740. The different schools of this university which offer a variety of programs are the medical school, business school, law school and other departments which offer humanities and social science programs.

8. Cornell University

Cornell University is located in Ithaca, New York and was founded by Ezra Cornell in 1865. Every year 20,633 students take admissions for different courses in this university.

A variety of courses spanning from agriculture, liberal arts, engineering to hotel administration are offered by this university. There are 7 graduate divisions and same number of undergraduate colleges in Cornell University.

9. Shanghai Jiao Tong University

One of the oldest universities in China, Shanghai Jiao Tong University is a member of C 9 League. The C 9 League contains top universities in China. Shanghai Jiao Tong University is a public university founded in 1896 as a result of issuing of an edict by Guang Xu Emperor. The university offers a wide range of courses like medicine, engineering, agriculture, law, humanities and many more.

10. Yale University

Yale University is the 3rd oldest of all universities providing higher education in the USA. Located in New Haven, Connecticut, the university is set in a sprawling 339 ha campus. Many prominent personalities have studied in Yale University. This university was established in 1701. Yale- educated Presidents since the Vietnam War include Gerald Ford, George H. W. Bush, Bill Clinton, and George W. Bush.

d) The Great Wall of China

The Great Wall of China is one of the new Seven Wonders of the World.

After 7 years of campaigning and one hundred million votes received, the results of the global ballet were announced on July 7, 2007, in Lisbon, Portugal during a spectacular gala show in the "Estadio da Luz" in the presence of 50,000 spectators and watched by hundreds of millions of T.V viewers worldwide, the new 7 wonders of the world were revealed:

1. The Pyramid at Chichen Itza (Pre 800 A.D), Yucatan Peninsula, Mexico.
2. Cristo Rendentor (1931), Rio De Janeiro, Brazil.
3. The Colosseum (A.D 70 – 82), Rome, Italy.
4. The Great Wall of China, (220 B.C and A.D 1368 – 1644), China.
5. Machu Picchu (1460 – 70), Peru.
6. Petra (9 B.C – A.D 40), Jordan
7. Taj Mahal (A.D 1630), Agra, India.

The Great Wall of China is a long wall stretching from SHANHAIGUAN in the east and LOP NUR in the west and is 8,851.8 km or 5,500.3 miles long. It is a series of stone and earthen fortifications in northern china, built, rebuilt, and maintained between 5th century B.C and 16th century, to protect northern border of the Chinese Empire during various successive dynasties.

In 2009, an additional 290 km (180 miles) of previously undetected portion of the wall, built during the Ming Dynasty were discovered. The newly discovered sections range from the HUSHAN mountains in the northern LIAONING province to JIAYUGUAN in western GANSU province. These sections had been submerged over time by sandstorms that moved across the arid region. Before the bricks were used, the Great Wall was mostly built from Earth or Taipei, stone and wood.

Some parts of the wall in the north of BEIJING and near tourist centers have been preserved and extensively renovated in many locations the wall is in disrepair. Sections of the wall are also prone to graffiti and vandalism. Parts have been destroyed because the wall is in the way of construction.

More than 60 km (37 miles) of the wall in GANSU province may fall in the next 20 years, due to erosions from sandstorms. In places height of the wall has been reduced from more than 5 meters to less than 2 meters. The Syros Lookout Towers that characterize the most form images of the wall have fallen down completely. Many western sections of the wall are constructed from mud, rather than brick and stone, and are therefore more susceptible to erosion.

Visibility from Space:

Visibility from the Moon

The apparent width of the Great Wall of China from the moon is the same as that of a human hair viewed from 2 miles away. To see the wall from the moon would require spatial resolution 17,000 times better than normal 20/20 vision. Not surprisingly, no human astronaut has ever claimed seeing the Great Wall of China from the moon.

Visibility from low earth orbit:

Some authors have argued that due to limitations of the optics of the eyes and low spatial resolution, it is impossible to see the Great Wall of China with the naked eyes, even from low orbit, and would require visual acuity of 20/3 (7.7 times better than the normal)

Interviewed reports:

Niel A. Armstrong stated about the view from Apollo 11: "I do not believe that, at least with my eyes, there would be any man-made object that I could see. I have not yet found somebody who has told me they've seen the wall of china from Earth orbit. … I've asked various people, particularly guys, that have been many orbits around China in the day time, and the ones I've talked to didn't see it.

44)

. . . .

a) Einstein's Special Relativity

Events and Inertial Reference Frames: - In theory of Special Relativity, an event, such as the launching of the space shuttle, is a physical "happening" that occurs at a certain place and time. The theory of Special Relativity deals with a special type of reference frames called the Inertial Reference Frames. As has been described in the discussion on Newton's laws of motion, an inertial reference frame is one in which Newton's law of inertia is valid. That is, if the net force acting on the body is zero, the body remains at rest or moves at constant velocity. In other words, the acceleration of such a body is zero when measured in an inertial reference frame.

The Postulates of Special Relativity: - Einstein built his theory of Special Relativity on two fundamental assumptions or postulates about the way nature behaves: -

The Postulates of Special Relativity:

1. The Relativity Postulate: - The laws of Physics are the same in every inertial reference frame.
2. The Speed of Light Postulate: - The speed of light in a vacuum, measured in any inertial reference frame, always has the same value of c, no matter how fast the source of light and the observer are moving relative to each other.

Since waves, such as water waves and sound waves, require a medium through which to propagate, it was natural for the scientists before Einstein to assume that light did too. This hypothetical medium was called the luminiferous ether and was assumed to fill all of space. Furthermore, it was believed that light travelled at the speed c only when measured with respect to ether. According to this view, an observer moving relative to the ether would measure a speed of light as slower as or faster than the constant magnitude c, depending on whether the observer moves with or against the light, respectively. During the year 1883-1887, however, the American scientists A.A. Michelson and E.W. Morley carried out a series of famous experiments whose results were not consistent with the ether theory. Their experiments, and others, led eventually to the demise of the ether theory and the acceptance of the theory of Special Relativity.

S. No. # Concept: -

1) Time Interval: -
   Classical Version: - Δt_0
   Relativistic Version: - $\Delta t = \Delta t_0 / \sqrt{[1 - v^2/c^2]}$
2) Length: -
   Classical Version: - L_0
   Relativistic Version: - $L = L_0 \sqrt{[1-v^2/c^2]}$
3) Momentum: -
   Classical Version: - $p = mv$
   Relativistic Version: - $p = mv/ \sqrt{[1-v^2/c^2]}$
4) Kinetic Energy: -
   Classical Version: - $K.E = (1/2) mv^2$
   Relativistic Version: - $K.E = mc^2 [(1/\sqrt{1-v^2/c^2}) - 1]$
5) Addition of Velocities: -
   Classical Version: - $v_{AB} = v_{AC} + v_{CB}$
   Relativistic Version: - $v_{AB} = [v_{AC} + v_{CB}]/ [1+v_{AC}v_{CB}/c^2]$

The Relativity of Time: Time Dilation: -

According to Special Relativity, the time passes more slowly for a person travelling in space at a speed close to the speed of light c than for an earth based observer. Hence we have the following equation for the dilation of time which means the lengthening of time: -

$$\Delta t = \Delta t_0/ \sqrt{(1-v^2/c^2)}$$

In this equation we have Δt_0 = proper time interval which is the time interval between two events as measured by an observer who is at rest with respect to the events and who views them as occurring at the same place (the astronaut travelling in deep outer space at a speed close to the speed of light in our case), and Δt = dilated time interval, which is the time interval as measured by an observer who is in motion with respect to the events and who views them as occurring at different places (earth-based observer). v = relative speed between the two observers, c = speed of light in vacuum. The time measured by the travelling astronaut is called the proper time interval and is denoted by Δt_0 and it is always less than Δt because $\sqrt{(1-v^2/c^2)} < 1$.

The Relativity of Length: Length Contraction: - According to Special Relativity, the length contraction equation is given as follows: -

$$L = L_0 \sqrt{(1 - v^2/c^2)}$$

The L_0 is the proper length and it is the length as measured by an observer who is at rest with respect to them (the astronaut in our case). The length contraction occurs only in one direction which is the direction of motion for an observer who is earth-based (i.e. the earth-based observer). Since $\sqrt{(1 - v^2/c^2)} < 1$ we have $L < L_0$. Hence a contraction of length occurs and L is less than L_0 by a factor of $\sqrt{(1 - v^2/c^2)}$

The Relativistic Momentum: -

According to the theory of Special Relativity, the magnitude of the relativistic momentum is defined as follows: -

$$p = mv / \sqrt{(1 - v^2/c^2)} = \text{magnitude of relativistic momentum}$$

The total relativistic momentum of an isolated system is conserved for all inertial reference frames.

We see that the relativistic momentum and non-relativistic momentum differ by the same factor $\sqrt{(1 - v^2/c^2)}$ that occurs in the time dilation and length contraction equation.

Hence relativistic momentum is greater than non-relativistic momentum by a factor of $\sqrt{(1 - v^2/c^2)}$.

The Equivalence of Mass and Energy: The Total Energy of an Object: -

$$E = mc^2 / \sqrt{(1 - v^2/c^2)} = \text{Total Energy of an Object}$$

Now when v = 0 ms^{-1}, the total energy is called rest energy and is given by the following relation.

$$E_0 = mc^2 = \text{Rest Energy of an Object}$$

We therefore have the following equation: -

$E = E_0 + K.E$

$K.E = E - E_0$

$K.E = [mc^2 / \sqrt{(1 - v^2/c^2)}] - mc^2$

$K.E = mc^2 [(1/\sqrt{1 - v^2/c^2}) - 1]$

Now we have the following series: -

$1 / \sqrt{(1 - v^2/c^2)} = 1 + (1/2)(v^2/c^2) + (3/8)(v^2/c^2)^2 + \ldots$

$K.E = mc^2 [1 + (1/2)(v^2/c^2) - 1] = (1/2)mv^2$

$K.E = (1/2) mv^2$

Hence $K.E = (1/2) mv^2$ is the classical equation for the kinetic energy.

The Relation between Total Energy and Momentum: -

It is possible to derive a useful relation between the total relativistic energy E and the relativistic momentum p, as follows:-

$p = mv / \sqrt{(1 - v^2/c^2)}$

$p / v = m / \sqrt{(1 - v^2/c^2)}$

$E = mc^2 / \sqrt{(1 - v^2/c^2)} = pc^2/v$

OR

$v/c = pc/E$

$E = mc^2 / \sqrt{(1 - v^2/c^2)} = mc^2 / \sqrt{(1 - p^2c^2/E^2)}$

$E^2 = m^2c^4 / (1 - p^2c^2/E^2)$

Solving this for E^2 gives the following relation: -

$E^2 = p^2c^2 + m^2c^4$

The Speed of Light is the ultimate Speed: -

One of the important consequences of the theory of Special Relativity is that objects with mass cannot reach the speed of light in vacuum. Hence the speed of light represents the ultimate speed. Consider the following equation: -

$K.E = E - E_0 = mc^2 [(1/\sqrt{1 - v^2/c^2}) - 1]$

In this equation as v approaches c, $\sqrt{(1 - v^2/c^2)}$ in the denominator approaches zero. Hence the K.E becomes infinitely large.

However the work-energy theorem tells us that an infinite amount of work would have to done to give the object an infinite kinetic energy. Since an infinite amount of work is not available, we are left with the conclusion that objects with mass cannot attain the speed of light c.

The Relativistic Addition of Velocities: -

The following is the relativistic velocity addition formula: -

$v_{AB} = (v_{AC} + v_{CB}) / (1 + v_{AC}v_{CB}/c^2)$

In this equation we have: -

v_{AB} = velocity of object A relative to object B,

v_{AC} = velocity of object A relative to object C,

v_{CB} = velocity of object C relative to object B.

Hence the relative velocity v_{AB} can be calculated from the given values of v_{AC} and v_{CB}.

Special Relativity: -

Numerical Problems: -

The Relativity of Time: Time Dilation: -

1. A radar antenna is rotating at an angular speed of 0.4 rad/s as measured on earth. To an observer moving past the antenna at a speed of 0.9c what is the angular speed?

    Solution: -

    $\Delta t = \Delta t_0 / \sqrt{(1 - v^2/c^2)}$

    $\Delta t = \Delta t_0 / \sqrt{[1 - (0.9c)^2 /c^2]}$

    $\Delta t = \Delta t_0 / \sqrt{(1 - 0.81)}$

    $\Delta t = \Delta t_0 / \sqrt{(0.19)}$

    $\Delta t_0 / \Delta t = \sqrt{(0.19)}$

    $w_0 = 2\pi r / \Delta t_0 = 0.4$ rad/s (Given)

    $w = (2\pi r/\Delta t_0) \times \Delta t_0 / \Delta t$

    $w = 0.4$rad/s $\times \sqrt{(0.19)}$

    $w = 0.174355958$ rad/s

2. An army commander is in an intergalactic jeep, turns on a red flashing light and sees it generate a flash every 2 seconds. An observer on earth measures that the time between flashes is 3 seconds. How fast is the jeep moving relative to the earth?

    Solution: -

    $\Delta t_0 = 2s$ and $\Delta t = 3s$

    $\Delta t = \Delta t_0 / \sqrt{(1 - v^2/c^2)}$

    $\Delta t_0 / \Delta t = \sqrt{(1 - v^2/c^2)} = 2/3$

    $1 - v^2/c^2 = (2/3)^2 = 0.44444444444$

$v^2/c^2 = 1 - 0.44444444 = 0.5555555556$
$v/c = \sqrt{(0.555555556)} = 0.745355993$
$v = 0.745355993c$
Hence the intergalactic jeep is moving at a speed of nearly 0.745c.
$v = 2.234521052 \times 10^8$ m/s

3. A 5kg object oscillates back and forth at the end of a spring whose spring constant is 75 N/m. An observer is travelling at a speed of 9×10^7 m/s relative to the fixed end of the spring. What does this observer measure for the period of oscillation?

Solution: -
$w = 2\pi L / T = \sqrt{(k/m)} = \sqrt{(75N/m/5kg)} = \sqrt{15}$
$T = 2\pi L/w = (2\pi/w) L = (2\pi/\sqrt{15}) L$
$L = L_0 \sqrt{(1 - v^2/c^2)}$
$L / L_0 = \sqrt{[1 - (9 \times 10^7)^2 / (3 \times 10^8)^2]} = \sqrt{(1 - 0.09)} = \sqrt{0.91}$
$T = (2\pi / \sqrt{15}) L$
$T_0 = (2\pi L / \sqrt{15}) (L_0 /L)$
$T_0 = (2\pi / \sqrt{15}) / \sqrt{0.91} = 1.7$ secs.

Therefore the observer measures, for the period of oscillation,
$T_0 = 1.7$ secs.

The Relativity of Length: Length Contraction: -

4. How fast must a meter stick be moving if its length is observed to shrink to one-third of a meter?

Solution: -
$L = L_0 \sqrt{(1 - v^2/c^2)}$
$1 = 3\sqrt{(1 - v^2/c^2)}$
$\sqrt{(1 - v^2/c^2)} = 1/3 = 0.33333333$
$1 - v^2/c^2 = (1/3)^2 = 0.11111111$
$v^2/c^2 = 0.88888889$
$v = 0.942809042c$
$v = 2.826470401 \times 10^8$ m/s

Hence the meter stick must be moving at a speed of 0.942809042c if its length is observed to shrink to one-third of a meter.

5. A UFO streaks across the sky at a speed of 0.7c relative to the earth. A person on the earth determines the length of the UFO to be 300 m along the direction of its motion. What length does the person measure for the UFO when it lands?

Solution: -

$L = L_0 \sqrt{(1 - v^2/c^2)}$

$L_0 = L / \sqrt{(1 - v^2/c^2)}$

$L_0 = 300m / \sqrt{[1 - (0.7c)^2/c^2]}$

$L_0 = 300m / \sqrt{(1 - 0.49)} = 300m/ \sqrt{0.51}$

$L_0 = 300m / 0.714142843$

$L_0 = 420.0840252m$

Hence the person measures the length of the UFO when it lands to be 420.0840252m.

6. A space traveler moving at a speed of $v_1 = 0.6c$ with respect to the earth makes a trip to a distant star that is stationary relative to the earth. He measures the length of this trip to be $L_1 = 7$ light years. What would be the length of this same trip (in light years) as measured by a traveler moving at a speed of 0.85c with respect to the earth?

Solution: -

$L_1 = L_0 \sqrt{(1 - v_1^2/c^2)}$

$L_0 = L_1 / \sqrt{(1 - v_1^2/c^2)} = 7$ light years$/\sqrt{[1 - (0.6c)^2/c^2]}$

$L_0 = (7/0.8)$ light years

$L = L_0 \sqrt{(1 - v^2/c^2)}$

$L = (7/0.8) \sqrt{[1 - (.85c)^2/c^2]}$

$L = 4.609348517$ light years

Hence the length of this same trip that the moving traveler measures to be 7 light years will be 4.6 light years as measured by another traveler moving at a speed of 0.85c with respect to the earth.

7. A rectangle has the dimensions of 5m x 4m when viewed by someone at rest with respect to it. When you are moving past the rectangle along one of its sides, the rectangle looks like a square. What dimensions do you observe when you move at the same speed along the adjacent side of the rectangle?

Solution: -

$L = L_0 \sqrt{(1 - v^2/c^2)}$
$4m = 5m \sqrt{(1 - v^2/c^2)}$
$(1 - v^2/c^2) = (4 / 5)^2 = 0.64$
$v^2/c^2 = 0.36$
$v = 0.6c$
$L = L_0 \sqrt{(1 - v^2/c^2)}$
$L = 4m \sqrt{[1 - (0.6c)^2/c^2]} = 4m \sqrt{(1 - 0.36)}$
$L = 4m \sqrt{(0.64)} = 4m \times 0.8 = 3.2m$
Hence the required dimensions are 5m x 3.2m
Relativistic Momentum: -

8. At what speed is the magnitude of the relativistic momentum of a particle four times the magnitude of the non-relativistic momentum?

Solution: -
$p = mv / \sqrt{(1 - v^2/c^2)} = p' / \sqrt{(1 - v^2/c^2)}$
$p = 4p'$
$4p' = p' / \sqrt{(1 - v^2/c^2)}$
$\sqrt{(1 - v^2/c^2)} = p'/ 4p' = 1/4$
$1 - v^2/c^2 = (1/4)^2 = 1/16 = 0.0625$
$v^2/c^2 = 1 - 0.0625 = 0.9375$
$v/c = \sqrt{0.9375} = 0.968245837$
$v = 0.968245837c$
$v = 2.902727993 \times 10^8$ m/s

Hence the speed of the particle at which the relativistic momentum is four times the non-relativistic momentum is 2.9×10^8 m/s.

9. Starting from rest, two skaters "push off" against each other on smooth level ice, where friction is negligible. One is a man and the other is a woman. The woman moves away with a velocity of + 1.4 m/s relative to the ice. The mass of the woman is 40 kg and the mass of the man is 70 kg. Assuming that the speed of light is 2m/s, so that relativistic momentum must be used, find the recoil velocity of the man relative to the ice.

Solution: -
$m_M v_M / \sqrt{[1 - v_M^2/c^2]} = m_W v_W / \sqrt{[1 - v_W^2/c^2]} = p_{relativistic}$

70 kg $v_M/\sqrt{[1 - v_M^2/(2m/s)^2]} = 40kgx\ 1.4m/s/\sqrt{[1 - (1.4/2)^2]}$

$v_M/\sqrt{[1 - v_M^2/4]} = 1.120224067$

$v_M^2 = (1 - v_M^2/4)\ (1.254901961)$

$v_M^2 = 0.955223881$

$v_M = -\ 0.977355555m/s$

Hence the recoil velocity of the man relative to the ice is given by $v_M = -\ 0.977m/s$. It is negative because it is a recoil velocity.

10. A rocket of mass $2.2x10^6$ kg has a relativistic momentum, the magnitude of which is $1.6x10^{14}$ kgm/ s. How fast is the rocket travelling?

Solution: -

mass $= 2.2x10^6$ kg and $p_{relativistic} = 1.6x10^{14}kgm/s$

$p = p'/\sqrt{(1 - v^2/c^2)} = mv\ /\ \sqrt{(1 - v^2/c^2)}$

$1.6x10^{14}kgm/s = 2.2x10^6kg\ x\ v\ /\ \sqrt{(1 - v^2/c^2)}$

$1.6x10^{14}kgm/s\ /\ 2.2x10^6kg = v/\ \sqrt{(1 - v^2/c^2)}$

$v\ /\ \sqrt{(1 - v^2/c^2)} = 0.727272727x10^8m/s$

$v^2/\ (1 - v^2/c^2) = 0.52892562x10^{16}$

Solving for v, keeping in mind that c is the velocity of light whose magnitude is $2.99792458x10^8m/s$, we have the following result.

$v = 7.06772909x10^7$ m/s

Hence the rocket is travelling at a speed of $7.06772909x10^7m/s$.

The Equivalence of Mass and Energy: -

11. How much work must be done on an electron to accelerate it from rest to a speed of 0.8c?

Solution: -

The work done is equal to the amount of kinetic energy involved.

$K.E = E - E_0$

$K.E = [mc^2/\ \sqrt{(1 - v^2/c^2)}] - mc^2$

$K.E = mc^2\ [(1/\sqrt{1-v^2/c^2}) - 1]$

Put $v = 0.8c$ in this equation and get the following result:

-

$K.E = mc^2\ [0.666666667]$

K.E = 9.11×10^{-31}kg x $(2.99792458 \times 10^8$m/s$)^2$ x 0.666666667

K.E = $5.458439786 \times 10^{-14}$ Joules

Hence the amount of work done on the electron to accelerate it from rest to a speed of 0.8c has been calculated as 5.458×10^{-14} Joule.

12. How close would two stationary electrons have to be positioned so that their total mass is three times what it is when the electrons are very far apart?

Solution: -

$E_0 = m'c^2 = 3mc^2$

$\Sigma E = E_1 - E_2 = ke^2/r_1 - ke^2/r_2$

$\Sigma E = 3mc^2 - mc^2 = 2mc^2$

$Ke^2 (1/r_1 - 1/r_2) = 2mc^2$

$E_2 / E_1 = ke^2/r_2 / ke^2/r_1 = r_1/r_2 = 3mc^2/mc^2 = 3$

$r_1 = 3r_2$

$Ke^2 (1/r_2 - 1/r_1) = 2mc^2$

$(1/r_2 - 1/3r_2) = 2mc^2/ke^2 = 2/3r_2$

$1/3r_2 = mc^2/ke^2$

$3r_2 = ke^2/mc^2$

$= 8.99 \times 10^9$ x $(1.6 \times 10^{-19}$C$)^2$ / 9.11×10^{-31}kgx$(3 \times 10^8$m/s$)^2$

$3r_2 = r_1 = 0.281086426 \times 10^{-14}$ m

$r_2 = 9.36954753 \times 10^{-16}$ m.

13. A nuclear power reactor generates 9×10^8 W of power. In one year, what is the change in the mass of the nuclear fuel due to the energy being taken from the nuclear reactor?

Solution: -

$P = 9 \times 10^8$ Watts = 9×10^8 Joules / sec.

E = total energy being taken in one year

1 year = 365days x 24 hours/day x 60 minutes/hour x 60 secs. /minute

1 year = 3.1536×10^7secs.

E = 3.1536×10^7 x 9×10^8 Joules / year

E = 2.83824×10^{16} Joules/ year

$E_0 = (\Delta m) c^2$

$(\Delta m) = E_0 / c^2 = 2.83824 \times 10^{16}$ / $(2.99792458 \times 10^8)^2$

$(\Delta m) = 0.31579679$kg

Hence the change in the mass of the fuel is given by $(\Delta m) = 0.31579679 kg$.

The Relativistic Addition of Velocities: -

14. A spacecraft approaching the earth launches an exploration vehicle. After the launch, an observer on earth sees the spacecraft approaching at a speed of 0.4c and the exploration vehicle approaching at a speed of 0.6c. What is the speed of the exploration vehicle relative to the spacecraft?

Solution: -

$v_{SE} = 0.4c$ and $v_{VE} = 0.6c$

$v_{VS} = [v_{VE} + v_{ES}]/ [1 + v_{VE}v_{ES}/c^2]$

$v_{VS} = [0.6c + (- 0.4c)]/ [1 + (0.6c)(-0.4c)/c^2]$

$v_{VS} = 0.2c/0.76 = 0.263157895c$

$v_{VS} = 0.263157895c$

Hence the speed of the exploration vehicle relative to the spacecraft is 0.263157895c.

15. The crew of a rocket that is moving away from the earth launches an escape pod, which they measure to be 50m long. The pod is launched toward the earth with a speed of 0.6c relative to the rocket. After the launch, the rocket's speed relative to the earth is 0.84c. What is the length of the escape pod as determined by an observer on earth?

Solution: -

$L_0 = 50m$, $v_{PR} = - 0.6c$, $v_{RE} = 0.84c$

$v_{PE} = [v_{PR} + v_{RE}]/ [1 + v_{PR}v_{RE} /c^2]$

$v_{PE} = [- 0.6c + 0.84c]/ [1 + (- 0.6c)(0.84c)/c^2]$

$v_{PE} = 0.403225806c$

$L = L_0 \sqrt{(1 - v^2/c^2)}$

$L = 50m \sqrt{[1 - (0.403225806c)^2/c^2]}$

$L = 50m \sqrt{(1 - 0.162591051)} = 50m \sqrt{(0.837408949)}$

$L = 50m \times 0.915100513 = 45.75502565m$

$L = 45.75502565m$

Hence the length of the escape pod as determined by an observer on earth is 45.75502565m.

Miscellaneous Problems: -

16. A spaceship is approaching the earth at a relative speed of 0.9c. The mass of the ship is 1×10^8 kg. Find the magnitude of (a) the classical momentum and (b) the relativistic momentum of the ship.

Solution: -

(a) $p_{classical}$ = mv = 1×10^8kg x 0.9 x 3×10^8m/s
= 2.7×10^{16}kgm/s

(b) $p_{relativistic}$ = mv / $\sqrt{[1 - v^2/c^2]}$
= 2.7×10^{16}kgm/s / $\sqrt{[1 - (0.9c)^2/c^2]}$
= 2.7×10^{16}kgm/s / $\sqrt{0.19}$
$P_{relativistic}$ = $6.194224815 \times 10^{16}$kgm/s

17. Twins who are 20 years of age leave the earth and travel to a distant planet 20 light years away. Assume that the planet and earth are at rest with respect to each other. The twins depart at the same time on different spaceships. One twin travels at a speed of 0.800c and the other twin travels at 0.600c. (a) According to the special theory of relativity, what is the difference between their ages when they meet again at the earliest possible time? (b) Which twin is older?

Solution: -

(a) D_0 = 20 light years
$D = D_0 \sqrt{(1 - v^2/c^2)}$
D_1 = 20 light years $\sqrt{[1 - (0.6c)^2/c^2]}$ = 16 light years
ΔD = 20 light years – 16 light years = 4 light years
Δt_1 = 4 light years / 0.6c = 6.666666667 years
D_2 = 20 light years $\sqrt{[1 - (0.8c)^2/c^2]}$ = 12 light years
ΔD = 20 light years – 12 light years = 8 light years
Δt_2 = 8 light years / 0.8c = 10 years
$\Delta t = \Delta t_2 - \Delta t_1$ = 10 years – 6.666666667years
Δt = 3.33 years

Hence the twins are 3.33 years apart when they meet again at the earliest possible time.

(b) The twin travelling at 0.6c is older.

18. Two spaceships A and B are exploring a new planet. Relative to this planet, spaceship A has a speed of 0.7c and spaceship B has a speed of 0.9c. What is the ratio of D_A/D_B of the values

for the planet's diameter that each spaceship measures in a direction that is parallel to its motion?

Solution: -

$D = D_0 \sqrt{(1 - v^2/c^2)}$

$D_A = D_0 \sqrt{[1 - (0.7c)^2/c^2]}$

$D_A = D_0 \sqrt{0.51}$

$D_B = D_0 \sqrt{[1 - (0.9c)^2/c^2]}$

$D_B = D_0 \sqrt{0.19}$

$D_A/D_B = D_0 \sqrt{0.51} / D_0 \sqrt{0.19} = \sqrt{0.51} / \sqrt{0.19}$

$D_A/D_B = 0.714142843 / 0.435889894$

$D_A/D_B = 1.638356045$

$D_A/D_B = 1.6$

Thus the required ratio D_A/D_B has the value of 1.6

19. Two atomic particles approach each other in a head-on collision. Each particle has a mass of 3×10^{-31}kg. The speed of each particle is 9×10^7m/s when measured by an observer standing in the laboratory. (a) What is the speed of one particle as seen by the other particle? (b) Determine the relativistic momentum of one particle, as it would be observed by the other.

Solution: -

(a) $v_{10} = 9 \times 10^7$m/s , $v_{20} = -9 \times 10^7$m/s

$v_{12} = [v_{10} + v_{02}] / [1 + (v_{10}v_{02})/c^2]$

$v_{12} = [9 \times 10^7 + 9 \times 10^7] / [1 + (9 \times 10^7)^2/(3 \times 10^8)^2]$

$v_{12} = 1.8 \times 10^8 / (1 + 9 \times 10^{-2})$

$v_{12} = 1.651376147 \times 10^8$m/s

$v_{12} = 1.65 \times 10^8$m/s

OR

$v_{21} = -1.65 \times 10^8$m/s

(b) $p = mv / \sqrt{(1 - v^2/c^2)}$

Put $m = 3 \times 10^{-31}$kg and $v = v_{12} = 1.65 \times 10^8$m/s

$p = (3 \times 10^{-31}$kg$) (1.65 \times 10^8$m/s$)/\sqrt{[1 - (1.65 \times 10^8m/s)^2/(3 \times 10^8m/s)^2]}$

$p = 4.954128441 \times 10^{-23}/\sqrt{0.696995202}$

$p = 4.954128441 \times 10^{-23}/0.834862385$

$p = 5.934065937 \times 10^{-23}$kgm/s

Hence relativistic momentum of one particle, as it would be seen

by the other particle, is given by: -
$p = 5.93 \times 10^{-23} \text{kgm/s}$

20. Determine the ratio of the relativistic kinetic energy to the non-relativistic kinetic energy $(1/2)mv^2$ when a particle has a speed of (a) $1 \times 10^{-2}c$ and (b) $0.85c$

Solution: -

$KE_{relativistic} = E - E_0 = mc^2 [1/ \sqrt{(1-v^2/c^2)} - 1]$

$KE_{non\text{-}relativistic} = (1/2) mv^2$

(a) $v = 1 \times 10^{-2}c$

$KE_{relativistic} = mc^2[1/\sqrt{(1 - 10^{-4}c^2/c^2)} - 1]$

$KE_{non\text{-}relativistic} = (1/2)m(1 \times 10^{-2}c)^2 = (1/2)mx10^{-4}c^2$

$KE_{relativistic} / KE_{non\text{-}relativistic}$

$= mc^2[1/\sqrt{(1 - 10^{-4})} - 1] / (1/2)mc^2 x \ 10^{-4}$

$= 2 \times 10^4 [5.0004 \times 10^{-5}]$

$= 1.00008$

(b) $KE_{relativistic} = mc^2[1/\sqrt{1} - (0.85)^2 - 1]$

$= mc^2[1/\sqrt{0.2775} - 1]$

$KE_{relativistic} = mc^2(0.898315992)$

$KE_{non\text{-}relativistic} = (1/2)mc^2(0.85)^2$

$KE_{relativistic} / KE_{non\text{-}relativistic} = mc^2(.898315992)/(1/2)mc^2(0.85)^2$

$= 2 \times 0.898315992 / 0.7225$

$= 1.796631984 / 0.7225$

$= 2.486687867$

Hence the required ratio is 2.486 which has been calculated above.

21. A certain star is 50 light years away. How long would it take a spacecraft travelling at .89c to reach that star from earth, as measured by the observer: (a) on earth: (b) on the spacecraft? (c) What is the distance travelled according to an observer on the spacecraft? (d) What will the spacecraft's occupants compute their speed to be from the results of (b) and (c)?

Solution: -

(a) $\Delta t = L/v = 50$ light years/ $0.89c = 56.17977528$ years

$\Delta t = 56.17977528$ years

(b) $\Delta t_0 = \Delta t \sqrt{(1 - v^2/c^2)} = 56.18 \times \sqrt{[1 - (.89c)^2/c^2]} = 25.6157598$

$\Delta t_0 = 25.6157598$ years

(c) $L = L_0 \sqrt{(1 - v^2/c^2)} = 50$ light years$\sqrt{[1 - (.89c)^2/c^2]}$

$L = 22.79802623$ light years

(d) $v = L/\Delta t_0 = 22.79802623$ light years/ 25.6157598 years $= .89c$

22. Suppose you decide to travel to a star 80 light years away. How fast would you have to travel so the distance would be only 30 light years?

Solution: -

$\Delta L = \Delta L_0 \sqrt{(1 - v^2/c^2)}$

30 light years $= 80$ light years $\sqrt{(1 - v^2/c^2)}$

$(1 - v^2/c^2) = (30/80)^2 = (0.375)^2 = 0.140625$

$v^2/c^2 = 1 - 0.140625 = 0.859375$

$v = 0.9270248110$

23. What is the mass and speed of an electron that has been accelerated by a voltage of 300kV?

Solution: -

$KE = Vq = 300$ kV $\times 10^3$V/kV $\times 1.6 \times 10^{-19}$J/V $= 4.8 \times 10^{-14}$J

$E_0 = m_0 c^2 = 9.11 \times 10^{-31}$kg $\times (3 \times 10^8 ms^{-1})^2 = 8.199 \times 10^{-14}$J

$KE/E_0 = [4.8 \times 10^{-14}/8.199 \times 10^{-14}] = 0.585437248$

$KE/E_0 = [1/ \sqrt{(1 - v^2/c^2)} - 1] = .585437248$

$m = m_0 /\sqrt{(1 - v^2/c^2)} = 1.585437248m_0 = 1.59m_0$

$\sqrt{(1 - v^2/c^2)} = .630740826 \Rightarrow v = .775993563c = .77c$

24. What is the speed and momentum of an electron ($m_0 = 9.11 \times 10^{-31}$kg) whose kinetic energy is one-third of its rest energy?

Solution: -

$KE = E - E_0$ and $K.E = E_0 [1/ \sqrt{(1 - v^2/c^2)} - 1]$

$(1/3) m_0 c^2 = m_0 c^2 [1/\sqrt{(1 - v^2/c^2)} - 1]$

$\sqrt{(1 - v^2/c^2)} = 3/4 = .75$

$v = .661437828c = .66c$

$E^2 = p^2 c^2 + m_0^2 c^4$

$$E - E_0 = E_0/3 = KE \Rightarrow E = (4/3)E_0$$
$$p^2c^2 = (4/3)^2 E_0^{\,2} - E_0^{\,2} = 7E_0^{\,2}/9$$
$$p = \sqrt{7}\, m_0 c/3$$
$$P = 9.11 \times 10^{-31}\ kg \times (3 \times 10^8\ ms^{-1})\ \sqrt{7}/3$$
$$p = 2.410279444 \times 10^{-22}\ kgms^{-1}$$
$$p = 2.4 \times 10^{-22}\ kgm/s$$

25. A person on a rocket travelling at 0.6c (with respect to the earth) observes a meteor come from behind and pass her at a speed she measures as 0.6c. How fast is the meteor moving with respect to the earth?

    Solution: -

    $$v = (v_R + v_M) / (1 + v_R v_M/c^2)$$
    $$v = (.6c + .6c) / (1 + (.6c)(.6c)/c^2) = 1.2c/1.36 = 0.882352941c$$

    $$v = 0.88c$$

    Hence the meteor is moving at .88c with respect to the earth.

Note that the effects of special relativity are observed in one dimension only and this implies that all relativistic calculation are to be done with the assumption that all motion is taking place along the same axis.

b) Forces and Newton's Laws of Motion

Isaac Newton developed three important laws of motion that pertain to force and mass, known as, "Newton's Laws of Motion". These are discussed as follows: -

Newton's First Law of Motion: -

An object continues in a state of rest or in a state of motion at a constant speed along a straight line, unless compelled to change that state by a net force.

Several forces may act simultaneously on an object and the net force is the vector sum of them all. "Newton's First Law of Motion" is also called, "The Law of Inertia".

Definition of Inertia and Mass: - Inertia is the natural tendency of an object to remain at rest or in motion at a constant speed along a straight line. The mass of an object is a quantitative measure of inertia.

SI unit of Inertia and Mass: kilogram (kg).

Definition of an Inertial Reference Frame: - An inertial reference frame is one in which Newton's Laws of Motion are valid. The acceleration of an inertial reference frame is zero, so it moves with a constant velocity. Earth, itself, is a good approximation of an inertial reference frame. Hence all of Newton's Laws of Motion are valid in an Inertial Reference Frame.

Newton's Second Law of Motion: -
When a net external force Σ F acts on an object of mass m, the acceleration, "a", that results is directly proportional to the net force and has a value that is inversely proportional to the mass. The direction of the acceleration is the same as the direction of the net force.

$a = \Sigma F / m$
OR
$\Sigma F = ma$
SI Unit of Force: - kgm/s^2 = newton (N)

The net forces are external forces that the environment exerts on an object and the internal forces are those that one part of the object exerts on the other part of the object. The external force in Newton's Second Law of Motion may have a vector component in the x and y directions.

$\Sigma F_x = ma_x$
$\& \Sigma F_y = ma_y$

Newton's Third Law of Motion: -
Whenever one body exerts a force on a second body, the second body exerts an oppositely directed force of equal value on the first body.

Hence three fundamental forces have been discovered viz. (1) Gravitational Force, (2) Strong Nuclear Force, and (3) Electroweak Force.

Newton's Law of Universal Gravitation: -
For two particles that have masses m_1 and m_2 and are separated by a distance r, the force that each exerts on the other is directed along the line joining the particles and has a value given by: -

$$F = G \, m_1 m_2 / r^2$$

The symbol G denotes the Universal Gravitational Constant, whose value is found experimentally to be: -

$$G = 6.673 \times 10^{-11} \text{ N-m}^2/\text{kg}^2$$

These are called the gravitational forces of action and reaction and are oppositely directed.

Definition of Weight: - The weight of an object on or above the earth is the gravitational force that the earth exerts on the object. The weight always acts downwards towards the center of the earth. On or above another astronomical body, the weight is the gravitational force exerted on the object by that body.

$$W = G \, M_E \, m / r^2 = mg$$
$$g = G \, M_E / r^2$$
SI Unit of Weight: newton (N)

Definition of the Normal Force: - The Normal Force F_N is one component of the force that a surface exerts on an object with which it is in contact – namely, the component that is perpendicular to the surface.

Apparent Weight and True Weight: - Suppose a man is moving in an elevator. This implies his weight $W = mg$ acts downward and the normal force perpendicular to the platform acts upward.

$$\Rightarrow \Sigma F_y = +F_N - mg = ma_y$$
$$\Rightarrow F_N = mg + ma_y$$
Apparent Weight = True Weight + mass x acceleration(y)

If the elevator accelerates upward, the acceleration, "a_y", is positive and apparent weight is greater than the true weight and if the elevator accelerates downward, the acceleration, "a_y", is negative and the apparent weight is less than the true weight.

Static Frictional Force: -
The magnitude f_s of the static frictional force can have any value from zero up to a maximum value of f_s^{MAX}, depending on the applied force. In other words, $f_s \leq f_s^{MAX}$ where the symbol " $\leq$ " is read "less than or equal to". The equality holds only when f_s attain its maximum value, which is: -

$$F_s^{MAX} = \mu_s F_N$$

Note that μ_s is the coefficient of static friction and F_N is the normal force.

Kinetic Frictional Force: -
The magnitude f_k of the kinetic frictional force is given by: -

$$F_k = \mu_k F_N$$

Note that μ_k is the coefficient of kinetic friction and F_N is the normal force.

The Tension Force: - The force of tension, "T", in the rope that is being pulled apart is not needed to accelerate the rope because the rope is idealized as a mass less rope. $\Sigma F = ma$, where $m = 0$ kg.

Hence the force, "T", is applied undiminished to the object attached to the other end of the rope.

Definition of Equilibrium: - An object is in equilibrium when it has zero acceleration.

This implies the x and y components of the acceleration of an object in equilibrium must also be zero.

$$\Sigma F_x = ma_x = 0 \text{ N } a_x = 0 \text{ m/s}^2$$
$$\Sigma F_y = ma_y = 0 \text{ N } a_y = 0 \text{ m/s}^2$$

The forces acting on an object in equilibrium must balance each other.

For non-equilibrium applications of Newton's Laws of Motion, the net force is not equal to zero, the acceleration is not equal to zero, and the x and y components of the net force are not equal to zero. The non-equilibrium forces do not balance each other.

Forces and Newton's Laws of Motion: -

Numerical Problems: -
Newton's Laws of Motion: -

1. An airplane has a mass of 4.2×10^5 kg and takes off under the influence of a constant net force of 5.3×10^5 N. What is the net force that acts on the plane's 80 kg pilot?
    Solution: -
    $F = ma = 4.2 \times 10^5$ kg x a = 5.3×10^5 N
    $a = F/m = 5.3 \times 10^5$ N$/4.2 \times 10^5$ kg = 1.261904762 m/s²
    $F_{net} = m_{pilot}$ a = 80 kg x 1.261904762 m/s² = 100.952381 N
    F_{net} = 100.95 N

2. Two forces F_A and F_B are applied to an object whose mass is 9 kg. The larger force is F_A. When both forces point due east, the object's acceleration has a value of 0.6 m/s². However when F_A points due east and F_B points due west, the acceleration is 0.5 m/s² due east. Find the values of (a) F_A and (b) F_B.
    Solution: -
    (a) $a_A + a_B$ = 0.6 m/s² due east
    $a_A - a_B$ = 0.5 m/s² due west
    a_A = (0.6 + 0.5)/2 = 1.1/2 = 0.55 m/s²
    a_B = 0.6 – 0.55 = 0.05 m/s²
    $F_A = ma_A$ = 9 kg x 0.55 m/s² = 4.95 N due east
    (b) $F_B = ma_B$ = 9 kg x 0.05 m/s² = 0.45 N due west
    $\Rightarrow$ (a) F_A = 4.95 N and (b) F_B = 0.45 N
    The Vector Nature of Newton's Second Law of Motion, Newton's Third Law of Motion: -

3. A duck has a mass of 3 kg. As the duck paddles a force of 0.2 N acts on it, in a direction due east. In addition, the current of the water exerts a force of 0.3 N in a direction of 40^0 South of East. When these forces begin to act, the velocity of the duck is 0.22 m/s in a direction due east. Find the magnitude and direction (relative to due east) of the displacement that the duck undergoes in 2 seconds while the forces are acting.

Solution: -

$x = v_0t + (1/2) a_1t^2 + (1/2) a_2t^2$

$x = 0.22$ m/s x 2s + ½(0.2 N/3 kg)(2s)² + ½(0.3 N cos40⁰/3 kg)(2)²

$x = 0.44$m + 0.133333333m + 0.153208889m

$x = 0.726542222$m

$y = (1/2) a_yt^2 = $ ½(0.3 N sin40⁰/3 kg)(2s)²

$y = 0.128557522$m

$d = \sqrt{(x^2 + y^2)} = \sqrt{[(0.726542222m)^2 + (0.128557522m)^2]}$

$d = \sqrt{(0.5278636 + 0.016527036)} = \sqrt{(0.544390636)}$

$d = 0.737828324$

$d = 0.7378$m

$\theta = \tan^{-1}(y/x) = \tan^{-1}(0.128557522/0.726542222)$

$\theta = \tan^{-1}(0.176944324) = 10.03^0$

$\theta = 10.03^0$ South of East

4. Only two forces act on an object (mass = 4 kg). One force F_1 = 50 N acts in a direction due east and the other force F_2 = 70 N acts at an angle $\theta = 50^0$ North of East. Find the magnitude and direction (relative to the x-axis) of the acceleration of the object.

Solution: -

$F_x = 50$ N + 70cos 50^0 N = 94.99513268 N

$F_y = 70$sin 50^0 N = 53.62311102 N

$F = \sqrt{(F_x^2 + F_y^2)} = \sqrt{[(94.99513268N)^2 + (53.62311102N)^2]}$

$F = \sqrt{(9024.075233 + 2875.438035)} = \sqrt{(11899.51327)}$

$F = 109.0848902$ N

$a = F/m = 109.0848902N/4kg = 27.27122255m/s^2$

$a = 27.27$ m/s²

$\theta = \tan^{-1}(F_y/F_x) = \tan^{-1}(53.62311102/94.99513268)$

$\theta = \tan^{-1} (0.564482721) = 29.4^0$
The Gravitational Force: -

5. On earth, two parts of a space probe weigh 49000 N and 9800 N. These parts are separated by a center to center distance of 10m and may be treated as uniform spherical objects. Find the magnitude of the gravitational force that each part exerts on the other out there in space, far from any other objects.
   Solution: -
   $m_1 = 49000/9.8 = 5000$ kg
   $m_2 = 9800/9.8 = 1000$ kg
   $F = Gm_1m_2/R^2$
   $F = 6.673 \times 10^{-11} N\text{-}m^2/kg^2 \times (5000kg)(1000kg)/(10m)^2$
   $F = 3.3 \times 10^{-6} N$

6. A space traveler whose mass is 160 kg leaves earth. What are his weight and mass (a) on earth and (b) in interplanetary space where there are no nearby planetary objects?
   Solution: -
   (a) m = 160 kg, W = 160kg x 9.8 m/s² = 1568 N
   (b) m = 160 kg, W = 160 kg x 0 m/s² = 0 N

7. The mass of a robot is 6000kg. This robot weighs 4000N more on planet A than it does on planet B. Both planets have the same radius of 2.8×10^6m. What is the difference ($M_A - M_B$) in the masses of these planets?
   Solution: -
   $\Delta W = G [6000kg/(2.8 \times 10^6)^2](M_A - M_B) = 4000N$
   $M_A - M_B = 4000N \times (2.8 \times 10^6)^2/(6.673 \times 10^{-11} N\text{-}m^2/kg^2)$
   (6000kg)
   $M_A - M_B = 0.7832559069 \times 10^{23}kg$
   $M_A - M_B = 7.832559069 \times 10^{22}kg$
   The difference ($M_A - M_B$) between the masses of these planets has been calculated and this value is given below:
   -
   $(M_A - M_B) = 7.8 \times 10^{22}$ kg

8. A planet has a mass of 7×10^{19}kg and a radius of 0.45×10^5m. (a) What is the acceleration due to gravity on this planet? (b) How much would a 70 kg person weigh on this planet?

Solution: -

(a) $g = G M/R^2 = 6.673 \times 10^{-11}$N-m^2/kg^2 x 7×10^{19}kg/ $(0.45 \times 10^5$m$)^2$

$g = 2.306716049$m/s^2 = 2.3067m/s^2

$g = 2.3067$ m/s^2

(b) $W = mg = 70$kg x 2.306716049m/s^2

$W = 161.4701235$kgm/s^2

$W = 161.47$ N

9. Several people are riding in a hot air balloon. The combined mass of the balloon and the people is 400kg. The balloon is motionless in the air because the downward-acting weight of the balloon and the people is balanced by an upward-acting "buoyant" force. If the buoyant force remains constant, how much mass should be dropped overboard so that the balloon acquires an upward acceleration of 0.2 m/s^2

Solution: -

m_1 = 400 kg = (mass of people and the balloon)

$a = 0.2$ m/s^2

$m_1(g - a) = m_2 g$

400kg $(9.8 - 0.2)$ m/s^2 = m_2 x 9.8m/s^2

m_2 = 400 kg x 9.6 m/s^2 / 9.8 m/s^2

m_2 = 391.8367347 kg

$M = m_1 - m_2$ = 400kg – 391.8367347kg

$M = 8.163265306$ kg

$M = 8.16$ kg

Hence a mass equal to 8.16 kg should be dropped overboard in order for the people and the balloon to acquire an upward acceleration of 0.2 m/s^2

10. At a distance H above the surface of a planet, the true weight of a remote probe is two per cent less than its true weight on the surface. The radius of the planet is R. Find the ratio H/R.

Solution: -

$F = G Mm/R^2$

$0.98F = G \, Mm/(R+H)^2$

$(R+H)^2/R^2 = F/0.98F = 1.020408163$

$(R+H)/R = \sqrt{(1.020408163)} = 1.010152545$

$1+H/R = 1.010152545$

$\Rightarrow H/R = 0.01$

The Normal Force, Static and Kinetic Frictional Forces: -

11. A rocket blasts off from rest and attains a speed of 50m/s in 10s. An astronaut has a mass of 60 kg. What is the astronaut's apparent weight during takeoff?
    Solution: -
    $v_0 = 0m/s$, $v = 50m/s$, $t = 10s$, and $m = 60kg$
    $a = (v - v_0)/t = [(50 - 0)/10] \, m/s^2 = 5m/s^2$
    $a = g + a = 9.8m/s^2 + 5m/s^2 = 14.8m/s^2$
    $W_{Apparent} = m \, (g + a) = 60kg \times 14.8m/s^2$
    $W_{Apparent} = 888 \, N$

12. A block whose weight is 50N rests on a horizontal table. A horizontal force of 40N is applied to the block. The coefficients of static and kinetic frictions are 0.74 and 0.53 respectively. Will the block move under the influence of the applied force, and if so, what will be the block's acceleration? Explain your reason.
    Solution: -
    $m = F/a = W/a = 50N/9.8m/s^2 = 5.102040816 \, kg$
    $F_s = \mu_s F_N = 0.74 \times 50N = 37N$
    The force of static friction of 37N is less than the applied force of 40N. Hence the block will move under the influence of this force.
    $F_k = \mu_k F_N = 0.53 \times 50N = 26.5N$
    $a = F/m = (40 - 26.5)N/5.102040816kg$
    $a = 13.5N/5.102040816kg$
    $a = 2.646m/s^2$
    The Tension Force, Equilibrium Application of Newton's Laws of Motion: -

13. A supertanker (mass $= 2 \times 10^9 kg$) is moving with a constant velocity. Its engines generate a forward thrust of $8 \times 10^6 N$. Determine (a) the magnitude of the resistive force exerted

on the tanker by the water, and (b) the magnitude of the upward buoyant force exerted on the tanker by the water.

Solution: -

(a) The resistive force exerted on the tanker by the water: -

$F_{resistive} = 8 \times 10^6 N$.

(b) The buoyant force exerted on the tanker by the water: -

$F_{buoyant} = mg = 2 \times 10^9 kg \times 9.8 m/s^2$

$F_{buoyant} = 1.96 \times 10^{10} N$

Miscellaneous: -

14. The coefficient of kinetic friction between an 18 kg crate and the floor is 0.40. What horizontal force is required to move the crate at a steady speed across the floor? What horizontal force is required if μ_k is zero?

Solution: -

a) $F = \mu_k F_N = \mu_k m (g\cos\theta)$

Now $\theta = 0^0$ (because the floor is horizontal)

$F = \mu_k mg$

$F = 0.4 \times 18 kg \times 9.8 ms^{-2} = 70.56N$

(b) $F = \mu_k F_N = \mu_k m (g\cos\theta)$

Now $\mu_k = 0$ and $\theta = 0^0$ (because the floor is horizontal)

$F = 0 N$

15. A 20 kg box is released on a 25^0 incline and accelerates down the incline at $0.4 m/s^2$. Find the friction force impeding its motion. How large is the coefficient of friction?

Solution: -

a) $F = m (g \sin\theta - a)$

$F = 20 kg (9.8 m/s^2 \sin 25^0 - 0.4 m/s^2)$

$F = 20 kg (4.141658965 - 0.4) ms^{-2}$

$F = 20 kg \times 3.741658965 ms^{-2} = 74.8331793N$

$F = 74.8N$

b) $F = m (g \sin\theta - a) = \mu_k mg \cos\theta$

$\mu_k = F/mg \cos\theta = 74.8331793N / [20 kg \times 9.8 ms^{-2} \times \cos 25^0]$

$\mu_k = 74.8331793 / 177.6363263 = 0.421271825$

Hence $\mu_k = .421$

45)

· ·

The Radiating Sun

The sun is a star in our solar system. In spite of its magnanimous distance from the earth it is the closest star in the universe, that is, closest to the planet earth. The mass of the sun is 1.99×10^{30} kg and its mean radius is 6.96×10^8 m. Its mean distance from the earth is 1.5×10^{11} m.

It takes about 8 minutes of time for the sun's rays to strike the surface of the planet earth and it is about 91 million miles away from the earth. In other words, the sun that is visible to the naked eye is about 8 minutes older.

(Time it takes for the sun's light rays to reach earth)
= (distance from the sun to earth)/ (velocity of light rays)
$\Rightarrow$ t = d/ v
$\Rightarrow$ 91,000,000 miles/[186,282 miles/second(60 seconds/minute)]
$\cong$ 8 minutes (approximately)
In SI units, similar result is obtained as follows: -
t =d/v=1.5×10^{11}m /[2.99792458×10^8m/sx(60s/minute)] $\cong$ 8 minutes

On planet earth, the solar radiation is in the form of electromagnetic radiation. The visible spectrum of light from the sun is a band of colors of distinct frequencies and distinct wavelengths. The speed of light in vacuum space is given as c = 2.99792458×10^8 m/s.

The visible spectrum of electromagnetic radiation starts from a frequency of 4×10^{14}Hz and continues till 7.9×10^{14}Hz. Likewise the wavelengths in the visible spectrum of light begin with $\lambda = 380$ nm and continue till they reach approximately $\lambda = 750$ nm.

The seven colors that are covered in the visible spectrum are violet followed by indigo, blue, green, yellow, orange, and finally red. The velocity of light is given by c = fλ, where f is the frequency and λ is the wavelength of the electromagnetic radiation. The band of colors, in the spectrum, comes into play because the electromagnetic waves have different speeds when they are refracted through a prism. This is called dispersion of light through a prism.

The visible light obeys certain laws of Physics, like reflection, refraction, diffraction, dispersion of light through a prism, polarization, resolution, interference, Doppler effects and relativistic effects. The speed of light in vacuum space is a constant for all inertial reference frames and it is 186,282 miles per second.

The space probes are usually sent in a direction which is away from the sun. Generally space probes are sent to the moon or a planet called Mars because these heavenly bodies are closest to the planet earth and deserve our wildest curiosities about them to be satisfied through a scientific astronomical research.

In the sun, there is a proton-proton cycle thought to occur continuously and it is given as follows: -

(1) $_1^1H + {}_1^1H \rightarrow {}_1^2H + {}_1^0e + \nu$
hydrogen + hydrogen $\rightarrow$ deuterium + positron + neutrino
(2) $_1^1H + {}_1^2H \rightarrow {}_2^3He + \gamma$
hydrogen + deuterium $\rightarrow {}_2^3He$ nuclei + gamma ray photon
(3) $_2^3He + {}_2^3He \rightarrow {}_2^4He + {}_1^1H + {}_1^1H$
$_2^3He$ nuclei + $_2^3He$ nuclei $\rightarrow \alpha$-particle + hydrogen + hydrogen

In these reactions, $_1^0e$ is a positron (mass = 0.000549 u), ν is a neutrino (mass = 0 u), and γ is a gamma ray photon (mass = 0 u), and $_1^1H$ is hydrogen, $_1^2H$ is an isotope of hydrogen known as deuterium, $_2^3He$ nuclei is an isotope of helium, and $_2^4He$ is an isotope of helium also called α - particle.

Hence hydrogen has three isotopes viz. $_1^1H$ (hydrogen), $_1^2H$ (deuterium), and $_1^3H$ (tritium), and helium has two isotopes viz. $_2^3He$ nuclei, and $_2^4He$ (helium) also called an α - particle.

The proton-proton cycle is actually a cycle of thermonuclear reactions, which is continuously taking place on the sun, releasing tremendous amounts of energy, and thereby bombarding the world with electromagnetic radiations. The sun has been shining for more than 5 billion years (5,000,000,000 years) and will continue to shine for that many more years. According to the Big Bang Theory, the universe is 14 billion years old, the Milky Way galaxy is 13.2 billion years old, and the solar system itself is 4.5 billion years old. It takes 230 million years for the sun to orbit the Milky Way Galaxy.

Farewell:

I do not fancy saying good bye in my books. Writing books to entertain my colleagues and to enlighten young readers on matters that seem trivial at first glance but are, somewhat, complicated in nature has become my way of spending my most sacred and immensely precious time. I wish to write about Arts and Science and I wish to produce the most beautiful works of Arts and Science, and sometimes in the future, I hope to attain great success towards my goal and become a writer of international reputation. My true goal in life is not to say good bye in my books but to continue saying hello for as long as there is a lovely moon shining, in this endless and merciless gloomy blue sky. I wish to congratulate my young and, somewhat, senior colleagues for successfully having read my book and I wish to them the best in this life and the life to come in the hereafter. I pray to God that He may shower His choicest blessings upon my somewhat senior colleagues. Some of them were members of the Lion's Club, I remember. Today I have been able to accomplish a great assignment of writing this book, by the grace and blessings of God and I only seek God's pleasure and appreciation. I hope it's a great success in both the faculty of Arts, as well as, the faculty of Science, of my alma-mater, for a good many academic years in the university, annual debates and annual seminars and symposiums. Furthermore I hope my book finds an intelligent academia in education for higher learning and continues enriching the world with more projects of a similar nature.

Finis

Glossary:

· ·

1) Albert Einstein – a famous mathematician and a physicist of 20th century A.D., page no. 199

2) A.M radio-wave – a radio wave in which the amplitude is being altered, amplitude modulation, page no. 202

3) Andromeda galaxy – the galaxy that is the closest neighbor of our own Milky Way Galaxy, page no. 343-346

4) Aphelion – the most distant point of the planet from the sun, page no. 312-340

5) Atmosphere – a sphere of air enclosing the surface of planet Earth, page no. 264-269

6) Audience- folks who lend ears to you, page no. 65-66

7) Aurora borealis – a glow in the night sky in the region near the magnetic north pole, also called northern lights, page no. 264-269

8) Aviation – the science and practice of flying powered, heavier-than-air craft such as airplane and helicopter, page no.221

9) Axis – the singular of axes, and the x, y, and z-axes of the three dimensional space, page no. 401-429 10) Barometer – an instrument for measuring atmospheric pressure, page no. 69

11) Black Hole – an area of time and space, whose gravitational field is so strong, that nothing is able to escape, not even light, page no. 351-352

12) C.N.G – compressed natural gas, page no. 383-384

13) Calcutta – a metropolitan city of the state of Bengal, India, page no. 383

14) Cyclone – a violent low pressure hurricane of limited diameter, page no. 264-269

15) Democracy – a government of the people, by the people, and for the people, page no. 211

16) Dumhal – a famous dance of Kashmir Valley, page no. 387

17) Equator – an imaginary line circling the earth midway between north and south poles, page no. 276

18) F.M radio-wave – a radio-wave in which frequency is being altered, frequency modulation, page no. 202

19) Far-sightedness – able to see objects, located farther away, page no. 74-76

20) Gravitation – natural force of attraction that tends to draw heavenly bodies together, page no. 301, 312, 341, 351

21) Hot Air Balloon – a large gas balloon in which passengers can be lifted up in a basket called gondola and enjoy a ride in the air, page no. 191

22) Hurricane – a storm with a violent wind, especially a cyclone in the West Atlantic, page no. 264-269

23) Incongruous – disharmonious, inconsistent, page no. 159

24) Jhelum River – a Himalayan river and the only major river that flows through the Kashmir Valley, page no. 387-388

25) Kohinoor – a diamond of great historical significance, page no. 101

26) Light – the visible spectrum of the electromagnetic radiation, velocity = 2.99792458×10^8m/s, page no. 401-429

27) Magnetic equator – an imaginary and irregular line circling the earth's surface; its shape and position vary from year to year, but

it is always close to the geographical equator. The attraction of magnetic north and magnetic south poles is equal at all points on this line, page no. 276 28) Mangrove forests – forests on the coast of Karachi, Pakistan, essential for its ecological balance, page no. 385-386

29) Meridian – an imaginary line extending from the north pole to the south pole at right angles to the equator, page no. 272

30) Metropolis – the chief city of a country or its capital city, page no. 207

31) Milky Way Galaxy – our own galaxy in which our own solar system revolves along with other solar systems, page no. 341

32) Navigation – the art and science of guiding a ship, airplane, space craft, or land vehicle from one place to another, page no. 216

33) Navigational Compass – a magnetic compass whose needle always points in the direction of the North Pole, page no. 70

34) Pasteurized Milk – milk heated to a certain degree for a certain time, page no.11 35) Perihelion – a planet's closest approach to the sun, page no. 266

36) Philosophy – a study of arts, page no. 85

37) Population Explosion – the world's annual rate of natural increase has risen to about 2%, almost double the pre-war record, causing what has been called a "population explosion", page no. 261

38) Prime meridian – the meridian or 0° longitude that passes through Greenwich in London, England, page no. 272

39) Purchase – obtain in exchange for money, page no. 387-388

40) Rouf – a famous folk dance of Kashmir Valley, page no. 387

41) Sagittarius A* - the galactic center of our own galaxy, the Milky Way Galaxy box, page no. 341-342

42) Shikara – a traditional wooden boat in Kashmir Valley, page no. 387-388 43) Shipyards – one of the largest shipping industry is located on the shores of Bombay, page no. 207-210

44) Shortsightedness – able to see better from a closer range, page no. 74-76

45) Simla Agreement – the treaty that had ensured that Pakistan recognize Bangladesh in exchange for its P.O.Ws., page no. 248-250

46) Simple pendulum – a pendulum made from a round, metallic bob tied to a string performing Simple Harmonic Motion by oscillating to and fro, page no. 52-53

47) Tesla & Marconi – the two inventors of the wireless radio, page no. 202

48) Tennis – an amateur game, page no. 160, 161

49) Tornado – a violently rotating column of air, visible as a funnel, with its vertex on the ground and its base in the clouds, page no. 264-269 50) Tropics – the region circling the earth between the Tropic of Cancer and the Tropic of Capricorn, page no. 274

51) Typhoon – a violent hurricane in East Asia, page no. 264-269

52) Urdu – a language of the Muslims of India, and Pakistan, page no. 387-388

53) Ursa Major and Ursa Minor – names of the two of the galaxies in the cosmos that are close to each other, page no. 347-350

54) Van Allen Radiation Belt – the greatest concentration of radio-active trapped particles occurs within the Magnetosphere or Exosphere in a region called Van Allen Radiation Belt, page no. 264-269

55) Zworykin and Farnsworth – the two inventors of the modern T.V, page no. 202

Bibliography

1) World Wide Websites on the computer via Internet.

2) Algebra and Trigonometry, by M.A.Munem and D.J.Foulis.

3) Calculus, by Boyce DiPrima.

4) Differential Equations, by Blanchard, Devaney, and Hall

5) Guinness World Records 2009.

6) The New Standard Encyclopedia.

7) Calculus and Analytical Geometry, by Thomas.

8) Wikipedia, the free Encyclopedia, on the Internet, on www.google.com.

9) Math Text: Modern Algebra & Trigonometry, by E. P. Vance.

10) Calculus: Earl W. Swokowski.

Further Suggestive Reading: -

1) General Theory of Relativity,

2) Einstein's Unified Field Theory,

3) Winners of the Nobel Peace Prize after WWII,

4) How to combat International Terrorism?

5) World Economy, (Depression, Recession, and Booming Economy), and Inflation,

6) Sources of Energy and the World's Energy Crisis,

7) Food and Drug Administration, (F.D.A),

8) Political Rights and Duties of US citizens,

9) The US Government, (Executive, Legislative, and the Judiciary),

10) The Indian Space Program.

"Fundamentals of Physics"

By: - Physicist Javed Naseer

Volume One

Dedication: - I dedicate my book to my colleagues who have been a great support in the preparation of this dissertation.

Newtonian Mechanics: -
Chapter No.1: Introduction and Mathematical Concepts: -
(a) Physics, (b) Units, (c) Conversion of Units, (d) Dimensional Analysis, (e) Trigonometry, (f) Scalars and Vectors, (g) Vector Addition and Subtraction, (1)Problems
Chapter No.2: Kinematics in One Dimension: - (a) Displacement, (b) Speed and Velocity, (c) Acceleration, (d) Equations of Kinematics for Constant Acceleration, (e) Freely Falling Bodies, (2)Problems
Chapter No.3: Kinematics in Two Dimensions: -
(a) Displacement, Velocity, and Acceleration, (b) Equations of Kinematics in Two Dimensions, (c) Projectile Motion, (d) Relative Velocity, (3)Problems
Chapter No.4: Forces and Newton's Laws of Motion: - (a) Newton's First Law of Motion, (b) Definition of Inertia and Mass, (c) Definition of an Inertial Reference Frame, (d) Newton's Second Law of Motion, (e) Newton's Third Law of Motion, (f) Newton's Law of Universal Gravitation, (g) Definition of Weight, (h) Definition of Normal Force, (i) Apparent Weight and True Weight, (j) Static Frictional Force, (k) Kinetic Frictional Force, (l) Tension Force, (m) Definition of Equilibrium, (4)Problems
Chapter No.5: Dynamics of Uniform Circular Motion: -
(a) Definition of Uniform Circular Motion, (b) Centripetal Acceleration, (c) Centripetal Force, (d) Banked Curves, (e) Vertical Circular Motion, (5) Problems
Chapter No.6: Work and Energy: - (a) Definition of Work Done by a Constant Force, (b) The Work-Energy Theorem, (c) Gravitational Potential Energy, (d) Conservative versus Non-Conservative Forces, (e) The Principle of Conservation of Mechanical Energy, (f) Non-Conservative Force and the Work-Energy Theorem, (g) Power, (h) Principle of Conservation of Energy, (i) Work Done by a Variable Force, (6)Problems
Chapter No.7: Impulse and Momentum: - (a) Definition of Impulse, (b) Definition of Linear Momentum,
(c) Impulse-Momentum Theorem, (d) Principle of Conservation of Linear Momentum, (e) Collision in One Dimension,
(f) Collision in Two Dimensions, (g) Center of Mass, (h) Momentum and Kinetic Energy, (7)Problems

Chapter No.8: Rotational Kinematics: - (a) Definition of Angular Displacement, (b) Definition of Angular Velocity,

(c) Definition of Angular Acceleration, (d) Equations of Rotational Kinematics, (e) Angular Variables and Tangential Variables, (f) Centripetal Acceleration and Tangential Acceleration, (g) Vector Nature of Angular Variables,

(8)Problems

Chapter No.9: Rotational Dynamics: - (a) Definition of Torque, (b) Equilibrium of a Rigid Body, (c) Definition of center of gravity, (d) Newton's Second Law for Rotational Motion about a fixed axis, (e) Moment of Inertia, (f) Comparison between Rotational and Translational Concepts, (g) Definition of Rotational Kinetic Energy, (h) Definition of Angular Momentum, (i) Principle of Conservation of Angular Momentum, (9) Problems

Chapter No.10: Simple Harmonic Motion and Elasticity: - (a) Hooke's Law, Restoring force of an Ideal Spring, (b) Simple Harmonic Motion and the Reference Circle, (c) Displacement, (d) Velocity, (e) Acceleration, (f) Frequency of Vibration, (g) Energy and Simple Harmonic Motion, (h) Definition of Elastic Potential Energy, (i) Conservation of Mechanical Energy, (j) The Pendulum, (k) Elastic Deformation, (l) Young's modulus, Shear modulus, and Bulk modulus, (10)Problems

Heat: -

Chapter No. 11: Pressure in Gases and Liquids: - (a) Mass Density, (b) Pressure and Depth in a Static Fluid, (c) Pascal's Principle, (d) Archimede's Principle, (e) The Equation of Continuity, (f) Bernoulli's Equation, (g) Viscous Flow. (11) Numerical Problems

Chapter No. 12: Temperature and Heat: (a) Common Temperature Scales, (b) The Kelvin Temperature Scale, (c) Linear Thermal Expansion, (d) Volume Thermal Expansion, (e) Heat and Internal Energy, (f) Heat and Temperature Change: Specific Heat Capacity, (g) Heat and Phase Change: Latent Heat, (h) Equilibrium Between Phases of Matter, (i) Humidity. (12) Numerical Problems

Chapter No. 13: The Transfer of Heat: - (a) Convection, (b) Conduction, (c) Radiation, (d) Applications. (13) Problems

Chapter No. 14: The Ideal Gas Law and Kinetic Theory: - (a) Molecular Mass, the Mole, and Avogadro's Number, (b) The Ideal Gas Law, (c) Kinetic Theory of Gases, (d) Diffusion. (14) Problems

Sound: -

Chapter No. 15: Waves and Sound: - (a) The Characteristics of Waves, (b) Sinusoidal Waves, (c) Wave Speed and Particle Speed on a String, (d) The Mathematical Description of a Wave, (e) The Characteristics of Sound, (f) Longitudinal Sound Waves, (g) The Frequency of a Sound Wave, (h) The Pressure Amplitude of a Sound Wave, (i) The Speed of Sound, (j) Sound Intensity, (k) Decibels, (l) Doppler Effect. (15) Numerical Problems

Chapter No. 16: The Principle of Linear Superposition and Interference Phenomena: - (a) The Priciple of Linear Superposition, (b) Constructive and Destructive Interference of Sound Waves, (c) Interference Phenomena, (d) Diffraction, (e) Beats, (f) Tranverse Standing Waves, (g) Longitudinal Standing Waves, (h) Complex Sound Waves. (16) Numerical Problems

Electromagnetism: -

Chapter No. 17: Electric Forces and Electric Fields: - (a) Origin of Electricity, (b) Charged Objects and Electric Force, (c) Conductors and Insulators, (d) Charging by Contact and by Induction, (e) Coulomb's Law, (f) Electric Field, (g) Electric Field Inside a Conductor: Shielding, (h) Gauss' Law. (17) Problems

Chapter No.18: Electric Potential Energy and the Electric Potential: - (a) Potential Energy, (b) The Electric Potential Difference, (c) Equipotential Surfaces and their Relation to Electric Field, (d) Capacitors and Dielectrics. (18) Problems

Chapter No. 19: Electric Circuits: - (a) Electromotive Force and Current, (b) Ohm's Law, (c) Resistance and Resistivity, (d) Electric Power, (e) Alternating Current, (f) Series Wiring, (g) Parallel Wiring, (h) Internal Resistance, (i) Kirchhoff's Rules, (j) The Measurement of Current and Voltage, (k) Capacitors in Series and Parallel, (l) RC Circuits, (m) Safety and Physiological Effects of Current. (19) Problems

Chapter No. 20: Magnetic Forces and Magnetic Fields: - (a) Magnetic Fields, (b) The Force that a Magnetic Field exerts on a Moving Charge, (c) The Motion of a Charged Particle in a Magnetic Field, (d) The Mass Spectrometer, (e) The Force on a Current in a Magnetic Field, (f) The Torque on a Current Carrying Coil, (g) Magnetic Fields Produced by Currents, (h) Ampere's Law, (i) Magnetic Materials. (20) Problems

Chapter No. 21: Electromagnetic Induction: - (a) Induced Emf and Induced Current, (b) Motional Emf, (c) Magnetic Flux, (d) Faraday's Law of Electromagnetic Induction, (e) Lenz's Law, (f) The Electric

Generator, (g) Mutual Inductance and Self Inductance, (h) Transformers. (21) Problems

Chapter No. 22: Alternating Current Circuits: - (a) Capacitors and Capacitive Reactance, (b) Inductors and Inductive Reactance, (c) Circuits containing Resistance, Capacitance, and Inductance, (d) Resonance in Electric Circuits, (e) Semiconductor Devices. (22) Problems

Chapter No. 23: Electromagnetic Waves: - (a) The Nature of Electromagnetic Waves, (b) The Electromagnetic Spectrum, (c) The Speed of Light, (d) The Energy Carried by Electromagnetic Waves, (e) Doppler Effect and Electromagnetic Waves, (f) Polarization. (23) Problems

Optics and Optical Instruments: -

Chapter No. 24: The Refraction of Light: Mirrors: - (a) The Refraction of Light, (b) The Formation of Images by a Plane Mirror, (c) Spherical Mirrors, (c) The Formation of Images by Spherical Mirrors, (d) The Mirror Equation and the Magnification Equation. (24) Problems

Chapter No.25: The Refraction of Light: Lenses and Optical Instruments: - (a) The Index of Refraction, (b) Snell's Law and the Refraction of Light, (c) Total Internal Reflection, (d) Polarization and the Reflection and Refraction of Light, (e) The Dispersion of Light: Prisms and Rainbows, (f) Lenses, (g) The Formation of Images by Lenses, (h) The Thin-Lens Equation and the Magnification Equation, (i) Lenses in Combination, (j) Human Eye, (k) Angular Magnification and the Magnifying Glass, (l) The Compound Microscope, (m) The Telescope, (n) Lens Aberrations: Chromatic Aberration and Spherical Aberration. (25) Problems

Chapter No. 26: Interference and the Wave Nature of Light: - (a) The Principle of Linear Superposition, (b) Young's Double-Slit Experiment, (c) Thin-Film Interference, (d) The Michelson's Interferometer, (e) Diffraction, (f) Resolving Power, (g) The Diffraction Grating, (h) X-Ray Diffraction. (26) Problems

Chapter No. 27: Special Relativity: - (a) Events and Inertial Reference Frames, (b) The Postulates of Special Relativity, (c) Time Dilation Equation, (d) Length Contraction, (e)Relativistic Momentum, (f) The Mass-Energy Equivalence, (g) The Relativistic Addition of Velocities. (27) Numerical Problems

Chapter No. 28: Particles and Waves: - (a) The Wave-Particle Duality, (b) Blackbody Radiation and Planck's Constant, (c) Photons and Photoelectric Effect, (d) The Momentum of a Photon and the Compton Effect, (e) The de-Broglie Wavelength and the Wave Nature of Matter. (28) Numerical Problems

Preface

· ·

This book contains ten chapters of Newtonian Mechanics in physics. I have written on mechanics because this is an application of the Physics of the car, besides a lot of other things. The efficient functioning of the car depends on its engine which is therefore related to the Physics of its motor. Numerous physical parameters that are involved in a car drive have been discussed in these chapters on mechanics. There are ten chapters from Newtonian Mechanics, comprising approximately 15 numerical problems from each chapter. Now and then the reader may stumble upon a numerical problem in this book that pertains to the motion and mechanics of the car, that is, displacement, velocity, acceleration, force, energy, and work done etc. associated with a car in motion.

The numerical problems that have been solved in this book of Physics are of paramount importance because these are related to the physical parameters that one encounters in the technology and the mobility of the car as well as other technological systems. The motor car is also developing into quite an essential technological product for commuting, both in the business sector and in political societies, in the present times. The car has been extensively exploited for a multitude of objectives, both in industry and administration. It is believed that the car is likely to find many other alternative undertakings besides business and industry, in due course of time. For instance, it may have a devastating feasibility in warfare in another period of great rivalry and conflicts.

It is conjectured that the car will be used to carry dangerous weapons of mass destruction in the future, the same way it is being manipulated to smuggle illegal drugs, and precious cargo in the metropolitan suburbs, in the present times. Car manufacturers should realize that, some day, the car may have a harmful and a devastating effect on society. The fast paced modernization with which the cars are developing more and more sophistication, and universal impact, in commuting has grown into a matter of concern for the philosophical mind, like me. It might become the cause for a great mass destruction in the world, sometimes in the future. To make this discussion brief, the car that saves human lives, in the present times, may also damage and destroy lives and property, on a large scale, many years from now. The car might be used as a dangerous weapon of a great mass destruction, not long from now, causing the largest massacre of human beings and livestock, the over growing world population has ever witnessed. This rocket like object, viz. the car, may become the legacy of an aristocratic monarchy someday. From the window of a low flying aircraft, these cars seem like rolling stones, crashing through the highway. I, however, do not mind driving around the town for a while because I have peaceful intensions, by the grace and mercy of God. I have included all the essential chapters on Newtonian Mechanics, Heat, Sound, Electromagnetism, Optics and Optical Instruments, Special Relativity, Particles and Waves, and last but not the least I have solved approximately 15 numerical problems for each of these chapters in this text book of Physics.

Physicist Javed Naseer
(University Graduate)
Newtonian Mechanics

Chapter No. 1

. . . .

Introduction and Mathematical Concepts: -

Physics: - Physics is that branch of science which deals with matter and motion.

Units: - There are three systems of units that are widely used, viz. "Le Systeme International d' Units", or simply SI system, Cgs units, and finally British Engineering System BE (the Gravitational version).

System SI Cgs BE
Length meter (m) centimeter (cm) foot (ft)
Mass kilogram (kg) gram (g) slug (sl)
Time second (s) second (s) second (s)

The Conversion of Units: -
1. 1 meter = 3.281 feet
2. 1 mile = 5280 feet
3. 1 hour = 3600 seconds
4. 1 day = 8.64×10^4 seconds
5. 1 year = 3.156×10^7 seconds
6. 1 slug = 14.59 kg
7. $9.8 \text{ m/s}^2 = 32.1538 \text{ ft/s}^2$ = acceleration due to gravity
8. $F = mg = 1 \text{ kg} \times 9.8 \text{ m/s}^2 = 9.8 \text{ N}$
    $F = ma = 1 \text{ kg} \times 1 \text{ m/s}^2 = 1\text{N}$
9. 1 mile/s = 1.609 km/s

Dimensional Analysis: -

In Physics, the term dimension is used to refer to the physical nature of a quantity and the type of units used to specify it. Dimensional analysis is used to check mathematical relation for the consistency of their dimensions.

Example: -

(a) h = (1/2) gt

$[L] = [(L) / (T)^2] \times [T] = [L] / [T]$
Hence this is dimensionally incorrect.
(b) $h = (1/2) gt^2$
$[L] = [(L) / (T)^2] \times [T]^2 = [L]$
Hence this is dimensionally correct.
Trigonometry: -
Suppose Hp = hypotenuse, Al = altitude and Ba = base of a right angled triangle, then we may have the following relations: -
Sin θ = Al /Hp θ = Sin^{-1} (Al /Hp)
Cos θ = Ba /Hp θ = Cos^{-1} (Ba /Hp)
Tan θ = (Sinθ / Cosθ) = Al /Ba θ = Tan^{-1} (Al /Ba)
Sin$^2\theta$ + Cos$^2\theta$ = 1
Sin ($\alpha \pm \beta$) = Sinα Cosβ $\pm$ Cosα Sinβ
Sin 2β = 2Sinβ Cosβ
Cos ($\alpha \pm \beta$) = Cosα Cosβ $\mp$ Sinα Sinβ
Cos 2β = Cos^2 β - Sin^2 β = 1 $-$ 2 Sin^2 β
Law of Cosines: $C^2 = A^2 + B^2 - 2AB$ Cosγ
Law of Sines: A / Sinα = B / Sinβ = C / Sinγ
Note that in the Law of Cosines and the Law of Sines A, B, and C are the three sides of the triangle, and the angles α, β, and γ are the three angles of the same triangle, respectively.
Scalars and Vectors: -
Scalars are physical quantities that have only a value, e.g. (mass and temperature). Vectors, on the other hand, are physical quantities that not only have a value but a direction also, e.g. (force, acceleration, velocity, and displacement). The fact that a quantity is negative or positive does not necessarily imply it is a scalar or a vector.
Mathematically a vector is represented by an arrow, in which, the length of the arrow specifies the value of the vector and the angle that the arrow makes with respect to the x, y, or z axis specifies the direction of the vector.

Vector Addition and Subtraction: -
The negative of a vector is the same vector with its direction reversed. There are two methods of adding or subtracting vectors, viz. (1) the Component Method and (2) the Law of Cosines Method.
The Component Method: -
$C_x = A_x + B_x$
$C_y = A_y + B_y$

$C = \sqrt{(C_x^2 + C_y^2)}$

$\theta = \tan^{-1}(C_y/C_x)$

Furthermore we may have as follows: -

$C_x = C \cos\theta$

$C_y = C \sin\theta$

The Law of Cosines Method: -

The Law of Cosines is as follows: -

$C^2 = A^2 + B^2 - 2AB \cos\gamma$

Note that γ is the angle between vector A and vector B.

Introduction and Mathematical Concepts: -

(1) Numerical Problems: -

Units, the Role of Units in Problem Solving: -

1) The mass of the parasite wasp Caraphractus Cintus can be as small as 6×10^{-7}kg. What is this mass in (a) gram (g), (b) milligram (mg), and (c) microgram (μg)?

Solution: -

(a) mass = 6×10^{-7}kg = 6×10^{-4}g

(b) mass = 6×10^{-7}kg = 6×10^{-1}mg

(c) mass = 6×10^{-7}kg = $6\times10^{2}\mu$g

2) How many seconds are there in (a) 2 hours and 25 minutes, and (b) half a day?

Solution: -

(a) 2 hours x 60 minutes/hour x 60 seconds/minute + 25 minutes x 60 seconds/minute = $7.2 \times 10^3 + 1.5 \times 10^3 = 8700$ seconds

(b) (½) day x 24 hours/day x 60 minutes/hour x 60 seconds/minute = 12 x $3.6 \times 10^3 = 4.32 \times 10^4$ seconds

3) The following are the dimensions of various physical parameters that will be discussed later in the text. Here [L], [T], and [M] denote respectively the dimensions of length, time, and mass.

e.g. Acceleration = a = $[L] / [T]^2$

Force = F = ma = $[M] [L] / [T]^2$

Energy = E = $(1/2) mv^2$ = mgh = $[M] [L]^2 / [T]^2$

Speed = v = $[L] / [T]$

Find out if the following statements are dimensionally correct.

(a) F = mv = $[M] [(L)/ (T)]$ Incorrect

(b) E = $(1/2) mv^2$ = $[M] [(L)^2/ (T)^2]$ correct

(c) E = mgh = [M] [(L)/ (T)²] [L] correct
(d) v = √(Ex/m) = √{[(M)(L)²/ (T)²] [L]/ [M]}
v = [[L]√[L]]/[T] Incorrect
(e) x = (1/2) at² = {[L]/ [T]²]}[T]² = [L] correct
Hence (b) E = (1/2) mv², (c) E = mgh, and (e) x = (1/2) at² are
dimensionally correct.

4) The depth of the ocean is sometimes measured in fathoms
(1fathom = 6 feet). Distance on the surface of the ocean is sometimes
measured in nautical miles (1nautical mile = 6076 feet). The water
beneath a surface rectangle, 3.4 nautical miles by 4.5 nautical miles
has a depth of 15 fathoms. Find the volume of water (in cubic meters)
beneath this rectangle.
Solution: -
V = 3.4 x 4.5 x 15 x 6/6076 (nautical mile)³
= .226629361 (nautical mile)³
V = .226629361 x (6076 feet)³
= 5.083577755 x 10¹⁰ cubic feet
V = 5.083577755 x 10¹⁰ x (.3048 meter)³
= 1.439508914 x 10⁹ cubic meters
Hence the answer is 1.4395 x 10⁹ m³.
Trigonometry: -
5) What is the angle θ that the diagonal of a cube makes with the
diagonal of the opposite face of the cube if the length of one of the edges
of the cube is 0.342 nm?
Solution: -
S = 0.342 nm x 10⁻⁹ m/nm = o.342 x 10⁻⁹ m
S` = √(S² + S²) = S√2
Tan θ = perpendicular / base = S / S√2 = 1 / √2
θ = tan⁻¹ (1/√2) = 35.26⁰ = 35.3⁰
Hence θ = 35.3⁰, which is the required angle.
6) What is the value of each of the angles of a triangle whose sides
are 80m, 120m, and 180m in length respectively? (Hint: Consider using
the law of cosines.)
Solution: -
C² = A² + B² – 2AB Cosθ
The above given is the Law of Cosines.
(a) (80)² = (120)² + (180)² - 2(120)(180) Cosα

$\Rightarrow Cos\alpha = \{(120)^2 + (180)^2 - (80)^2\} / 2(120)(180)$

$Cos\alpha = 0.935185185$

$\alpha = Cos^{-1}(0.935185185)$

$\alpha = 20.7^0$ opposite 80m side

(b) $(120)^2 = (80)^2 + (180)^2 - 2(80)(180) \cos\beta$

$\Rightarrow Cos\beta = \{(80)^2 + (180)^2 - (120)^2\} / 2(80)(180)$

$Cos\beta = 0.847222222$

$\beta = Cos^{-1}(0.847222222)$

$\beta = 32.1^0$ opposite 120m side

(c) $(180)^2 = (80)^2 + (120)^2 - 2(80)(120) \cos\gamma$

$\Rightarrow Cos\gamma = \{(80)^2 + (120)^2 - (180)^2\} / 2(80)(120)$

$Cos\gamma = -0.604166667$

$\gamma = Cos^{-1}(-0.604166667)$

$\gamma = 127.2^0$ opposite 180m side

We may check the result by adding $\alpha + \beta + \gamma = 180^0$.

Vector Addition and Subtraction: -

7) A car is being pulled out of the mud by two forces that are applied by two ropes. The value of each force applied by each rope is 3000N. The two ropes make an angle of $\theta = 9^0$ with respect to a perpendicular line that bisects the car into two equal halves. (a) How much force would a single rope have to apply to accomplish the same effect as that due to the combined effect of the two ropes? (b) How would the single rope be directed with respect to the perpendicular line that bisects the car into two equal halves?

Solution: -

(a) $F = 2F_1 \cos\theta_1 = 2F_2 \cos\theta_2$

Note $F_1 = F_2 = 3000N$, and $\theta_1 = \theta_2 = 9^0$

$\Rightarrow F = 2 \times 3000N \times \cos 9^0 = 5926.13$ N

(b) The single rope will be directed along the perpendicular line that bisects the car into two equal halves.

8) Vector A has a value of 10 units and points due west and vector B points due north. (a) What is the value of vector B if A+B has a value of 20 units? (b) What is the direction of A+B relative to due west? (c) What is the value of vector B if A-B has a value of 20 units? (d) What is the direction of A-B relative to due west?

Solution: -

(a) A+B = 20 units & A = 10 units

$B = \sqrt{\{(20)^2 - (10)^2\}} = \sqrt{300} = 17.32050808$ units

(b) $\theta = \tan^{-1}(B/A) = \tan^{-1}(17.32050808/10) = \tan^{-1}(1.732050808)$

$\theta = 60^0$ North of West

(c) A-B = 20 units & A = 10 units

$B = - \sqrt{\{(20)^2 - (10)^2\}}$

B = - 17.32050808 units

(d) $\theta = \tan^{-1}(B/A) = \tan^{-1}(-17.32050808/10)$

$\theta = \tan^{-1}(-1.732050808)$

$\theta = - 60^0$ South of West

The Components of a Vector: -

9) The value of the force vector F is 90N. The x- component of this vector is directed along the +x-axis and has a value of 60N. The y-component points along the +y-axis. (a) Find the direction of F relative to the +x-axis. (b) Find the component of F along the +y-axis.

Solution: -

$F = \sqrt{(F_x^2 + F_y^2)}$

$F_x = F \cos\theta$

$F_y = F \sin\theta$

(a) $F_x/F = \cos\theta$

$\theta = \cos^{-1}(F_x/F) = \cos^{-1}(60/90) = \cos^{-1}(0.666666667) = 48.2^0$

$\theta = 48.2^0$

(b) $F_y = \sqrt{(F^2 - F_x^2)} = \sqrt{\{(90)^2 - (60)^2\}} = \sqrt{(4500)}$

$F_y = 67.1N$

10) The speed of an object and the direction in which it moves constitutes a vector quantity known as velocity. An ostrich is running at a speed of 20m/s in a direction of 70^0 N of W. What is the magnitude of the ostrich's velocity component that is directed (a) due north and (b) due west?

Solution: -

(a) $v_N = 20$m/s x $\sin70^0 = 18.79385242$ m/s

(b) $v_W = 20$m/s x $\cos70^0 = 6.840402867$ m/s

Addition of Vectors by Means of Components: -

11) Vector A has a value of 10 units and points due east and vector B points due north. (a) What is the value of B, if the vector (A+B) points 30^0 north of East? (b) Find the value of the vector (A+B).

Solution: -

(a) $\tan \theta = B/A$ σ B = A tan θ

B = 10 units (tan 30^0) = 5.77 units

(b) $R = A + B = \sqrt{\{(10)^2 + (10 \tan 30^0)^2\}}$

$R = 10\sqrt{(1 + \tan^2 30^0)} = 11.547$ units

12) You are driving into a metropolis and in the distance you see the famous Gateway-to-the-arch. This monument rises to a height of 180m. You estimate your line of sight with the top of the arch to be 3^0 above the horizontal. Approximately how far (in km) are you from the base of the arch?

Solution: -

$\tan \theta$ = height/ base = h/ b

base = height/ $\tan\theta$ = 180m / $\tan 3^0$ = 3434.604604m

base = 3.4km

13) A highway is to be built between two towns, one of which lies 40km south and 80km west of the other. What is the shortest length of highway that can be built between the towns, and at what angle would the highway be directed with respect to due west?

Solution: -

$AB = \sqrt{[(40km)^2 + (80km)^2]} = \sqrt{[1600 + 6400]} = \sqrt{[8000km^2]}$

AB = 89.4 km

$\theta = \tan^{-1}(40/ 80) = \tan^{-1}(0.5) = 26.6^0$

$\theta = 26.6^0$ south of west

14) A chimpanzee sitting against his favorite tree gets up and walks 60m due east and 45m due south to reach a termite mound, where he eats his lunch. (a) What is the shortest distance between the tree and the termite mound? (b) What angle does the shortest distance make with respect to due west?

Solution: -

$R = [(60m)^2 + (45m)^2] = \sqrt{[3600 + 2025]} = \sqrt{[5625]} = 75m$

$\Rightarrow R = 75m$

$\theta = \tan^{-1}(45/ 60) = \tan^{-1}(0.75) = 36.86989765^0$

$\Rightarrow \theta = 37^0$ south of east

15) The x-vector component of a displacement vector r has a magnitude of 200m and points along the negative x-axis. The y-vector component has a magnitude of 250m and points along the negative y-axis. Find the magnitude and direction of r; specify the direction with respect to negative x-axis.

Solution: -

$r = \sqrt{[x^2 + y^2]}$

$r = \sqrt{[(200m)^2 + (250m)^2]}$

$r = \sqrt{[40000 + 62500]}$

"The Morning Echo"

$r = \sqrt{[102,500]}$

$r = 320.1562119m$

$\Rightarrow r = 320m$

$\theta = \tan^{-1}(y/x)$

$\theta = \tan^{-1}(250/200)$

$\theta = \tan^{-1}(1.25) = 51.34019175^0$

$\Rightarrow \theta = 51.3^0$ below the negative x-axis.

Miscellaneous: -

16) The x-component of a vector r is + 4m/s and the y-component of that same vector r is + 8 m/s. What is the magnitude and direction of vector r? Give the direction with respect to + x-axis.

Solution: -

$r = \sqrt{[x^2 + y^2]}$

$r = \sqrt{[(4\ m/s)^2 + (8\ m/s)^2]} = \sqrt{[16 + 64]} = \sqrt{[80]} = 8.94427191\ m/s$

$\Rightarrow r = 8.9\ m/s$

$\tan \theta = y/x = 8/4 = 2 \Rightarrow \theta = \tan^{-1}[2] = 63.4^0$

Hence $r = 8.9\ m/s$ and $\theta = 63.4^0$ are the magnitude and direction of the vector r.

Chapter No.2:

. . . .

Kinematics in One Dimension: -

Concepts: -

1) Displacement: - The displacement is a vector that points from the object's initial position to its final position and has a value that equals the shortest distance between the two positions.

$\Delta x = (x - x_0) =$ displacement

SI unit of displacement = meter or designated by (m)

2) Speed and Velocity: - The average speed is the distance travelled divided by the time required to cover the distance.

$\Rightarrow$ Average Speed = distance / elapsed time (m/s)

The average velocity is the displacement Δx divided by the elapsed time $\Delta t = t - t_0$

SI unit of average velocity is meters/second or (m/s)

$\overline{v} = (x - x_0)/ (t - t_0) = \Delta x/\Delta t$

Instantaneous Velocity: - The instantaneous velocity, "v", of an object in motion indicates how fast the object is moving and its direction of motion at each instant of time. The value of the instantaneous velocity is the instantaneous speed. If Δt, the time interval, is small enough the instantaneous velocity becomes approximately equal to the average velocity. In the limit Δt becomes infinitesimally small, the instantaneous velocity and average velocity become equal, so that: -

$v = \lim_{\Delta t \to 0} (\Delta x/\Delta t)$

In our discussion we will use the word velocity to mean instantaneous velocity and speed to mean instantaneous speed.

3) Acceleration: - Acceleration is defined as the rate at which the velocity is changing. It is a vector like velocity and force.

Average acceleration = Change in velocity/Elapsed time

$\overline{a} = (v - v_0)/ (t - t_0) = \Delta v/\Delta t$

Hence average acceleration $\overline{a}$ is a vector that points in the same direction as Δv, the change in velocity.

Instantaneous acceleration is the limiting case of the average acceleration when Δt approaches zero and is defined as follows: -

$a = \lim_{\Delta t \to 0} (\Delta v / \Delta t) = \bar{a}$

When Δt approaches zero in the limit given above, the instantaneous acceleration and average acceleration become equal. In our discussion we will use the word acceleration to mean instantaneous acceleration.

Equations of Kinematics for Constant Acceleration: - In the equations, $v = (v_0 + at)$ and $x = \frac{1}{2}(v + v_0) t$, there are five kinematic variables involved, viz. (1) x = displacement, (2) $a = \bar{a}$ = acceleration (constant), (3) v = final velocity at time t, (4) v_0 = initial velocity at time $t_0 = 0$ seconds, and (5) t = time elapsed since $t_0 = 0$ seconds.

The equations of kinematics for constant acceleration are as follows: -

1) $v = v_0 + at$
2) $x = \frac{1}{2}(v_0 + v) t$
3) $x = v_0 t + (\frac{1}{2})at^2$
4) $v^2 = v_0^2 + 2ax$

Freely Falling Bodies: - The idealized motion of an object falling from a height, in which air resistance is neglected and the acceleration is approximately constant, is known as free fall. Since the acceleration is constant in a free fall, the equations of kinematics can be used.

The acceleration of a freely falling body is called its acceleration due to gravity and its value without any algebraic sign is denoted by the symbol g. The acceleration due to gravity is directed downward towards the center of the earth. Near the surface of the earth, g is approximately $g = 9.8$ m/s^2.

In reality, however, g decreases with increasing altitude and varies slightly with latitude. The acceleration due to gravity on the surface of the moon is one sixth as large as that on the earth.

The equations of Kinematics for constant acceleration for freely falling bodies are as follows: -

1) $v = v_0 + gt$
2) $y = \frac{1}{2}(v + v_0) t$
3) $y = v_0 t + (\frac{1}{2}) gt^2$
4) $v^2 = v_0^2 + 2gy$

In these equations, the x-axis becomes the y-axis and the constant acceleration, "a", becomes the acceleration due to gravity, "g".

Kinematics in One Dimension: -
(2) Numerical Problems: -
Displacement, Speed, and Velocity: -
1) A whale swims due east for a distance of 7km, turns around and goes due west for 2km and finally turns around and heads 4km due east. (a) What is the total distance travelled by the whale? (b) What are the magnitude and direction of the displacement of the whale?
Solution: -
(a) S = total distance
S = 7km + 2km + 4km = 13km
(b) d = total displacement
d = 7km − 2km + 4km = 11km due east
2) A woman and her husband are out for a morning run to the river, which is located 5km away. The woman runs at 3m/s in a straight line. The husband runs back and forth at 5m/s between his wife and the river, until the wife reaches the river. What is the total distance run by the husband?
Solution: -
t = d/v = 5km/3m/s = 5000m/3m/s = 1.667 x 10^3 s
d = vt = 5m/s x 1.667 x 10^3 s = 8.333 x 10^3 m
⇒ d = 8.333 x 10^3m
Hence the total distance run by the husband is 8.333 km.
3) A plane is sitting on a runway, awaiting take off. On an adjacent parallel runway, another plane lands and passes the stationary plane at a speed of 55m/s. The arriving plane has a length of 50m. By looking out of a window (very narrow), a passenger on the stationary plane can see the moving plane. For how long a time is the plane visible?
Solution: -
t = d/v = 50m/55m/s = 0.909 seconds
⇒ t = 0.909 secs.
Hence the plane is visible for 0.909 seconds only.
4) A tourist being chased by an angry bear is running in a straight line towards his car at a speed of 5m/s. The car is a distance d away. The bear is 30m behind the tourist and running at 8m/s. The tourist reaches the car safely. What is the maximum possible value for d?
Solution: -
The speed of the tourist relative to the bear is given by the following: -
v` = 8m/s − 5m/s = 3m/s

$\Rightarrow t = d'/v' = 30m/3m/s = 10$ seconds

$d = vt = 5m/s \times 10s = 50m$

Hence the maximum possible value for d is 50m.

Acceleration: -

5) A motorcycle has a constant acceleration of $4m/s^2$. Both the velocity and acceleration of the motorcycle point in the same direction. How much time is required for the motorcycle to change its speed from (a) 15 to 40m/s and (b) 40 to 70m/s?

Solution: -

$v = v_0 + at \Rightarrow t = (v - v_0)/a$

a) $t = (40m/s - 15m/s)/4m/s^2 = 25m/s / 4m/s^2 = 6.25$ seconds.

b) $t = (70m/s - 40m/s)/ 4m/s^2 = 30m/s/ 4m/s^2 = 7.5$ seconds

Hence the answers are (a) $t = 6.25$ seconds and (b) $t = 7.5$ seconds.

6) A runner accelerates to a velocity of 6m/s due west in 2 secs. His average acceleration is $0.7m/s^2$, also directed due west. What was the velocity when he began accelerating?

Solution: -

$v = v_0 + at \Rightarrow v_0 = v - at$

$\Rightarrow v_0 = 6m/s - 0.7m/s^2 \times 2s = 6m/s - 1.4m/s = 4.6m/s$

Hence the velocity of the runner when he began accelerating has been 4.6m/s.

Equations of kinematics for constant acceleration, Application of the equations of kinematics: -

7) The speed ramp at an airport is basically a large conveyor belt on which you can stand and be moved along. The belt of one ramp moves at a constant speed such that a person who stands still on it, leaves the ramp 80 seconds after getting on. Jack is in a real hurry, however, and skips the speed ramp. Starting from rest with an acceleration of $0.4ms^{-2}$, he covers the same distance as the ramp does, but in one-fourth the time. What is the speed at which the belt of the ramp is moving?

Solution: -

$x = (\frac{1}{2}) at^2 = vt$

$x = (\frac{1}{2}) (0.4ms^{-2}) (80s/4)^2 = 80m$

$x = vt = 80m = v (80s)$

$v = 80m/ 80s = 1ms^{-1}$

Hence the speed at which the belt of the ramp is moving is $1 ms^{-1}$.

8) A car is travelling at a constant speed of 25m/s on a highway. At the instant this car passes an entrance ramp, a second car enters the highway from the ramp. The second car starts from rest and has a

constant acceleration. What acceleration must it maintain so that the two cars meet for the first time at the next exit which is 3km away?

Solution: -

$x = x_0 + vt = 3000m = 25m/s \times t(s)$

$\Rightarrow t = 3000/25 = 120 seconds$

$x = (1/2) at^2 \Rightarrow a = 2x/t^2$

$a = (2 \times 3000)/ (120)^2 = 6000/ (120)^2$

$a = 0.41666667 m/s^2$

Hence the second car must maintain an acceleration of 0.41666667m/s^2 if it wants to meet the first car for the first time at the next exit 3km away.

9) A train has a length of 100m and starts from rest with a constant acceleration at time t = 0 seconds. At this instant, a car just reaches the end of the train. The car is moving with a constant velocity. At a time t = 15 seconds, the car just reaches the front of the train. Ultimately, however, the train pulls ahead of the car and at t = 30 seconds, the car is again at the rear of the train. Find the value of (a) the car's velocity and (b) the train's acceleration.

Solution: -

(a) $v/2 = 100m / 15s \Rightarrow v = 200/15 = 13.3m/s$

$\Rightarrow v = 13.3m/s$

(b) acc. $= v/t = 13.3/15 = 0.88m/s^2$

$\Rightarrow a = 0.88m/s^2$

Hence (a) the car's velocity is 13.3m/s and (b) the train's acceleration is 0.88m/s^2

10) A jetliner, travelling northward, is landing with a speed of 70m/s. Once the jet touches down, it has 800m of runway, in which to reduce its speed to 7m/s. Compute the average acceleration of the plane during landing.

Solution: -

$v^2 - v_0^2 = 2\bar{a}x$

$\Rightarrow \bar{a} = (v^2 - v_0^2)/2x$

$\bar{a} = \{(7)^2 - (70)^2\}/ (2 \times 800)$

$\bar{a} = (49 - 4900)/1600$

$\bar{a} = - 4851/1600 = -3.03m/s^2$

$\Rightarrow \bar{a} = - 3.03m/s^2$ northward

Hence the average acceleration of the plane during landing has been computed and its value is – 3.03m/s^2.

Freely Falling Bodies: -

11) An astronaut on a distant planet wants to determine its acceleration due to gravity. The astronaut throws a rock straight up with a velocity of 21m/s and measures the time of 18 seconds before the rock returns to his hand. What is the acceleration due to gravity on this planet?

Solution: -

v = 21m/s

t = 18s/2 = 9s

$\Rightarrow$ v = v$_0$ + gt = 9g

v = 21m/s = 9g

$\Rightarrow$ g = 21m/s/9s = 2.33m/s^2

Hence the acceleration due to gravity on this planet is 2.33m/s^2 directed towards the center of this planet.

12) A stone is dropped from a sea cliff and the sound of it striking the ocean bed is heard 2 seconds later. How high is the cliff, assuming the speed of sound to be 343m/s?

Solution: -

h = (1/2) gt^2 and t = (2 – h/343) s

$\Rightarrow$ h = (1/2) g (2 – h/343)^2

h = (1/2) g {4 + h^2/ (343)^2 – 4h/343}

h = 2g + gh^2/2(343)^2 – 2gh/343 = h

$\Rightarrow$ h^2 – 4(343) h – 2(343)^{2}h/g + 4(343)^2 = 0

$\Rightarrow$ h^2 – 1372h – 24010h + 470596 =0

h^2 – 25382h + 470596 = 0

Now this is a quadratic equation in h and therefore it can be solved for h. The value thus found comes out to be 18.55m or approximately 18.6m. It is left as an exercise for the student to solve.

$\Rightarrow$ h = 18.55m

13) A ball is thrown straight upward and rises to a maximum height of 9m above its launch point. At what height above its launch point has the speed of the ball decreased to one third of its initial value?

Solution: -

v = $\sqrt{}$(2gh) = $\sqrt{}$(2x9.8x9) = $\sqrt{}$(176.4) = 13.28156617m/s

$\Rightarrow$ v = 13.28m/s

v^2 – v$_0$^{2} = 2gh

v^2 – (v/3)^2 = v^2 – v^2/9 = 2gh

8v^2/9 = 2gh

h = 8v^2/18g = 8 x (13.28)^2/18g = 7.99m

h = 7.99m

Hence it will rise to a height of 7.99m above its launch point when its speed has decreased to one third of its initial value.

14) A woman on a bridge 80m high sees a raft floating at a constant speed on the river below. She drops a stone from rest in an attempt to hit the raft. The stone is released when the raft has 8m more to travel before passing under the bridge. The stone hits the water 5m in front of the raft. Find the speed of the raft.

Solution: -

$v = (8 - 5)/t = 3/t$

$t = \sqrt{(2h/9.8)} = \sqrt{(2 \times 80/9.8)}$

$v = 3/t = 3\sqrt{(9.8/160)} = \sqrt{(9 \times 9.8/160)}$

$v = \sqrt{(88.2/160)}$

$v = \sqrt{(0.55125)}$

$v = 0.74246212 m/s$

$v = 0.742 m/s$

Therefore the speed of the mentioned raft is $v = 0.742 m/s$.

15) Two identical pallet guns are fired simultaneously from the edge of a cliff. These guns impart an initial speed of 20m/s to each pallet. Gun A is fired straight upward, with the pallet going up and then falling back down, eventually hitting the ground beneath the cliff. Gun B is fired straight downward. In the absence of air resistance, how long after pallet B hits the ground does pallet A hit the ground?

Solution: - The time it takes for the pallet A to return to the level of the cliff is how long it will take for pallet A to hit the ground after pallet B has already hit the ground.

$v^2 - v_0^2 = 2gh$

$(20)^2 - (0)^2 = (20)^2 = 2gh$

$\Rightarrow h = (20)^2/2g = 20.40816327 m$

$h = (1/2) gt^2 \Rightarrow t = \sqrt{(2h/g)} = \sqrt{(2 \times 20.4040816327 /9.8)}$

$\Rightarrow t = 2.040816327$

$\Rightarrow t` = 2t = 2 \times 2.040816327 = 4.081632653$ seconds

Hence the required time $t` = 4.081632653$ seconds.

Miscellaneous: -

16) A stone is dropped from the top of a cliff and it takes 3 seconds for it to hit the ground below. Determine the height of the cliff.

Solution: -

$h = (1/2) gt^2$

$\Rightarrow h = (1/2) (9.8 m/s^2) (3 s)^2 = 44.1 m$

$\Rightarrow h = 44.1 m$

Hence the height of the cliff has been determined to be 44.1 m.

Chapter No.3

· ·

Kinematics in Two Dimensions: -

Concepts: -

Displacement, Velocity and Acceleration: - The displacement has been defined in Chapter No.2 along x and y axes. The displacement vector, however, may lie anywhere in the plane.

Displacement $= \Delta r = r - r_0$

The average velocity of a moving object is a vector and may lie anywhere in the x-y plane.

$\bar{v} = (r - r_0)/ (t - t_0) = \Delta r/\Delta t$

The velocity of a moving object at an instant of time is its instantaneous velocity. The average velocity becomes equal to the instantaneous velocity, "v", in the limit that Δt becomes infinitesimally small and approaches zero.

$v = \text{Lim}_{\Delta_t \to 0} (\Delta r/\Delta t)$

The average acceleration, "$\bar{a}$", is defined as the change in velocity divided by the elapsed time.

$\bar{a} = (v - v_0)/ (t - t_0) = \Delta v/\Delta t$

The average acceleration, "$\bar{a}$", becomes equal to the instantaneous acceleration, "a", when Δt becomes infinitesimally small.

$a = \text{Lim}_{\Delta_t \to 0} (\Delta v/\Delta t)$

The acceleration may have a vector component, "a_x", along the x-direction and a vector component, "a_y", along the y-direction.

Equation of Kinematics in Two Dimensions: -

For the motion in two dimensions, we may have x and y components of the vector variable and these may have positive or negative signs. The x and y components are scalars and comprise five kinematic variables.

Serial Number: Variable (x and y components): -

1) Displacement: -

x - Component: - x

y - Component: - y

2) Acceleration: -

x - Component: - a_x

y - Component: - a_y

3) Final Velocity: -

x - Component: - v_x

y - Component: - v_y 4) Initial Velocity: -

x - Component: - v_{ox}

y - Component: - v_{oy}

5) Elapsed Time: -

x - Component: - t

y - Component: - t

The following are the equations of kinematics for constant acceleration in two dimensions: -

$\Rightarrow$ For the x-component we may have the following equations: -

1) $v_x = v_{ox} + a_x t$

2) $x = (\frac{1}{2})(v_{ox} + v_x) t$

3) $x = v_{ox} t + (1/2) a_x t^2$

4) $v_x^2 = v_{ox}^2 + 2a_x x$

$\Rightarrow$ For the y-component we may have the following equations: -

1) $v_y = v_{oy} + a_y t$

2) $y = (1/2)(v_{oy} + v_y)t$

3) $y = v_{oy} t + (1/2)a_y t^2$

4) $v_y^2 = v_{oy}^2 + 2a_y y$

Projectile Motion: -

A projectile is like a cannon ball that has been fired. The path followed by a projectile is called its trajectory which is a parabolic path. The following is a brief discussion on the various parameters encountered in the study of the motion of a projectile.

a) The fall time of a projectile can be calculated as follows: -

$y = v_{oy} t + (1/2) a_y t^2$

$\Rightarrow t = \sqrt{(2y/ a_y)}$ where $v_{oy} = 0$ m/s

b) The velocity of a projectile is determined from the equations which are given below: -

$v_y = v_{oy} + a_y t$

$v = \sqrt{(v_x^2 + v_y^2)}$

$\theta = \cos^{-1}(v_x/v)$

c) The height of a projectile is calculated as follows: -

$v_{oy} = v_o \sin\theta$

$y = H = (v_y^2 - v_{oy}^2)/2a_y$

d) The time of flight of a projectile is determined from the equations which are given below: -

$y = v_{oy}t + (1/2) a_y t^2 \Rightarrow y = 0$

$v_{oy}t = (1/2) a_y t^2$

$\Rightarrow t = 2v_{oy}/a_y$

e) The range of a projectile is measured as follows: -

$v_{ox} = v_o \cos\theta = v_x$

$x = R = v_x t = v_{ox} t$

f) The final parameters can be used to calculate initial parameters from the same kind of equations that we have already given, viz.

$v_o = \sqrt{(v_{ox}^2 + v_{oy}^2)} \quad \theta = \tan^{-1}(v_{oy}/v_{ox})$

$v_{ox} = v_x = v_o \cos\theta$

$v_y^2 = v_{oy}^2 + 2a_y y$ or $v_{oy} = \sqrt{(v_y^2 - 2a_y y)}$

There are two ways of throwing an object from a cliff. It can be thrown either with an angle θ above the horizontal or with the same angle θ below the horizontal. In any case it will strike the ground beneath with the same velocity.

Relative Velocity: -

Along one direction, the relative velocity can be understood by the equation: -

$v_{AB} = v_{AC} + v_{CB}$

Along perpendicular directions the relative velocity, "v_{AB}" is given by the equation of Pythagoras as follows: -

$v_{AB} = \sqrt{(v_{AC}^2 + v_{CB}^2)}$

$\theta = \tan^{-1}(v_{CB}/v_{AC})$

Note, "v_{CB}" is the velocity along the vertical direction and, "v_{AC}" is the velocity along the horizontal direction. Note also while the velocity of object A relative to object B is v_{AB} that of object B relative to object A is $v_{BA} = -v_{AB}$.

Kinematics in Two Dimensions: -

(3) Numerical Problems: -

Displacement, Velocity, and Acceleration: -

1) In diving to a depth of 800m, an elephant seal also moves 500m due east of his starting point. What is the value of the seal's displacement?

Solution: -

$R = \sqrt{(x^2 + y^2)} = \sqrt{[(500)^2 + (-800)^2]}$

$R = \sqrt{890000} \Rightarrow R = 9.43 \times 10^2$ m

2) A jetliner is moving at a speed of 300m/s. The vertical component of the plane's velocity is 50m/s. What is the value of the horizontal component of the plane's velocity?

Solution: -

$v^2 = \sqrt{(v_x^2 + v_y^2)} \Rightarrow v_x = \sqrt{(v^2 - v_y^2)}$

$v_x = \sqrt{[(300m/s)^2 - (50m/s)^2]} = \sqrt{87500} = 295.8m/s$

$\Rightarrow v_x = 295.8m/s$

3) A dolphin leaps out of the water at an angle of 40^0 above the horizontal. The horizontal component of the dolphin's velocity is 8.8m/s. Find the value of the vertical component of the velocity.

Solution: -

$v_x = v \cos\theta \Rightarrow v = v_x/\cos\theta = (8.8m/s)/\cos40^0$

$v_y = v \sin\theta = [(8.8/\cos40^0] \sin40^0 = 8.8 \tan40^0 \Rightarrow v_y = 7.38m/s$

4) An object moves around a circular orbit of radius 2×10^{10}m. It moves ¼ of the circumference of this great circle in a period of 8×10^5 seconds. (a) What is the average speed of this object for the given period? (b) What is the value of the average velocity of the object during this period?

Solution: -

(a) Average Speed = distance/time

$\overline{S} = (C/4)/t = (1/4) (2\pi \times 2\times10^{10}m)/ (8\times10^5s) \Rightarrow S = 3.9\times10^4m/s$

(b) Average Velocity = displacement/time

$\overline{V} = \sqrt{(R^2 + R^2)}/t = R (\sqrt{2})/t = (2\times10^{10}m) (\sqrt{2})/ (8\times10^5s)$

$\Rightarrow \overline{V} = 3.5\times10^4m/s$

Equation of Kinematics in Two Dimensions, Projectile Motion: -

5) A tennis ball is struck such that it leaves the racket horizontally with a speed of 30m/s. The ball hits the court at a horizontal distance of 20m from the racket. What is the height of the tennis ball when it leaves the racket?

Solution: -

$v_{ox} = 30m/s$, $x = 20m$, $h = ?$

$x = v_{ox}t = v_x t \Rightarrow t = x/v_{ox}$

$t = 20m/30m/s = (2/3) s = 0.66666s$

$h = (½) gt^2 = (1/2) \times 9.8m/s^2 \times (0.66666s)^2 = 2.177m$

$\Rightarrow$ h = 2.177m

6) A diver runs horizontally with a speed of 2m/s off a platform that is 8m above the water. What is his speed just before striking the water?

Solution: -

$v_y = \sqrt{(2gh)} = \sqrt{(2 \times 9.8 \times 8)} = \sqrt{(156.8)} = 12.52198067$

$v = \sqrt{(v_x^2 + v_y^2)} = \sqrt{[(2)^2 + (12.52198067)^2]} = \sqrt{(4 + 156.8)}$

$v = \sqrt{(160.8)} = 12.68$m/s

$\Rightarrow$ v = 12.68m/s

7) A horizontal rifle is fired at a bull's eye. The muzzle speed of the bullet is 700m/s. The barrel is pointed directly at the center of the bull's eye but the bullet strikes the target 0.015m below the center. What is the horizontal distance between the end of the rifle and the bull's eye?

Solution: -

h = (½) gt² = 0.015m

t = $\sqrt{(2h/g)}$ = $\sqrt{[(2 \times 0.015)/9.8]}$ = $\sqrt{(0.003061224)}$

$\Rightarrow$ t = 0.055328334s

x = R = v_xt = (700m/s) (0.055328334s) = 38.72983346m

$\Rightarrow$ x = 38.7m

8) An Olympic long jumper leaves the ground at an angle of 30⁰ and travels through the air for a horizontal distance of 9m before landing. What is the take off speed of the jumper?

Solution: -

x = 9m,

y = x tanθ = 9 tan 30⁰ = (1/2) gt²

$\Rightarrow$ t = $\sqrt{[(2 \times 9 \tan 30^0)/9.8]}$ = 1.02977632s

d = $\sqrt{(x^2 + y^2)}$ = $\sqrt{[(9m)^2 + (9\tan 30^0)^2]}$ = $9\sqrt{(1 + \tan^2 30^0)}$

$\Rightarrow$ d = 10.39230485m

v = d/t = 10.39230485m/1.02977632s = 10.09180795m/s

$\Rightarrow$ v = 10.09m/s

Therefore the take off speed of the Olympic jumper, when he leaves the ground, is 10.09 m/s.

9) The two stones have identical initial speeds of v_0 = 14m/s and are thrown at an angle θ = 40⁰, one below and one above the horizontal. What is the distance between the two points where the two stones strike the ground?

Solution: -

h = (½) gt² = $v_y^2/2g$ = $(v_0 \sin θ)^2/2g$ = $(14 \sin 40^0)^2/(2 \times 9.8)$

$\Rightarrow$ h = 4.131759112m

$t = \sqrt{(2h/g)} = \sqrt{(2 \times 4.131759112/9.8)} = 0.918268014s$

$\Rightarrow t` = 2t = 2 \times 0.918268014 = 1.836536028s$

$v_x = v \cos\theta = 14 \cos40^0 = 10.7246222m/s$

$x = v_x t` = 10.7246222m/s \times 1.836536028s = 19.69615506m$

$\Rightarrow x = 19.696m$

Therefore the distance between the two points where the two stones strike the ground is x = 19.696m.

10) An eagle is flying horizontally at 7m/s with a fish in its claws. It accidentally drops the fish. (a) How much time passes before the fish's speed triples? (b) How much additional time would be required for the fish's speed to triple again?

Solution: -

(a) $v = \sqrt{[(3 \times 7)^2 - (7)^2]} = \sqrt{(441 - 49)} = \sqrt{(392)}$

$v = 19.79898987m/s = 19.8m/s$

$t = v/g = 19.79898987m/s /9.8m/s^2 = 2.020305089s$

$\Rightarrow t = 2.02s$

(b) $v = \sqrt{[(3 \times 21)^2 - (7)^2]} = \sqrt{(3969 - 49)} = \sqrt{(3920)}$

$v = 62.60990337m/s$

$t` = v/g = 62.60990337m/s /9.8m/s^2 = 6.38876565s$

$t`` = t` - t = 6.38876565 - 2.020305089 = 4.368460561s$

$\Rightarrow t`` = 4.368s$

11) A fire hose rejects a stream of water at an angle of 40^0 above the horizontal. The water leaves the nozzle with a speed of 30m/s. Assuming that the water behaves like a projectile, how far from a building should the fire hose be located to hit the highest possible fire?

Solution: -

$h = v_y^2/2g = (v \sin\theta)^2/2g = (30\sin40^0)^2/2g$

$\Rightarrow h = 18.97236327m$

$h = (½) gt^2 \Rightarrow t = \sqrt{(2h/g)}$

$t = \sqrt{[2(30\sin40^0)^2/2g^2]} = 30\sin40^0/g = 19.28362829/9.8$

$\Rightarrow t = 1.967717173s$

$v_x = v \cos\theta = 30\cos40^0 = 22.98133329m/s$

$x = R = v_x t = 22.98133329m/s \times 1.967717173s = 45.22076418m$

$\Rightarrow x = R = 45m$

12) Suppose a ball is kicked on the moon where the acceleration due to gravity is one sixth that on earth. If the velocity of the ball is v_0 = 30m/s and the angle above the horizontal is 30^0 find (a) the height of the ball and (b) the range of the ball.

Solution: -

(a) $h = v^2/2g = (30\sin30^0)^2/2g = (30\sin30^0)^2/ (2g/6)$
$h = 68.87755102m$
$\Rightarrow h = 68.877m$
(b) $x = v_x t = R = (v_0\cos\theta)t$
$v_x = v_0\cos\theta = 30\cos30^0 = 25.98076211m/s$
$t = \sqrt{(2h/g)} = \sqrt{[(2x68.87755102)/9.8]} = 3.749218994s$
$x = v_x t = 25.98x3.749 = 97.40756678m$
$\Rightarrow x = R = 97.4m$
Therefore (a) the height of the ball is 68.877m and (b) the range of the ball is 97.4m respectively.

Relative Velocity: -

13) Two passenger trains are passing each other on adjacent tracks. Train A is moving east with a speed of 15m/s and train B is travelling west with a speed of 30m/s. (a) What is the velocity of train A as seen by passengers in train B? (b) What is the velocity of train B as seen by passengers in train A?

Solution: -

(a) Train A as seen by passengers in train B: -
$V_{WE} = V_W + V_E = 30m/s + 15m/s = 45m/s$ due east.
(b) Train B as seen by passengers in train A: -
$V_{EW} = V_E + V_W = 15m/s + 30m/s = 45m/s$ due west.

14) At some airports there are speed ramps to help passengers get from one place to another. A speed ramp is a moving conveyor belt that you can either stand or walk on. Suppose a speed ramp has a length of 200m and is moving at a speed of 3m/s relative to the ground. In addition, suppose you can cover this distance in 100s when walking on ground. If you walk at the same rate with respect to the speed ramp that you walk with respect to the ground, how long does it take for you to travel the 200m using the speed ramp?

Solution: -

$V_{PG} = V_{PR} + V_{RG}$
Note that V_{PG} is the velocity of the person with respect to the ground, V_{PR} is the velocity of the person with respect to the ramp, and V_{RG} is the velocity of the ramp with respect to the ground.
$\Rightarrow V_{PR} = $ Length/time $= 200m/100s = 2m/s$ and $V_{RG} = 3m/s$
$\Rightarrow V_{PG} = V_{PR} + V_{RG} = 2m/s + 3m/s = 5m/s$
$\Rightarrow t = $ Length/$V_{PG} = 200m/5m/s = 40s$
Hence it takes, for that person, 40 seconds to travel 200m using the speed ramp.

15) A swimmer capable of swimming at a speed of 2m/s in still water (i.e. the swimmer can swim with a speed of 2m/s relative to the water), starts to swim directly across a 3km wide river. However, the current is 1m/s and it carries the swimmer downstream. (a) How long does it take the swimmer to cross the river? (b) How far downstream will the swimmer be upon reaching the other side of the river?

Solution: -

(a) t = distance/velocity = 3000m/2m/s = 1500 seconds

$\Rightarrow$ t = 1.5x10^3 seconds

(b) s = vt = 1m/s x 1500s = 1500m

$\Rightarrow$ s = 1.5x10^{3}m

Hence it takes 1500s for the swimmer to cross the river and he is 1500m downstream upon reaching the other side of the river

Chapter No.4

· ·

Forces and Newton's Laws of Motion: -
Isaac Newton developed three important laws of motion that pertain to force and mass, known as, "Newton's Laws of Motion". These are discussed as follows: -
Newton's First Law of Motion: -
An object continues in a state of rest or in a state of motion at a constant speed along a straight line, unless compelled to change that state by a net force.

Several forces may act simultaneously on an object and the net force is the vector sum of them all. "Newton's First Law of Motion" is also called, "The Law of Inertia".

Definition of Inertia and Mass: - Inertia is the natural tendency of an object to remain at rest or in motion at a constant speed along a straight line. The mass of an object is a quantitative measure of inertia.

SI unit of Inertia and Mass: kilogram (kg).

Definition of an Inertial Reference Frame: - An inertial reference frame is one in which Newton's Laws of Motion are valid. The acceleration of an inertial reference frame is zero, so it moves with a constant velocity. Earth, itself, is a good approximation of an inertial reference frame. Hence all of Newton's Laws of Motion are valid in an Inertial Reference Frame.

Newton's Second Law of Motion: -
When a net external force Σ F acts on an object of mass m, the acceleration, "a", that results is directly proportional to the net force and has a value that is inversely proportional to the mass. The direction of the acceleration is the same as the direction of the net force.

$a = \Sigma F / m$

OR

$\Sigma F = ma$

SI Unit of Force: - kgm/s^2 = newton (N)

The net forces are external forces that the environment exerts on an object and the internal forces are those that one part of the object exerts on the other part of the object. The external force in Newton's Second Law of Motion may have a vector component in the x and y directions.

$$\Rightarrow \Sigma F_x = ma_x$$
$$\& \Sigma F_y = ma_y$$

Newton's Third Law of Motion: -

Whenever one body exerts a force on a second body, the second body exerts an oppositely directed force of equal value on the first body.

Hence three fundamental forces have been discovered viz. (1) Gravitational Force, (2) Strong Nuclear Force, and (3) Electroweak Force.

Newton's Law of Universal Gravitation: -

For two particles that have masses m_1 and m_2 and are separated by a distance r, the force that each exerts on the other is directed along the line joining the particles and has a value given by: -

$$F = G\, m_1 m_2 / r^2$$

The symbol G denotes the Universal Gravitational Constant, whose value is found experimentally to be: -

$$G = 6.673 \times 10^{-11} \text{ N-m}^2/\text{kg}^2$$

These are called the gravitational forces of action and reaction and are oppositely directed.

Definition of Weight: - The weight of an object on or above the earth is the gravitational force that the earth exerts on the object. The weight always acts downwards towards the center of the earth. On or above another astronomical body, the weight is the gravitational force exerted on the object by that body.

$$W = G\, M_E\, m / r^2 = mg$$
$$\Rightarrow g = G\, M_E / r^2$$

SI Unit of Weight: newton (N)

Definition of the Normal Force: - The Normal Force F_N is one component of the force that a surface exerts on an object with which it is in contact – namely, the component that is perpendicular to the surface.

Apparent Weight and True Weight: - Suppose a man is moving in an elevator. This implies his weight W = mg acts downward and the normal force perpendicular to the platform acts upward.

$\Rightarrow \Sigma F_y = +F_N - mg = ma_y$

$\Rightarrow F_N = mg + ma_y$

Apparent Weight = True Weight + mass x acceleration(y)

If the elevator accelerates upward, the acceleration, "a_y", is positive and apparent weight is greater than the true weight and if the elevator accelerates downward, the acceleration, "a_y", is negative and the apparent weight is less than the true weight.

Static Frictional Force: -

The magnitude f_s of the static frictional force can have any value from zero up to a maximum value of f_s^{MAX}, depending on the applied force. In other words, $f_s \leq f_s^{MAX}$ where the symbol " $\leq$ " is read "less than or equal to". The equality holds only when f_s attain its maximum value, which is: -

$F_s^{MAX} = \mu_s F_N$

Note that μ_s is the coefficient of static friction and F_N is the normal force.

Kinetic Frictional Force: -

The magnitude F_k of the kinetic frictional force is given by: -

$F_k = \mu_k F_N$

Note that μ_k is the coefficient of kinetic friction and F_N is the normal force.

The Tension Force: - The force of tension, "T", in the rope that is being pulled apart is not needed to accelerate the rope because the rope is idealized as a mass less rope. $\Sigma F = ma$, where m = 0 kg.

Hence the force, "T", is applied undiminished to the object attached to the other end of the rope.

Definition of Equilibrium: - An object is in equilibrium when it has zero acceleration.

$\Rightarrow$ The x and y components of the acceleration of an object in equilibrium must also be zero.

$\Sigma F_x = ma_x = 0$ N $a_x = 0$ m/s^2

$\Sigma F_y = ma_y = 0$ N $a_y = 0$ m/s^2

The forces acting on an object in equilibrium must balance each other.

"The Morning Echo"

For non-equilibrium applications of Newton's Laws of Motion, the net force is not equal to zero, the acceleration is not equal to zero, and the x and y components of the net force are not equal to zero. The non-equilibrium forces do not balance each other.

Forces and Newton's Laws of Motion: -
(4) Numerical Problems: -
Newton's Laws of Motion: -
1) An airplane has a mass of 4.2×10^5 kg and takes off under the influence of a constant net force of 5.3×10^5 N. What is the net force that acts on the plane's 80 kg pilot?
Solution: -
$F = ma = 4.2 \times 10^5$ kg x a $= 5.3 \times 10^5$ N
$\Rightarrow a = F/m = 5.3 \times 10^5$ N$/4.2 \times 10^5$ kg $= 1.261904762$ m/s^2
$F_{net} = m_{pilot}$ a $= 80$ kg x 1.261904762 m/s$^2 = 100.952381$ N
$\Rightarrow F_{net} = 100.95$ N
2) Two forces F_A and F_B are applied to an object whose mass is 9 kg. The larger force is F_A. When both forces point due east, the object's acceleration has a value of 0.6 m/s^2. However when F_A points due east and F_B points due west, the acceleration is 0.5 m/s^2 due east. Find the values of (a) F_A and (b) F_B.
Solution: -
(a) $a_A + a_B = 0.6$ m/s^2 due east
$a_A - a_B = 0.5$ m/s^2 due west
$a_A = (0.6 + 0.5)/2 = 1.1/2 = 0.55$ m/s^2
$a_B = 0.6 - 0.55 = 0.05$ m/s^2
$\Rightarrow F_A = ma_A = 9$ kg x 0.55 m/s$^2 = 4.95$ N due east
(b) $F_B = ma_B = 9$ kg x 0.05 m/s$^2 = 0.45$ N due west
$\Rightarrow$ (a) $F_A = 4.95$ N and (b) $F_B = 0.45$ N
The Vector Nature of Newton's Second Law of Motion, Newton's Third Law of Motion: -
3) A duck has a mass of 3 kg. As the duck paddles a force of 0.2 N acts on it, in a direction due east. In addition, the current of the water exerts a force of 0.3 N in a direction of 40^0 South of East. When these forces begin to act, the velocity of the duck is 0.22 m/s in a direction due east. Find the magnitude and direction (relative to due east) of the displacement that the duck undergoes in 2 seconds while the forces are acting.

Solution: -

$x = vt + (1/2) a_1t^2 + (1/2) a_2t^2$

$x = 0.22$ m/s x 2s + ½(0.2 N/3 kg)(2s)^2 + ½(0.3 N cos40^0/3 kg)(2)^2

$x = 0.44$m + 0.133333333m + 0.153208889m

$\Rightarrow x = 0.726542222$m

$y = (1/2) a_yt^2$ = ½(0.3 N sin40^0/3 kg)(2s)^2

$\Rightarrow y = 0.128557522$m

$d = \sqrt{(x^2 + y^2)} = \sqrt{[(0.726542222m)^2 + (0.128557522m)^2]}$

$d = \sqrt{(0.5278636 + 0.016527036)} = \sqrt{(0.544390636)}$

$d = 0.737828324$

$\Rightarrow d = 0.7378$m

$\theta = \tan^{-1} (y/x) = \tan^{-1} (0.128557522/0.726542222)$

$\theta = \tan^{-1} (0.176944324) = 10.03^0$

$\Rightarrow \theta = 10.03^0$ South of East

4) Only two forces act on an object (mass = 4 kg). One force F_1 = 50 N acts in a direction due east and the other force F_2 = 70 N acts at an angle θ = 50^0 North of East. Find the magnitude and direction (relative to the x-axis) of the acceleration of the object.

Solution: -

$F_x = 50$ N + 70cos 50^0 N = 94.99513268 N

$F_y = 70$sin 50^0 N = 53.62311102 N

$F = \sqrt{(F_x^2 + F_y^2)} = \sqrt{[(94.99513268N)^2 + (53.62311102N)^2]}$

$F = \sqrt{(9024.075233 + 2875.438035)} = \sqrt{(11899.51327)}$

$F = 109.0848902$ N

$\Rightarrow a = F/m = 109.0848902N/4kg = 27.27122255$m/s^2

$\Rightarrow a = 27.27$ m/s^2

$\theta = \tan^{-1} (F_y/F_x) = \tan^{-1} (53.62311102/94.99513268)$

$\Rightarrow \theta = \tan^{-1} (0.564482721) = 29.4^0$

The Gravitational Force: -

5) On earth, two parts of a space probe weigh 49000 N and 9800 N. These parts are separated by a center to center distance of 10m and may be treated as uniform spherical objects. Find the magnitude of the gravitational force that each part exerts on the other out there in space, far from any other objects.

Solution: -

$m_1 = 49000/9.8 = 5000$ kg

$m_2 = 9800/9.8 = 1000$ kg

$\Rightarrow F = Gm_1m_2/R^2$

$F = 6.673x10^{-11}$N-m^2/kg^2 x (5000kg)(1000kg)/(10m)^2

$\Rightarrow F = 3.3 \times 10^{-6} N$

6) A space traveler whose mass is 160 kg leaves earth. What are his weight and mass (a) on earth and (b) in interplanetary space where there are no nearby planetary objects?

Solution: -

(a) m = 160 kg, W = 160kg x 9.8 m/s² = 1568 N

(b) m = 160 kg, W = 160 kg x 0 m/s² = 0 N

7) The mass of a robot is 6000kg. This robot weighs 4000N more on planet A than it does on planet B. Both planets have the same radius of 2.8×10^6 m. What is the difference $(M_A - M_B)$ in the masses of these planets?

Solution: -

$\Delta W = G \, [6000kg/(2.8 \times 10^6)^2](M_A - M_B) = 4000N$

$M_A - M_B = 4000N \times (2.8 \times 10^6)^2/(6.673 \times 10^{-11} N\text{-}m^2/kg^2)(6000kg)$

$M_A - M_B = 0.7832559069 \times 10^{23} kg$

$M_A - M_B = 7.832559069 \times 10^{22} kg$

$\Rightarrow$ The difference $(M_A - M_B)$ between the masses of these planets has been calculated and this value is given below: -

$(M_A - M_B) = 7.8 \times 10^{22} \, kg$

8) A planet has a mass of 7×10^{19} kg and a radius of 0.45×10^5 m. (a) What is the acceleration due to gravity on this planet? (b) How much would a 70 kg person weigh on this planet?

Solution: -

(a) $g = G \, M/R^2 = 6.673 \times 10^{-11} N\text{-}m^2/kg^2 \times 7 \times 10^{19} kg/(0.45 \times 10^5 m)^2$

$\Rightarrow g = 2.306716049 m/s^2 = 2.3067 m/s^2$

$\Rightarrow g = 2.3067 \, m/s^2$

(b) W = mg = 70kg x 2.306716049m/s²

$W = 161.4701235 m/s^2$

$\Rightarrow W = 161.47 \, N$

9) Several people are riding in a hot air balloon. The combined mass of the balloon and the people is 400kg. The balloon is motionless in the air because the downward-acting weight of the balloon and the people is balanced by an upward-acting "buoyant" force. If the buoyant force remains constant, how much mass should be dropped overboard so that the balloon acquires an upward acceleration of 0.2 m/s²

Solution: -

$m_1 = 400 \, kg = $ (mass of people and the balloon)

$a = 0.2 \, m/s^2$

$\Rightarrow m_1(g - a) = m_2 g$

$\Rightarrow$ 400kg (9.8 – 0.2) m/s^2 = m$_2$ x 9.8m/s^2

$\Rightarrow$ m$_2$ = 400 kg x 9.6 m/s^2 / 9.8 m/s^2

m$_2$ = 391.8367347 kg

$\Rightarrow$ M = m$_1$ – m$_2$ = 400kg – 391.8367347kg

M = 8.163265306 kg

$\Rightarrow$ M = 8.16 kg

Hence a mass equal to 8.16 kg should be dropped overboard in order for the people and the balloon to acquire an upward acceleration of 0.2 m/s^2

10) At a distance H above the surface of a planet, the true weight of a remote probe is two per cent less than its true weight on the surface. The radius of the planet is R. Find the ratio H/R.

Solution: -

F = G Mm/R^2

0.98F = G Mm/(R+H)^2

(R+H)^2 / R^2 = F/0.98F = 1.020408163

(R+H)/R = $\sqrt{}$(1.020408163) = 1.010152545

1+H/R = 1.010152545

$\Rightarrow$ H/R = 0.01

The Normal Force, Static and Kinetic Frictional Forces: -

11) A rocket blasts off from rest and attains a speed of 50m/s in 10s. An astronaut has a mass of 60 kg. What is the astronaut's apparent weight during takeoff?

Solution: -

v$_0$ = 0m/s, v = 50m/s, t = 10s, and m = 60kg

$\Rightarrow$ a = (v – v$_0$)/t = [(50 – 0)/10] m/s^2 = 5m/s^2

a = g + a = 9.8m/s^2 + 5m/s^2 = 14.8m/s^2

W$_{Apparent}$ = m (g + a) = 60kg x 14.8m/s^2

$\Rightarrow$ W$_{Apparent}$ = 888 N

12) A block whose weight is 50N rests on a horizontal table. A horizontal force of 40N is applied to the block. The coefficients of static and kinetic frictions are 0.74 and 0.53 respectively. Will the block move under the influence of the applied force, and if so, what will be the block's acceleration? Explain your reason.

Solution: -

m = F/a = W/a =50N/9.8m/s^2 = 5.102040816 kg

F$_s$ = μ_sF$_N$ = 0.74x50N = 37N

$\Rightarrow$ The force of static friction of 37N is less than the applied force of 40N. Hence the block will move under the influence of this force.

$F_k = \mu_k F_N = 0.53 \times 50N = 26.5N$

$a = F/m = (40 - 26.5)N/5.102040816kg$

$a = 13.5N/5.102040816kg$

$\Rightarrow a = 2.646m/s^2$

The Tension Force, Equilibrium Application of Newton's Laws of Motion: -

13) A supertanker (mass = $2 \times 10^9 kg$) is moving with a constant velocity. Its engines generate a forward thrust of $8 \times 10^6 N$. Determine (a) the magnitude of the resistive force exerted on the tanker by the water, and (b) the magnitude of the upward buoyant force exerted on the tanker by the water.

Solution: -

(a) The resistive force exerted on the tanker by the water: -

$F_{resistive} = 8 \times 10^6 N$.

(b) The buoyant force exerted on the tanker by the water: -

$F_{buoyant} = mg = 2 \times 10^9 kg \times 9.8m/s^2$

$F_{buoyant} = 1.96 \times 10^{10} N$

Miscellaneous: -

14) The coefficient of kinetic friction between an 18 kg crate and the floor is 0.40. What horizontal force is required to move the crate at a steady speed across the floor? What horizontal force is required if μ_k is zero?

Solution: -

a) $F = \mu_k F_N = \mu_k m (g\cos\theta)$

Now $\theta = 0^0$ (because the floor is horizontal)

$\Rightarrow F = \mu_k mg$

$F = 0.4 \times 18 kg \times 9.8ms^{-2} = 70.56N$

(b) $F = \mu_k F_N = \mu_k m (g\cos\theta)$

Now $\mu_k = 0$ and $\theta = 0^0$ (because the floor is horizontal)

$\Rightarrow F = 0N$

15) A 20 kg box is released on a 25^0 incline and accelerates down the incline at $0.4m/s^2$. Find the friction force impeding its motion. How large is the coefficient of friction?

Solution: -

a) $F = m (g \sin\theta - a)$

$\Rightarrow F = 20kg (9.8m/s^2 \sin25^0 - 0.4m/s^2)$

$F = 20kg (4.141658965 - 0.4)ms^{-2}$

$F = 20kg \times 3.741658965ms^{-2} = 74.8331793N$

$\Rightarrow$ F =74.8N

b) F = m (g sinθ - a) = μ_k mg cosθ

$\Rightarrow \mu_k$ = F/mg cosθ = 74.8331793N/ [20kg x 9.8ms^{-2} x cos25^0]

$\Rightarrow \mu_k$ = 74.8331793/ 177.6363263 = 0.421271825

Hence μ_k = .421

Chapter No.5

. . . .

Dynamics of Uniform Circular Motion: -
Uniform Circular Motion: -
Definition of Uniform Circular Motion: - Uniform Circular Motion is the motion of an object travelling at a constant (uniform) speed on a circular path.

$v = 2\pi r/T$

If the radius of the circular path is known, the speed can be calculated from the period or vice versa.

Centripetal Acceleration: - The centripetal acceleration of an object moving with a speed v on a circular path of radius r has a value a_c given by: -

$a_C = v^2/r$

The centripetal acceleration vector always points toward the center of the circle and continually changes direction as the object moves.

$\Delta v/v = v\Delta t/r$

$\Rightarrow \Delta v/\Delta t = v^2/r$

Centripetal Force: - The centripetal force is the name given to the net force required to keep an object of mass m, moving at a speed v, on a circular path of radius r, and it has a value given by: -

$F_C = mv^2/r$

The centripetal force always points toward the center of the circle and continually changes direction as the object moves.

Banked Curves: - For banked curves, the centripetal force and its direction is given by: -

$F_C = F_N\sin\theta = mv^2/r$

$F_N\sin\theta/F_N\cos\theta = [mv^2/r]/mg$

$\text{Tan } \theta = v^2/rg$

Satellites in Circular Orbits: - The gravitational force or the centripetal force of a satellite in circular orbit, its velocity, and period are given as follows: -

$$F_C = GM_E m/r^2 = mv^2/r$$
$$\Rightarrow v = \sqrt{[GM_E/r]} = 2\pi r/T$$
$$\Rightarrow T = 2\pi r^{3/2}/\sqrt{[GM_E]}$$

Apparent Weightlessness and Artificial Gravity: - Artificial gravity can be created in outer space by the circular motion of the space station whose centripetal acceleration equals the acceleration due to gravity on earth. Apparent weightlessness occurs when a person in an elevator falls freely so that there is no net force to balance his weight.

$$F_C = mv^2/r = mg$$
$$\Rightarrow v = \sqrt{[rg]}$$

Vertical Circular Motion: - The centripetal force with which the object moves in a vertical circular motion, the object's weight mg, which always acts downward and the normal force, which acts perpendicular to the object and directed towards the center are related as follows: -

Starting from the bottom of the circle and moving anti clockwise, the centripetal force at the four locations of the circle 90^0 apart is given by:-

1) $F_{C1} = F_{N1} - mg = mv_1^2/r$

At the bottom of the circle, the normal force and the weight of the object, which is being whirled around in a vertical circle, are acting in opposite directions. The weight of the object acts downwards and the normal force acts upwards towards the center of the circle.

2) $F_{C2} = F_{N2} = mv_2^2/r$

At this 3 O'clock position, the weight of the object acts tangent to the circle and points downward.

3) $F_{C3} = F_{N3} + mg = mv_3^2/r$

In this 12 O'clock position, the normal force as well as the weight of the object act downward and towards the center.

4) $F_{C4} = F_{N4} = mv_4^2/r$

In this 9 O'clock position, like in the 3 O'clock position, the weight of the object acts tangent to the circle and points downward. The normal force equals the centripetal force and as always is directed toward the center of the circle.

The propulsion and braking forces are omitted for simplicity because they do not act along the radial direction. Furthermore this is not a uniform motion but we are able to use the concepts that apply to a uniform circular motion.

Dynamics of Uniform Circular Motion: -

(5) Numerical Problems: -

Uniform Circular Motion, Centripetal Acceleration: -

1) How long does it take a plane, travelling at a constant speed of 200 m/s to fly once around a circle whose radius is 3000 m?

Solution: -

$v = 2\pi r/T$

$\Rightarrow T = 2\pi r/v = 2\pi \times 3000m/200m/s$

$T = 30\pi$ secs.

$\Rightarrow T = 94$ secs.

2) The blade of a windshield viper moves through an angle of 90^0 in 0.5 secs. The tip of the blade moves on the arc of a circle that has a radius of 0.6 m. What is the value of the centripetal acceleration of the tip of the blade?

Solution: -

$v = 2\pi r/T$

$a_C = v^2/r = (2\pi r/T)^2/r$

$a_C = 4\pi^2 r/T^2 = 4\pi^2 \times 0.6m /(4 \times 0.5s)^2$

$a_C = \pi^2 \times 0.6m/s^2 = 5.921762641m/s^2$

$\Rightarrow a_C = 5.9$ m/s²

3) Computer-controlled display screens provide drivers in the Indianapolis 500 with a variety of information about how their cars are performing. For instant as a car is going through a turn, a speed of 50 m/s, and a centripetal acceleration of 2g (two times the acceleration due to gravity) are displayed. Determine the radius of the turn (in meters).

Solution: -

$v = 2\pi r/T$ and centripetal acceleration $= 2g$

$a_C = v^2/r$

$\Rightarrow r = v^2/a_C = v^2/2g = (50m/s)^2/2 \times 9.8m/s^2$

$r = 25 \times 10^2/19.6$

$\Rightarrow r = 127.55$ m

Hence the radius of the turn is 127.55 m.

4) A bicycle chain is wrapped around a rear sprocket ($r_1 = 0.04$ m) and a front sprocket ($r_2 = 0.09$ m). The chain moves with a speed of 2 m/s around the sprockets, while the bike moves at a constant velocity. Find the value of the acceleration of a chain link that is in contact with (a) the rear sprocket, (b) neither sprocket, and (c) the front sprocket.

Solution: -

(a) $a_C = v^2/r_1 = (2m/s)^2/0.04m = 100$ m/s²

$\Rightarrow a_C = 1\times10^2 \, m/s^2$

(b) $a_C = v^2/r = (2m/s)^2/\alpha = 0 \, m/s^2$ where α = infinity

$\Rightarrow a_C = 0 \, m/s^2$

(c) $a_C = v^2/r_2 = (2m/s)^2/0.09m = 44.4 \, m/s^2$

$\Rightarrow a_C = 44.4 \, m/s^2$

Therefore the values of the accelerations for the rear sprocket, neither sprocket, and the front sprocket have been determined.

Centripetal Force: -

5) A 0.02 kg ball is shot from the plunger of a pinball machine. Because of a centripetal force of 0.03 N, the ball follows a circular arc whose radius is 0.3 m. What is the speed of the ball?

Solution: -

$F_C = mv^2/r = (0.02 \, kg) \, v^2/0.3 \, m = 0.03 \, N$

$\Rightarrow v = \sqrt{[0.03N \times 0.3m/0.02kg]}$

$v = \sqrt{(0.45)} = 0.67m/s$

$\Rightarrow v = 0.67m/sec.$

6) A car is safely negotiating an unbanked circular turn at a speed of 30 m/s. The maximum static frictional force acts on the tires. Suddenly a wet patch in the road reduces the maximum static frictional force by a factor of four. If the car is to continue safely around the curve, to what speed must the driver slow the car?

Solution: -

$F_S = mv^2/r \Rightarrow (1/4) \, F_S = (1/4) \, mv^2/r \Rightarrow (1/4) \, mv^2/r = mv_1^2/r$

$\Rightarrow v_1^2 = v^2/4 \Rightarrow v_1 = v/2 \Rightarrow v_1 = 30m/s/2 = 15 \, m/s$

Hence $v_1 = 15$ m/s is the speed to which the driver must slow down the car.

Banked Curves: -

A jet (mass = 3×10^4 kg) flying at 200m/s banks to make a horizontal circular turn. The radius of the turn is 4000m. Determine the necessary lifting force.

Solution: -

$F = mv^2/r = 3\times10^4kg \times (200m/s)^2 /4000m$

$F = 3\times10^5 \, N$

$F_{Lift} = \sqrt{[F^2 + F^2]} = (\sqrt{2}) \, F = (\sqrt{2}) \times 3\times10^5 \, N = 4.24\times10^5 \, N$

$\Rightarrow F_{Lift} = 4.24\times10^5 \, N$

A curve of radius 200m is banked at an angle of 20^0. At what speed can it be negotiated under icy conditions where friction is negligible?

Solution: -

$g \tan\theta = v^2/r$

$\Rightarrow v = \sqrt{(rg\ tan\theta)} = \sqrt{[200m \times 9.8m/s^2 \times tan20^0]}$

$v = \sqrt{(713.3816592)} = 26.70920551$

$\Rightarrow v = 26.7m/s$

Satellites in Circular Orbits, Apparent Weightlessness, and Artificial Gravity

A satellite is placed in orbit ($r = 5x10^8$ m) above the surface of a planet. This planet has a mass of $M_p = 2x10^{30}$kg and a radius of $R = 9x10^9$m. Find the orbital speed of the satellite.

Solution: -

$R_1 = R + r = 9x10^9m + 0.5x10^9m = 9.5x10^9m$

$v = \sqrt{[GM_p/R_1]}$

$v = \sqrt{[6.673x10^{-11}N\text{-}m^2/kg^2 \times 2x10^{30}kg/9.5x10^9m]}$

$v = \sqrt{(1.404842105x10^{10})} = 1.18526x10^5m/s$

$\Rightarrow v = 1.18526x10^5$ m/s

Two satellites, A and B, are in different circular orbits around the earth. The orbital speed of satellite A is four times that of satellite B. Find the ratio T_A/T_B of the periods of the satellites.

Solution: -

$T = 2\pi r^{3/2}/\sqrt{(GM_E)} = 2\pi r/v = (2\pi/v)(GM_E/v^2) = 2\pi GM_E/v^3$

$\Rightarrow T_A/T_B = v_B^3/v_A^3 = (1)^3/(4)^3 = 1/64$

$\Rightarrow T_A/T_B = 1/64$

A satellite has a mass of 6000kg and is in a circular orbit $5x10^6$ m above the surface of a planet. The period of the orbit is three hours. The radius of the planet is $5.2x10^7$m. What is the true weight of the satellite when it is at rest on the planet's surface?

Solution: -

$R = 5.2x10^7m + 0.5x10^7m = 5.7x10^7m$

$v = \sqrt{(GM_E/R)} = 2\pi R/T$

$\Rightarrow M_p = 4\pi^2 R^3/GT^2$

$M_p = 4\pi^2 \times (5.7x10^7m)^3/6.673x10^{-11}N\text{-}m^2/kg^2 \times (3x3600s)^2$

$\Rightarrow M_p = 9.3932454x10^{26}kg$

F = Weight of the Satellite = $G (M_pm/R^2)$

$F = 6.673x10^{-11}Nm^2/kg^2 \times 9.3932454x10^{26}kg \times 6000kg/(5.2x10^7m)^2$

$\Rightarrow F = 1.390853398x10^5N$

Hence the weight of the satellite is $1.39x10^5N$ on the surface of the planet.

12) A satellite is in a circular orbit around an unknown planet. The satellite has a speed of $v_1 = 2x10^5m/s$ and the radius of the orbit is ($R_1 = 6x10^7$m). A second satellite also has a circular orbit around the same

planet. The orbit of this second satellite has a radius of 9x10^{7}m. What is the orbital speed of the second satellite?

Solution: -

$v = \sqrt{(GM_p/R)}$

$v_1 = v_2 \sqrt{(R_2/R_1)}$

$v_2 = v_1 \sqrt{(R_1/R_2)} = 2\text{x}10^5 \text{ms}^{-1}\sqrt{(6\text{x}10^7 \text{m}/9\text{x}10^7)}$

$v_2 = 1.6\text{x}10^5 \text{m/s}$

Vertical Circular Motion: -

13) A motorcycle has a speed of 50m/s as it passes over the top of a hill whose radius of curvature is 200m. The mass of the motorcycle and the driver is 400kg. Find the value of (a) the centripetal force, and (b) the normal force that acts on the cycle.

Solution: -

(a) $F_C = mv^2/r = 400\text{kg} \times (50\text{m/s})^2 /200\text{m}$

$\Rightarrow F_C = 5\text{x}10^3\text{N}$

(b) $F_N = F_C - mg = mv^2/r - mg = 5000\text{N} - 400\text{kg} \times 9.8\text{m/s}$

$\Rightarrow F_N = 5000\text{N} - 3920\text{N} = 1.08 \text{ x}10^3 \text{ N}$

14) The condition of apparent weightlessness for the passengers can be created for a brief instant when a plane flies over the top of a vertical circle. At a speed of 300m/s, what is the radius of the vertical circle that the pilot must use?

Solution: -

At the top of the circle the normal force has to be zero.

$\Rightarrow F_N = 0\text{N}$

$mv^2/r = mg$

$\Rightarrow r = v^2/g = (300\text{m/s})^2/9.8\text{m/s}^2$

$r = 9.18\text{x}10^3\text{m}$

Miscellaneous Problem: -

15) Speed boat A negotiates a curve whose radius is 95 m and speed boat B negotiates a curve whose radius is 285m. Each boat experiences the same centripetal acceleration. What is the ratio v_A/v_B of the speeds of the boats?

Solution: -

$a_C = v_A^2/r_A = v_B^2/r_B$

$\Rightarrow v_A^2/v_B^2 = r_A/r_B = 95\text{m}/285\text{m} = 1/3$

$v_A/v_B = \sqrt{(1/3)} = 0.577350269$

$\Rightarrow v_A/v_B = 0.577$

Chapter No.6:

· ·

Work and Energy: -

Definition of Work done by a Constant Force: - The work done on an object by a constant force F is given by: -

$W = (F \cos\theta) s$

Where F is the magnitude of the force, s is the magnitude of the displacement, and θ is the angle between the force and displacement.

SI system: Unit of work done is newton-meter = joule (J)

CGS system: Unit of work done is dyne-centimeter = erg

BE system: Unit of work done is foot-pound = foot-pound (ft-lb)

Definition of Kinetic Energy: - The Kinetic Energy KE of an object of mass m and speed v is given by: -

$KE = (\frac{1}{2}) mv^2$

SI Unit of Kinetic Energy: - joules (J)

The Work-Energy Theorem: - When a net external force does work on an object, the kinetic energy of the object changes from its initial value of KE_0 to a final value of KE_f, the difference between the two values being equal to the work.

$W = KE_f - KE_0 = (\frac{1}{2})mv_f^2 - (\frac{1}{2})mv_0^2$

Definition of Gravitational Potential Energy: - The gravitational Potential Energy is the energy that an object of mass m has by virtue of its position relative to the surface of the earth. This position is a measurement of the height h of the object relative to an arbitrary zero level.

$PE = mgh$

SI Unit of Gravitational Potential Energy = joule (J)

The work done by the force of gravity is given by: -

$W_{gravity} = (mg \cos0^0) (h_0 - h_f) = mg (h_0 - h_f)$

$W_{gravity} = mgh_0 - mgh_f$

$\Rightarrow W_{gravity} = PE_0 - PE_f$

$\Rightarrow W_{gravity} =$ (Initial Gravitational - (Final Gravitational Potential Energy) Potential Energy)

Conservative Forces versus Non-Conservative Forces: -
Definitions of a Conservative Force: -
1) A force is conservative when the work it does on a moving object is independent of the path between the object's initial and final positions.

2) A force is conservative when it does no net work on an object moving around a closed path, starting and finishing at the same point.

Conservative Forces: - The examples of a conservative force are (a) Gravitational Force, (b) Elastic Spring Force, and (c) Electric Force.

Non-Conservative Forces: - The examples of non-conservative force are (a) Static and Kinetic Frictional Forces, (b) Air Resistance, (c) Tension, (d) Normal Force, (e) Propulsion Force of a rocket.

In normal situations, conservative forces (such as gravity) and non-conservative forces (such as friction and air resistance) act simultaneously on an object.

$\Rightarrow$ The work done by the net external force is given by: -

$$W = W_c + W_{nc} = (\tfrac{1}{2})mv_f^2 - (\tfrac{1}{2})mv_0^2$$

If the only non-conservative force acting is the frictional force, then we have as follows: -

$$W_c = W_{gravity} = mg\,(h_0 - h_f)$$
$$\Rightarrow W_{nc} = (\tfrac{1}{2})mv_f^2 - (\tfrac{1}{2})mv_0^2 - mg(h_0 - h_f)$$
$$\Rightarrow W_{nc} = \Delta KE + \Delta PE$$

The Principle of Conservation of Mechanical Energy: - The total mechanical energy ($E = KE + PE$) of an object remains constant as the object moves, provided that the net work done by external non-conservative forces is zero. $W_{nc} = 0J$

$$W_{nc} = KE_f - KE_0 + PE_f - PE_0$$
$$W_{nc} = (KE_f + PE_f) - (KE_0 + PE_0)$$
$$W_{nc} = E_f - E_0 = 0J$$
$$\Rightarrow E_f = E_0$$
$$(\tfrac{1}{2})\,mv_f^2 + mgh_f = (\tfrac{1}{2})\,mv_0^2 + mgh_0$$

Hence the mechanical energy is conserved.

Non-Conservative Forces and the Work-Energy Theorem: - Sometimes the work done by external non-conservative force, such as air resistance and friction is not zero. In other words, the mechanical energy is not conserved.

$$\Rightarrow W_{nc} = E_f - E_0 \neq 0$$

Power: -

Definition of Average Power: - Average power, $\overline{P}$, is the average rate at which work W is done, and it is obtained by dividing W by the time t required to perform the work.

$\overline{P}$ = Average Power = Work /Time = W/t

SI Unit of Power: joule/second = watt (w)

The Principle of Conservation of Energy: - Energy can neither be created nor destroyed, but can only be converted from one form to another.

Work done by a Variable Force: - The work done by a constant force is W = (F cosθ) s. The work done by a variable force is given by: -

$W = (F \cos\theta)_1 \Delta s_1 + (F \cos\theta)_2 \Delta s_2 + \dots$

The work done by a variable force, which is not constant, in moving an object is equal to the area under the graph of Fcosθ versus s.

Work and Energy: -

(6) Numerical Problems: -

Work done by a Constant Force: -

1) The brakes of a truck cause it to slow down by applying a retarding force of 4×10^4 N to the truck over a distance of 1000m. What is the work done by this force on the truck? Is the work positive or negative? Why?

Solution: -

W = Fs

$\Rightarrow$ W = (- 4×10^4N) x 1000m

$\Rightarrow$ W = - 4×10^7 J

This is a retarding force; therefore the work done is negative.

2) A person pulls a toboggan for a distance of 50m along the snow with a rope directed 30° above the snow. The tension in the rope is 100N. (a) How much work is done on the toboggan by the tension force? (b) How much work is done if the same tension is directed parallel to the snow?

Solution: -

(a) W = (F cosθ) s = (100N cos30°) x 50m = 4330J

(b) W = Fs = 100N x 50m = 5000 (N-m) or Joule.

3) A husband and a wife take turns pulling their child in a wagon along a horizontal sidewalk. Each exerts a constant force and pulls the wagon through the same displacement. They do the same amount of work but the husband's pulling force is directed 60° above the horizontal and the wife's pulling force is directed 40° above the horizontal. The

husband pulls with a force whose value is 70N. What is the magnitude of the pulling force exerted by his wife?

Solution: -

$F = F_h \cos 60^0 = F_w \cos 40^0$ But $F_h = 70N$

$\Rightarrow F_w = 70N \cos 60^0/\cos 40^0 = 45.689N$

Hence the pulling force exerted by the wife has a value of 45.689N

The Work Energy Theorem and Kinetic Energy: -

4) The hammer throw is a track and field event in which an 8kg ball ("the hammer"), starting from rest, is whirled around in a circle several times and released. It then moves upward on the familiar cruising path of projectile motion. In one throw, the hammer is given a speed of 30m/s. For comparison a bullet has a mass of 3g and starting from rest, exits the barrel of a gun with a speed of 390m/s. Determine the work done to launch the motion of (a) the hammer and (b) the bullet.

Solution: -

(a) $W = KE = (\frac{1}{2}) mv^2$

$W = (\frac{1}{2}) (8kg) (30ms^{-1})^2 = 3600N\text{-}m = 3.6 \times 10^3 J$

(b) $W = KE = (\frac{1}{2}) mv^2$

$W = (\frac{1}{2}) (3 \times 10^{-3} kg) (390ms^{-1})^2 = 228.15N\text{-}m = 2.28 \times 10^2 J$

5) Two cars A and B, are travelling with the same speed of 30m/s, each having started from rest. Car A has a mass of 2.1×10^3kg and car B has a mass of 3×10^3kg. Compared to the work required to bring car A up to speed, how much additional work is required to bring car B up to speed?

Solution: -

$W_A = KE_A = (\frac{1}{2}) m_A v_A^2 = (\frac{1}{2}) (2.1 \times 10^3 kg) (30ms^{-1})^2 = 9.45 \times 10^5 J$

$W_B = KE_B = (\frac{1}{2}) m_B v_B^2 = (\frac{1}{2}) (3 \times 10^3 kg) (30ms^{-1})^2 = 13.5 \times 10^5 J$

$\Rightarrow \Delta KE = 13.5 \times 10^5 - 9.45 \times 10^5 = 4.05 \times 10^5 J$

Hence the additional work required to bring car B up to speed is given by the value, $\Delta KE = 4.05 \times 10^5 J$.

Gravitational Potential Energy, Conservative versus Non-Conservative Forces: -

6) A bicyclist rides 6km due east, while the resistive force from the air has a magnitude of 4N and points due west. The rider then turns around and rides 6km due west back to her starting point. The resistive force from the air, on the return trip, has a magnitude of 4N and points due east. (a) Find the work done by the resistive force during

the round trip. (b) Based on your answer to part (a), is the resistive force a conservative force? Explain.

Solution: -

(a) W = (-4Nx6km) x10^3m/km + (-4Nx6km) x10^3m/km

W = - 4.8x10^4J

(b) The force of static and kinetic friction, air resistance, normal force, and force of propulsion of a rocket are the examples of a non-conservative force. It is therefore a non-conservative force.

7) Relative to the ground, what is the gravitational potential energy of a 60kg person, who is at the top of a tower, a height of 513m above the ground?

Solution: -

$E_{\text{(Gravitational Potential Energy)}}$ = mgh

$E_{\text{(Gravitational Potential Energy)}}$ = 60kg x 9.8ms^{-2} x 513m

$E_{\text{(Gravitational Potential Energy)}}$ = 301,644J = 3x10^5J

8) An 80kg skier rides a 3100m long lift to the top of a mountain. The lift makes an angle of 15^0 with the horizontal. What is the change in the skier's gravitational potential energy?

Solution: -

Change in Gravitational Potential Energy = ΔGPE

ΔGPE = mgh` = mg x hsinθ = 80kg x 9.8ms^{-2} x 3100m sin15^0

ΔGPE = 629,033.8072J

$\Rightarrow$ ΔGPE = 6.29 x 10^5J

9) "Rocket man" has a propulsion unit strapped to his back. He starts from rest on the ground, fires the unit, and is propelled straight upward. At a height of 20m, his speed is 6ms^{-1}. His mass, including the propulsion unit, has the approximate constant value of 200kg. Find the work done by the force generated by the propulsion unit.

Solution: -

W_{nc} = KE + PE

KE = (½) mv^2 = (½) (200kg) (6ms^{-1})^2 = 3.6 x 10^3J

PE = mgh = 200kg x 9.8ms^{-2} x 20m = 39.2 x 10^3J

W_{nc} = KE + PE = (½) mv^2 + mgh = 3.6 x 10^3J + 39.2 x 10^3J

W_{nc} = 4.28 x 10^4J

The Conservation of Mechanical Energy: -

10) A slingshot fires a pebble from the top of a building at a speed of 15m/s. The building is 40m tall. Ignoring air resistance, find the speed

with which the pebble strikes the ground when the pebble is fired (a) horizontally, (b) vertically straight up, and (c) vertically straight down.

Solution: -

(a) $v_y = \sqrt{(2gh)} = \sqrt{(2 \times 9.8ms^{-2} \times 40m)} = \sqrt{(784)}\ ms^{-1} = 28ms^{-1}$

$v_x = 15ms^{-1}$

$\Rightarrow v = \sqrt{(v_x^2 + v_y^2)} = \sqrt{[(15ms^{-1})^2 + (28ms^{-1})^2]} = \sqrt{(1009)}\ ms^{-1}$

$\Rightarrow v = 31.76m/s$

(b) $v^2 - v_0^2 = 2gh$

$\Rightarrow h = (v^2 - v_0^2)/2g$

$h = (15ms^{-1})^2/2 \times 9.8ms^{-2} = 11.47959184m$

$\Rightarrow$ Total height $= 11.47959184m + 40m = 51.47959184m$

$v = \sqrt{(2gh)} = \sqrt{(2 \times 9.8ms^{-2} \times 51.48m)} = \sqrt{(1009)}\ ms^{-1} = 31.76ms^{-1}$

(c) $v^2 = v_0^2 + 2gh = (15ms^{-1})^2 + 2 \times 9.8ms^{-1} \times 40m$

$\Rightarrow v = \sqrt{(225 + 784)}\ ms^{-1} = \sqrt{(1009)}\ ms^{-1} = 31.76ms^{-1}$

11) A cyclist approaches the bottom of a gradual hill at a speed of 9m/s. The hill is 4m high, and the cyclist estimates that she is going fast enough to coast up and over it without pedaling. Ignoring air resistance and friction, find the speed at which the cyclist crests this hill.

Solution: -

$v^2 = v_0^2 + 2gh$

$v_0^2 = v^2 - 2gh = (9ms^{-1})^2 - 2 \times 9.8ms^{-2} \times 4m$

$v_0^2 = 81 - 78.4 = 2.6$

$\Rightarrow v_0 = \sqrt{2.6} = 1.6m/s$

Non-Conservative Forces and the Work-Energy Theorem: -

12) A roller coaster (300kg) moves from A (4m above ground) to B (19m above ground). Two non-conservative forces are present: friction does $- 3 \times 10^3J$ of work on the car, and a chain mechanism does $+4 \times 10^3J$ of work to help the car up a long climb. What is the change in the car's kinetic energy, $\Delta KE = KE_f - KE_0$, from A to B?

Solution: -

$W_{nc} = 4 \times 10^3J - 3 \times 10^3J = 1 \times 10^3J = E$

$\Delta PE = mg\ (h_f - h_0) = 300kg \times 9.8ms^{-2} \times (19m - 4m)$

$\Delta PE = 300 \times 9.8 \times 15\ J = 44100\ J = 44.1 \times 10^3J$

$E = \Delta KE + \Delta PE$

$\Rightarrow \Delta KE = E - \Delta PE$

$\Rightarrow \Delta KE = 1 \times 10^3J - 44.1 \times 10^3J = - 4.31 \times 10^4J$

13) The (non-conservative) force propelling a 2×10^2kg car up a mountain road does 5.6×10^6J of work on the car. The car starts from rest at sea level and has a speed of $30ms^{-1}$ at an altitude of 300m above sea

level. Obtain the work done on the car by the combined forces of friction and air resistance, both of which are non-conservative forces.

Solution: -

$W_{nc} = \Delta KE + \Delta PE = (\frac{1}{2}) mv^2 + mgh$

$W_{nc} = (\frac{1}{2}) (2x10^2kg) (30ms^{-2})^2 + 2x10^2kg \times 9.8ms^{-2} \times 3x10^2m$

$W_{nc} = 9x10^4J + 58.8x10^4J = 67.8x10^4J$

$W_{(friction + air\ resistance)} = 0.678x10^6J - 5.6x10^6J = -4.922x10^6J$

Power: -

14) One kilowatt-hour (KWh) is the amount of work done or energy generated when one kilowatt of power is supplied for a time of one hour. A kilowatt-hour is the unit of energy used by power companies when computing your electric bill. Determine the number of joules of energy in two kilowatt-hours.

Solution: -

$E/2KWh = 2x10^3 \times 60 \times 60 \ J/ 2KWh = 7.2x10^6J /2KWh$

Hence there are $7.2x10^6J$ in 2KWh.

15) The motor of a ski boat generates an average power of $6.3x10^3W$ when the boat is moving at $10ms^{-1}$. When the boat is pulling a skier at the same speed, the engine must generate an average power of $8.1x10^3W$. What is the tension in the tow bar that is pulling the skier?

Solution: - $\Delta \overline{P} = 8.1x10^3W - 6.3x10^3W = 1.8x10^3W$

$T = $ Force of tension $= \Delta \overline{P}/v = 1.8x10^3W/10ms^{-1} = 180N$

Hence the tension in the tow bar that is pulling the skier is 180N.

Chapter No.7: -

. . . .

Impulse and Momentum: -

The Impulse-Momentum Theorem: -

Definition of Impulse: - The impulse J of a force is the product of the average force $\bar{F}$ and the time interval Δt during which the force acts:

$$J = \bar{F}\Delta t$$

Impulse is a vector quantity and has the same direction as the force. SI Unit of Impulse: newton-second (N-s).

Definition of Linear Momentum: - The linear momentum p of an object is the product of the object's mass m and the velocity v:

$$p = mv$$

Linear momentum is a vector quantity that points in the same direction as the velocity. SI Unit of Linear Momentum: kgm/s.

Impulse-Momentum Theorem: - When a net force acts on an object, the impulse of this force is equal to the change in momentum of the object:

$$(\Sigma\bar{F})\Delta t = mv_f - mv_0$$

Impulse = Change in Momentum

This is a version of Newton's Second Law of Motion.

Principle of Conservation of Linear Momentum: - The total linear momentum of an isolated system remains constant (is conserved). An isolated system is one for which the vector sum of the average external forces acting on the system is zero.

$\Sigma\,\bar{F}$ = sum of average external forces

$$\Rightarrow \Sigma F\,(\Delta t) = P_f - P_0 = 0$$
$$\Rightarrow P_f = P_0$$

The total momentum of two balls in an isolated system is conserved and the total momentum of one ball in an isolated system is not conserved. It is so because in the two ball case the sum of the average external forces is zero but not in one ball case.

336

Collision in One Dimension: - Collisions are often classified according to whether the total kinetic energy changes during the collision.

1) Elastic Collision: - One in which the total kinetic energy of the system after the collision is equal to the total kinetic energy before the collision.

2) Inelastic Collision: - One in which the total kinetic energy of the system is not the same before and after the collision. If the objects stick together after colliding, the collision is completely inelastic.

The total linear momentum of the two ball system is conserved because no external forces act on the balls. The momentum conservation applies whether or not the collision is elastic.

$\Rightarrow m_1v_{f1} + m_2v_{f2} = m_1v_{01} + 0$

Total momentum = total momentum
after collision before collision

Before and after an elastic collision, the kinetic energy is the same.

$\Rightarrow (\frac{1}{2})m_1v_{f1}^2 + (\frac{1}{2})m_2v_{f2}^2 = (\frac{1}{2})m_1v_{01}^2 + 0$

Total kinetic energy = total kinetic energy
after collision before collision

$\Rightarrow v_{f1} = [(m_1 - m_2)/ (m_1 + m_2)] v_{01}$

$\Rightarrow v_{f2} = [2m_1/ (m_1 + m_2)] v_{01}$

Collision in Two Dimensions: - In two dimensions the x and y components are considered separately as follows: -

x - Component

$m_1v_{f1x} + m_2v_{f2x} = m_1v_{01x} + m_2v_{02x}$

$P_{fx} = P_{0x}$

y - Component

$m_1v_{f1y} + m_2v_{f2y} = m_1v_{01y} + m_2v_{02y}$

$P_{fy} = P_{0y}$

Center of Mass: - The center of mass is a point that represents the average location for the total mass of a system.

$\Rightarrow x_{cm} = (m_1x_1 + m_2x_2)/ (m_1 + m_2)$

If $m_1 = m_2$ then we may have as follows: -

$x_{cm} = (x_1 + x_2)/ 2$

$\Delta x_{cm} = (m_1\Delta x_1 + m_2\Delta x_2)/ (m_1 + m_2)$

$v_{cm} = (m_1v_1 + m_2v_2)/ (m_1 + m_2)$

The velocity of center of mass is the same before and after collision if the total linear momentum is conserved.

Momentum and Kinetic Energy: -

$KE = (½) mv^2$

$p = mv \Rightarrow v = p/m$

$\Rightarrow KE = (½) m (p/m)^2 = p^2/2m$

Both momentum and kinetic energy depend on the mass of the object.

Impulse and Momentum: -

(7) Numerical Problems: -

The Impulse – Momentum Theorem: -

1) A volley ball is spiked so that its increasing velocity of $+5ms^{-1}$ is changed to an outgoing velocity of $-19ms^{-1}$. The mass of the volley ball is 0.40 kg. What impulse does the player apply to the ball?

Solution: -

$J = (\Sigma\overline{F}) \Delta t = mv_f - mv_0 = m (v_f - v_0)$

$\Rightarrow J = 0.40kg (-19ms^{-1} - 5ms^{-1}) = 0.4kg \times (-24ms^{-1})$

$J = - 9.6$ N-s

2) A golfer, driving a golf ball off the tee, gives the ball a velocity of $+40ms^{-1}$. The mass of the ball is 0.055kg and the duration of the impact with the golf club is $0.4 \times 10^{-2}s$. (a) What is the change in momentum of the ball? (b) Determine the average force applied to the ball by the club.

Solution: -

(a) $(\Sigma\overline{F}) \Delta t = mv_f - mv_0$

$(\Sigma\overline{F}) \Delta t = 0.055kg \times 40ms^{-1} - 0 = 2.2$ N-s

$\Rightarrow$ The change in momentum is 2.2N-s

(b) $(\Sigma\overline{F}) = (mv_f - mv_0)/ \Delta t = 2.2$ N-s/ $0.4 \times 10^{-2}s = 550$ N

$\Rightarrow$ The average force applied to the ball is 550N.

3) A 50kg skater is standing still in front of a wall. By pushing against the wall she propels herself backward with a velocity of
- 0.9 ms^{-1}. Her hands are in contact with the wall for 0.9s. Ignore friction and wind resistance, find the magnitude and direction of the average force she exerts on the wall (which has the same magnitude but opposite direction as the force that the wall applies to her).

Solution: -

$(\Sigma\overline{F}) \Delta t = mv_f - mv_0 = 50kg \times (- 0.9 ms^{-1}) = - 45$ N-s

$\Sigma\overline{F} = (mv_f - mv_0)/ \Delta t = - 45$ N-s/ 0.9s

$\Rightarrow \Sigma\overline{F} = - 50$ N

Hence the magnitude of the average force she exerts on the wall is – 50 N and the direction of this force is the same as the direction of the velocity.

The Principle of Conservation of Linear Momentum: -

4) A cannon of mass 62×10^2 kg is rigidly bolted to the earth, so it can recoil only by a negligible amount. The cannon fires a 90 kg shell horizontally with an initial velocity of 600 ms^{-1}. Suppose the cannon is then unbolted from the earth, and an external force hinders its recoil. What would be the velocity of a shell fired by this loose cannon? (Hint: In both cases assume that the burning gunpowder imparts the same KE to the system).

Solution: -

$m_1 v_1 + m_1 v_1 = m_2 v_2$
$\Rightarrow m_1 v_1 = (½) m_2 v_2$
$v_1 = m_2 v_2 / 2m_1 = (90$ kg x 600 ms$^{-1}) / 2 \times 62 \times 10^2$ kg
$v_1 = 4.35483871$ms^{-1} = 4.4ms^{-1}
$\Rightarrow v = v_2 - v_1 = 600$ms^{-1} – 4.35483871ms^{-1} = 595.6451613 ms^{-1}

Hence the velocity of a shell fired by the given loose cannon is 595.6ms^{-1}.

5) In a science fiction novel two enemies Kirk and Gorn are fighting in outer space. From starting position, they push against each other. Kirk flies off with a velocity of +2ms^{-1} while Gorn recoils with a velocity of -3ms^{-1}. (a) Without doing any calculations, describe which person has the greater mass. Give your reasoning. (b) Determine the ratio of the masses of these two people, m_{Kirk} / m_{Gorn}.

Solution: -

(a) $m_{Kirk} v_{Kirk} = m_{Gorn} v_{Gorn}$
$M_{Kirk} (+2$ms$^{-1}) = m_{Gorn} (+3$ms$^{-1})$
$\Rightarrow m_{Kirk} > m_{Gorn}$

For their momentum to be equal, the mass of Kirk is greater than the mass of Gorn.

(b) $m_{Kirk} / m_{Gorn} = 3$ms$^{-1} / 2$ ms$^{-1} = 1.5$
$\Rightarrow m_{Kirk} / m_{Gorn} = 1.5$

6) A fireworks rocket is moving at a speed of 35m/s. The rocket suddenly breaks into two pieces of equal masses, which fly off with velocities v_1 and v_2 in a direction of 25^0 and 50^0 with respect to the direction of the original rocket respectively. What is the magnitude of the velocities (a) v_1 and (b) v_2?

Solution: -
(a) v_1 = 2x35cos25^0 = 63.44154509 m/s
(b) v_2 = 2x35cos50^0 = 44.99513268 m/s
Hence the velocities of the two pieces given are v_1 = 63.44ms^{-1} and v_2 = 44.99 ms^{-1}.

Collision in One Dimension, Collision in Two Dimensions: -
7) In a football game, a receiver is standing still, having just caught a pass. Before he can move, a tackler running at a velocity of +5.5 ms^{-1} grabs him. The tackler holds on to the receiver and the two move off together with a velocity of +3 ms^{-1}. The mass of the tackler is 99 kg. Assume that the momentum is conserved find the mass of the receiver.
Solution: -
$m_1v_{f1} + m_2v_{f2} = m_1v_{01} + 0$
99 kg x 3 ms^{-1} + m_2 x 3 ms^{-1} = 99 kg x 5.5 ms^{-1}
$\Rightarrow m_2$ = 99kg x (5.5 – 3) ms^{-1} / 3 ms^{-1}
$\Rightarrow m_2$ = 82.5 kg
8) A golf ball bounces down a flight of steel stairs, striking each stair once on the way down. The ball starts at the top step with a vertical velocity component of zero. If all the collisions with the stairs are elastic, and if the vertical height of the staircase is 4 m, determine the bounce height when the ball reaches the bottom of the stairs. Neglect air resistance.
Solution: -
$\Delta KE = (½) mv_f^2 – (½) mv_0^2 = (½) mv_f^2 – 0 = (½) mv_f^2$
h = (½) gt^2 = 4m
$v_f = \sqrt{(2gh)} = \sqrt{[2 \times 9.8ms^{-2} \times 4m]} = \sqrt{[78.4]} = 8.85ms^{-1}$
Hence bounce height is 4m because all collisions are elastic and momentum is conserved.
9) A cue ball (mass = 0.2 kg) is at rest on a frictionless pool table. The ball is hit dead center by a pool stick, which applies an impulse of + 2.2 N-s to the ball. The ball then slides along the table and makes an elastic head-on collision with a second ball of equal mass that is initially at rest. Find the velocity of the second ball just after it is struck.
Solution: -
$(\Sigma \overline{F}) \Delta t = mv_f – mv_0 = mv_f – 0 = mv_f = 2.2$ N-s
$\Rightarrow v_f = (\Sigma \overline{F}) \Delta t/ m = + 2.2$ Ns/ 0.2 kg = 11ms^{-1}

10) A 6 kg ball, moving to the right at a velocity of 1 ms^{-1} on a frictionless table, collides head-on with a stationary 8 kg ball. Find the final velocities of the balls if the collision is (a) elastic and (b) completely inelastic.

Solution: -

(a) $m_1 v_{f1} + m_2 v_{f2} = m_1 v_{01} + m_2 v_{02}$

(½) $m_1 v_{f1}^2$ + (½) $m_2 v_{f2}^2$ = (½) $m_1 v_{01}^2$ + 0

$v_{f1} = [(m_1 - m_2)/ (m_1 + m_2)]\ v_{01}$

$v_{f2} = [2m_1/ (m_1 + m_2)]\ v_{01}$

$\Rightarrow v_{f1} = [(6kg - 8kg)/ (6kg + 8kg)]$ x 1ms^{-1} = - 0.142857

$v_{f2} = [(2x6kg)/ (6 + 8)\ kg]$ x 1 ms^{-1} = 0.857142857ms^{-1}

(b) $(m_1 + m_2)\ v_f = m_1 v_{01} + m_2 v_{02}$

(6 + 8) kg x v_f = 6 kg x 1 ms^{-1} + 0

$\Rightarrow v_f$ = 0.428571429 ms^{-1}

In an inelastic collision the KE_f is not equal to KE_0. For the Conservation of Momentum to hold the net external force acting on the system should be zero.

11) An automobile has a mass of 3000 kg and a velocity of + 20 ms^{-1}. It makes a rear end collision with a stationary car whose mass is 2000 kg. The cars lock bumpers and skid off together with the wheels locked.

(a) What is the velocity of the two cars just after the collision?

(b) Find the impulse (magnitude and direction), that acts on the skidding cars from just after the collision until they come to a halt.

(c) If the coefficient of kinetic friction between the wheels of the cars and the pavement is μ_k = 0.70, determine how far the cars skid before coming to rest.

Solution: -

(a) $(m_1 + m_2)\ v_f = m_1 v_{01}$

(3000 kg + 2000 kg) v_f = 3000 kg x 20 ms^{-1}

v_f = 3000 kg x 20 ms^{-1}/ 5000 kg = 12 ms^{-1}

(b) $(\Sigma \overline{F})\ \Delta t = 0 - (m_1 + m_2)\ v_f = - (3000 kg + 2000 kg)$ x 12 ms^{-1}

J = Impulse = - 5000 kg x 12 ms^{-1} = - 6x10^4 N-s

The impulse has a magnitude of – 6x10^4 N-s and has the same direction as the velocity of the car.

(c) $v_f^2 - v_0^2 = 2\mu_k gs$

$\Rightarrow s = (v_f^2 - v_0^2)/ 2\mu_k g = v_f^2/ 2\mu_k g = (12\ ms^{-1})^2/ 2$ x 0.7 x 9.8 ms^{-2}

$\Rightarrow s$ = 1440/ 14x9.8 = 10.49562682 m

12) A 60 kg skater is travelling due east at a speed of 4 ms⁻¹. An 80 kg skater is moving due south at a speed of 8 ms⁻¹. They collide and hold on to each other after collision, managing to move off at an angle θ south of east, with a speed of v_f. Find the (a) angle θ and (b) speed v_f assuming that friction can be ignored.

Solution: -

(a) $m_1 v_{fx} + m_2 v_{fx} = m_1 v_{0x}$

(60 kg + 80 kg) v_{fx} = 60 kg x 4 ms⁻¹

$\Rightarrow v_{fx}$ = 240 kgms⁻¹/ 140 kg = 1.714285714 ms⁻¹

(60 kg + 80 kg) v_{fy} = 80 kg x (- 8 ms⁻¹)

$\Rightarrow v_{fy}$ = - 640 kgms⁻¹/ 140 kg = - 4.571428571 ms⁻¹

$\theta = \tan^{-1}(v_{fy}/ v_{fx}) = \tan^{-1}$ (- 4.571428571/ 1.714285714)

$\theta = \tan^{-1}$ (- 2.6666666667) = - 69.4⁰ south of east

(b) $v_f = \sqrt{[v_{fx}^2 + v_{fy}^2]}$

$v_f = \sqrt{[(1.714285714ms^{-1})^2 + (- 4.571428571ms^{-1})^2]}$

$v_f = \sqrt{(2.938775509 + 20.89795918)}$

$v_f = \sqrt{(23.83673469)}$ = 4.882287854 ms⁻¹

$\Rightarrow v_f$ = 4.88 ms⁻¹

Hence the magnitude of v_f is given by 4.88 ms⁻¹ and the direction is given by the angle θ = - 69.4⁰ south of east

Center of Mass: -

13) A planet and it's only natural satellite are separated by a center to center distance of 4x10⁹m. The mass of the planet is 6x10²⁵ kg and that of its natural satellite is 8x10²³ kg. How far does the center of mass lie from the center of the planet?

Solution: -

$x_{cm} = (m_1 x_1 + m_2 x_2)/ (m_1 + m_2)$

x_{cm} = (8x10²³ kg x 4x10⁹ m)/ (8x10²³ + 600x10²³) kg

x_{cm} = 5.2631579x10⁷ m

14) A molecule consists of an atom A and an atom B separated by a distance of 2x10⁻¹¹ m. The mass of atom A is 0.80 times the mass of atom B. $\Rightarrow m_A$ = 0.8m_B. Determine the location of the center of mass of the molecule relative to the atom A.

Solution: -

$x_{cm} = (m_1 x_1 + m_2 x_2)/ (m_1 + m_2)$

$\Rightarrow x_{cm}$ = (2x10⁻¹¹m x m_B)/ (m_B + 0.8m_B)

x_{cm} = 1.11x10⁻¹¹m

Miscellaneous: -

15) A 0.02 kg bullet is fired straight up at a falling wooden block that has a mass of 2 kg. The bullet has a speed of 900ms⁻¹ when it strikes the block. The block originally was dropped from rest from the top of a building and had been falling for a time t when the collision with the bullet occurred. As a result of this collision, the block (with the bullet in it) reverses direction, rises, and comes to a momentary halt at the top of the building. Find the time t.

Solution: -

$v_f = [2m_1/ (m_1 + m_2)] \, v_{01}$

$v_f = [2x.02kg/ (2 + .02) \, kg] \times 450ms^{-1} = 900x0.02/ \, 2.02$

$v_f = 8.910891089 \, ms^{-1}$

$v_f^2 = 2gh \Rightarrow h = v_f^2/ \, 2g$

$h = v_f^2/ \, 2g = (8.910891089ms^{-1})^2/ \, 2x9.8ms^{-2}$

$h = 79.40398/ \, 2x9.8 = 4.051223469 \, m = (½) \, gt^{`2}$

$t` = \sqrt{[2h/g]} = \sqrt{[2x4.051223469m/ \, 9.8ms^{-2}]} = 0.909274601$

$\Rightarrow t = t`/2 = 0.909/ \, 2 = 0.45s$

Chapter No.8:

. . . .

Rotational Kinematics: -

Definition of Angular Displacement: - When a rigid body rotates about a fixed axis, the angular displacement $\Delta\theta$ is the angle swept out by a line passing through any point on the body and intersecting the axis of rotation perpendicularly. By convention the angular displacement is positive if it is counterclockwise and negative if it is clockwise.

SI Unit of Angular Displacement: radian (rad). The radian is neither a base SI unit nor a derived one. It is regarded as a supplementary SI unit.

θ (in radian) = arc length/ radius = S/ r

$\theta = 2\pi r/ r = 2\pi$ rad $\Rightarrow$ 1 full rotation

1 rad = $360^0/ 2\pi^c$ = 57.3^0

Definition of Angular Speed: - Angular Speed w is the derivative of the angle θ with respect to the time t.

w = dθ/dt

SI Unit of Angular Speed: radian per second (rad/ second).

Definition of Angular Acceleration: - Angular acceleration is equal to the second derivative of the displacement θ with respect to the time t.

$\alpha = d^2\theta/dt^2$

SI Unit of Angular Acceleration: (rad/ s^2)

For the definition of a derivative, consider y = f(x) = x^n.

Then dy/dx = nx^{n-1} $\Rightarrow$ d^2y/dx^2 = n (n-1) x^{n-2}. Hence y, the function of x, is the dependent variable and x is the independent variable and n is the exponent, which is a constant, in this definition of a derivative.

The Equations of Rotational Kinematics: - Before we give the equations of rotational kinematics, we symbolize certain parameters as follows: -

S. No. Quantity: -

1) Displacement: -
Rotational Motion: - θ
Linear Motion: - x
2) Initial Velocity: -
Rotational Motion: - w_0
Linear Motion: - v_0
3) Final Velocity: -
Rotational Motion: - w
Linear Motion: - v
4) Acceleration: -
Rotational Motion: - α
Linear Motion: - a
5) Time: -
Rotational Motion: - t
Linear Motion: - t
The equations of kinematics for rotational and linear motions are as follows: -
Serial No. # Rotational Motion
(α = Constant)
1) $w = w_0 + \alpha t$
2) $\theta = (\frac{1}{2}) (w_0 + w) t$
3) $\theta = w_0 t + (\frac{1}{2})\alpha t^2$
4) $w^2 = w_0^2 + 2\alpha\theta$
Serial No. # Linear Motion
(a = constant)
1) $v = v_0 + at$
2) $x = (1/2)(v_0 + v)t$
3) $x = v_0 t + (1/2)at^2$
4) $v^2 = v_0^2 + 2ax$
Angular Variables and Tangential Variables: -
Suppose S is the arc length and t is the time to cover it then the tangential speed is given as follows: -
$v_T = S/ t = r\theta/ t = r (\theta/ t) = rw$
($\because$ S = $r\theta$ and w is an angular speed variable in rad/ second)
Note that v_T is the tangential speed variable given by the above equation.
Now the tangential acceleration is given as follows: -
$a_T = (v_T - v_{0T})/ t = (rw - rw_0)/ t = r [(w - w_0)/ t]$
$a_T = r\alpha$ (α is the angular acceleration variable in rad/ s^2)

Centripetal Acceleration is given as follows: -

$a_C = v_T^2/ r = (rw)^2/ r = rw^2$ (w is the angular speed in rad/s)

$\Rightarrow a_C = rw^2$

While the tangential speed is changing, the motion is called a non-uniform circular motion.

The linear acceleration is found as follows: - Let, a, denote the linear acceleration, then we have as follows: -

$a = \sqrt{[a_C^2 + a_T^2]} = \sqrt{[(rw^2)^2 + (r\alpha)^2]}$

$a = r \sqrt{[w^4 + \alpha^2]}$

$\Rightarrow a = r \sqrt{[w^4 + (w - w_0)^2/ t^2]}$

$\Rightarrow \varphi = \tan^{-1}(a_T/a_C) = \tan^{-1}(r\alpha/ rw^2)$

$\Rightarrow \varphi = \tan^{-1}(\alpha/ w^2)$

Hence for a rolling motion of a car tire which does not slip relative to the surface, we may have as follows: -

$v = rw$ (w in rad/ s)

Linear Speed = Tangential speed (v_T)

$a = r\alpha$ (α in rad/ s^2)

Linear acceleration = Tangential acceleration (a_T)

Vector Nature of Angular Variables: - If the motion is anticlockwise like the curled fingers of your right hand, it is taken positive and the direction of the vector is your extended thumb as the axis at right angle to the motion. When the angular velocity is increasing, the angular acceleration vector points in the same direction as the angular velocity. Conversely, when the angular velocity is decreasing, the angular acceleration vector points in the opposite direction to the angular velocity.

Rotational Kinematics: -

(8) Numerical Problems: -

Rotational Motion and Angular Displacement, Angular Velocity and Angular Acceleration: -

1) A diver completes 4 somersaults in 2 seconds. What is the average angular speed in radian per second of the diver?

Solution: - θ = angular displacement

$w = \Delta\theta/ \Delta t = (\theta - \theta_0)/ (t - t_0) = 2\pi \times 4$ radians/ 2 seconds

$w = 4\pi$ radian/second = 12.566 rad/s

2) In Europe, surveyor often measure angles in grads. There are 100 grads in one quarter of a circle. How many grads are there in one degree?

Solution: -

$90^0 = \pi/2$ rad = 100 grads

$\Rightarrow 1^0 = 100/90 = 1.11$ grads

Equations of Rotational Kinematics: -

3) A flywheel has a constant angular deceleration of 4 rad/s². (a) Find the angle through which the flywheel turns as it comes to rest from an angular speed of 400 rad/s. (b) Find the time required for the flywheel to come to rest.

Solution: -

(a) $\alpha = 4$ rad/s² and $w = 400$ rad/s

$w^2 - w_0^2 = 2\alpha\theta$

$\theta = w^2/2\alpha = (400 \text{ rad/s})^2 / 2\text{x}4\text{rad/s}^2$

$\Rightarrow \theta = 2 \times 10^4$ radians

(b) $w = w_0 + \alpha t$

$t = (w - w_0)/ \alpha = [400 \text{ rad/s} - 0]/4 \text{ rad/s}^2$

$t = 1\text{x}10^2$ seconds

4) A top is a toy that is made to spin on its pointed end by pulling on a string wrapped around the body of the top. The string has a length of 100 cm and is wrapped around the top at a place where its radius is 3 cm. The thickness of the string is negligible. The top is initially at rest. Someone pulls the free end of the string, thereby, unwinding it and giving the top an angular acceleration of +9 rad/s². What is the final angular velocity of the top when the string is completely unwound?

Solution: - S = 100 cm, r = 3 cm, and $\alpha = + 9$ rad/s²

$\Rightarrow \theta = S/r = 100\text{cm}/3\text{cm} = 33.33$ radian

$w^2 - w_0^2 = 2\alpha\theta$

$\Rightarrow w = \sqrt{[2\alpha\theta]} = \sqrt{[2 \times 9\text{rad/s}^2 \times 33.33\text{rad}]}$

$w = \sqrt{(600)} = 24.49$ rad/s

$\Rightarrow w = 24.49$ rad/s

Angular Variables and Tangential Variables: -

5) A disc (radius = 3 mm) is attached to a high speed drill at a workshop and is turning at 8x10⁵ rad/s. Determine the tangential speed of a point on the outer edge of this disc.

Solution: -

$r = 3$ mm = 3×10^{-3} m = 0.003m

$w = 8 \times 10^5$ rad/s

$\Rightarrow v_T = rw = 0.003\text{m} \times 8 \times 10^5 \text{ rad/s} = 24 \times 10^2 \text{ ms}^{-1}$

$v_T = 2400$ ms⁻¹

6) One type of a slingshot can be made from a length of a rope and a leather pocket for holding the stone. The stone can be thrown by whirling it rapidly in a horizontal circle and releasing it at the right moment. Such a slingshot is used to throw a stone from the edge of a cliff, the point of release being 40m above the base of the cliff. The stone lands on the ground below the cliff at a point x. The horizontal distance of point x from the base of the cliff (directly beneath the point of release) is 40 times the radius of the circle on which the stone is whirled. Determine the angular speed of the stone at the moment of release.

Solution: -

$h = (\frac{1}{2}) gt^2 = 40m$

$\Rightarrow t = \sqrt{[2h/g]} = \sqrt{[2 \times 40/9.8]}$

$t = \sqrt{[8.163265306]} = 2.857142857s$

$v_T = rw \Rightarrow w = v_T/r = \Delta\theta/\Delta t$

$\Delta\theta = S/r = 40r/r = 40$ radians

$\Delta t = t = 2.857142857s$

$w = [40r/r]$ rad $/ [2.857142857]$ s

$\Rightarrow w = 14$ rad/s

Centripetal Acceleration and Tangential Acceleration: -

7) A race car travels with a constant tangential speed of 80ms^{-1} around a circular track of radius 700m. Find (a) the magnitude of the car's total acceleration, and (b) the direction of its total acceleration relative to the radial direction.

Solution: -

(a) $v_T = 80ms^{-1} = rw = 700m \times w$

$w = v_T /r = 80m/ 700m = 0.114285714$ rad/ s

$a_C = rw^2 = v_T^2 /r = (80ms^{-1})^2/ 700m = 9.1ms^{-2}$

$\Rightarrow a_C = 9.1$ ms^{-2}

(b) Direction: - radially inward

8) A 300 kg speedboat is negotiating a circular turn (r = 40m) around buoy. During the turn, the engine causes a net tangential force of magnitude 600N to be applied to the boat. The initial speed of the boat going into the turn is 7ms^{-1}. (a) Find the tangential acceleration, (b) After the boat is 3 seconds into the turn, find the centripetal acceleration.

Solution: - m = 300 kg, r = 40 m, F_T = 600N, and v_{0T} = 7ms^{-1}

(a) $F_T = ma_T = 600N = 300kg \times a_T$

$\Rightarrow a_T = F_T/m = 600N/300kg = 2$ ms^{-2}

(b) $v_T = v_{0T} + a_T t = 7ms^{-1} + 2ms^{-2} \times 3s = 7ms^{-1} + 6ms^{-1} = 13ms^{-1}$

$a_C = v_T^2/r = (13ms^{-1})^2/40m = (169/40) \, ms^{-2}$

$\Rightarrow a_C = 4.225 \, ms^{-2}$

Rolling Motion: - Note: - All problems in this section assume that there is no slipping of the surfaces in contact during the rolling motion: -

9) A car is travelling with a speed of 30 ms^{-1} along a straight horizontal road. The wheels have a radius of 0.4m. If the car speeds up with a linear acceleration of 2 ms^{-2} for 10 seconds, find the angular displacement of each wheel during this period.

Solution: - The given data is as follows: - $v_0 = 30 \, ms^{-1}$, r = 0.4m, $a_T = 2ms^{-2}$, and t = 10s

$v = v_0 + a_T t = 30 \, ms^{-1} + 2 \, ms^{-2} \times 10s = 50 \, ms^{-1}$

$\Rightarrow v_0 = 30 \, ms^{-1}$ and v = 50 ms^{-1}

$w_0 = v_0/r = 30 \, ms^{-1}/0.4m = 75 \, rad/s$

$w = v/r = 50 \, ms^{-1}/0.4m = 125 \, rad/s$

$\alpha = a_T/r = 2 \, ms^{-2}/0.4m = 5 \, rad/s^2$

$w^2 - w_0^2 = 2\alpha\theta \Rightarrow \theta = [w^2 - w_0^2]/2\alpha$

$\Rightarrow \theta = [(125rad/s)^2 - (75rad/s)^2]/ (2 \times 5rad/s^2)$

$\theta = 1 \times 10^3$ radians

10) A ball of radius 0.3m rolls along a horizontal table top with a constant linear speed of 4 ms^{-1}. The ball rolls off the edge and falls a vertical distance of 3m before hitting the floor. What is the angular displacement of the ball while the ball is in the air?

Solution: -

r = 0.3m, v = 4 m/s, and h = 3m

$w = v/r = 4 \, m/s /0.3m = 13.33 \, rad/s$

$h = (½) gt^2 = 3m$

$t = \sqrt{[2h/g]} = \sqrt{[2 \times 3m/9.8ms^{-2}]}$

$t = \sqrt{[0.612244898]} = 0.782460796s$

$\Rightarrow \theta = wt = 13.3333rad/s \times 0.782460796s$

$\theta = 10.4$ radians

Miscellaneous: -

11) During a tennis serve, a racket is given an angular acceleration of magnitude 200 rad/s^2. At the top of the serve, the racket has an angular speed of 9 rad/s. If the distance between the top of the racket and the shoulder is 2m, find the magnitude of the total acceleration of the top of the racket.

Solution: - $\alpha = 200rad/s^2$, w = 9 rad/s, and r = 2m

$a_C = rw^2$ and $a_T = r\alpha$

$\Rightarrow a = \sqrt{[a_c^2 + a_T^2]}$

$a_C = rw^2 = 2m \times (9rad/s)^2 = 162ms^{-2}$

$a_T = r\alpha = 2m \times 200rad/s^2 = 400ms^{-2}$

$\Rightarrow a = \sqrt{[(162ms^{-2})^2 + (400ms^{-2})^2]}$

$a = \sqrt{(26244 + 160000)} = \sqrt{(186244)} = 431.5599611ms^{-2}$

$\Rightarrow a = 431.559m/s^2$

12) The take up reel of a cassette tape has an average radius of 2 cm. Find the length of the tape (in meters) that passes around the reel in 9 seconds when the reel rotates at an average angular speed of 4 rad/s.

Solution: -

$r = 2$ cm $= 0.02$m, t = 9 seconds, and w = 4rad/s

$\Rightarrow \Delta\theta = \theta - \theta_0 = wt = 4$ rad/s $\times$ 9s = 36 rad

$S = r\Delta\theta = 2$cm $\times$ 36 rad = 72 cm

$\Rightarrow S = 0.72$m

13) A record is rotating on the turn table at an angular velocity of w = 5 radians / second. What is the total angular displacement in t = 5 seconds?

Solution: -

$w = \Delta\theta / \Delta t$

$\Rightarrow \Delta\theta = w\Delta t = 5$ radians/ second $\times$ 5 seconds = 25 radians

$\Rightarrow \Delta\theta = 25$ radians

Hence the total angular displacement in t = 5 seconds, when the angular velocity is 5 radians / seconds is 25 radians.

14) A person lowers a basket into a well by turning the hand crank whose diameter is 0.6 m. The crank handle moves with a constant tangential speed of 1.5 m/s on its circular path. Find the linear speed with which the basket moves down the well, unwinding a long handle whose diameter is 0.2 m.

Solution: -

$v_T = 1.5$ m/s

$r = 0.3$ m

$\Rightarrow w = v_T/r = 1.5$m/s $/ 0.3$ m = 5 radians/s

$r = 0.2$ m/2 = 0.1 m

$\Rightarrow v = rw = 0.1$ m $\times$ 5 radians/s = 0.5m/s

Hence the linear speed with which the basket moves down the well is v = 0.5 m/s.

Chapter No.9

. . . .

Rotational Dynamics: -

The translational motion can occur along a curved line. It is, therefore, also called curvilinear motion or linear motion. Another possibility is rotational motion, which may occur in combination with translational motion. Before we actually give the definition of torque, let us define three concepts viz. lever arm, line of action, and axis of rotation. The lever arm is just the perpendicular distance between the line of action and the rotational axis. Secondly, the line of action is a line that is collinear with the direction of applied force which produces torque. Thirdly, the axis of rotation is the axis about which the object rotates as a consequence of torque that is being generated.

Definition of Torque: -

Torque = (magnitude of Force) (Lever Arm)

$\tau = F\ell$

Direction: The torque is positive when the force tends to produce a counterclockwise rotation about the axis, and negative when the force tends to produce a clockwise rotation.

SI Unit of Torque: - newton-meter or simply (N-m).

Equilibrium of a Rigid Body: - A rigid body is in equilibrium if it has zero translational acceleration and zero angular acceleration. In equilibrium, the sum of the externally applied forces is zero, and the sum of the externally applied torques is zero.

$\Rightarrow \Sigma F_x = 0$ N $\Sigma F_y = 0$ N and $\Sigma \tau = 0$ N-m

Definition of Center of Gravity: - The center of gravity of a rigid body is the point at which its weight can be considered to act when the torque due to the weight is being calculated.

$x_{cg} = [W_1 x_1 + W_2 x_2 + ...] / [W_1 + W_2 + ...]$

x_{cg} = center of gravity

Newton's Second Law for Rotational Motion about a Fixed Axis:-

The moment of inertia of a model plane flying on a guideline on a circle of radius r and having a mass m is given by: -

$I = \Sigma\, mr^2$

A tangential force F_T acts on the plane and the torque is given by: -

$F_T = ma_T$

$\tau = F_T r = m\, a_T r$ But $a_T = r\alpha$

$\Rightarrow \tau = mr^2\, \alpha = I\alpha$ ($\because I = mr^2$)

Rotational analog of Newton's Second Law for a rigid body rotating about a fixed axis:

Net external torque = (Moment of x (Angular

Inertia) Acceleration)

$\Sigma\tau = I\alpha$

Note that α must be expressed in rad/s^2.

The moment of inertia of an object depends on its mass and its radius: -

1) For a thin walled hollow cylinder or hoop with axis through the center, we have: -

$I = MR^2$

2) For a solid cylinder or disc with axis through the center, we have: -

$I = (1/2)MR^2$

3) For a thin rod with axis perpendicular to the rod and passing through the center, we have: -

$I = (1/12)ML^2$

4) For a thin rod with axis perpendicular to the rod and passing through one end, we have: -

$I = (1/3)ML^2$

5) For a solid sphere with axis through the center, we have: -

$I = (2/5)MR^2$

6) For a solid sphere with axis tangent to the surface, we have: -

$I = (7/5)MR^2$

7) For a thin walled spherical shell with axis through the center, we have: -

$I = (2/3)MR^2$

8) For a thin rectangular sheet with axis parallel to one edge and passing through the center of the other edge, we have: -

$I = (1/12)ML^2$

9) For a thin rectangular sheet with axis along one edge, we have:-
$I = (1/3)ML^2$
Comparison between Rotational and Translational Concepts: -
Physical Concept: -
Displacement:-
Rotational: - θ
Translational: - s
Velocity:-
Rotational: - w
Translational: - v
Acceleration:-
Rotational: - α
Translational: - a
The Cause of Acceleration:-
Rotational: - Torque τ
Translational: - Force F
Inertia: -
Rotational: - Moment of Inertia I
Translational: - Mass m
Newton's Second Law: -
Rotational: - $\Sigma\tau = I\alpha$
Translational: - $\Sigma F = ma$
Work: -
Rotational: - $\tau\theta$
Translational: - Fs
Kinetic Energy: -
Rotational: - $(1/2)Iw^2$
Translational: - $(1/2)mv^2$
Momentum: -
Rotational: - $L = Iw$
Translational: - $p = mv$
Definition of Rotational Work: - The rotational work W_R done by a constant torque τ in turning an object through an angle θ is given by: -
$W_R = \tau\theta$
The angle θ must be expressed in radians. SI Unit of Rotational Work: Joule (J)
Definition of Rotational Kinetic Energy: -

The rotational kinetic energy KE_R of a rigid object rotating with an angular speed w about a fixed axis and having a moment of inertia I is given by: -

$KE_R = (1/2) Iw^2$

The angular speed w must be expressed in rad/s. SI Unit of Rotational Kinetic Energy: Joule (J)

Definition of Angular Momentum: -

The angular momentum L of a body rotating about a fixed axis is the product of the body's moment of inertia I and its angular velocity w with respect to that axis: -

$L = Iw$

The angular velocity w must be expressed in rad/s. SI Unit of angular momentum:- $kg\ m^2/s$

Principle of Conservation of Angular Momentum: -

The total angular momentum of a system remains constant (is conserved) if the net average external torque acting on the system is zero.

$\Sigma\tau = I\alpha = 0\ Nm$

The angular acceleration α must be expressed in rad/s^2 and the moment of inertia I must be expressed in kgm^2. SI Unit of torque: Nm

Rotational Dynamics: -

(9) Numerical Problems: -

The Action of Forces and Torques on Rigid Objects: -

1) A square 0.5m on a side is mounted so that it can rotate about an axis that passes through the center of the square. The axis is perpendicular to the plane of the square. A force of 20N lies in this plane and is applied to the square. What is the magnitude of the maximum torque that such a force could produce?

Solution: -

$\tau = F\ell = 20N \times 0.5cos45^0 = 7.07Nm$

$\Rightarrow \tau = 7.07Nm$

2) The wheel of a car has a radius of 0.4m. The engine of the car applies a torque of 300Nm to this wheel, which does not slip against the road surface. Since the wheel does not slip, the road must be applying a force of static friction to the wheel that produces a counter torque. Moreover, the car has a constant velocity, so this counter torque balances

the applied torque. What is the magnitude of the static frictional force?

Solution: - $\tau = F\ell = 300Nm$

$\Rightarrow F = \tau/\ell = 300Nm/0.4m = 750N$

$\Rightarrow F$ = Static Frictional Force = 750N

Rigid Objects in Equilibrium, Center of Gravity: -

3) A guy is involved in doing push-ups. His weight is W= 600N. His center of gravity is 0.5m from his hands and 0.9m from his feet. Find the normal force exerted by the floor on each hand and each foot, assuming that that guy holds this position.

Solution: -

$0.5F_N = 0.9F_N' = 0.9(600 - F_N) = 540 - 0.9F_N$

$1.4F_N = 540 \Rightarrow F_N = 540/1.4 = 385.7N$

$\Rightarrow F_{N1}$ (normal force on each hand) $= F_N/2 = 385.7/2 = 192.85N$

$\Rightarrow F_{N1} = 192.85N$

Similarly $F_N' = 600n - 385.7 = 214.3$

$\Rightarrow F_{N2}$ (normal force on each foot) $= F_N'/2 = (214.3)/2 = 107.1N$

$\Rightarrow F_{N2} = 107.1N$

Hence the normal force on each hand is 192.85N and the normal force on each foot is 107.1N respectively.

4) An inverted, "V", is made of uniform boards and weighs 434N. Each side has the same length and makes a 29^0 angle with the vertical. Find the magnitude of the static frictional force that acts on the lower end of each leg of the "V".

Solution: -

$(\frac{1}{2})W \sin\theta = 2F_S \cos\theta$

$\Rightarrow F_S = (1/4)W \tan\theta$

$F_S = (1/4) \times 434N \tan29^0 = 60.14253208N$

$\Rightarrow F_S = 60.14N$

5) A jet transport has a weight of 1×10^7N and is at rest on the runway. The two rear wheels are 20m behind the front wheel and the plane's center of gravity is 16m behind the front wheel. Determine the normal force F_N exerted by the ground on (a) the front wheel and on (b) each of the two rear wheels.

Solution: -

(a) $F_{N1} = 1\times10^7N (20m - 16m)/20m = 1\times10^7N \times 4m/20m$

$\Rightarrow F_{N1} = 2\times10^6N$

(b) $F_{N2} = 1\times10^7N (16m/2)/20m = 0.4\times10^7N$

$\Rightarrow F_{N2} = 4x10^6N$

Hence the normal force F_N on the front wheel and each of the two rear wheels is given by: -

$F_{N1} = 2x10^6N$

and $F_{N2} = 4x10^6N$

6) A uniform board is leaning against a smooth vertical wall. The board is at an angle θ above the horizontal ground. The coefficient of static friction between the ground and the lower end of the board is μ_S = 0.7. Find the smallest value of θ, such that the lower end of the board does not slide along the ground.

Solution: -

$\tau = (W\ell/2) \sin\theta' - \mu_S(W\ell)\cos\theta' = 0$

$(W\ell/2) \sin\theta' = \mu_S(W\ell)\cos\theta'$

$\Rightarrow \tan\theta' = \sin\theta'/\cos\theta' = 2\mu_S$

$\Rightarrow \theta' = \tan^{-1}(2\mu_S) = \tan^{-1}(2x0.7) = \tan^{-1}(1.4) = 54.46^0$

$\Rightarrow \theta = 90^0 - 54.46^0 = 35.5^0$

Hence the smallest required angle θ is 35.5^0.

Newton's Second Law for Rotational Motion about a Fixed Axis:-

7) A clay vase on a potter's wheel experiences an angular acceleration of 7 rad/s² due to the application of a 20Nm net torque. Find the total moment of inertia of the vase and the potter's wheel.

Solution: -

$\tau = I\alpha \Rightarrow I = \tau/\alpha$ = moment of inertia

$I = \tau/\alpha = 20Nm/7rad/s^2 = 2.857kgm^2$

$\Rightarrow I = 2.857kgm^2$

Hence the moment of inertia of the vase and the potter's wheel is given by: -

$I = 2.857 kgm^2$

SI Unit of moment of inertia: kgm^2.

8) A uniform solid disc with a mass of 30 kg and a radius of 0.4m is free to rotate about a frictionless axle. Forces of 100N and 200N are applied to the disc. What is (a) the net torque produced by the two forces and (b) the angular acceleration of the disc?

Solution: -

(a) $\Sigma\tau = F\ell - F'\ell$

$\Sigma\tau = -200N \times 0.4m + 100N \times 0.4m$

$\Rightarrow \Sigma\tau = -40Nm$

(b) $\alpha = \Sigma\tau / I = \Sigma\tau/[(1/2)mR^2]$

$\alpha = -40Nm/[(1/2)(30kg)(0.4m)^2]$

$\alpha = -40Nm/2.4kgm^2 = -16.66666667 \text{ rad/s}^2$

$\Rightarrow \alpha = -16.67 \text{ rad/s}^2$

Hence the net torque produced by the two forces is $-40Nm$ and the angular acceleration of the disc is -16.67rad/s^2.

Rotational Work and Energy: -

9) Three objects lie in the x-y plane. Each rotates about the z-axis with an angular speed of 7rad/s. The mass m of each object and its perpendicular distance r from the z-axis are: - (i) $m_1 = 7kg$ and $r_1 = 3m$, (ii) $m_2 = 5kg$ and $r_2 = 2.1m$, and (iii) $m_3 = 5.9kg$ and $r_3 = 4m$. (a) Find the tangential speed of each object. (b) Determine the total KE of this system using the expression: -

$KE = (\frac{1}{2})m_1v_1^2 + (\frac{1}{2})m_2v_2^2 + (\frac{1}{2})m_3v_3^2$. (c) Obtain the moment of inertia of the system. (d) Find the rotational KE of the system using the relation $(\frac{1}{2})Iw^2$ to verify that the answer is the same as that in (b).

Solution: -

(a) (i) $v_{1T} = r_1w = 3m \times 7rad/s = 21m/s$

(ii) $v_{2T} = r_2w = 2.1m \times 7rad/s = 14.7m/s$

(iii) $v_{3T} = r_3w = 4m \times 7rad/s = 28m/s$

(b) $KE = (\frac{1}{2})m_1v_{1T}^2 + (\frac{1}{2})m_2v_{2T}^2 + (\frac{1}{2})m_3v_{3T}^2$

$KE = $ Kinetic Energy $= (\frac{1}{2})(7kg)(21ms^{-1})^2+(\frac{1}{2})(5kg)(14.7ms^{-1})^2+(\frac{1}{2})(5.9kg)(28ms^{-1})^2$

$KE = 1543.5J + 540.225J + 2312.8J = 4396.525J$

(c) $I = \Sigma mR^2 = m_1R_1^2 + m_2R_2^2 + m_3R_3^2$

$I = 7kg \times (3m)^2 + 5kg \times (2.1m)^2 + 5.9kg \times (4m)^2$

$I = 63 \text{ kgm}^2 + 22.05 \text{ kgm}^2 + 94.4 \text{ kgm}^2 = 179.45 \text{ kgm}^2$

(d) $KE_R = (\frac{1}{2})Iw^2 = (\frac{1}{2})(179.45kgm^2) \times (7rad/s)^2 = 4.396525 \times 10^3J$

$\Rightarrow KE_R = 4.396525 \times 10^3J$

10) A merry-go-round has a mass of 2000kg and a radius of gyration of 20m. How much work is required to accelerate it from rest to a rotation rate of one revolution in 8 seconds?

Solution: -

$I = mR^2 = 2000kg \times (20m)^2 = 8 \times 10^5 \text{ kgm}^2$

$\alpha = (w - w_0)/t = 2\pi \text{ rad}/ (8seconds)^2 = (\pi/32) \text{ rad/s}^2$

$\tau = I\alpha = 8 \times 10^5 \text{ kgm}^2 \times (\pi/32) \text{ rad/s}^2 = \pi/4 \times 10^5 \text{ Nm}$

$\theta = \pi \text{ radians}$

$W = \tau\theta = \pi/4 \times 10^5Nm \times \pi \text{ rad} = (\pi^2/4) \times 10^5J = 2.4674011 \times 10^5J$

$\Rightarrow W = 2.467 \times 10^5J$

Angular Momentum: -

11) Two discs are rotating about the same axis. Disc A has a moment of inertia of 4kgm² and an angular velocity of +8rad/s. Disc B is rotating with an angular velocity of -10rad/s. The two discs are then linked together without the aid of any external torques, so that they rotate about a single unit with an angular velocity of -3rad/s. The axis of rotation for this unit is the same as that for the separate discs. What is the moment of inertia of disc B?

Solution: -

$I_A w_A + I_B w_B = I_{AB} w_{AB}$

$\Rightarrow$ 4kgm²x8rad/s + I_B (- 10rad/s) = (4 + I_B) kgm² x (- 3rad/s)

$32 - 10I_B = - 12 - 3I_B$

$\Rightarrow +7I_B = 44$

$\Rightarrow I_B = 44/7 = 6.2857$kgm²

Hence the moment of inertia of disc B is 6.2857kgm².

12) A thin rod has a length of 0.3m and rotates in a circle on a frictionless table top. The axis is perpendicular to the length of the rod at one of its ends. The rod has an angular velocity of 0.4rad/s and a moment of inertia of 2.2x10⁻⁴kgm². A bug standing on the axis decides to crave out to the other end of the rod. When the bug (mass = 5x10⁻⁴kg) gets where it's going, what is the angular velocity of the rod?

Solution: -

$I_1 w_1 + I_2 w_2 = (I_1 + I_2) w_3$ and $w_2 = 0$ rad/s

$\Rightarrow I_1 w_1 = (I_1 + I_2) w_3$

Now $I_2 = MR^2 = (5x10^{-4}kg)(0.3m)^2 = 0.45x10^{-4}$kgm² for the bug

$I_1 + I_2 = 2.2x10^{-4}$kgm² + 0.45x10⁻⁴kgm² = 2.65x10⁻⁴kgm²

$\Rightarrow w_3 = I_1 w_1 / (I_1 + I_2) = 2.2x10^{-4}$kgm²x0.4rad/s / (2.65x10⁻⁴kgm²)

$\Rightarrow w_3 = 0.33$ rad/s

Miscellaneous: -

13) A post is driven perpendicularly into the ground and serves as the axis about which a gate rotates. A force of 9N is applied perpendicular to the gate and acts parallel to the ground. How far from the post should the force be applied to produce a torque with a magnitude of 2.7 Nm?

Solution: -

$\tau = F\ell$

$\ell = \tau / F = 2.7$Nm/9N = 0.3m

$\Rightarrow \ell = 0.3$m

Hence the force should be applied perpendicularly 0.3m from the axis of rotation to produce the given torque.

14) A baggage carousel at an airport is rotating with an angular speed of 0.3 rad/s when the baggage begins to be loaded on to it. The moment of inertia of the carousel is 2000kgm². Eleven pieces of baggage with an average mass of 20kg each are dropped vertically onto the carousel and come to rest at a perpendicular distance of 3m from the axis of rotation. (a) Assuming that no net external torque acts on the system of carousel and baggage, find the final angular speed. (b) In reality, the angular speed of the baggage carousel does not change. Therefore what can you say qualitatively about the net external torque acting on the system?

Solution: -

(a) $I = MR^2 = M(3m)^2 = 2000kgm^2$

$\Rightarrow M = 2000kgm^2/9m^2 = 222.22kg$

$\Sigma M = 222.22kg + 20kg \times 11 = 222.22kg + 220kg = 442.22kg$

$I' = 442.22kg \times (3m)^2 = 3979.9998 = 3980kgm^2$

$Iw = I'w'$

$2000kgm^2 \times 0.3 \text{ rad/s} = 3980kgm^2 \times w'$

$\Rightarrow w' = 2000kgm^2 \times 0.3 \text{ rad/s}/3980kgm^2$

$w' = 0.150753769 \text{ rad/s}$

$\Rightarrow w' = 0.15 \text{ rad/s}$

Hence the final angular speed of the system of carousel and baggage comes out to be 0.15rad/s.

(b) A net external torque must be applied to the system in a direction opposite to the angular deceleration to keep the system of carousel and baggage in motion.

15) A mass less, rigid board is placed across two bathroom scales that are separated by a distance of 1.9m. A person lies on the board. The scale under his head reads 500N, and the scale under his feet reads 400N. (a) Find the weight of the person. (b) Locate the center of gravity of the person relative to a scale beneath his head.

Solution: -

(a) $W = 500N + 400N = 900N = 9 \times 10^2 N$

$\Rightarrow$ Weight of the person $= 900N$

(b) $x_{cg} = [400N \times 1.9m + 500N \times 0m]/[400N + 500N] = 760/900$

$\Rightarrow x_{cg} = 0.844m$

16) The moment of inertia of an airport carousel is 4000 kgm² and the radius of the carousel is 5 m. Determine the mass placed on the carousel.

Solution: -

$I = MR^2$

$\Rightarrow M = I / R^2 = 4000 \text{ kgm}^2 / (5 \text{ m})^2 = 4000/ 25 = 160 \text{ kg}$

$\Rightarrow M = 160 \text{ kg}$

Hence the mass placed on the carousel is 160 kg.

Chapter No.10

· ·

Simple Harmonic Motion and Elasticity: -

Hooke's Law, Restoring Force of an Ideal Spring: - The restoring force of an ideal spring is given by: -

$F = - Kx$

where K is the spring constant, and x is the displacement of the spring from its unstrained length. The minus sign indicates that the restoring force always points in a direction opposite to the displacement of the spring.

Simple Harmonic Motion and the Reference Circle: - Simple Harmonic Motion, like any other motion, can be described in terms of displacement, velocity, and acceleration.

Displacement: - Suppose a ball is moving in a circular path along what is known as the reference circle. The ball starts on the x-axis at x = + A, and moves through an angle θ in a time t. Since the circular motion is uniform, the ball moves with a constant angular speed w (in rad/s). Therefore wt = θ

$x = A \cos\theta = A \cos (wt)$

$w = 2\pi/T = 2\pi f$ (w in rad/s)

where T is called the period and f is called the frequency, given in number of seconds per cycle and number of cycles per second, respectively.

The equation of a sinusoidal wave, or a periodic wave, or a harmonic wave is given by: -

$y(x,t) = A \sin (2\pi ft \pm 2\pi x/\lambda)$

Note y(x,t) is the displacement on the y-axis, A is the amplitude of the wave, f is the frequency of the wave, x is the distance on the x-axis, and λ is the wavelength of the sinusoidal wave, or the periodic wave, or the harmonic wave.

Velocity: - The velocity in simple harmonic motion is given by the following relationship.

$v = - Aw \sin\theta = - Aw \sin (wt)$ (w in rad/s)

361

$v_{max} = Aw$ (w in rad/s)

Acceleration: - In simple harmonic motion, the velocity is not constant; consequently, there must be an acceleration. This acceleration can be determined with the aid of the reference circle.

$a = - Aw^2 \cos\theta = - Aw^2 \cos(wt)$

$a_{max} = Aw^2$ (w in rad/s)

Frequency of Vibration: - The restoring force is given as follows:-

$F = - Kx = ma$

$\Rightarrow - K(A \cos wt) = m(- Aw^2 \cos wt)$

$\Rightarrow w = 2\pi f = \sqrt{[K/m]}$ (w in rad/s)

Energy and Simple Harmonic Motion: - Since the dependence of the spring force on x is linear, the magnitude of the average force is just one-half the sum of the initial and final values or we have: -

$\bar{F} = (1/2)(Kx_0 + Kx_f)$

The work $(W_{elastic})$ done by the average spring force is given by:-

$W_{elastic} = (\bar{F} \cos\theta)s = (1/2)(Kx_0 + Kx_f) \cos 0^0 (x_0 - x_f)$

$\Rightarrow W_{elastic} = (\frac{1}{2})Kx_0^2 - (\frac{1}{2})Kx_f^2$

$W_{elastic}$ = [Initial elastic - Final elastic (Potential Energy)]

Definition of Elastic Potential Energy: - The elastic potential energy $PE_{elastic}$ is the energy that a spring has by virtue of being stretched or compressed. For an ideal spring that has an spring constant K and is stretched or compressed by an amount x relative to its unstrained length, the elastic potential energy is given by: -

$PE_{elastic} = (\frac{1}{2})Kx^2$

SI Unit of Elastic Potential Energy: joule(J)

Hence the total mechanical energy is now given by the following equation: -

$E = (\frac{1}{2})mv^2 + (\frac{1}{2})Iw^2 + mgh + (\frac{1}{2})Kx^2$

The total mechanical energy is the sum of the translational kinetic energy, rotational kinetic energy, gravitational potential energy and elastic potential energy.

Conservation of Mechanical Energy: - According to the conservation of mechanical energy, we have as follows: -

$E_f = E_0$

$[(\frac{1}{2})mv_f^2 + (\frac{1}{2})Iw_f^2 + mgh_f + (\frac{1}{2})Kx_f^2]$

$= [(\frac{1}{2})mv_0^2 + (\frac{1}{2})Iw_0^2 + mgh_0 + (\frac{1}{2})Kx_0^2]$

Suppose the object is moving on a horizontal table, then $h_f = h_0$. The object is not rotating, so its angular speed is zero, that is ($w_0 = w_f = 0$ rad/s). Suppose the initial translational speed of the object $v_0 = 0$m/s. With these substitutions, the conservation of energy equation becomes as follows: -

$(\frac{1}{2})mv_f^2 + (\frac{1}{2})Kx_f^2 = (\frac{1}{2})Kx_0^2$

$\Rightarrow v_f = \sqrt{[K/m \ (x_0^2 - x_f^2)]}$

The Pendulum: - If θ is expressed in radians, the arc length S and the radius L of the circular path are related, according to the equation as given below: -

$S \equiv \ell = L\theta$

The torque created by gravity is given by: -

$\tau \equiv - K'\theta = - mgL \ \theta$

$\Rightarrow w = 2\pi f = \sqrt{[K/m]} = \sqrt{[mgL/I]}$

Hence for rotational motion we have as follows: -

$w = \sqrt{[mgL/I]}$

where K has been replaced by mgL and the mass m has been replaced by I, the moment of inertia.

For a simple pendulum, which is a string tied to a round metallic bob, performing simple harmonic motion, we have as follows: -

$I = mL^2 = $ moment of inertia

$\Rightarrow w = 2\pi f = \sqrt{[mgL/I]} = \sqrt{(g/L)}$

$\Rightarrow T = 1/f = 2\pi\sqrt{(L/g)}$

A quantum unit of gravitational force field, called the "graviton", has not yet been discovered.

Damped Harmonic Motion: - In simple harmonic motion, an object oscillates with constant amplitude because there is no mechanism for dissipation of energy. In reality, however, friction or some other energy dissipation mechanism is always present.

In the presence of energy dissipation mechanism, the amplitude of oscillation decreases as time passes and the motion is no longer simple harmonic. It is referred to as damped harmonic motion because the decrease in amplitude is being called "damping".

Damping is present in the mechanism of shock absorbers of the suspension system of a car, where the vibrations are reduced for a bumpy ride.

Elastic Deformation: - Stretching, Compression, and Young's Modulus: -

If the amount of stretching is small compared to the original length of the object, we have as follows: -

$F = Y \ (\Delta L/L_0) \ A$

where "F" denotes the magnitude of the stretching force applied perpendicularly to the surface at the end of the rod, "A" is the cross-sectional area of the rod, ΔL is the increase in length, and L_0 is the original length of the rod. The term "Y" is the proportionality constant called "Young's modulus". Hence the unit of Y is N/m^2.

Shear Deformation and the Shear Modulus: - An object may expand in a number of ways. For instant, it may stretch or be compressed lengthwise or the total original area may become stretched or compressed or finally the whole volume may suffer a slight change in magnitude.

The deformation in area is called shear deformation and the shear modulus is represented by the letter S in the following equation: -

$F = S \ (\Delta X/X_0) \ A$

where ΔX is the slight deformation in area, X_0 is the original area, and S is the shear modulus and has units of N/m^2.

Volume Deformation and the Bulk Modulus: - The magnitude of the perpendicular force per unit area is called pressure, which is defined as follows: -

$P = F/A$

SI Unit of pressure: $N/m^2 = $ Pascal (Pa)

$\Rightarrow \Delta P = - B \ (\Delta V/V_0)$

Hence during compression or expansion of any volume the fractional change $(\Delta V/V_0)$ is proportional to the applied pressure ΔP. Here B is a constant of proportionality, called Bulk modulus.

Hooke's Law for Stress and Strain: - Stress is directly proportional to strain.

SI Unit of stress: $N/m^2 = $ Pa (Pascal)

SI Unit of strain: Strain is a unit less quantity because it is a ratio of two similar physical parameters.

$F/A = Y \ (\Delta L/L_0)$

$F/A = S \ (\Delta X/X_0)$

$\Delta P = B \ (- \Delta V/V_0)$

Stress (is proportional to) Strain.

Note that Y, S, and B denote the Young's modulus, the Shear modulus, and the Bulk modulus, respectively. These are the constants of proportionality.

Simple Harmonic Motion and Elasticity: -
(10) Numerical Problems: -
The Ideal Spring and Simple Harmonic Motion: -
1) A hand exerciser utilizes a coiled spring. A force of 90N is required to compress the spring by 0.022m. Determine the force needed to compress the spring by 0.073m.
Solution: -
$F' = - Kx'$
$K = - F'/x' = - 90N/0.022m = - 4090.909091N/m$
$F = - Kx = 4090.909091N/m \times 0.073m$
$F = 298.6363636N$
$\Rightarrow F = 298.636N$

2) A car is hauling a 100 kg trailer, to which it is connected by a spring. The spring constant is 3100N/m. The car accelerates with an acceleration of 0.5m/s². By how much does the spring stretch?
Solution: -
$F = ma = - Kx$
$F = 100kg \times 0.5m/s^2 = 50N$
$\Rightarrow x = F/K = 50N/3100N/m = 0.016129032m$
$\Rightarrow x = 0.016m$
Hence the spring stretches by $x = 0.016m$

Simple Harmonic Motion and the Reference Circle: -
3) The shock absorbers in the suspension system of a car are in such bad shape that they have no effect on the behavior of the springs attached to the axles. Each of the identical springs attached to the front axle supports 400kg. A person pushes down on the middle of the front end of the car and notices that it vibrates through six cycles in 2 seconds. Find the spring constant of either spring.
Solution: -
$f = 6$ cycles/2seconds $= 3$ Hz
$f = (1/2\pi) \sqrt{[g/\ell]} \Rightarrow \ell = g/4\pi^2f^2$
$\Rightarrow \ell = x = 9.8m/s^2/4\pi^2(3Hz)^2 = 0.027581878m$
$F = mg = 400kg \times 9.8m/s^2 = 3920N = Kx$
$\Rightarrow K = F/x = 3920N/ 0.027581878m = 142,122.3022N/m$
$\Rightarrow K = 1.42 \times 10^5N/m$

This problem can also be solved by putting the values directly in the equation given below: -
$w = 2\pi f = \sqrt{(K/m)}$
$\Rightarrow K = 4\pi^2f^2m = 4\pi^2 \times (3Hz)^2 \times 400kg = 1.421223022 \times 10^5N/m$

4) Objects of equal mass are oscillating up and down in Simple Harmonic Motion on two different vertical springs. The spring constant of spring 1 is 215N/m. The motion of the object, on spring 1 has three times the amplitude as the motion of the object on spring 2. The magnitude of the maximum velocity is the same in each case. Find the spring constant of spring 2.

Solution: -

$v_{max} = Aw = 3Aw_1 = Aw_2$

$\Rightarrow 3w_1 = w_2 = 3\sqrt{(K_1/m)} = \sqrt{(K_2/m)}$

$K_2 = 9K_1 = 9 \times 215N/m = 1935N/m$

$\Rightarrow K_2 = 1935N/m$

Energy and Simple Harmonic Motion: -

5) A heavy duty stapling gun uses a 0.2 kg metal rod that rams against the staple to eject it. The rod is pushed by a stiff spring called a "ram spring" (K = 25000N/m). The mass of the spring may be ignored. Squeezing the handle of the gun first compresses the ram spring by 9×10^{-3}m from its unstrained length and then releases it. Assuming that the ram spring is oriented vertically and is still compressed by 0.2×10^{-3}m when downward moving ram hits the staple; find the speed of the ram at the instant of contact.

Solution: -

$KE = (\frac{1}{2})mv^2 = PE_{elastic} = (\frac{1}{2})Kx_0^2 - (\frac{1}{2})Kx_f^2$

$\Rightarrow v = \sqrt{[(K/m)(x_0^2 - x_f^2)]}$

$v = \sqrt{[(25000N/m/0.2kg)[(9\times10^{-3}m)^2 - (0.2\times10^{-3}m)^2]]}$

$v = \sqrt{(10.12)} = 3.18m/s$

Hence the speed of the ram at the instant of contact is 3.18 ms^{-1}.

6) A 0.9kg object is suspended from a vertical spring whose spring constant is 99N/m. (a) Find the amount by which the spring is stretched from its unstrained length. (b) The object is pulled straight down by an additional distance of 0.3m and released from rest. Find the speed with which the object passes through its original position on the way up.

Solution: -

(a) $F = mg = Kx$

$x = F/K = mg/K = 0.9kg \times 9.8m/s^2/99N/m = 0.089090909$ m

$\Rightarrow x = 0.089m$

(b) $KE = PE_{elastic}$

$(\frac{1}{2})mv^2 = (\frac{1}{2})Kx^2$

$\Rightarrow v = \sqrt{(Kx^2/m)} = \sqrt{[(99N/m) \times (0.3m)^2/0.9kg]}$

$v = \sqrt{(9.9)} = 3.146426545m/s$

$\Rightarrow$ v = 3.146m/s

The Pendulum: -

7) Astronauts on a distant planet set up a simple pendulum of length 0.99m. The pendulum executes simple harmonic motion and makes 99 complete vibrations in 500 seconds. What is the acceleration due to gravity?

Solution: -

$T = 1/f = 2\pi\sqrt{[\ell/g]}$

$\Rightarrow g = 4\pi^2\ell/T^2$

$g = 4\pi^2 \times 0.99m/ (500seconds/99vibrations)^2$

$g = 4\pi^2(0.99m)/(5.050505051s)^2$

$g = 1.532234765m/s^2$

$\Rightarrow g = 1.53m/s^2$

Hence the acceleration due to gravity on the planet is 1.53m/s² and the time period of the given simple pendulum is 5.05s.

8) A point on the surface of a solid sphere (radius = r) is attached directly to a pivot on the ceiling. The sphere swings back and forth as a physical pendulum with a small amplitude. What is the length of a simple pendulum that has the same period as this physical pendulum? Give your answer in terms of r.

Solution: -

For a physical pendulum we have for its period as follows: -

$T = 2\pi\sqrt{[I/mgL]} = 2\pi\sqrt{[I/mgr]}$

Now for a solid sphere with its axis of rotation tangent to the surface, its moment of inertia, "I", given by: -

$I = (7/5) mr^2$

$\Rightarrow T = 2\pi\sqrt{(7r/5g)}$ _____ eqn.(i)

For a simple pendulum, the time period is given by: -

$T = 2\pi\sqrt{(L/g)}$ _____eqn.(ii)

Equating eqn. (i) equal to eqn. (ii), we have: -

$T = 2\pi\sqrt{(7r/5g)} = 2\pi\sqrt{(L/g)} \Rightarrow L = 7r/5$

$\Rightarrow L = (7/5) r$

Elastic Deformation, Stress, Strain, and Hooke's Law: -

9) A 4000kg statue is placed on top of a cylindrical material (Y = 3x10¹¹N/m²) stand. The stand has a cross-sectional area of 8x10⁻³m² and a height of 2m. By how much does the statue compress the stand?

Solution: -

$F/A = Y (\Delta L/L_0)$

$4000kg \times 9.8m/s^2/8x10^{-3}m^2 = (3x10^{11}N/m^2)(\Delta L/2m)$

$\Delta L = 4000kg \times 9.8m/s^2 \times 2m/(8x10^{-3}m^2 \times 3x10^{11}N/m^2)$

$\Delta L = 3266.666667x10^{-8}m$

$\Rightarrow \Delta L = 3.26x10^{-5}m$

10) Two metal beams are joined together by four rivets, each rivet has a radius of $6x10^{-2}m$ and is to be exposed to a shearing stress of no more than $6x10^7$pascals. What is the maximum tension T that can be applied to each beam, assuming that each rivet carries one-fourth of the total load? Solution: -

$F/A = S (\Delta X/X_0)$

$F/A = 6x10^7$pascals

$\Rightarrow T = 6x10^7$pascals $\times$ Area

$T = 6x10^7Pa \times \pi(6x10^{-2}m)^2 \times 4$

$T = 2714.336053 \times 10^3N$

$\Rightarrow T = 2.7x10^6N$

The rivets are circular and therefore the area of each rivet is πR^2.

11) The shovel of a backhoe is controlled by hydraulic cylinders that are moved by oil under pressure. Determine the volume strain $(\Delta V/V_0)$, including algebraic sign, experienced by the oil, when the pressure increases from $2x10^5Pa$ to $7x10^5Pa$ while the shovel is digging a trench.

Solution: -

$B = 1.7x10^9N/m^2$ for oil

$\Delta P = 7x10^5Pa - 2x10^5Pa = 5x10^5Pa$

$\Delta P = - B (\Delta V/V_0)$

$\Rightarrow \Delta V/V_0 = - \Delta P/B = - 5x10^5$pascal$/ 1.7x10^9 N/m^2$

$\Delta V/V_0 = 2.941176471x10^{-4}$

$\Rightarrow \Delta V/V_0 = 2.94x10^{-4}$

Hence the volume strain $\Delta V/V_0$ that has been determined comes out to be $\Delta V/V_0 = 2.94x10^{-4}$.

12) A solid brass sphere is subject to a pressure of $2.2x10^6$ Pa due to the atmosphere of a planet. On another planet, the pressure due to the atmosphere is $8x10^6$ Pa. By what fraction $\Delta r/r_0$ (including the algebraic sign) does the radius of the sphere change when it is exposed to the atmosphere of another planet (given above)? Assume that the change in radius is very small relative to the initial radius.

Solution: -

$\Delta P = 8x10^6$ Pa $- 2.2x10^6$ Pa $= 5.8x10^6 N/m^2$

$B = 6.7x10^{10} N/m^2$ for brass.

The volume of a sphere is given by: $- V = (4/3)\pi r^3$

$- \Delta P/B = (r^3 - r_0^3)/r_0^3 = -5.8 \times 10^6$ Pa$/6.7 \times 10^{10}$ N/m^2

$(r^3 - r_0^3)/r_0^3 = -8.656716418 \times 10^{-5}$

$\Rightarrow r^3/r_0^3 = 1 - 8.656716418 \times 10^{-5}$

$r^3/r_0^3 = 0.999913433$

$r/r_0 = \sqrt[3]{r^3/r_0^3} = \sqrt[3]{(0.999913433)} = .999971143$

$r/r_0 - 1 = (r - r_0)/r_0 \Rightarrow \Delta r/r_0 = 0.999971143 - 1$

$\Delta r/r_0 = -0.000028857$

$\Delta r/r_0 = -2.8857 \times 10^{-5}$

Hence the answer of this problem is $\Delta r/r_0 = -2.8857 \times 10^{-5}$.

Miscellaneous: -

13) Atoms in a solid are not stationary, but vibrate about their equilibrium position. Typically, the frequency of vibration is about $f = 9 \times 10^{11}$ Hz and the amplitude is about $A = 9 \times 10^{-12}$m. For a typical atom, what is its (a) maximum speed and (b) maximum acceleration?

Solution: -

(a) $w = 2\pi f = 2\pi (9 \times 10^{11}\text{Hz}) = 18\pi \times 10^{11}\text{rad/s}$

$v_{max} = Aw = (9 \times 10^{-12}\text{m}) \times 18\pi \times 10^{11}\text{rad/s}$

$\Rightarrow v_{max} = 50.89380099$ m/s $= 50.89$ m/s

(b) $a_{max} = Aw^2 = 9 \times 10^{-12}\text{m} (18\pi \times 10^{11}\text{ rad/s})^2$

$a_{max} = 2.8779766 \times 10^{14}$ m/s^2

$\Rightarrow a_{max} = 2.8779 \times 10^{14}$ m/s^2

Hence the maximum speed is 50.9m/s and the maximum acceleration is 2.8779×10^{14} m/s^2.

14) A spiral staircase winds up to the top of a tower in an old castle. To measure the height of the tower, a rope is attached to the top of the tower and hung down the center of the staircase. However, nothing is available with which to measure the length of the rope. Therefore at the bottom of the rope, a small object is attached so as to form a simple pendulum that just clears the floor. The period of the pendulum is measured to be 8 seconds. What is the height of the tower?

Solution: -

$T = 2\pi \sqrt{(\ell/g)}$

$\Rightarrow \ell = T^2 g/4\pi^2 = (8s)^2 \times 9.8\text{m/s}^2/4\pi^2$

$\ell = 15.887$m

$\Rightarrow \ell = 15.89$m

Hence the height of the tower has been computed to be, as given below: -

$\ell = 15.89$m.

15) A CD player is mounted on four cylindrical rubber blocks. Each cylinder has a height of 0.50m and a cross-sectional area of 2.1×10^{-2} m^2 and the shear modulus for rubber is 2.6×10^6 N/m^2. If a horizontal force of magnitude 50 N is applied to the CD player, how far will the unit move sideways? Assume that each block is subjected to one-fourth of the force.

Solution: -

$F/A = S (\Delta X/X_0)$

$\Rightarrow \Delta X = (F/A) (X_0/S)$

$\Delta X = [50N / (4 \times 2.1 \times 10^{-2}m)][0.5m/2.6 \times 10^6 \text{ N/m}^2]$

$\Rightarrow \Delta X = 1.144688645 \times 10^{-4}$m

Hence the unit will move sideways by a magnitude of $\Delta X = 1.144688645 \times 10^{-4}$m.

16) The spring constant of a spring is 400 N/m and the force applied is 200 N. What is the magnitude of the amount of stretching produced?

Solution: -

$F = - Kx$

$\Rightarrow x = - F/K = - 200 N/ 400 N/m = - 0.50 m$

$\Rightarrow x = - 0.50 m$

Hence the magnitude of the amount of stretching produced is x = - 0.50 m.

Heat: -

Chapter No. 11

· ·

Pressure in Gases and Liquids: -
Fluids are materials that can flow and these include both liquids and gases. The most familiar gas is the atmospheric air and the most familiar liquid is the water. The mass density of a liquid or a gas is an important factor that determines its behavior as a fluid.

Definition of Mass-Density: - The mass-density ρ is the mass m of a substance divided by its volume: -

$\Rightarrow \rho = m / V$

$\Rightarrow$ SI Unit of Mass Density: kg/ m^3

Definition of Specific Gravity: - The specific gravity of a substance is its density divided by the density of a standard reference material, usually chosen to be water at 4^0C.

Specific gravity = density of a substance / density of water at 4^0C

$\Rightarrow$ Sp. Gravity = density of a substance / 1×10^3kg/m^3

Hence the specific gravity of various substances are ice, 0.917; concrete, 2.2; silver, 10.5; gold, 19.3; diamond, 3.52; lead, 11.3; copper, 8.89; iron (steel), 7.86; aluminum, 2.7; brass, 8.47; mercury, 13.6; hydrolic oil, 0.8; and water, 1. Since specific gravity is a ratio, it has no units.

Pressure: - The pressure is defined as force divided by area over which the force acts.

$\Rightarrow P = F/ A$

The SI Unit of Pressure is Newton / meter^2 (N/m^2) or Pascal (Pa). Another unit of pressure is pounds / inches^2 or (lb/ in^2) abbreviated as "psi". Now 1 Pa is a very small magnitude, therefore we use 10^5 Pa called one bar of pressure.

Atmospheric Pressure at sea level = 1.013×10^5 Pa = 1 atmosphere

Pressure and Depth in a Static Fluid: - For a static fluid in equilibrium we have the following: -

$P_2 A - P_1 A = mg$

Note P_2 and P_1 are the pressure at the bottom and at the top of a column of static fluid and m is the mass of the fluid.

$\Rightarrow P_2 = P_1 + \rho gh$

Where $P_1 = 1.013 \times 10^5$ Pa is the atmospheric pressure equal to one atmosphere.

Now $P_2 = (P_{atm} + \rho gh)$ is called the absolute pressure and $(P_2 - P_{atm})$ = ρgh is called the gauge pressure.

Pascal's Principle: - According to the Pascal's principle, any change in the pressure applied to a completely enclosed fluid is transmitted undiminished to all parts of the fluid and the enclosing walls.

$\Rightarrow F_2 = F_1 (A_2/ A_1)$

This is derived from the equation $P_2 = P_1 + \rho gh$. When the two pressures, P_2 and P_1 are at the same level so that the pressure increment $\rho gh = 0$, and $P_2 = P_1$.

Archimede's Principle: - According to Archimede's Principle, any fluid applies a buoyant force to an object that is partially or completely immersed in it: the magnitude of the buoyant force equals the weight of the fluid that the object displaces.

$\Rightarrow F_B = W_{FLUID}$

(magnitude of the buoyant force) = (weight of the displaced fluid)

Ideal Fluid: - When the fluid particles passing at a point in a fluid, flow at the same velocity, it is called a steady flow, otherwise it is termed an unsteady flow. There is also an incompressible flow and compressible flow. In an incompressible flow the density remains constant e.g a liquid. In a compressible flow, the density

of flowing fluid changes like in most gases. Fluid flow can be viscous and non-viscous. Now honey has high viscosity where as water is much less viscous. A fluid with zero viscosity flows in an unhindered way without dissipation of energy. No fluid, however, has zero viscosity at normal temperature but some fluids still exhibit negligibly small viscosity.

$\Rightarrow$ An incompressible, non-viscous fluid is called an ideal fluid.

The Equation of Continuity: - The equation of continuity is an expression of the fact that mass is conserved (i.e neither created nor destroyed) as the fluid flows. According to the equation of continuity, the mass flow rate (ρAv) has the same value at every position along a tube that has a single entry and a single exit point for fluid flow. For two positions along such a tube, we have as follows: -

$\Rightarrow \rho_1 A_1 v_1 = \rho_2 A_2 v_2$

Where ρ = fluid density (kg/ m^3)

A = cross-sectional area of tube (m²)

v = fluid velocity (m/s)

SI unit of Mass Flow Rate: kg/s

For an incompressible fluid, the density does not change.

$\Rightarrow A_1 v_1 = A_2 v_2$ ($\because \rho_1 = \rho_2$)

$\Rightarrow Q$ = Volume flow rate = Av

Bernoulli's Equation: - For steady flow, the speed, pressure, and elevation of an incompressible, non-viscous fluid are related by an equation known as Bernoulli's equation.

The pressure within a fluid is caused by collisional forces, which are non-conservative. The work done by non-conservative forces is not equal to zero, $\Rightarrow W_{nc} \neq 0$. We use work-energy theorem to derive Bernoulli's equation as follows: -

$W_{nc} = E_f - E_0 = (1/2\ mv_f^2 + mgh_f) - (1/2\ mv_0^2 + mgh_0)$

F = PA

$\Rightarrow F + \Delta F = (P + \Delta P)\ A$

$\Rightarrow \Delta F = (\Delta P)\ A$

$W = (\Delta F)\ s = (\Delta P)\ As = (\Delta P)\ V$ ($\because V = As$)

$\Rightarrow W_{nc} = (P_2 - P_1)\ V = (1/2\ mv_1^2 + mgy_1) - (1/2\ mv_2^2 + mgy_2)$

Dividing by V and noting $\rho = m/V$, we have as follows: -

$P_2 - P_1 = (1/2\ \rho v_1^2 + \rho g y_1) - (1/2\ \rho v_2^2 + \rho g y_2)$

$\Rightarrow P_1 + 1/2\ \rho v_1^2 + \rho g y_1 = P_2 + 1/2\ \rho v_2^2 + \rho g y_2$

Hence according to Bernoulli's equation, in the steady flow of a non-viscous, incompressible fluid of density ρ, the pressure P, the fluid speed v, and the elevation y at any two points (1 and 2) are related by: -

$\Rightarrow P_1 + 1/2\ \rho v_1^2 + \rho g y_1 = P_2 + 1/2\ \rho v_2^2 + \rho g y_2$

When the speed of the fluid is the same $v_1 = v_0$ as it is when the cross-sectional area remains constant we have as follows: -

$P_2 = P_1 + \rho g(y_1 - y_2) = P_1 + \rho g \Delta y$

When the moving fluids are contained in a horizontal pipe and the elevations are equal i.e. $y_1 = y_2$ we have as follows: -

$P_1 + 1/2\ \rho v_1^2 = P_2 + 1/2\ \rho v_2^2$

Hence the quantity $(P + 1/2\ \rho v^2)$ remains constant and when v increases P decreases.

Viscous Flow: -

Forces needed to move a layer of Viscous fluid with a constant velocity: -

The magnitude of the tangential force F required to move a fluid layer at a constant speed v, when the layer has an area A and is located a

perpendicular distance y from an immobile surface is given as follows:
-

$F = \eta Av / y$

where η is the coefficient of viscosity.

SI Unit of Viscosity: Pa.s

Common unit of Viscosity: Poise (P) = (0.1) Pa.s

Poiseuille's Law: - According to Poiseuille's law, a fluid whose viscosity is η, flowing through a pipe of radius R and length L, has a volume flow rate Q given as follows: -

$Q = \pi R^4 (P_2 - P_1) / 8\eta L$

where P_1 and P_2 are the pressures at the two ends of the pipe.

Pressure in Gases and Liquids: -

(11) Numerical Problems: -

Mass Density: -

1) A bar of gold measures (0.14m x 0.04m x 0.04m). How many gallons of water have the same mass as this bar?

Solution: -

$V_{Au} = 0.14m \times 0.04m \times 0.04m = 2.24 \times 10^{-4}$ m³

Mass of gold $= \rho_{Au} \times V_{Au} = 19,300$ kg/ m³ x 2.24×10^{-4} m³

Mass$_{Au} = 4.3232$ kg

$V (H_2O) = m/\rho = 4.3232$ kg / $[1 \times 10^3$ kg/ m³] $= 4.3232 \times 10^{-3}$ m³

1 US gallon $= 3.785 \times 10^{-3}$ m³

$\Rightarrow V = 4.3232 \times 10^{-3}$ m³ / 3.785×10^{-3} m³ $= 1.142192867$ gallons

$\Rightarrow V = 1.14$ gallons

Hence there will be approximately 1.14 gallons of water which have the same mass as the given bar of gold.

2) An antifreeze solution is made by mixing ethylene glycol ($\rho = 1116$ kg/m³) with water. Suppose the specific gravity of such a solution is 1.089. Assume that the total volume of the solution is the sum of its components; determine the volume percentage of ethylene glycol in the solution.

Solution: -

$\rho_1 V_1 + \rho_2 V_2 = \rho V$

$\Rightarrow 1116 V_1 + 1000 V_2 = 1089 V$ equation (i)

$V_1 + V_2 = V$ equation (ii)

$\Rightarrow 1116 V_1 + (V - V_1)1000 = 1089 V$

$116 V_1 = 1089 V - 1000 V$

$\Rightarrow V_1/V = 89/116$

$\Rightarrow \% V_1/V = [89/116] \times 100 = 76.7\%$

Pressure: -

3) A cylinder (with circular ends) and a hemisphere are solid throughout and made from the same material. They are resting on the ground, the cylinder on one of its ends and the hemisphere on one of its sides. The weight of each causes the same pressure to act on the ground. The cylinder is 1/3 m high. What is the radius of the hemisphere?

Solution: -

$P = F/A = \rho ghA/A = \rho gh$

$V = 1/2 [(4/3) \pi r^3] = \pi r^2 h$

Volume of hemisphere = Volume of cylinder ($\because P_1 = P_2$)

$\Rightarrow 1/2 [(4/3)\pi r^3] = \pi r^2(1/3)$ ($\because V_1 = V_2$)

$\Rightarrow 2\pi r^3 = \pi r^2$

$\Rightarrow r = 1/2 = 0.5$ m

Hence the radius of the hemisphere is 0.5 m.

Pressure and Depth in a Static Fluid: -

Pressure Gauges: -

4) A water tower is a familiar sight in many towns. The purpose of such a tower is to provide storage capacity and to provide sufficient pressure in the pipes that deliver the water to customers. There is a spherical reservoir that contains 6×10^6 kg of water when full. The reservoir is vertical to the atmosphere at the top. For a full reservoir, find the gauge pressure that the water has at the faucet in (a) House A (20 m underneath the bottom of the reservoir) and (b) House B (12.5 m underneath the bottom of the reservoir).

Solution: -

$P_2 = P_1 + \rho gh$ = Absolute Pressure

$P_2 - P_1 = \rho gh$ = Gauge Pressure

$\rho = M/V$

$V = (6 \times 10^6$ kg$)/ (1 \times 10^3$ kg/m$^3) = 6 \times 10^3$ m^3

$V = (4/3) \pi r^3 = 6 \times 10^3$ m^3

$\Rightarrow r^3 = [(6 \times 3 \times 10^3)/4\pi]$ m$^3 = 1.432394488 \times 10^3$ m^3

$\Rightarrow r = \sqrt[3]{(1.432394488 \times 10^3)} = 11.27251652$ m

$d = 2r = 2 \times 11.27251652$ m $= 22.54503304$ m

$\Rightarrow h_A = 20 + 2r = 42.54503304$ m

$\Rightarrow h_B = 12.5 + 2r = 35.04503304$ m

(a) $P_A = \rho gh_A = 1 \times 10^3 \times 9.8 \times 42.54503304$

$\Rightarrow P_A = 4.16941 \times 10^5$ Pa

(b) $P_B = \rho g h_B = 1 \times 10^3 \times 9.8 \times 35.04503304$

$\Rightarrow P_B = 3.43441 \times 10^5$ Pa

5) Mercury is poured into a tall glass. Ethyl alcohol is then poured on top of the mercury until the height of ethyl alcohol itself is 90 cm. The two fluids do not mix, and the air pressure at the top of ethyl alcohol is one atmosphere. What is the absolute pressure at a point that is 5.2 cm below the ethyl-alcohol-mercury interface?

Solution: -

P_2 is absolute pressure.

$P_2 = P_1 + \rho_1 g h_1 + \rho_2 g h_2 = 1$ atmosphere $+ \rho_1 g h_1 + \rho_2 g h_2$

$\Rightarrow P_2 = 1.013 \times 10^5 + 806 \times 9.8 \times 0.9 + 13,600 \times 9.8 \times 0.052$

$P_2 = (1.013 + 0.0710892 + 0.0693056) \times 10^5$

$P_2 = 1.1533948 \times 10^5$ Pa

$\Rightarrow P_2 = 1.153 \times 10^5$ Pa

Hence the required absolute pressure is 1.153×10^5 Pascals.

6) A 2m tall container is filled to the brim, partway with mercury and the rest of the way with water. The container is open to the atmosphere. What must be the depth of the mercury so that the absolute pressure on the bottom of the container is three times the atmospheric pressure?

Solution: -

$P_2 = P_1 + \rho_1 g h_1 + \rho_2 g h_2 = 3$ atmosphere

$\Rightarrow \rho_1 g h_1 + \rho_2 g h_2 = 3$ atmosphere $- 1$ atmosphere $= 2$ atmosphere

$13,600 g h_1 + 1000 g (2 - h_1) = 2 \times 1.013 \times 10^5$ Pa

$(133280 - 9800) h_1 = (2.026 - 0.196) \times 10^5 = 1.83 \times 10^5$ Pa

$123480 h_1 = 1.83 \times 10^5$ Pa

$h_1 = 1.83 \times 10^5 / 1.23480 \times 10^5 = 1.48202138$ m

$\Rightarrow h_1 = 1.48202138$ m

Hence the required depth of the mercury should be 1.48 m approximately.

Pascal's Principle: -

7) The atmospheric pressure above a swimming pool changes from 749 mm to 771 mm of mercury. The bottom of the swimming pool is 16m x 19 m rectangle. By how much does the force on the bottom of the swimming pool increase?

Solution: -

1 atmosphere $= 1.013 \times 10^5$ N/ m² or Pascals $= 760$ mm of mercury

$\Rightarrow \Delta F = (\Delta P) A$

$\Delta P = [(771mm - 749mm)/ 760mm] \times 1.013 \times 10^5$ N/m²

$\Rightarrow \Delta P = 2932.368421$ N/m^2

A = total area of the pool = 16m x 19m = 304m^2

$\Rightarrow \Delta F = (\Delta P)$ A

$\Rightarrow \Delta F = 2932.368421$N /m^2 x 304m^2 = 8.9144x10^5 N

$\Rightarrow \Delta F = 8.9144$x10^{5}N

Hence as the pressure over the swimming pool changes from 749mm to 771mm of mercury, the increase in force on the bottom of the pool is 8.9144x10^{5}N.

Archimede's Principle: -

8) What is the radius of a helium filled balloon that would carry a load of 6000 N (in addition to the weight of the helium) when the density of the air is 1.29 kg/m^3?

Solution: -

weight of helium + weight of load = weight of balloon

$(.179)(4/3)\pi r^3 kg \times 9.8m/s^2 + 6000$ N $= (1.29)(4/3)\pi r^3 kg \times 9.8m/s^2$

$\Rightarrow (4/3)\pi r^3 (10.8878) = 6000$ N

$\Rightarrow r^3 = 6000 \times 3/(4\pi \times 10.8878) = 131.5595885$

$\Rightarrow r = {}^3\sqrt{(131.5595885)} = 5.085974388$m

Hence the radius of the given balloon has been calculated to be r = 5.0859m.

9) A solid cylinder (radius = 0.25m, height = 0.2m) has a mass of 30kg. This cylinder is floating in water. Then oil (ρ = 700kg/m^3) is poured on top of the water until the cylinder is partly inside the water and part of it on top is inside the oil. How much height of the cylinder is inside the oil?

Solution: -

$\rho = m/ \pi r^2 h = 30kg/ \pi(0.25m)^2 \times 0.2m$

$\Rightarrow \rho = 763.9437267$ kg/m^3

$700 \times 9.8 \times \pi(0.25)^2(0.2 - h) + 10^3 \times 9.8 \times \pi(0.25)^2 h = 30kg \times 9.8m/s^2$

$\Rightarrow 269.39157 - 1346.95785h + 1924.2255h = 294$

$\Rightarrow 1924.2255h - 1346.95785h = 294 - 269.39157$

$\Rightarrow 577.2676503h = 24.60843$

$\Rightarrow h = 24.60843/ (577.2676503) = 0.042629151$m

$\Rightarrow h = 4.262915 \times 10^{-2}$ m

Hence the height of the cylinder which is inside the oil is 4.2629cm.

The Equation of Continuity: -

10) A room has a volume of 200 m^3. An air conditioning system is to replace the air in this room every fifteen minutes (15 minutes), using

ducts that have a square cross-section. Assuming that the air can be treated as an incompressible fluid, find the length of a side of the square if the air speed within the ducts is (a) 2m/s and (b) 4 m/s.

Solution: -

Q = Volume/ time = 200 m^3 / 15x60s = 200/900 = 2/9 m^3/s

(a) $Q = A_1v_1$ = (2/9) m^3/s

$\Rightarrow A_1 = Q/v_1$ = (2/9) m^3/s /2m/s = (1/9) m^2

$1 = \sqrt{(A_1)} = \sqrt{1^2} = \sqrt{(1/9)}$ = 1/3 = 0.333333333 m^2

(b) $Q = A_2v_2$ = (2/9) m^3/s

$\Rightarrow A_2 = Q/v_2$ = (2/9) m^3/s / 4m/s = (1/18) m^2

$1 = \sqrt{(A_2)} = \sqrt{1^2} = \sqrt{(1/18)}$ = 0.23570226 m

$\Rightarrow$ (a) 1 = 0.33m and (b) 1 = 0.2357 m.

Bernoulli's Equation: -

Application of Bernoulli's Equation: -

11) The construction of a flat rectangular roof (4mx7m) allows it to withstand a maximum net outward force of 30,000 N. The density of air is 1.29 kg/m^3. At what wind speed will this roof blow outward?

Solution: -

P = F/A = 30,000N/(4mx7m) = 30,000/28 = 1071.428571 Pa

$P = (1/2) \rho v^2$

$\Rightarrow v = \sqrt{(2P/\rho)} = \sqrt{(2x1071.428571/1.29)} = \sqrt{(1661.129567)}$

$\Rightarrow v$ = 40.75695729 m/s

Hence the roof will blow outward at a wind speed of 40.76m/s.

12) A ventri meter is a device for measuring the speed of a fluid within a pipe. There is a gas flowing at a speed v_2 through a horizontal section of a pipe whose cross-sectional area is A_2 = 0.09m^2. The gas has a density of 1.4kg/m^3. The ventri meter has a cross-sectional area of A_1 = 0.06m^2 and has been substituted for a section of the larger pipe right in the middle. The pressure difference between the two sections is $P_2 - P_1$ = 140Pa. Find (a) the speed v_2 of the gas in the larger original pipe and (b) the volume flow rate Q of the gas.

Solution: -

(a) $P_2 - P_1 = (1/2)\rho(v_1^2 - v_2^2) = (1/2) \rho v_1^2[1 - (A_1/A_2)^2]$

$v_1^2 = 2(P_2 - P_1)/ \rho[1 - (A_1/A_2)^2] = 2x140$ Pa/ 1.4[1 - (.06/.09)^2]

$\Rightarrow v_1^2 = 360$

$\Rightarrow v_1 = \sqrt{(360)}$ = 18.97366596m/s

$\Rightarrow v_2 = (.06/.09) x 18.97366596 = 12.64911064$ m/s

$\Rightarrow v_1 = 18.97m/s$ and $v_2 = 12.649$ m/s

(b) $Q = A_2v_2 = .09$ x $12.64911064 = 1.138419958$ m³/s

$\Rightarrow Q = 1.138$ m³/s

Viscous Flow: -

13) When an object moves through a fluid, the fluid exerts a viscous force F on the object that tends to slow it down. For a small sphere of radius R, moving slowly with speed v, the magnitude of the viscous force is given by Stoke's Law viz. $F = 6\pi\eta Rv$, where η is the viscosity of the fluid. (a) What is the viscous force on a sphere of radius $R = 9x10^{-3}$ m falling through water ($\eta = 1x10^{-2}Pa.s$), when the sphere has a speed of 4 m/s?

(b) The speed of the falling sphere increases until the viscous force balances the weight of the sphere. Therefore no net force acts on the sphere, and it falls with a constant speed called the "terminal speed". If the sphere has $m = 1x10^{-3}kg$, what is its terminal speed?

Solution: -

(a) $F = 6\pi\eta Rv$ Stoke's Law

$\Rightarrow F = 6\pi x(1x10^{-2} Pa.s)x(9x10^{-3}m)x(4m/s)$

$\Rightarrow F = 6.7858x10^{-3}$ N

(b) $F = 1x10^{-3}kg$ x $9.8m/s^2 = 9.8x10^{-3}N$

$\Rightarrow F = 6\pi x(1x10^{-2} Pa.s)(9x10^{-3}m)v = 9.8x10^{-3}N$

$\Rightarrow v = 9.8x10^{-3}N/[6\pi(1x10^{-2}Pa.s)(9x10^{-3}m)]$

$\Rightarrow v = 5.776735m/s$

Miscellaneous: -

14) A pressure difference of $2x10^4$ Pa is needed to drive water ($\eta = 1x10^{-4}$ Pa.s) through a pipe whose radius is $9x10^{-4}$ m. The volume flow rate of the water is $3x10^{-5}$ m³/s. What is the length of the pipe?

Solution: -

$Q = \pi R^4 (P_2 - P_1) / 8\eta L$

$\Rightarrow L = \pi R^4(P_2 - P_1)/ (8\eta Q)$

$L = \pi(9x10^{-4}m)^4(2x10^4 Pa) / [8x(1x10^{-4} Pa.s)x3x10^{-5} m^3/s]$

$\Rightarrow L = 1.717$ m

Hence the length of the pipe is 1.717m.

15) Water is running out of a faucet, falling straight down, with an initial speed of 1.0 m/s. At what distance below the faucet is the radius of the stream reduced to one-third of its value at the faucet?

Solution: -

$A_1 = \pi r_1^2$

$A_2 = \pi r_2^2$

$A_1 v_1 = A_2 v_2$

$(\because r_1 = 3r_2 \Rightarrow A_1 = 9A_2)$

$v_1 = 9v_2 = 9 \times 1 m/s = 9 m/s$

$v_2 = 1\ m/s$

$v_1^2 - v_2^2 = 2gy$

$\Rightarrow y = (v_1^2 - v_2^2)/\ 2g = [(9)^2 - (1)^2]/2 \times 9.8 = [81 - 1]/19.6$

$\Rightarrow y = 80/19.6 = 4.081632653\ m$

Hence the distance below the faucet at which the radius of the stream is one-third of its value at the faucet is $y = 4.08 m$.

Chapter No. 12

· ·

Temperature and Heat: -

Common Temperature Scale: -

On the Celsius temperature scale or the centigrade temperature scale, there are 100 equal divisions between the ice point (0⁰C) and the steam point (100⁰C). On the Fahrenheit temperature scale, there are 180 equal divisions between the ice point (32⁰F) and the steam point (212⁰F).

To change from Fahrenheit scale to Centigrade scale, we use the following relation: -

$(F - 32)5/9 = C$

To change from Centigrade scale to Fahrenheit scale, we use just the reverse operation as follows: -

$\Rightarrow (9/5)C + 32 = F$

The Kelvin Temperature Scale: -

For scientific work, the Kelvin temperature scale is the scale of choice. One Kelvin (K) is equal in size to one centigrade degree. However, the temperature T on the Kelvin scale differs from the temperature T_C on the centigrade scale by an additive constant, 273.15, as follows: -

$T = T_C + 273.15$

The lower limit of temperature is called absolute zero and is designated as 0 K on the Kelvin scale. Absolute zero is equal to -273.15⁰C, $\Rightarrow$ 0 K = - 273.15⁰C. No substance can be cooled beyond absolute zero and the volume of all substances becomes zero at absolute zero. Cooling beyond absolute zero would imply having a negative volume of a substance which is not possible in the realm of science.

Thermometers: -

The operation of any thermometer is based on the change in some physical property with temperature; this physical property is called a thermometric property. Examples of thermometric properties are the length of a mercury column in mercury thermometers, pressure of a gas in a constant volume gas thermometer, electrical resistance in an electrical resistance thermometer, electrical voltage in a thermocouple, infrared radiation in a thermogram or a thermograph.

Linear Thermal Expansion: -

Most substances expand when heated. For linear expansion, an object of length L_0 experiences a change in length ΔL when the temperature changes by ΔT as follows: -

$\Delta L = \alpha L_0 \Delta T$

where α is the coefficient of linear expansion.

For an object held rigidly in place, a thermal stress can occur when the object attempts to expand or contract. The stress can be large, even for small temperature changes.

When the temperatures change, a hole in a plate of solid material expands or contracts as if the hole were filled with the surrounding material.

Volume Thermal Expansion: -

For volume expansion, the change ΔV in the volume of an object of volume V_0 is given by the following equation: -

$\Delta V = \beta V_0 \Delta T$

where β is the coefficient of volume expansion.

When the temperatures change, a cavity in a piece of solid material expands or contracts as if the cavity were filled with the surrounding material.

Heat and Internal Energy: -

The internal energy of a substance is the sum of the kinetic, potential, and other kinds of energy that the molecules of the substance have: - Heat is energy that flows from a higher temperature object to a lower temperature object because of the difference in temperatures. The SI unit of heat is the Joule (J).

Although heat may originate in the internal energy supply of a substance, it is not correct to say that a substance contains heat. The substance has internal energy, not heat. The word "heat" is used only when referring to the energy actually in transit from hot to cold.

Heat and Temperature Change: Specific Heat Capacity: -

The amount of heat Q that must be supplied or removed to change the temperature of a substance of mass m by an amount ΔT is given by the following relation: -

$Q = Cm\Delta T$

Note C is a constant, known as Specific Heat Capacity.

When materials are placed in thermal contact within a perfectly insulated container, the principle of energy conservation requires that the heat lost by warmer materials equals the heat gained by cooler materials.

Heat is sometimes measured with a unit called the kilocalorie (kcal). The conversion factor between kilocalories and joules is known as the mechanical equivalent of heat.

1 kilocalorie = 4186 joules

This is also the specific heat capacity of water at 15^0C. $\Rightarrow$ The specific heat capacity of water is c = 4186 J/kg.C^0 or 1 kcal/kgC^0.

Heat Units other than the Joule: -

According to the equation Q = CmΔT, the specific heat capacity of water can be given as c = 1 kcal/kg.C^0 or it can be given as c = 1 cal/g. C^0. Nutritionists use the word Calorie with a capital C, to specify energy contents of foods; this use is unfortunate since 1 Calorie = 1000 calories = 1 kilocalorie. The British thermal unit (Btu) is the other commonly used unit and was defined historically as the amount of heat needed to raise the temperature of one pound of water by one Fahrenheit degree.

$\Rightarrow$ 1 kilocalorie = 4186 Joules

OR

1 calorie = 4.186 Joules

A calorimeter is used to measure the thermal change or change in thermal energy of a substance.

Heat and Phase Change: Latent Heat: -

Heat must be supplied or removed to make a material change from one phase to another. The heat Q that must be supplied or removed to change the phase of mass m of a substance is given as follows: -

Q = mL

where L is the latent heat of the substance and has SI unit of J/kg.

The latent heats of fusion, vaporization, and sublimation refer, respectively, to the solid/liquid, liquid/vapor, and the solid/vapor phase changes.

Equilibrium between Phases of Matter: -

The equilibrium vapor pressure of a substance is the pressure of the vapor phase that is in equilibrium with the liquid phase. For a given substance, vapor pressure depends only on temperature. For a liquid, a plot of the equilibrium vapor pressure versus temperature is called the vapor pressure or vaporization curve.

The fusion curve gives the combination of temperature and pressure for equilibrium between solid and liquid phases.

Humidity: -

The relative humidity is defined as follows: -

% relative humidity = [Partial Pressure of water vapor / Equilibrium vapor pressure

of water at the existing temperature] x100

The dew point is the temperature below which the water vapor in the air condenses. On the vaporization curve of water, the dew point is the temperature that corresponds to the actual pressure of the water vapor in the air.

Temperature and Heat: -

(12) Numerical Problems: -

Common Temperature Scales; the Kelvin Temperature Scale; Thermometers: -

1) The normal body temperature is 98.4^0F. What does this temperature correspond to on the Centigrade scale?

Solution: -

The expression applied for converting a reading on Fahrenheit Scale to a reading on Centigrade Scale is as follows: -

$(F - 32)5/9 = C$

$\Rightarrow (98.4 - 32)$ x5/9 = 66.4x5/9 = 332/9 = 36.88888889

$\Rightarrow 98.4^0F \equiv 36.89^0C$

Hence 98.4^0F is equivalent to 36.89^0C on the Centigrade scale.

2) A personal computer is designed to operate over the temperature range from 41 to113^0F. To what do these temperatures correspond to (a) on the Centigrade scale and (b) on the Kelvin scale?

Solution: -

(a) $(41F^0 - 32)5/9 = 9x5/9 = 5^0C$

$(113F^0 - 32)5/9 = 81x5/9 = 9x5 = 45^0C$

(b) $T = T_c + 273.15 = 5^0C + 273.15 = 278.15$ K

$T = T_c + 273.15 = 45^0C + 273.15 = 318.15$ K

3) What does the temperature 45^0C on the Centigrade scale correspond to on the Fahrenheit Scale?

Solution: -

The expression used for converting a reading on the Centigrade scale to a reading on the Fahrenheit scale is as follows: -

$(9/5)C + 32 = F$

$\Rightarrow (9/5) \times 45 + 32 = 9 \times 9 + 32 = 81 + 32 = 113^0F$

$\Rightarrow T = 45^0C \equiv 113^0F$

Hence the reading of 45^0C on the Centigrade scale that corresponds to a reading on the Fahrenheit scale is 113^0F.

4) Evaluate the readings (a) 50^0C and (b) 70^0C that correspond to the readings on the Kelvin temperature scale.

(Hint: $0 K = -273^0C$)

Solution: -

(a) $T = T_C + 273.15 = 50^0C + 273.15 = 323.15 K$

$\Rightarrow T = 323.15 K$

(b) $T = T_C + 273.15 = 70^0C + 273.15 = 343.15 K$

$\Rightarrow T = 343.15 K$

Hence 50^0C corresponds to $323.15 K$ on the Kelvin temperature scale and 70^0C corresponds to $343.15 K$ on the Kelvin temperature scale.

Linear Thermal Expansion: -

5) A steel aircraft carrier is 390 m long when moving through the icy North Atlantic at a temperature of 3^0C. By how much does the carrier lengthen when it is travelling in the warm Mediteranean Sea at a temperature of 23^0C?

Solution: -

α (Steel) $= 12 \times 10^{-6} (C^0)^{-1} =$ coefficient of linear expansion of steel

$\Delta L = \alpha L_0 \Delta T = 12 \times 10^{-6}(C^0)^{-1} \times 390m \times (23 - 3) C^0$

$\Rightarrow \Delta L = .0936m = 9.36$ cm

Hence the aircraft carrier will lengthen by 0.0936m.

6) Find the approximate length of the Golden Gate Bridge if it is known that the steel in the roadbed expands by 0.6m when the temperature changes from +3 to 36.3^0C.

Solution: -

α (Steel) $= 12 \times 10^{-6} (C^0)^{-1}$

$\Delta L = \alpha L_0 (\Delta T)$

$\Rightarrow L_0 = \Delta L / \alpha(\Delta T) = 0.6m / [12 \times 10^{-6}(C^0)^{-1} \times (36.3 - 3) C^0]$

$\Rightarrow L_0 = 1500m$

Hence the approximate length of the Golden Gate Bridge is 1500m.

Volume Thermal Expansion: -

7) A copper kettle contains water at 30^0C. When the water is heated to its boiling point, the volume of the kettle expands by 2.1×10^{-5} m^3. Determine the volume of the kettle at 30^0C.

Solution: -

β(Cu) = $51 \times 10^{-6}(C^0)^{-1}$ = coefficient of volume expansion of Cu.

$\Delta V = \beta V_0 (\Delta T)$

$\Rightarrow V_0 = \Delta V / \beta(\Delta T)$

$V_0 = 2.1 \times 10^{-5}$ $m^3 / [51 \times 10^{-6} \times (100 - 30)]$

$\Rightarrow V_0 = 5.88 \times 10^{-3}$ m^3

Hence the volume of the kettle is 5.88×10^{-3} m^3, which is the value for its volume at 30^0C.

8) A thin spherical shell of silver has an inner radius of 54×10^{-3} m, when the temperature is 20^0C. The shell is heated to 150^0C. Find the change in the interior volume of the shell. The coefficient of thermal volume expansion of silver is given as $\beta = 57 \times 10^{-6}$ $(C^0)^{-1}$.

Solution: -

$\beta = 57 \times 10^{-6}$ $(C^0)^{-1}$ = coefficient of thermal expansion for silver

$\Delta V = \beta V_0 (\Delta T) = 57 \times 10^{-6}$ $(C^0)^{-1} \times (4/3)\pi(54 \times 10^{-3}$ m$)^3 \times (150-20)C^0$

$\Rightarrow \Delta V = 57 \times (4/3)\pi(5.4)^3 \times 130 \times 10^{-12}$

$\Rightarrow \Delta V = 4.887514927 \times 10^{-6}$ m^3

Hence the change in the interior volume of the given shell will be 4.8875×10^{-6} m^3, which we have calculated above.

Heat and Internal Energy; Heat and Temperature: Specific Heat Capacity: -

9) A rock of mass 0.3 kg falls from rest from a height of 20 m into a pail containing 0.4 kg of water. The rock and water have the same initial temperature. The specific heat capacity of the rock is 1930 J/kg.C^0. Ignore the heat absorbed by the pail itself, and determine the rise in temperature of the rock and water.

Solution: -

P.E = potential energy = mgh = Q = heat energy = Cm (ΔT)

$\Rightarrow$ P.E = mgh = 0.3kg $\times$ 9.8m/s^2 $\times$ 20m = 58.8J

$\Rightarrow$ Q = C_1 m_1 (ΔT) + C_2 m_2 (ΔT)

$\Rightarrow$ Q = 0.4kg $\times$ 4186J/kg.C^0 $\times$ ΔT + 0.3kg $\times$ 1930J/kg.C^0 $\times$ ΔT

$\Rightarrow$ Q = 58.8J = (0.4 $\times$ 4186 + 0.3 $\times$ 1930) ΔT

$\Rightarrow$ ΔT = 58.8J/ [2253.4J/C^0] = $0.026093903C^0$

$\Rightarrow \Delta T = 0.02609 \ C^0$

Hence the rise in temperature of the rock and water is $0.02609 \ C^0$.

10) In a passive solar house, the sun heats water stored in barrels to a temperature of 40^0C. The stored energy is then used to heat the house on cloudy days. Suppose that $3 \times 10^9 J$ of heat is needed to maintain the inside of the house at 19^0C. How many barrels (1barrel $= 2.2 \ m^3$) of water are needed?

Solution: -

$Q = Cm \ (\Delta T)$

$\Rightarrow 3 \times 10^9 J = 4186 J/kg.C^0 \ x \ m \ x \ (40 - 19) \ C^0$

$\Rightarrow m = 3 \times 10^9 J / \ [4186 J/kg.C^0 \ x \ 21 C^0] = 34127.36332 \ kg$

$\Rightarrow V = m \ / \ \rho = 34127.36332 \ kg / \ 1 \times 10^3 \ kg/m^3 = 34.12736332 \ m^3$

No. of barrels $= 34.12736332 \ m^3 \ / \ 2.2 \ m^3 = 15.5$ barrels

Hence approximately 16 barrels of water are needed.

11) If the price of electrical energy is $0.08 per kilowatt-hour, what is the cost of using electrical energy to heat the water in a swimming pool (15m x 7m x 2m) from 19 to 30^0C?

Solution: -

$Q = Cm \ (\Delta t)$

$C = 4186 \ J/kg.C^0$ for water

$\Delta T = 30 - 19 = 11 C^0$

$m = V\rho = (15m \ x \ 7m \ x \ 2m) \ x \ 1 \times 10^3 \ kg/m^3 = 2.1 \times 10^5 kg$

$\Rightarrow Q = Cm \ (\Delta T) = 4186 J/kg.C^0 \ x \ 2.1 \times 10^5 kg \ x \ 11 C^0$

$\Rightarrow Q = 9.66966 \times 10^9 J$

$1 \ KWh = 3.6 \times 10^6 J$

$\Rightarrow E = 9.66966 \times 10^9 J / \ 3.6 \times 10^6 J = 2686.016667 \ KWh$

$\Rightarrow Cost = 2686.016667 \ KWh \ x \ \$0.08/KWh = \$214.88$

Hence the cost of heating the water in the given swimming pool by electrical energy will be \$214.88.

12) At a fabrication plant, a hot metal forging has a mass of 80kg and a specific heat capacity of $500 J/kg.C^0$. To harden it, the forging is immersed in 800kg of oil that has a temperature of 40^0C and a specific heat capacity of $3,000 \ J/kg.C^0$. The final temperature of the oil and the forging at thermal equilibrium is 50^0C. Assuming that heat flows only between the forging and the oil, determine the initial temperature of the forging.

Solution: -

$Q = C_1 m_1 \ (\Delta T_1) = C_2 m_2 \ (\Delta T_2)$

Heat gained = Heat lost

500J/kg.C⁰x 80kg (T – 50) C⁰ = 3000J/kg.C⁰x 800kg (50 – 40) C⁰

$500J/kg.C^0 \times 80kg (T – 50) C^0 = 3000J/kg.C^0 \times 800kg (50 – 40) C^0$

$\Rightarrow 40,000T – 2,000,000 = 24,000,000$

$\Rightarrow 40,000T = 26,000,000$

$\Rightarrow T = 26,000,000/ 40,000 = 650^0C$

Hence the initial temperature of the forging is 650^0C.

Heat and Phase Change: Latent Heat: -

13) How much heat must be added to 0.5kg of aluminum to change it from a solid at 99^0C to a liquid at 660^0C (its melting point)? [Hint: The latent heat of fusion L_f for aluminum is $4 \times 10^5 J/kg$.]

Solution: -

$Q = Cm (\Delta T) + mL_f$

$\Rightarrow Q = 9 \times 10^2 J/kg.C^0 \times 0.5kg \times (660 – 99) C^0 + 0.5kg \times 4 \times 10^5 J/kg$

$\Rightarrow Q = 2.5245 \times 10^5 J + 2 \times 10^5 J = 4.5245 \times 10^5 J$

Hence $Q = 4.5 \times 10^5 J$ is the amount of heat that must be added to the given sample of aluminum in order to melt it down under stated conditions.

Equilibrium between Phases of Matter, Humidity: -

14) If the partial pressure of water vapor is 1200Pa and the equilibrium vapor pressure of water at the existing temperature is 3600Pa, determine the relative humidity.

Solution: -

% relative humidity = [Partial Pressure of Water Vapor/ Equilibrium Vapor Pressure of Water at the Existing temperature] x 100

% relative humidity = [1200 Pa/ 3600 Pa] x 100% = 33.3%

Hence the relative humidity under the stated conditions is 33.3%.

15) Find the partial pressure of water vapor when the relative humidity is 60% and the equilibrium vapor pressure of water at the existing temperature is 5000Pa.

Solution: -

Partial Pressure of Water Vapor = % relative humidity x [Equilibrium Vapor Pressure of Water at the existing temperature]

$\Rightarrow$ Partial Pressure of Water Vapor = 60% x 5000Pa = 5000x 0.6

$\Rightarrow$ Partial Pressure of Water Vapor = 3000Pa

Hence the Partial Pressure of Water Vapor under the stated conditions is 3000 Pascals.

Chapter No.13

· ·

The Transfer of Heat: -
The heat energy is transferred to us from a substance through convection, conduction, and radiation. Let us now discuss these three processes of heat transfer stepwise.

Convection: -
When heat is transferred to us from a substance, the internal energy of the substance can change. This change in internal energy is accompanied by a change in temperature or a change in phase. Virtually all our energy originates in the sun and is transferred to us over a distance of 150 million kilometers through the void of space. Today's sunlight provides energy to drive photosynthesis in the plants that provide our food and hence metabolic energy. Ancient sunlight nurtured the organic matter that became fossil fuels of oil, natural gas, and coal. Hence we examine three processes by which heat is transferred: convection, conduction, and radiation.

When part of a fluid is warmed, like the air over a fire, it becomes heated and expands, decreasing in density, during this process. According to Archimede's principle the surrounding cooler and denser air pushes the warmer fluid upward. As the warmer fluid rises, the surrounding cooler fluid replaces it. This cooler fluid is subsequently warmed and pushed upward in the same way. Hence a continuous flow is established, which carries along heat.

Whenever heat is transferred by the bulk movement of a gas or a liquid, the heat is said to be transferred by convection. The fluid flow itself is called as convection current. Hence convection is the process in which heat is carried from place to place by the bulk movement of a fluid.

A volcanic eruption is one visible example of convection and less visible convection currents are set up in a pot of water which is boiling on a gas burner. Another example of convection is the thermal. When sun's rays heat the ground, which in turn warms up the neighboring air, the cooler denser air pushes the warmer air upward resulting in an updraft or thermal. These thermals can be quite strong depending on the amount of heat the ground can supply. These thermals can be used by glider pilots to gain considerable altitudes. Birds utilize thermals in a similar fashion.

The temperature usually decreases with increasing altitude but sometimes meteorological conditions cause a layer to form in the atmosphere where the temperature increases with increasing altitude. Such a layer is called Inversion Layer because its temperature profile is inverted. This causes smog layer that can often be seen hovering over large cities. This is an example of natural convection. There is also forced convection such as in an automobile where a pump or a fan in the radiator circulates the cooler and warmer portions of the fluid. Hence forced convection takes place in an automobile engine.

Conduction: -

Conduction is the process whereby heat is transferred directly through a material, with any bulk movement of the material playing no role in the transfer.

Those materials that conduct heat well are called thermal conductors, and those materials that conduct heat poorly are known as thermal insulators. Most metals are excellent thermal conductors, and wood, glass, and most plastics are common insulators. Thermal insulation has many practical applications. For example in housing, thermal insulators are used in attics and walls to reduce heating and cooling costs. Thermal insulators viz. wooden handles or plastic handles on many pots and pans reduce the flow of heat to the cook's hands.

Conduction of Heat through a Material: -

The heat Q conducted during a time t through a bar of length L and cross-sectional area A is given by: -

$$\Rightarrow Q = (kA\Delta T)t / L$$

Where ΔT is the temperature difference between the ends of the bar and k is the thermal conductivity of the material.

SI unit of Thermal Conductivity: J/ smC^0

Radiation: -

Radiation is a process in which energy is transferred by means of electromagnetic waves.

Energy from the sun is brought to earth by large amounts of visible light waves as well as by substancial amounts of infrared and ultraviolet waves.

These waves belong to a class of waves known, as electromagnetic waves, a class that also includes the microwaves used for cooking and the radio waves used for AM and FM broadcasts.

The process of transferring energy via electromagnetic waves is called radiation, and unlike convection or conduction, it does not require a material medium. Electromagnetic waves from the sun travel through the void of space during their journey to earth. Every object in the universe radiates energy. A material that is a good absorber, like a blackbody, is also a good emitter and a material that is a poor absorber, like a polished silver surface, is also a poor emitter. A perfect blackbody, being a perfect absorber, is also a perfect emitter. Since the color black is associated with nearly complete absorption of visible light, the term perfect blackbody or simply blackbody is used when referring to an object that absorbs all the electromagnetic waves falling on it.

The Stefan-Boltzmann Law of Radiation: -

The radiant energy Q, emitted in a time t by an object that has a Kelvin temperature T, a surface area A, and an emissivity e, is given by: -

$Q = e \sigma T^4 A t$

Where σ is the Stefan-Boltzmann constant which has a value of 5.67×10^{-8} J/ $(s.m^2.K^4)$.

Hence it is possible to calculate the size of a star with the help of Stefan-Boltzmann law of radiation if the temperature in kelvin is known along with other parameters like emissivity e, time t in seconds, and the energy radiated Q.

When an object has a higher temperature than its surroundings, the object emits a net radiant power $P_{net} = (Q/t)_{net}$. The net power is the power the object emits minus the power it absorbs. Applying the Stefan-Boltzmann law leads to the following expression for P_{net} when the temperature of the object is T and the temperature of the environment is T_0: -

$P_{net} = e \sigma A (T^4 - T_0^4)$

Applications: - To keep the heating and air-cinditioning bills to a minimum, it pays to use good thermal insulation in your home. Insulation inhibits heat loss due to convection between the inner and outer walls and minimizes heat transfer by conduction. Consider the following equation for example: -

$Q/t = A\Delta T/ (L/k)$

The term L/k in the denominator is called the R value of the insulation. For a building material, it is convenient to talk about an R value because it expresses in a single number the combined effects of thermal conductivity and thickness. Larger R values mean better insulation because it reduces loss of heat due to conduction. Hence a smaller value of k and a larger value of L yield a larger value of R and lead to a better insulation.

The Transfer of Heat: -
(13) Numerical Problems: -
Conduction: -

1) A person's body is covered with 2 m² of wool clothing. The thickness of the wool is 4×10^{-3} m. The temperature of the outside surface of the wool is 5°C and the skin temperature is 37°C. How much heat per second does the person lose due to conduction?

Solution: -

$Q/t = kA\Delta T/ L$

$k = 0.04$ J/smC° for wool.

$\Rightarrow Q/t = kA\Delta T/ L = [0.04 \text{J/smC}° \times 2\text{m}^2 \times (37–5) \text{ C}°] / (4\times10^{-3}\text{m})$

$\Rightarrow Q/t = 6.4\times10^2 \text{J/s} = 640\text{J/s}$

Hence the heat lost per second due to conduction is 6.4×10^2J/s.

2) In an electrically heated home, the temperature of the ground in contact with a concrete basement wall is 20°C. The temperature at the inside surface of the wall is 30°C. The wall is 0.2m thick and has an area of 20 m². Assume that one kilowatt-hour of electrical energy costs $0.20. How many hours are required for two dollar's worth of energy to be conducted through the wall?

Solution: -

$Q = (kA\Delta T) \, t /L$

$k = 1.1$J/smC° for concrete

$\Rightarrow Q/t = [1.1 \text{J/smC}° \times 20\text{m}^2 \times (30 – 20) \text{ C}°]/0.2\text{m}$

$\Rightarrow Q/t = 1.1\times10^3 \text{J/s} = 1.1$ KW

Now the price of electricity is $0.20 per KWh. This implies for $2.0 there are 10KWh that can be purchased.

$\Rightarrow t = Q/ (Q/t) = 10\text{KWh}/1.1\text{KW} = 9.09$ hours

Hence the time required for $2.00 worth of energy to be conducted through the wall will be 9.09 hours.

3) Due to a temperature difference ΔT, heat is conducted through an aluminum plate that is 0.04m thick. The plate is then replaced by a stainless steel plate that has the same temperature difference and cross-sectional area. How thick should the stainless steel be so that the same amount of heat per second is conducted through it?

Solution: -

$Q = (kA\Delta T) \, t/ \, L$

$k_1 = 240 \text{J/smC}^0$ for aluminum.

$k_2 = 14 \text{J/smC}^0$ for stainless steel.

$Q/t = [k_1 A\Delta T]/L_1 = [k_2 A\Delta T]/L_2$

$\Rightarrow k_1/ L_1 = k_2/L_2$

$\Rightarrow L_2 = k_2 L_1/k_1 = [14 \text{J/smC}^0 \times .04\text{m}]/240 \text{J/smC}^0$

$\Rightarrow L_2 = 2.33 \times 10^{-3}\text{m}$

Therefore the steel plate should be $L_2 = 2.33 \times 10^{-3}\text{m}$ thick, in order for it to conduct the same amount of heat per second as the aluminum plate.

4) In the conduction equation $Q = (kA\Delta T) \, t \, / \, L$, the combination of factors kA/L is called the conductance. The human body has the ability to vary the conductance of the tissue beneath the skin by increasing or decreasing the flow of blood to veins and capillaries underlying the skin. The conductance can be adjusted over a range such that the tissue beneath the skin is equivalent to a thickness of 0.06mm of Styrofoam or 2.4mm of air. By what factor can the body adjust the conductance?

Solution: -

$Q = (kA\Delta T) \, t \, / \, L =$ amount of heat conducted

$\Rightarrow C = kA/L =$ conductance of heat

$k_2 = 0.01 \text{J/smC}^0$ for Styrofoam

$L_2 = 0.06 \text{ mm} = 0.06 \times 10^{-3} \text{ m}$

$k_1 = 0.0256 \text{ J/smC}^0$ for air

$L_1 = 2.4 \text{ mm} = 2.4 \times 10^{-3} \text{ m}$

$\Rightarrow C_1 = k_1 A/L_1 = (0.0256 \text{ J/smC}^0) \, A \, / \, (2.4 \times 10^{-3} \text{ m}) = 10.6666A$

$\Rightarrow C_2 = k_2 A/L_2 = (0.01 \text{ J/smC}^0) \, A \, / \, (0.06 \times 10^{-3} \text{ m}) = 166.6666A$

$\Rightarrow \text{Factor} = C_2 \, / \, C_1 = 166.6666A/ \, 10.6666A = 15.625 \equiv 16$

Hence the body can adjust the conductance by a factor of 15.625.

5) Three building materials, glass ($k = 0.8 \text{ J/smC}^0$), concrete ($k = 1.1 \text{ J/smC}^0$), and asbestos ($k = 0.09 \text{ J/smC}^0$) are sandwiched together.

"The Morning Echo"

The temperatures at the inside and outside surfaces are 30°C and 0°C respectively. Each material has the same thickness and cross-sectional area. Find the temperatures (a) at the glass-concrete interface and (b) the concrete-asbestos interface.

Solution: -

$$Q = kA(\Delta T)t/ L = k_1 A(\Delta T_1)t/ L = k_2 A(\Delta T_2)t/ L$$
$$\Rightarrow k(\Delta T) = k_1(\Delta T_1) = k_2(\Delta T_2)$$

$$0.8(30 - t_1) = 1.1(t_1 - t_2) = 0.09(t_2 - 0)$$
$$24 - 0.8t_1 = 1.1t_1 - 1.1t_2 = 0.09t_2$$
$$\Rightarrow 24 = 1.9t_1 - 1.1t_2 \ (1)$$
$$24 = 0.8t_1 + 0.09t_2 \ (2)$$

Now equations (1) and (2) are simultaneous equations in t_1 and t_2 and these can be solved for the values of t_1 and t_2. The values thus obtained are as follows: -

$$t_1 = 27.17 \ ^0C$$
and $t_2 = 25.11 \ ^0C$

Hence the temperature of the (a) glass-concrete interface is 27.17°C and the temperature of the (b) concrete-asbestos interface is 25.11°C.

6) In a house the temperature at the surface of a window is 30°C. The temperature outside at the window surface is 20°C. Heat is lost through the window via conduction, and the heat lost per second has a certain value. The temperature outside begins to fall while the condition inside the house remains the same. As a result, the heat lost per second increases. What is the temperature at the outside window surface when the heat lost per second triples?

Solution: -

$t_2 = 30°C$ and $t_1 = 20°C$
$$Q/t = kA(\Delta T)/ L = kA(30 - 20) \ C^0/ L = 10 \ kA/L$$
$$\Rightarrow 3(Q/t) = 30 \ kA/L$$
$$\Rightarrow 30 = (30 - t_1) \ C^0$$
$$\Rightarrow t_1 = (30 - 30) \ C^0 = 0°C$$

Hence when the heat lost per second triples the outside the window surface temperature is 0°C, which is the freezing point of water.

7) Two rods, one of iron and the other of brass are joined end to end. The cross-sectional area of each is $6 \times 10^{-3} \ m^2$, and the length of each is 0.06 m. The free end of the iron rod is kept at 200°C while the free end of the brass rod is kept at 10°C. The loss of heat through the sides may be

ignored. (a) What is the temperature at the iron-brass interface? (b) How much heat is conducted through the unit in one second? (c) What is the temperature in the iron rod at a distance of 0.02 m from the hot end?

Solution: -

(a) $k_1 = 79$ J/msC^0 for iron

$k_2 = 110$ J/smC^0 for brass

$Q = (k_1 A \Delta T_1)t/ L = (k_2 A \Delta T_2)t /L$

$\Rightarrow k_1(\Delta T_1) = k_2(\Delta T_2)$

$79(200 - t_1) = 110(t_1 - 10)$

$\Rightarrow t_1 = 16900/189 = 89.4^0$C

Hence the temperature at the iron-brass interface is $t_1 = 89.4^0$C.

(b) $Q/t = [k_2 A (200-10)]/0.06 - [k_1 A (200-10)]/0.06$

$\Rightarrow Q/t = (110 \times 6 \times 10^{-3} \times 190)/0.06 - (79 \times 6 \times 10^{-3} \times 190)/0.06$

$\Rightarrow Q/t = [(110-79) \times 6 \times 10^{-3} \times 190]/0.06 = (31 \times 6 \times 10^{-3} \times 190)/0.06$

$\Rightarrow Q/t = 589$ J

Hence 589 J of heat is conducted through the unit in 1 second.

(c) $Q = 79 \times 6 \times 10^{-3} \times (200-t_1)/ 0.02 = 79 \times 6 \times 10^{-3} \times (t_1-89.4)/ 0.04$

$\Rightarrow (200 - t_1)/0.02 = (t_1 - 89.4)/ 0.04$

$\Rightarrow t_1 = 489.4/3 = 163.1^0$C

Hence the temperature of the iron rod at a distance of 0.02m from the hot end is $t_1 = 163.1^0$C.

8) One end of an aluminum bar is maintained at 270^{0}C, while the other end is kept at a constant but lower temperature. The cross-sectional area of the bar is 3.5×10^{-3} m^2. Because of insulation, there is negligible heat loss through the sides of the bar. Heat flows through the bar, however, at the rate of 6.3 J/s. What is the temperature of the bar at a point 0.2 m from the hot end?

Solution: -

$Q/t = (k A \Delta T)/ L$

k (for aluminum) $= 240$ J/smC^0

$\Rightarrow 6.3$J/s $= [240$J/smC$^0 \times 3.5 \times 10^{-3}$ m$^2 \times (270 - t_2)]/ 0.2$m

$\Rightarrow 270 - t_2 = (6.3 \times 0.2)/ [240 \times 3.5 \times 10^{-3}] = 1.5$

$\Rightarrow t_2 = 270 - 1.5 = 268.5^0$C

Hence the temperature of the aluminum bar at a point 0.2 m from the hot end is 268.5^{0}C.

Radiation: -

9) How many days does it take for a perfect blackbody cube (0.02m on a side, 25^0C) to radiate the same amount of energy that a 75W light bulb uses in one hour?

Solution: -
75W in 1 hour uses = 75W x 60x60s/h = $27x10^4J/h$
$\Rightarrow Q = e\sigma AT^4t$
$\Rightarrow t = Q/e\sigma AT^4$
$t = (27x10^4J /h)/ [(1)(5.67x10^{-8}J/sm^2K^4)(0.02m)^2(273+25)^4 x6]$
$t = (27x10^4)/[5.67x10^{-8} x (0.02)^2 x (298)^4x6]$
$\Rightarrow t = 251596.3911s$
$\Rightarrow t = (251596.3911s)/3.6x10^3s/h = 69.88788641$ hours
$\Rightarrow t = 69.88788641h/24h/d = 2.91$ days
Hence it takes 2.91 days for a perfect blackbody cube to radiate the same amount of energy that a 75W bulb uses in one hour.

10) An object emits 40W of radiant power. If it were a perfect blackbody, other things being equal, it would emit 80W of radiant power. What is the emissivity of the object?
Solution: -
$Q/t = e\sigma AT^4 = 40W$
$Q/t = \sigma AT^4 = 80W$ (e = 1 for a perfect blackbody)
$\Rightarrow e = e\sigma AT^4/\sigma AT^4 = 40W/80W = 0.5$
Hence the emissivity of the object is e = 0.5.

11) A car parked in the sun absorbs energy at a rate of 600 Watts per square meter of surface area. The car reaches a temperature at which it radiates energy at the same rate. Treating the car as a perfect radiator (e = 1), find the temperature.
Solution: -
$Q/tA = e\sigma T^4 = 600W/m^2 = 600 J/sm^2$
$\Rightarrow T^4 = 600 J/sm^2/ [5.67x10^{-8}J/sm^2K^4]$
$\Rightarrow T = \sqrt[4]{[600/5.67x10^{-8}]} = 320.73K$
Hence the temperature of the car that we have determined above is T = 320.73K.

12) A glass wall of a building is 0.2 m thick. The temperature inside the building is 30^0C while the temperature outside is 0^0C. Heat is conducted through the wall. When the building is unheated, the inside temperature falls to 0^0C and heat conduction ceases. However, the wall does emit radiant energy when its temperature is 0^0C. The radiant energy emitted per second per square meter is the same as the heat lost

per second per square meter due to conduction. What is the emissivity of the wall?

Solution: -
$Q/t = e\sigma AT^4 = kA\Delta T/L$
k (for glass) = $0.8J/smC^0$
$\Rightarrow$ e $(5.67x10^{-8}J/sm^2K^4)(1)(273K)^4 = 0.8x(1)x(30 - 0)/0.2$
$\Rightarrow$ e $= (0.8x30)/[0.2x5.67x10^{-8}x(273)^4] = 0.381019848$
Hence the emissivity of the glass is 0.38 which we have determined above.

Miscellaneous: -

13) One end of an iron poker is placed in a fire where the temperature is 600^0C and the other end is kept at a temperature of 30^0C. The poker is 1.3 m long and has a radius of $6x10^{-3}$m. Ignoring the heat lost along the length of the poker, find the amount of heat conducted from one end of the poker to the other in 6 seconds.
Solution: -
$Q = (kA\Delta T) t/ L$
k (for iron) = 79 J/smC^0
$\Rightarrow$ Q $= [79 \times \pi(6x10^{-3}m)^2 \times (600 - 30)C^0 \times 6s]/ 1.3m = 23.5J$
$\Rightarrow$ Q = 23.5J
Therefore the amount of heat conducted through one end of the poker to the other end in 6 seconds is Q = 23.5J.

14) Suppose a stove has an area of 1.5 m^2 and an emissivity of 0.7. The room warms to a temperature of 30^0C or (303K) when the stove surface reaches a temperature T. Suppose the net power generated by the stove is 8500W, find the temperature T.
Solution: -
$P = Q/t = e\sigma A [T^4 - (303)^4] = 8500W$
$\Rightarrow$ $T^4 - (303)^4 = 8500W/[0.7x5.67x10^{-8} \times (1.5m^2)]$
$\Rightarrow$ $T^4 = 1427.731586x10^8 + 84.28892481x10^8$
$\Rightarrow$ $T^4 = 1512.020511x10^8$
$\Rightarrow$ T $= {}^4\sqrt{[1512.020511x10^8]} = 623.57K$
Therefore the temperature T = 623.57K.

15) A solid cylindrical rod is made from a center cylinder of lead and an outer concentric jacket of copper. Except for its ends, the rod is insulated so that the heat loss from the curved surfaces is negligible. When the temperature difference is maintained between its ends, the rod conducts one third the amount of heat that it would conduct if it were

solid copper. Determine the ratio of the inner radius of the lead to the total radius of the rod i.e r_1/r_2.

Solution: -
$Q/t = (kA\Delta T)/L$
k (for copper) $= 390$ J/smC^0
k (for lead) $= 35$ J/smC^0
$3[35\pi r_1^2\Delta T/L + 390(\pi r_2^2 - \pi r_1^2)\Delta T/L] = 390\pi r_2^2\Delta T/L$
$\Rightarrow 105\pi r_1^2 + 1170\pi r_2^2 - 1170\pi r_1^2 = 390\pi r_2^2$
$\Rightarrow 780r_2^2 = 1065r_1^2$
$\Rightarrow r_1^2/r_2^2 = 780/1065 = (0.732394366)$
$\Rightarrow r_1/r_2 = \sqrt{(0.732394366)} = 0.85$
$\Rightarrow r_1/r_2 = 0.85$
Hence the ratio of the radii r_1/r_2 comes out to be 0.85.

Chapter No. 14

. . . .

The Ideal Gas Law and Kinetic Theory: -
Molecular Mass, the Mole, and Avogadro's number: -
Frequently we wish to compare the mass of one atom with another atom. To facilitate the comparison, a mass scale, known as the atomic mass scale has been established. The unit is called atomic mass unit (symbol: u). By international agreement, the reference element is chosen to be the most abundant isotope of carbon, which is called carbon-12. Its atomic mass is defined to be exactly twelve atomic mass units or 12u. The relationship between atomic mass unit and the kilogram is as follows: -

$$\Rightarrow 1u = 1.6605 \times 10^{-27} \text{ kg}$$

In the periodic table, the atomic mass of carbon (C) is given as 12.011u rather than exactly 12u, because small amount (about 1%) of the naturally occurring material is an isotope called carbon-13. The molecular mass of a molecule is the sum of the atomic masses of its atoms.

One gram-mole of a substance contains as many particles (atoms or molecules) as there are atoms in 12 grams of the isotope carbon-12. Experiments show that 12 grams of carbon-12 contain 6.022×10^{23} atoms. The number of atoms per mole is known as Avogadro's number N_A, after the Italian scientist Amedeo Avogadro (1776-1856).

$$\Rightarrow N_A = 6.022 \times 10^{23} \text{ mol}^{-1}$$

Hence the number of moles n contained in any sample is the number of particles N in the sample divided by the number of particles per mole N_A (Avogadro's number).

$$\Rightarrow n = N/N_A$$
$$\Rightarrow n = m_{particle} N / m_{particle} N_A$$
$$\Rightarrow n = m/ \text{ Mass per mole}$$

Hence mass per mole (in g/mole) of a substance has the same numerical value as the atomic or molecular mass of the substance (in atomic mass units).

$\Rightarrow m_{particle} = $ Mass per mole$/N_A$

The Ideal Gas Law: -

The absolute pressure P of an ideal gas is directly proportional to the Kelvin temperature T and the number of moles n of the gas and is inversely proportional to the volume V of the gas: $P = R(nT/V)$. In other words,

$PV = nRT$

where R is the universal gas constant and has the value of 8.31J/(mol.K).

$\Rightarrow PV = nRT = nN_A (R/N_A)T = N (R/N_A)T$

The term R/N_A is referred to as Boltzmann's constant in honor of Austrian physicist Ludwig Boltzmann (1844–1906), and is represented by the symbol k: -

$\Rightarrow k = R/N_A = 8.31J/(mol.K)/6.022x10^{23}mol^{-1} = 1.38x10^{-23}J/K$

$\Rightarrow PV = NkT$

The Ideal Gas Law is derived from Boyle's Law and Charle's Law which are as follows: -

Boyle's Law: - According to Boyle's Law at constant temperature T and a constant n, the pressure of an ideal gas in inversely proportional to its volume or we may have as follows: -

$P_1 \alpha 1/V_1$ and $P_2 \alpha 1/V_2$

$\Rightarrow P_1V_1 = P_2V_2$

Charle's Law: - According to Charle's Law at constant pressure P and a constant n, the volume of an ideal gas is directly proportional to its temperature or we may have as follows: -

$V_1 \alpha T_1$ and $V_2 \alpha T_2$

$\Rightarrow V_1/T_1 = V_2/T_2$

By combining Boyle's Law with Charle's Law, we arrive at the Ideal Gas Law, which we have already stated.

$\Rightarrow P_1V_1/T_1 = P_2V_2/T_2$

$\Rightarrow PV = nRT = NkT$

An ideal gas is any gas that obeys the equation of Ideal Gas Law and gives the readings in an experiment in accordance with the Ideal Gas Law.

Kinetic Theory of Gases: -

From the concepts of External Forces e.g (1) Gravitational Force, (2) Normal Force, (3) Frictional Forces, (4) Tension Forces, (5) Restoring Force of a spring, (6) Collisional Forces exerted by a fluid pressure; we arrive at Newton's Second Law of Motion, ΣF = ma and Newton's Third Law of Motion. Combining these with Ideal Gas Law, we arrive at Kinetic Theory of Gases viz. (1) Average Translational Kinetic Energy per particle, KE = (3/2) kT and (2) Internal Energy of a Monatomic Ideal Gas, U = (3/2) nRT.

To calculate the pressure that a gas exerts by the collision of its molecules with the walls of the container we proceed as follows: -

Average Force =

(Final – Initial) Momentum/ Time between successive collisions

$\Rightarrow$ Average Force = [(- mv) – (+mv)]/[2L/v] = - mv^2/L

The total force on the wall of the container is given as follows: -

$\bar{F}$ = (N/3) $(m\bar{v}^2/L)$

$\Rightarrow$ F = (N/3) (mv_{rms}^2/L)

where v_{rms} is the root mean squared speed, $v_{rms} = \sqrt{[\bar{v}^2]}$

$\Rightarrow$ P = F/A = F/L^2 = (N/3)(mv_{rms}^2/L^3)

But V = L^3 and therefore this equation becomes as follows: -

PV = (2/3)N (1/2)mv_{rms}^2

$\Rightarrow$ PV = (2/3) N (KE) = NkT

$\Rightarrow \overline{KE}$ = (1/2)mv_{rms}^2 = (3/2)kT

The Internal Energy of a Monatomic Ideal Gas: - The internal energy U is the total translational kinetic energy of the N atoms that constitute the gas: U = N[(1/2)mv_{rms}^2]. Since (1/2)mv_{rms}^2 = (3/2)kT, the internal energy can be written in terms of the Kelvin temperature as follows: -

$\Rightarrow$ U = N(3/2)kT

But k = R/N_A and N/N_A = n therefore we have as follows: -

U = (3/2)nRT

Diffusion: -

Diffusion is the process whereby solute molecules move through a solvent from a region of higher solute concentration to a region of lower solute concentration. Fick's law of diffusion states that the mass m of solute that diffuses in a time t through the solvent in a channel of length L and cross-sectional area A is given as follows: -

$\Rightarrow$ m = (DAΔC)t/L

where ΔC is the solute concentration difference between the ends of the channel and D is the diffusion constant.

SI unit for the Diffusion Constant: m^2/s

As you recall for the conduction of heat through a solid bar of length L, cross-sectional area A, and the temperature difference of $\Delta T = T_2 - T_1$ we have as follows: -

$\Rightarrow Q = (kA\Delta T)\ t/L$

In the equation for Fick's Law of Diffusion, the parameters are as follows: - $\Delta C = kg/m^3$, $t = $ seconds, $A = m^2$, $L = m$, $D = m^2/s$, and $m = $ kg. Hence both of these equations are similar in form.

The Ideal Gas Law and Kinetic Theory: -

(14) Numerical Problems: -

Molecular Mass, the Mole, and Avogadro's number: -

1) A mass of 434.4735 g of an element is known to contain 40×10^{23} atoms. What this element could possibly be?

Solution: -

40×10^{23} atoms contain 434.4735g of the unknown element.

$\Rightarrow 6.022 \times 10^{23}$ atoms contain $[434.4735g\ /40 \times 10^{23}] \times 6.022 \times 10^{23}$

$\Rightarrow m = [6.022 \times 10^{23}\ /\ 40 \times 10^{23}]\ \times 434.4735 = 65.41g$

This value of m = 65.41 suggests Zinc. Hence this element is Zinc because 65.41 is the atomic mass of Zinc (Zn).

(2) What are (a) the molecular mass (in atomic mass units) and (b) the mass (in kg) of sodium chloride (NaCl) molecule?

Solution: -

(a) Na: 22.9898u + Cl: 35.4530u = NaCl: 58.4428u

$\Rightarrow$ Molecular Mass of NaCl = 58.4428u

(b) Mass of the NaCl molecule in kg is given by the following: -

$1u = 1.6605 \times 10^{-27}\ kg$

$\Rightarrow$ Mass (in kg) of NaCl molecule = 1.6605×10^{-27}kg/u x 58.4428u

$\Rightarrow$ Mass of NaCl molecule (in kg) = $97.0442694 \times 10^{-27}\ kg$

Another method of finding out the mass of NaCl molecule in kilogram is as follows:-

$m = 58.4428u/6.022 \times 10^{23}\ mol^{-1} = 97.04882099 \times 10^{-24}g$

$\Rightarrow m = 97.04882099 \times 10^{-27}\ kg$

Hence we obtain similar results by both the methods.

3) A certain substance has a molecular mass of 75,600 u. Find the mass (in kg) of one molecule of this substance.

Solution: -

Mass (in kg) of 1 molecule of the given substance = m

$m = 75,600u/6.022 \times 10^{23} mol^{-1} = 12553.96878 \times 10^{-23} g$

$m = 75,600u/6.022 \times 10^{23} mol^{-1} = 12.55396878 \times 10^{-23} kg$

Another method which should give a similar result is as follows: -

$1u = 1.6605 \times 10^{-27} kg$

$\Rightarrow m = 75,600u \times 1.6605 \times 10^{-27} kg/u = 12.55338 \times 10^{-23} kg$

The Ideal Gas Law: -

4) A Goodyear blimp typically contains 6000 m³ of helium (He) at an absolute pressure of $1.2 \times 10^5 Pa$. The temperature of the helium is 300K. What is the mass (in kg) of the helium in the blimp?

Solution: -

$V = 6000 \ m^3$

$P = 1.2 \times 10^5 Pa$

$T = 300K$

$PV = nRT$

$\Rightarrow n = PV/RT = 1.2 \times 10^5 Pa \times 6000 \ m^3 / [8.31 J/mol.K \times 300K]$

$n = 2.888086643 \times 10^5$ moles

$\Rightarrow m = n \times m_{particle} = 2.888086643 \times 10^5$ moles $\times 4.0026 g/mole$

$\Rightarrow m = 1.15598556 \times 10^6 g = 1.15598556 \times 10^3 kg$

Hence mass of helium (in kg) in the blimp under the conditions mentioned is 1.15598556×10^3 kg.

5) A bicycle tire whose volume is 1×10^{-3} m³ has a temperature of 300K and an absolute pressure of $5 \times 10^5 Pa$. A cyclist brings the pressure up to $9 \times 10^5 Pa$ without changing the temperature or the volume. How many moles of air must have been pumped into the tire?

Solution: -

$P_1 V = n_1 RT$

$P_2 V = n_2 RT$

$\Rightarrow n = n_2 - n_1 = (P_2 - P_1) V/RT$

$\Rightarrow n = (9 - 5) \times 10^5 Pa \times 1 \times 10^{-3} \ m^3 / [8.31 J/mol.K \times 300K]$

$\Rightarrow n = 4 \times 10^2 / 8.31 \times 300 = 0.1604492579$ moles

Hence n = 0.16044 moles of air have been pumped into the tire.

6) An ideal gas at 20°C and a pressure of $2 \times 10^5 Pa$ occupies a volume of 3.1 m³. (a) How many moles of gas are present? (b) If the volume is raised to 5.1 m³ and the temperature is raised to 25°C, what will be the pressure of the gas?

Solution: -

$T = 20 + 273.15 = 293.15K$

$P = 2 \times 10^5 Pa$

$V = 3.1 \text{ m}^3$

$PV = nRT$

$\Rightarrow n = PV/RT = 2\times10^5\text{Pa} \times 3.1 \text{ m}^3 / 8.31\text{J/(mol.K)} \times 293.15\text{K}$

$\Rightarrow n = 254.5076 \text{ mol}$

(b) $PV = nRT$

$n = 254.5076 \text{ moles}$

$V = 5.1 \text{ m}^3$

$T = 25 + 273.15 = 298.15\text{K}$

$P = nRT/V = 254.5076\text{mol} \times 8.31\text{J/(mol.K)} \times 298.15\text{K}/[5.1\text{m}^3]$

$\Rightarrow P = 1.236421159\times10^5\text{Pa}$

Hence under the given conditions the pressure of the gas will be P $= 1.2364\times10^5\text{Pa}$.

Kinetic Theory: -

7) The temperature near the surface of earth is 300K. A Xenon atom (atomic mass = 131.29u) has a kinetic energy equal to the average translational kinetic energy and is moving straight up. If the atom does not collide with any other atom or molecule, how high up would it go before coming to rest? Assume that the acceleration due to gravity is constant throughout the ascent.

Solution: -

$\overline{KE} = (1/2) m (v_{rms})^2 = (3/2)kT$

$v = \sqrt{[3kT/m]} = \sqrt{[3\times(1.38\times10^{-23}\text{J/K})\times300/(131.29\times1.6605\times10^{-27})]}$

$\Rightarrow v = \sqrt{[5.697063597\times10^4]} = 238.6852236 \text{ m/s}$

$h = v^2/2g = 5.697063597\times10^4/[2\times9.8\text{m/s}^2] = 2906.6651 \text{ m}$

8) The average values of the squared speeds $\overline{v^2}$ does not equal the square of the average speeds $(\overline{v})^2$. To verify this fact consider three particles with the following speeds: $v_1 = 2$ m/s, $v_2 = 5$ m/s, and $v_3 = 8$ m/s. Calculate (a) $\overline{v^2} = (1/3) (v_1^2 + v_2^2 + v_3^2)$ and (b) $(\overline{v})^2 = [(1/3)(v_1 + v_2 + v_3)]^2$.

Solution: -

(a) $\overline{v^2} = (1/3)(v_1^2 + v_2^2 + v_3^2) = (1/3)(2^2+5^2+8^2) = (1/3)(4+25+64)$

$\Rightarrow \overline{v^2} = (1/3)(93) = 31 \text{ m}^2/\text{s}^2$

(b) $(\overline{v})^2 = [(1/3)(v_1+v_2+v_3)]^2 = [(1/3)(2+5+8)]^2$

$(\overline{v})^2 = [(1/3)15]^2 = (5)^2 = 25\text{m}^2/\text{s}^2$

Hence we find the value of $\overline{v^2}$ is not equal to $(\overline{v})^2$.

Diffusion: -

9) A tube has a length of 0.02m and a cross-sectional area of 8x10^{-5}m^2. The tube is filled with a solution of sucrose in water. The diffusion constant of sucrose in water is 5x10^{-10} m^2/s. A difference in concentration of 4x10^{-3} kg/m^3 is maintained between the ends of the tube. How much time is required for 9x10^{-14}kg of sucrose to be transported through the tube?

Solution: -

According to Fick's Law we have the following equation: -

m = (DAΔC)t / L

$\Rightarrow$ t = mL /(DAΔC)

$\Rightarrow$ t = 9x10^{-14}kg x 0.02m/[5x10^{-10} m^2/sx8x10^{-5} m^2 x 4x10^{-3}kg/m^3]

$\Rightarrow$ t = 11.25s

Hence the time required for the solute to be transported through the tube will be t = 11.25s.

10) For water vapor in air at 293K, the diffusion constant is D = 2.4x10^{-5} m^2/s. (a) The time required for the first solute molecules to traverse a channel of length L is t = L^2/2D according to Fick's Law. Find the time t for L = 0.02m. (b) For comparison, how long would a water molecule take to travel L = 0.02m at the translational rms speed of water molecule (assumed to be an ideal gas) at a temperature of 293K? (c) Explain why the answer in part (a) is so much larger than the answer in part (b).

Solution: -

(a) t = L^2/2D = (0.02m)^2/ [2(2.4x10^{-5}m^2/s)] = 8.3333s

$\Rightarrow$ t = 8.3333 seconds

Hence the time t for L = 0.02m, according to Fick's law has been calculated as t = 8.3333s.

(b) KE = (1/2) m (v$_{rms}$)^2 = (3/2)kT

m = 18.01528g/mol/[6.022x10^{23}mol^{-1}] = 2.991577549x10^{-23}g

$\Rightarrow$ m = 2.991577549x10^{-26}kg

(v$_{rms}$) = $\sqrt{}$(v$_{rms}$)^2 = $\sqrt{}$[3kT/m]

v$_{rms}$ = $\sqrt{}$[3(1.38x10^{-23}J/K)(293K)/(2.991577549x10^{-26}kg)]

$\Rightarrow$ v$_{rms}$ = $\sqrt{}$[40.54783739x10^4] = 636.7718382 m/s

$\Rightarrow$ t = L/v$_{rms}$ = 0.02 m / [636.7718382m/s] = 3.1408x10^{-5} s

$\Rightarrow$ t = 3.1408x10^{-5}s

(c) In part (a) there is a zigzag motion of the solute particles involved, therefore the time taken for the water molecule to traverse the length L = 0.02m is larger in part (a) compared to part (b).

Miscellaneous: -

11) In a diesel engine, the piston compresses air at 295K to a volume that is one-eighteenth of the original volume and a pressure that is 50 times the original pressure. What is the temperature of the air after the compression?

Solution: -

$P_1V_1/T_1 = P_2V_2/T_2$

$\Rightarrow PV/295 = [50PxV/18]/T$

$\Rightarrow T = [50x295/18]$ K

$T = 819.4K$

Hence the temperature of the air after compression is $T = 819.4K$.

12) The diffusion constant of ethanol in water is $12.4x10^{-10}$ m^2/s. A cylinder has a cross-sectional area of 5 cm^2 and a length of 3 cm. A difference in ethanol concentration of 12 kg/m^3 is maintained between the ends of the cylinder. In one hour, what mass of ethanol diffuses through the cylinder?

Solution: -

$m = (DA\Delta C) t/ L$

$\Rightarrow m = [12.4x10^{-10}$ m^2/s x $5x10^{-4}$ m^{2}x12 kg/m^{3}x3600s]/ $(3x10^{-2}$m)

$\Rightarrow m = 8.928x10^{-7}$kg $= 8.928x10^{-3}$ g

Hence the mass of the ethanol that diffuses through the cylinder has been calculated as $m = 8.928x10^{-3}$ g.

13) Very fine smoke particles are suspended in air. The translational rms speed of a smoke particle is $3x10^{-4}$ m/s and the temperature is 295K. Find the mass of the particle.

Solution: -

$\overline{KE} = (1/2)$ m $(v_{rms})^2 = (3/2)kT$

$\Rightarrow m = 3kT/(v_{rms})^2 = [3(1.38x10^{-23}$J/K)x295K]/$(3x10^{-4}$m/s)^2

$\Rightarrow m = 1.357x10^{-13}$kg

Hence the mass of the smoke particle is $m = 1.357x10^{-13}$kg.

14) A drop of water has a radius of $8x10^{-5}$ m. How many water molecules are in the drop?

Solution: -

$V = (4/3) \pi R^3$

$\Rightarrow V = (4/3) \pi (8x10^{-5}m)^3 = 2.144660585x10^{-12}$ m^3

$m = \rho V = 1x10^3$kg/m^3 x $2.144660585x10^{-12}$ m^3

$\Rightarrow m = 2.144660585x10^{-6}$ g

n = total mass/ $m_{particle}$ = 2.144660585x10⁻⁶ g/ 18.01528 g/mol
$\Rightarrow$ n = 0.119046753x10⁻⁶
N = nN_A = 0.119046753x10⁻⁶ mol x 6.022x10²³mol⁻¹
$\Rightarrow$ N = 7.16899545x10¹⁶ molecules

15) At the normal boiling point of a material, the liquid phase has a density of 890kg/m³ and the vapor phase has a density of 0.630kg/m³. Determine the ratio of the distances between the neighbouring molecules in the gas phase to that in the liquid phase. (Hint: Assume that the volume of each phase is filled with many cubes, with one molecule at the center of each cube.)

Solution: -

ρ = m/V
$\Rightarrow$ V = m/ρ = L^3
L_1^3 = m/ρ_1
L_2^3 = m/ρ_2
$\Rightarrow L_1$ = $\sqrt[3]{(m/\rho_1)}$ = $\sqrt[3]{(m/890)}$
L_2 = $\sqrt[3]{(m/\rho_2)}$ = $\sqrt[3]{(m/0.630)}$
$\Rightarrow L_2 /L_1$ = $\sqrt[3]{(890)}$/ $\sqrt[3]{(0.63)}$ = 9.619001716/0.857261888
$\Rightarrow L_2/L_1$ = 11.22061047

Hence the ratio of the distances between the neighboring molecules in the gas phase to that in the liquid phase is L_2/L_1 = 11.22.

Chapter No. 15: -

. . . .

Waves and Sound: -
The characteristics of Waves: - Water waves have two characteristics common to all waves and these are as follows: -
1) A wave is a traveling disturbance.
2) A wave carries energy from place to place.
We will consider two types of waves, viz. transverse and longitudinal waves. A transverse wave is one in which the disturbance occurs perpendicular to the direction of travel of the wave. A longitudinal wave is one in which the disturbance occurs parallel to the line of travel of the wave. Hence electromagnetic waves, like the light waves, are transverse waves and mechanical waves like sound are longitudinal waves.

Some waves are neither transverse nor longitudinal. For example, in a water wave, the motion of the water particles is not entirely perpendicular or entirely parallel to the line along which the wave travels. Instead the motion includes both the transverse and the longitudinal components, since the water particles at the surface move on nearly circular paths.

Sinusoidal Waves: - These waves are also referred to as periodic waves or harmonic waves. These originate as a consequence of simple harmonic motion, which we discussed in chapter no. 10.

Hence the concepts that pertain to simple harmonic motion, viz. 1) cycle, 2) amplitude, 3) period, and 4) frequency also pertain to periodic, harmonic, or sinusoidal waves. We meticulously define these concepts as follows: -
1) Cycle: - A cycle is defined as one complete vibration of the wave or the disturbance between two consecutive crests or two consecutive troughs.
2) Amplitude, A: - It is defined as the distance between a crest or the highest point on the wave, and the undisturbed position. It is also the distance between a trough or the lowest point on the wave and the undisturbed position.

3) Period, T: - It is defined as the time it takes a wave to undergo one complete vibration that is one full wavelength. It is measured in seconds.

4) Frequency, f: - It is defined as the reciprocal of period, T. Frequency is measured as cycles/ second or Hertz.

$\Rightarrow f = 1/T$

Furthermore, we define the velocity as the product of the frequency and the wavelength of a wave both transverse and longitudinal.

$\Rightarrow v = f\lambda = \lambda/T$

Wave Speed and Particle Speed on a String: -

The wave speed on the string of a guitar, violin, or a piano is given by the following expression: -

$\Rightarrow v_{WAVE} = \sqrt{[F/(m/L)]}$

Note F is the tension in the string and m/L is mass per unit length of the string which is called the linear density. Hence the speed of a wave is determined by the properties of the string – that is, the tension, F, and the mass per unit length, m/L.

The speed of a particle on the string is determined by the properties of the source creating the wave and it is given by the following expression: -

$\Rightarrow v_{PARTICLE} = Aw \sin wt$

Note $w = 2\pi f$ is the angular frequency, t = time in seconds, and A is the amplitude.

The Mathematical Description of a Wave: -

The following expressions describe the displacements of a particle caused by a wave travelling in the +x direction to the right, and also – x direction to the left, with an amplitude, A, frequency, f, and wavelength, λ.

Wave Motion towards (+ x): -

$y = A \sin (2\pi ft + 2\pi x/ \lambda)$

Wave Motion towards (– x): -

$y = A \sin (2\pi ft + 2\pi x/ \lambda)$

The expressions $(2\pi ft \pm 2\pi x/ \lambda)$ are called the phase angles and when a calculator is used to evaluate the function, $\sin (2\pi ft \pm 2\pi x/\lambda)$, it must be set to its radian mode.

The Characteristics of Sound: -

Longitudinal Sound Waves: - Sound is a longitudinal wave which is created by a vibrating object like a guitar string. Moreover sound can be created or transmitted only in a medium, such as a gas, liquid, or solid. Sound cannot exist in a vacuum.

The sound wave, which is a longitudinal wave, consists of regions of compressed air called condensations and regions of rarefied air called rarefactions. These regions travel exactly one behind the other and their motion is caused by molecules of air executing simple harmonic motion. The wavelength, λ, of a sound wave is defined as the distance between two successive rarefactions or two successive condensations.

The Frequency of a Sound Wave: - Each cycle of a sound wave consists of one condensation and one rarefaction and the frequency is the number of cycles per second that passes by a given location. For example if the object vibrates back and forth in simple harmonic motion at a frequency of 100 Hz, then 100 condensations, each followed by a rarefaction, are generated every second, thus forming a sound wave, whose frequency is also 100 Hz. Sound with a single frequency is called a pure tone.

Experiments have shown that a healthy young person can hear sounds of frequencies from approximately 20 Hz to 20 kHz. The ability to hear high frequencies decreases with age and a middle aged adult person hears frequencies up to only 12 kHz – 14 kHz.

Pure tones are used in push button telephones. Sound can be generated whose frequencies lie below 20 Hz or above 20 kHz although human beings normally do not hear it. Sound waves with frequencies below 20 Hz are called infrasonic, while those above 20 kHz are called ultrasonic. Rhinoceroses use infrasonic frequencies as low as 5 Hz to call one another while bats use ultrasonic frequencies as high as 100 kHz for navigating.

Frequency is an objective propert of a sound wave because frequency can be measured by an electronic frequency counter. A listener, however, interprets frequency as a subjective property. The human brain interprets frequency in terms of a subjective quality called pitch. A pure tone with a large frequency is interpreted as high pitched sound, and a pure tone with a low frequency is interpreted as low pitched sound.

The Pressure Amplitude of a Sound Wave: - When a sound wave travels from one end of an air filled tube to the other end there are regions of condensations and rarefactions, which show that the air pressure varies sinusoidally along the length of the tube. The Pressure Amplitude is the maximum change in pressure, measured relative to the undisturbed position or atmospheric pressure.

In a typical conversation between two persons, the change in air pressure that occurs is of the order of 3×10^{-2} Pa which is very small compared to the atmospheric pressure of 1.01×10^5 Pa. The ear is remarkable for detecting such small changes in pressure.

Loudness is an attribute of sound that depends mainly on the amplitude of the wave; the larger the amplitude, the louder the sound. The pressure amplitude is an objective property of a sound wave because it can be measured. Loudness, on the other hand, is subjective. Every person determines what is loud, depending on the sensitivity of his or her hearing.

The Speed of Sound: - Generally sound travels slowest in gases, faster in liquids, and fastest in solids. For example at 20^0C the speed of sound in air is 343 m/s, while the speed of sound in fresh water is 1482 m/s (almost four times faster than in air), and the speed of sound in steel is 5960 m/s (almost seventeen times faster than in air).

Gases: - Like the speed of a wave on a guitar string, the speed of sound depends on the properties of the medium. In a gas, it is only when molecules collide that the condensations and rarefactions of a sound wave can move from one place to another. The average molecular speed between collisions therefore should have the same order of magnitude as the speed of sound in a gas. For an ideal gas, this average speed is the translational rms speed given by the expression: -

$\Rightarrow v_{rms} = \sqrt{[3kT/m]}$

Note k = Boltzmann constant = 1.38×10^{-23} J/K, and T = Kelvin temperature.

Careful analysis shows that the speed of sound in an ideal gas is given by the expression: -

$\Rightarrow v = \sqrt{[\gamma kT/m]}$

Note $\gamma = C_p/C_V$, where C_p = specific heat capacity at constant pressure, and C_V = specific heat capacity at constant volume. The term $\gamma = C_p/C_V$ appears in the expression because the process of compression and expansion in a sound wave is adiabatic, that is, there is no transfer of heat.

Liquids: - The speed of sound occurs adiabatically rather than isothermally in liquids. Hence the speed of sound in liquids depends on, ρ, the density of that liquid, and the adiabatic bulk modulus, B_{ad}, of the liquid.

$\Rightarrow v = \sqrt{[B_{ad}/\rho]}$

Solid Bars: - When sound travels through a long slender solid bar, the speed of sound depends on the properties of the medium and is given by the following expression: -

$\Rightarrow v = \sqrt{[Y/\rho]}$

Note Y = Young's modulus, and ρ = density of the medium.

Sound Intensity: -

Sound waves carry energy that can be used to do work, like forcing the eardrums to vibrate. In an extreme case, such as a sonic boom, the energy can be sufficient to cause damage to windows and buildings. The amount of energy transported per second by a sound wave is called the power of the wave and is measured in SI units of Joules/second (J/s) or watts (W).

The sound intensity I is defined in terms of the power P of sound that passes perpendicularly through an area A of the surface as follows: -

$\Rightarrow I = P/A$

The unit of sound intensity, I, is power per unit area or W/m^2.

For a 1000 Hz tone, the smallest sound intensity that the human ear can detect is $I = 1 \times 10^{-12}$ W/m^2, which is called the threshold of hearing. Sound intensity of the order of $1 W/m^2$ can be very painful and cause permanent damage to the hearing. The sound source at the center of a sphere emits sound uniformly in all directions. For a spherically uniform radiation, the intensity, I, is given by the following expression: -

$\Rightarrow I = P/ [4\pi R^2]$

$\Rightarrow I_1/I_2 = [P/4\pi R_1^2]/ [P/4\pi R_2^2] = R_2^2/R_1^2$

The equation for intensity $I = P/4\pi R^2$ underestimates the sound intensity from the bathroom singing because it does not take into account the reflected sound.

Hence in the bathroom the sound power passing through part of an imaginary spherical surface is the sum of the direct sound power, and the reflected sound power from the walls of the bathroom.

Decibels: -

The decibel (dB) is a measurement unit used when comparing two sound intensities. The intensity level B (expressed in decibels) is defined as follows: -

$\Rightarrow B = (10\ dB)\ \log (I/I_0)$

Note I_0 is the intensity of the reference level to which I is being compared and it is often the threshold of hearing, which is $I_0 = 1 \times 10^{-12}$ W/m^2. Decibel, like the radian, is dimensionless. Note also that the intensity level B = 0dB does not mean that the sound intensity is zero; it means that $I = I_0$.

Hence at the threshold of hearing, the intensity is $I = 1 \times 10^{-12}$ W/m^2 corresponding to an intensity level B = 0 dB. During a whisper, the intensity is $I = 1 \times 10^{-10}$ W/m^2, which corresponds to an intensity level of B = 20 dB. At a normal conversation from about 1 meter away, the intensity is $I = 3.2 \times 10^{-6}$ W/m^2, which corresponds to B = 65 dB of intensity level. At a live rock concert, the intensity of sound of $I = 1$ W/m^2 corresponds to the intensity level B = 120 dB and at the threshold of pain, the intensity $I = 10$ W/m^2 corresponds to an intensity level of B = 130 dB.

Hearing tests have revealed that one decibel change in the intensity level corresponds to approximately the smallest change in loudness that an average listener with normal hearing can detect.

Experiments have shown that if the intensity level changes by 10 dB the new sound seems approximately twice as loud as the original sound.

$\Rightarrow B_2 - B_1 = 10$ dB [log (I_2/I_0) – log (I_1/I_0)] = 10 dB

Solving this reveals that $I_2/I_1 = 10$. Hence increasing the sound intensity by a factor of ten will double the perceived loudness.

Doppler Effect: -

For the Doppler Effect to occur the velocity of sound source and the velocity of the observer must be different and the wavelength and frequency of sound must be taken into account in order to calculate the magnitude of the Doppler Effect.

Hence the equations of Doppler Effect are as follows: -

Let f_0 and f_S be the frequencies of the observer and the source respectively and v_S, v_0, and v be the velocities of the moving source, the moving observer, and the sound respectively, then we have the following equations: -

1) Source moving toward stationary observer: -
$\Rightarrow f_0 = f_S [1/ (1 - v_S/v)]$
2) Source moving away from stationary observer: -
$\Rightarrow f_0 = f_S [1/ (1 + v_S/v)]$

3) Observer moving toward stationary source: -
$\Rightarrow f_0 = f_S [1 + v_0/v]$
4) Observer moving away from stationary source: -

$\Rightarrow f_0 = f_S [1 - v_0/v]$

5) The general case for all these four equations, when the source and the observer are both moving, will be as follows: -

$\Rightarrow f_0 = f_S [(1 \pm v_0/v)/ (1 \mp v_S/v)]$

In this equation, in the numerator, (+) implies the observer moves toward the source, and (-) implies the observer moves away from the source; and in the denominator, (-) implies the source moves toward the observer, and (+) implies the source moves away from observer.

Waves and Sound: -

(15) Numerical Problems: -

The Characteristics of Waves, Periodic Waves: -

1) A person standing in the ocean notices that after a wave crest passes by 8 more crests pass by in a time of 72 seconds. What is the frequency of the wave?

Solution: -

T = Total time for the crests to pass/ No. of crests that have passed

$\Rightarrow$ T = 72 seconds/ 8 crests = 9 seconds/ crest

$\Rightarrow$ f = 1/T = 1 crest/9 seconds = 0.11Hz

Hence the frequency of the wave is f = 0.11 Hz or f = 0.11 cycles/ seconds.

2) A longitudinal wave with a frequency of 5 Hz takes 2 seconds to travel the length of a 3 m slinky. Determine the wavelength of the wave.

Solution: -

v = d/t = 3 m/2 seconds = 1.5 m/s = fλ

$\Rightarrow \lambda$ = v/ f = (1.5 m/s)/ 5 Hz = 0.3 m

Hence the wavelength of the wave is λ = 0.3 m, which we have determined above.

3) A water skier is moving at a speed of 15m/s. When she skis in the same direction as a traveling wave, she springs upward every 0.9 seconds because of the wave crests. When she skis in the direction opposite to that in which the wave moves, she springs upward every 0.8 seconds in response to the crests. The speed of the skier is greater than the speed of the wave. Determine (a) the speed and (b) the wavelength of the wave.

Solution: - The following two simultaneous equations have been derived from the data given in the statement of the problem.

v − 15 = - λ/ 0.9

$v + 15 = \lambda/ 0.8$

$\Rightarrow v/ 0.8 - 15/ 0.8 = - \lambda/ 0.72$

$\Rightarrow v/ 0.9 + 15/ 0.9 = \lambda/ 0.72$

$\Rightarrow v(1/0.8 + 1/0.9) = 15/ 0.8 - 15/ 0.9$

$\Rightarrow v(1.7/0.72) = (13.5 - 12)/ 0.72 = 1.5/ 0.72$

$\Rightarrow v = 1.5/ 1.7 = 0.882352944$ m/s

$\Rightarrow \lambda = (15 + 0.882352944) \times 0.8 = 12.7058823552$ m

Hence the velocity, v, and the wavelength, λ, of the wave have been determined to be (a) v = 0.88 m/s, and (b) λ = 12.7058 m, respectively.

The Speed of a Wave on a String: -

4) The linear density of the A string on a violin is 8×10^{-4} kg/m. A wave on the string has a frequency of 500 Hz and a wavelength of 70 cm. What is the tension in the string?

Solution: -

$\rho = m//L = 8 \times 10^{-4}$ kg/m

f = 500 Hz

λ = 70 cm = 0.7m

F = tension in the string = ?

$\Rightarrow v = \sqrt{[F/(m/L)]} = \sqrt{[F/\rho]} = f\lambda = 500$ Hz x 0.7m = 350 m/s

$\Rightarrow F = v^2 \times \rho = (350$ m/s$)^2 \times 8 \times 10^{-4}$ kg/m = 12.25 x 8 = 98 N

$\Rightarrow F = 98$ N

Hence the tension in the string has a magnitude of F = 98 N.

5) A transverse wave is travelling with a speed of 250 m/s on a horizontal string. If the tension in the string is increased by a factor of four, what is the speed of the wave?

Solution: -

v = 250 m/s

$v = \sqrt{[F/\rho]} = \sqrt{[F/(m/L)]}$

The tension F in the string increases to 4F.

$\Rightarrow v` = \sqrt{[4F/\rho]} = 2\sqrt{[F/\rho]} = 2v$

$\Rightarrow v` = 2v = 2 \times 250$ m/s = 500 m/s

Hence the speed of the wave when the tension in the string is increased by a factor of four is given by v` = 500 m/s

6) To measure the acceleration due to gravity on a distant planet, an astronaut hangs a 0.06 kg ball from the end of a wire. The wire has a length of 1.00 m and a linear density of $\rho = m/L = 0.9 \times 10^{-4}$ kg/m. Using electronic equipment, the astronaut measures the time for a transverse pulse to travel the length of the wire and obtain a value of 0.02 seconds.

The mass of the wire is negligible compared to the mass of the ball. Determine the acceleration due to gravity.

Solution: -

$v = d/t = \sqrt{[F/\rho]} = \sqrt{[mg'/(\rho)]}$

$v = 1.00m/ 0.02s = \sqrt{[(0.06 \text{ kg} \times g')/0.9 \times 10^{-4} \text{ kg/m}]}$

$\Rightarrow v = 50 \text{ m/s} = \sqrt{[0.06g'/(0.9 \times 10^{-4})]}$

$\Rightarrow 2500 = 0.06g'/(0.9 \times 10^{-4})$

$\Rightarrow g' = (2500 \times 0.9 \times 10^{-4})/0.06 = 0.225/ 0.06 = 22.5/6 = 3.75 m/s^2$

$\Rightarrow g' = 3.75 \text{ m/s}^2$

Hence the acceleration due to gravity on the distant planet is given by $g' = 3.75 \text{ m/s}^2$.

The Mathematical Description of a Wave: -

(Angles are in radians)

7) A wave has the following properties: amplitude = 0.4 m, period = 0.8 second, wave speed = 15 m/s. The wave is travelling in the –x direction. What is the mathematical expression for the wave?

Solution: -

$y = A \sin (2\pi ft \pm 2\pi x / \lambda)$ for – x and + x directions respectively.

$v = f\lambda = \lambda/T$

$\Rightarrow \lambda = v \times T = 15 \text{ m/s} \times 0.8s = 9.6 \text{ m}$

$\Rightarrow f = 1/T = 1/0.8s = 1.25 \text{ Hz}$

$\Rightarrow y = 0.4 \sin (2 \times 1.25\pi t + 2\pi x / 9.6)$

$\Rightarrow y = 0.4 \sin (2.5\pi t + 0.20833\pi x)$

Hence the mathematical expression for the wave is given as follows: -

$y = 0.4 \sin (2.5\pi t + 0.208\pi x)$

8) A wave causes a displacement y that is given in meters according to $y = (0.5) \sin (10\pi t + 10\pi x)$, where t and x are expressed in seconds and meters respectively. (a) Find the amplitude, the frequency, the wavelength, and the speed of the wave. (b) Is this wave travelling in the + x or – x direction?

Solution: -

(a) $y = (0.5) \sin (10\pi t + 10\pi x)$

$\Rightarrow$ Compare with the equation, $y = A \sin (2\pi ft + 2\pi x/ \lambda)$ for a wave travelling in the – x direction.

$\Rightarrow A = 0.5 \text{ m}$

$f = 5 \text{ Hz}$

$\lambda = 5 \text{ m}$

$\Rightarrow v = f\lambda = 5 \text{ Hz} \times 5 \text{ m} = 25 \text{ m/s}$

(b) The wave, which is a sinusoidal wave, is travelling in the – x direction.

The Nature of Sound, The Speed of Sound: -

9) The speed of a sound in a container of hydrogen at 199K is 1190 m/s. What would be the speed of sound if the temperature was raised to 399K? Assume that hydrogen behaves like an ideal gas.

Solution: -

$v_1 = \sqrt{[\gamma kT_1/m]}$

$v_2 = \sqrt{[\gamma kT_2/m]}$

$\Rightarrow v_1/v_2 = \sqrt{[T_1/T_2]} = \sqrt{[199K/399K]} = (1190 \text{ m/s})/v_2$

$\Rightarrow v_2 = 1190 \text{ m/s} \sqrt{[399K/199K]}$

$\Rightarrow v_2 = 1685 \text{ m/s}$

The speed of sound, therefore, will be $v_2 = 1685$ m/s.

10) The distance between a loudspeaker and the left ear of a listener is 3 m. (a) Calculate the time required for sound to travel this distance if the air temperature is 20°C. (b) Assuming that the sound frequency is 600 Hz, how many wavelengths of sound are contained in this distance?

Solution: -

(a) $t = d/v = 3 \text{ m}/(343 \text{ m/s}) = 8.746356 \times 10^{-3} \text{s}$

$\Rightarrow t = 8.74 \times 10^{-3} \text{s}$

(b) $v = f\lambda = 600 \text{ Hz} \times \lambda = 343 \text{ m/s}$

$\Rightarrow \lambda = (343 \text{ m/s})/(600 \text{ Hz}) = 0.571666667 \text{ m}$

$n\lambda = d$

$\Rightarrow n = d/\lambda = 3 \text{ m}/0.571666667 \text{ m}$

$\Rightarrow n = 5.247813408$

Hence the answers are (a) $t = 8.74 \times 10^{-3}$s and (b) n = 5.24 respectively.

Sound Intensity: -

11) A loudspeaker has a circular opening with a radius of 0.089m. The electrical power needed to operate the speaker is 30W. The average sound intensity at the opening is 20 W/m². What percentage of electrical power is converted by the speaker into sound power?

Solution: -

$I = P/A = 20 \text{ W/m}^2 = P/[\pi (0.089 \text{ m})^2]$

$\Rightarrow P = 20 \text{ W/m}^2 \times \pi(0.089 \text{ m})^2 = 0.497691108 \text{ W}$

$\% P = (0.497691108/30) \times 100 = 1.65897 \%$

$\Rightarrow \% P = 1.658 \%$

12) Suppose that sound is emitted uniformly in all directions by a public address system. The intensity at a location 30 m away from the

sound source is 2×10^{-4} W/m^2. What is the intensity at a spot that is 80 m away?

Solution: -

$P = I_1 A_1 = I_2 A_2$

$\Rightarrow 2 \times 10^{-4}$ W/m^2 x $4\pi(30m)^2 = I_2$ x $4\pi(80m)^2$

$\Rightarrow I_2 = [2 \times 10^{-4}$ W/m^2 x $4\pi(30m)^2] / 4\pi(80m)^2$

$\Rightarrow I_2 = 2.8125 \times 10^{-5}$ W/m^2

Decibels: -

13) The bellow of a territorial bull hippopotamus has been measured at 110 dB above the threshold of hearing. What is the sound intensity?

Solution: -

$\beta = 10$ dβ log $[I/I_0]$

$\Rightarrow 110$ d$\beta = 10$ dβ log $[I/ 1 \times 10^{-12}]$

$11 = \log [I/1 \times 10^{-12}]$

$\Rightarrow 1 \times 10^{11} = I/[1 \times 10^{-12}]$

$\Rightarrow I = 1 \times 10^{-1}$ W/m$^2 = 0.1$ W/m^2

Hence the sound intensity is 0.1 W/m^2.

14) In a discussion person A is talking 2 dβ louder than person B, and person C is talking 3 dβ louder than person A. What is the ratio of the sound intensity of person C to the sound intensity of person B?

Solution: -

$\beta = 10$ dβlog $[I/I_0]$

$\Rightarrow 2$ d$\beta = 10$ dβ log $[I_A/ I_B]$

$\Rightarrow I_A/ I_B = $ antilog $(0.2) = 1.584893192$

$\Rightarrow 3$ d$\beta = 10$ dβ log $[I_C/ I_A]$

$\Rightarrow I_C/ I_A = $ antilog $(0.3) = 1.995262315$

$\Rightarrow I_C / I_B = [I_A/ I_B]$ x $[I_C/ I_A]$

$\Rightarrow I_C / I_B = (1.584893192)$ x (1.995262315)

$\Rightarrow I_C / I_B = 3.16$

The Doppler Effect: -

15) The security alarm on a parked car goes off and produces a frequency of 1000 Hz. The speed of sound is 343 m/s. As you drive towards this parked car, pass it, and drive away, you observe the frequency to change by 100 Hz. At what speed are you driving?

Solution: -

$f_0 = f_S (1 + v_0/v)$ for an observer moving towards stationary source.

$f_0 = f_s (1 - v_0/v)$ for an observer moving away from stationary source.

$\Rightarrow f_0 = 900$ Hz and $f_s = 1000$ Hz in both cases.

900 Hz $= 1000$ Hz $(1 + v_0/v)$

$\Rightarrow 0.9 = 1 + v_0/343$

$\Rightarrow v_0 = 34.3$ m/s

Now this is the speed when the car is approaching the source and this is also the speed with which it is receding away from the source. Hence the speed of the car that you are driving wll be the average of these two speeds.

$\Rightarrow v_0 = (34.3$ m/s $+ 0$ m/s$)/2 = 17.15$ m/s

$\Rightarrow v_0 = 17.15$ m/s

Hence the speed at which you are driving is given by $v = 17.15$ m/s.

Chapter No.16: -

. . . .

The Principle of Linear Superposition and Interference Phenomena: -

The Principle of Linear Superposition: -

When two or more waves are present simultaneously at the same place, the resultant disturbance is the sum of the disturbances from the individual waves.

Constructive and Destructive Interference of Sound Waves: -

When two waves always meet condensation to condensation and rarefaction to rarefaction (or crest to crest and trough to trough), they are said to be exactly in phase and to exhibit constructive interference.

When two waves always meet condensation to rarefaction (or crest to trough), they are said to be exactly out of phase and to exhibit destructive interference.

When two waves meet, they interfere constructively if they always meet exactly in phase and destructively if they always meet out of phase. In either case, this means that the wave patterns do not shift relative to one another as time passes. Sources that produce waves in this fashion are called coherent sources. Destructive interference is applied in techniques for reducing the loudness of sound such as the noise cancelling or eliminating devices like the headphones.

For two waves vibrating in phase, a difference in path lengths that is zero or an integer number (1,2,3,...) of wavelengths leads to constructive interference; a difference in path lengths that is half integer number (1/2, 1½, 2½,...) of wavelengths leads to destructive interference.

Interference Phenomena: -

By combining our knowledge of sound waves with the principle of linear superposition, we are able to understand the interference phenomena of diffraction, beats, and transverse and longitudinal standing waves.

Diffraction: -

The bending of sound waves around the edges of a doorway is an example of diffraction. When the waves are bent due to diffraction, there is an angle of diffraction through which they are bent. This angle is given in terms of sinθ.

If the angle θ defines the location of the first minimum intensity point on either side of the center of doorway then the following equation gives θ in terms of the wavelength λ and the width D of the doorway and assumes that the doorway can be treated like a slit whose height is very large compared to its width.

$\Rightarrow \sin \theta = \lambda / D$ single slit (first minimum)

For a circular opening other than a single slit such as that in a loudspeaker, the angle θ is related to the wavelength λ and the diameter D of the opening by the following equation: -

$\Rightarrow \sin \theta = 1.22 \lambda / D$ circular opening (first minimum)

For a low diffraction, θ is small, λ is small, and D is large, and we have a narrow dispersion for high frequency sound waves with small wavelengths. For a high diffraction, θ is large, λ is large, and D is small, and we have a wide dispersion for low frequency sound waves with large wavelengths. In a stereo system, wide dispersion of sound waves is desirable.

Beats: -

When two identical tuning forks are sounded simultaneously with a frequency of 440 Hz and 438 Hz respectively, the loudness of the resulting sound rises and falls periodically. The periodic variations in loudness are called beats and result from the interference between two sound waves with slightly different frequencies. The number of times per second that the loudness rises and falls is the beat frequency and is the difference between the two sound frequencies. Hence in the case of tuning forks with frequencies of 440 Hz and 438 Hz, the beat frequency is 440 Hz – 438 Hz = 2 Hz, which implies 2 times per second. Audible and inaudible sound waves, however, behave in exactly the same way. Musicians often tune their instruments, like the guitar, by listening to a beat frequency. The guitarist, for example, adjusts the tension in the string until the beats vanish, ensuring that the string is vibrating at the correct frequency.

Transverse Standing Waves: -

A standing wave is another interference effect that can occur when two waves overlap. Standing waves can arise with transverse waves, such as those on a guitar string, and also with longitudinal sound waves, such as those in a flute. In any case, the principle of linear superposition provides an explanation of the effect, just as it does for diffraction and beats. In a transverse standing wave pattern, there are places called nodes and antinodes. The nodes are places that do not vibrate at all, and antinodes are the ones that exhibit maximum vibration. In a transverse standing wave pattern, the one loop pattern corresponds to the smallest frequency f_1, and the larger frequencies are integer multiples of f_1. For a two loop pattern, the frequency corresponds to $2f_1$ and for a three loop pattern, the frequency corresponds to $3f_1$ etc. Hence the frequencies are f_1, $2f_1$, $3f_1$, etc. and these are called harmonics, that is, the first harmonic, the second harmonic, and the third harmonic, etc. These are also referred to as the fundamental f_1, the first overtone $f_2 = 2f_1$, and the second overtone $f_3 = 3f_1$, etc. Hence the frequencies above the fundamental are called overtones.

Standing waves arise because identical waves travel in opposite directions and combine in accordance with the principle of linear superposition. A standing wave seems to be standing because it does not travel in any direction like the individual waves that produce it.

Repeated reinforcement between newly created and reflected cycles causes a large amplitude standing wave to develop on the string, even when the hand, itself vibrates with only a small amplitude. Hence the motion of the string is a resonance effect. The frequency f_1 at which resonance occurs is sometimes called the natural frequency of the string. There are a series of natural frequencies that lead to standing waves on a string fixed at both ends and these are given by the following equation: -

$\Rightarrow f_n = n\ (v/2L)$ $n = 1, 2, 3, 4,\ldots$ string fixed at both ends

When the standing wave pattern corresponds to one half wavelength, the two fixed ends of the string are nodes, and the length, L, of the string must contain an integer number n of half wavelengths.

$\Rightarrow L = n\ (1/2)\ \lambda_n$

$\Rightarrow \lambda_n = 2L/n$

$\Rightarrow v = f_n\ \lambda_n = f_n\ (2L/\ n)$

Longitudinal Standing Waves: -

To determine the natural frequencies of the air columns in a tube open at both ends, there are antinodes at each end of the open tube. As in a transverse standing wave, the distance between two successive antinodes is one half of a wavelength, so the length L of the tube must be an integer number, n, of half wavelengths.

$\sigma\ L = n\ (1/2)\ \lambda_n$

$\sigma\ \lambda_n = 2L/n$

$\Rightarrow f_n = v/\lambda_n = n\,(v/2L)\quad n = 1, 2, 3, 4,\ldots$

At these frequencies large amplitude standing waves develop within the tube due to resonance.

Standing waves can also exist in a tube with only one end open. Here the standing waves have an antinode at the open end and a node at the closed end. The distance between a node and an antinode is one-fourth of a wavelength. Hence the length L of the tube must be an odd number of quarter wavelengths.

$\Rightarrow L = n\,(1/4)\,\lambda_n\quad n = 1, 3, 5,\ldots$

$\Rightarrow \lambda_n = 4L/n$

$\Rightarrow f_n = v/\lambda_n = n\,(v/4L)\quad n = 1, 3, 5,\ldots$

Hence a tube open at one end only can develop standing waves only at the odd harmonic frequencies f_1, f_3, f_5, etc. and a tube open at both ends can develop standing waves at all harmonic frequencies f_1, f_2, f_3, etc. Moreover the fundamental frequency f_1 of a tube open at one end only is one half that of a tube open at both ends. In other words, a tube open at one end only, needs to be only one half as long as a tube open at both ends in order to produce the same fundamental frequency.

Energy of the standing waves is also conserved, either on a string or in a tube of air. The energy of the standing wave is the sum of the energies of the individual waves that comprise the standing wave. Interference redistributes the energy of the individual wave to create locations of greatest energy (antinodes) and locations of no energy (nodes).

Complex Sound Waves: -

Musical instruments sound different even when they are playing at the same frequencies because the relative amplitudes of the harmonics that the instruments create are different. The sound wave corresponding to a note produced by a musical instrument or a singer is called a complex sound wave because it consists of a mixture of the fundamental and harmonic frequencies. The pattern of pressure fluctuations in a complex wave can be obtained by using the principle of linear superposition. When the individual pressure patterns for each of the harmonics are added together, they yield the complex pressure pattern in accordance with the principle of linear superposition. The spectrum analyzer is useful in determining the amplitude and frequency of each harmonic present in a complex wave and displays the result on a screen.

"The Morning Echo"

The Principle of Linear Superposition and Interference Phenomena: -

16) Numerical Problems: -

The Principle of Linear Superposition, Constructive and Destructive Interference of Sound Waves: -

1) a) When two identical waves meet crest to crest and trough to trough, do these interfere constructively or destructively? b) When the same two identical waves meet crest to trough and trough to crest, do these interfere constructively or destructively?

Solution: -

a) When two identical waves meet condensation to condensation and rarefaction to rarefaction (or crest to crest and trough to trough) they will interfere constructively, reinforcing one another and combining into a single wave of twice the frequency because they are exactly in phase.

b) When two identical waves meet condensation to rarefaction and vice versa (or crest to trough and vice versa), they will interfere destructively, cancelling one another leading to zero frequency because they are exactly out of phase.

2) Two loudspeakers are vibrating in phase. Speaker A is located 4m horizontally to the left of speaker B. The speed of sound is 343 m/s. The speakers are playing the same tone. What is the smallest frequency that will produce destructive interference at point C located vertically downward at a distance of 3m from speaker B, such that σ ABC = 90^0.

Solution: -
AC = $\sqrt{[(AB)^2 + (BC)^2]}$
AC = $\sqrt{[(4m)^2 + (3m)^2]}$
AC = $\sqrt{[16 + 9]} = \sqrt{[25]} = 5$ m
$\lambda/2 = 5$ m $- 3$ m $= 2$ m
$\Rightarrow \lambda = 2 \times 2$ m $= 4$ m
$\Rightarrow f = v/\lambda = (343$ m/s$)/4$m $= 85.75$ Hz

Hence the smallest frequency that will produce destructive interference at point C will be 85.75 Hz.

Diffraction: -

3) The entrance to a large lecture room consists of two side-by-side doors, one hinged on the left and the other hinged on the right. Each door is 0.8 m wide. Sound of frequency 595 Hz is coming through the entrance from within the room. The speed of sound is 343 m/s. What is the diffraction angle θ of the sound after it passes through the doorway when (a) one door is open and (b) both doors are open?

Solution: -
(a) $\sin \theta = n\lambda / D$
$\Rightarrow \sin \theta = [(343 \text{ m/s})/ 595 \text{ Hz}]/ 0.8 \text{ m} = 0.720588235$
$\Rightarrow \theta = \sin^{-1} (0.720588235) = 46^0$
(b) $\sin \theta = n\lambda / D$
$\Rightarrow \sin \theta = [(343 \text{ m/s})/ 595 \text{ Hz}]/ 1.6 \text{ m} = 0.360294118$
$\Rightarrow \theta = \sin^{-1} (0.360294118) = 21^0$

4) A speaker has a diameter of 0.2 m. (a) Assuming that the speed of sound is 343 m/s, find the diffraction angle θ for a 3 kHz tone. (b) What speaker diameter D should be used to generate a 4 kHz tone whose diffraction angle is as wide as that for the 3 kHz tone in part (a)?
Solution: -
(a) $\sin \theta = 1.22 \lambda / D$
$\Rightarrow \sin \theta = [1.22 \times (343 \text{ m/s})/ (3 \times 10^3 \text{ Hz})]/ 0.2 \text{ m} = 0.6974333$
$\Rightarrow \theta = 44.2^0$
(b) $\sin \theta = 1.22 \lambda / D$
$\Rightarrow \sin 44.2^0 = [1.22 \times (343 \text{ m/s})/ (4 \times 10^3 \text{ Hz})]/ D$
$\Rightarrow D = [1.22 \times (343 \text{ m/s})/ (4 \times 10^3 \text{ Hz})]/ \sin 44.2^0$
$\Rightarrow D = 0.15 \text{ m}$

5) Sound exits a diffraction horn loudspeaker through a rectangular opening like a small doorway. A person is sitting at an angle θ off to the side of a diffraction horn that has a width D of 0.08m. The speed of sound is 343 m/s. This individual does not hear a sound wave that has a frequency of 6000 Hz. When she is sitting at an angle of $\theta/2$, there is a different frequency that she does not hear. What is it?
Solution: -
$\sin \theta = n\lambda / D$ n = 1,2,3, … for destructive interference
$\sin \theta = [(343\text{m/s})/ 6000 \text{ Hz}]/0.08\text{m} = 0.714583333333$
$\Rightarrow \theta = \sin^{-1} (0.71458333333) = 45.60906222^0$
$\Rightarrow \theta/2 = 22.80453111^0$
$\Rightarrow \sin (\theta/2) = \sin (22.80453111^0) = [(343\text{m/s})/f]/0.08\text{m}$
$\Rightarrow f = [(343\text{m/s})/0.08\text{m}]/\sin (22.80453111^0)$
$\Rightarrow f = 11061.99003 \text{ Hz} = 11.06 \text{ kHz}$

6) A 4 kHz tone is being produced by a speaker with a diameter of 0.2m. The air temperature changes from 0 to 30^{0}C. Assuming air to be an ideal gas, find the change in the diffraction angle θ.
Solution: -
$v_{273.15K}/ v_{303.15K} = (331 \text{ m/s})/ v_{303.15K} = [\sqrt{273.15}]/ [\sqrt{303.15}]$
$\Rightarrow v_{303.15K} = [331\text{m/s} \times \sqrt{303.15}]/ \sqrt{273.15} = 348.7033965 \text{ m/s}$

sin θ_1 = [1.22 x (331 m/s)/ 4000 Hz]/ 0.2m = 0.504775

$\Rightarrow \theta_1$ = sin^{-1} (0.504775) = 30.3164175^0

sin θ_2 = [1.22 x (348.7033965 m/s)/4000 Hz]/0.2m = 0.53177268

$\Rightarrow \theta_2$ = 32.1253060$7^0$

$\Delta\theta$ = 32.125306$07^0$ – 30.316417$5^0$ = 1.80888857$4^0$

$\Rightarrow \Delta\theta$ = 1.8^0

Hence the change in the diffraction angle $\Delta\theta$ has been determined to be 1.8^0.

Beats: -

7) Two pure tones are sounded together. The pressure variation of the two sound waves is measured with respect to the atmospheric pressure. The time period of the first pure tone is T_1 = 0.02s and the time period of the second pure tone is T_2 = 0.024s. What is the beat frequency?

Solution: -

f = 1/T

f_1 = 1/T_1 = 1/0.02s = 50 Hz

f_2 = 1/T_2 = 1/0.024s = 41.6666 Hz = 42 Hz

Beat frequency = f_1 – f_2 = 50 Hz – 42 Hz = 8 Hz

Hence the beat frequency is 8 Hz.

8) Two ultrasonic sound waves combine and form a beat frequency that is in the range of human hearing. The frequency of one of the ultrasonic waves is 60 kHz. What are (a) the smallest possible and (b) the largest possible value for the frequency of the other ultrasonic wave?

Solution: -

(a) 60,000 Hz

- 40,000 H

_____

+ 40,000 Hz

$\Rightarrow$ f = 40,000 Hz = 40 kHz is the smallest frequency of the other ultrasonic wave.

(b) 60,000 Hz

+ 20,000 Hz

_____

+ 80,000 Hz

$\Rightarrow$ f = 80,000 Hz = 80 kHz is the largest possible frequency of the other ultrasonic wave.

9) A sound wave is travelling in sea water where the adiabatic bulk modulus and density are ΔP = 3.41 x 10^8 Pa and ρ = 1025 kg/m^3

respectively. The wavelength of the sound is 2.25 m. A tuning fork is struck underwater and vibrates at 250 Hz. What would be the beat frequency heard by an underwater swimmer?

Solution: -

$\Delta P = - \beta (\Delta V/V_0)$

$\Rightarrow \Delta P = 3.41 \times 10^8$ Pa

$\Rightarrow v = \sqrt{[F/\rho]} = \sqrt{[3.41 \times 10^8 \text{ Pa}/ 1025 \text{ kg/m}^3]}$

$\Rightarrow v = 576.7867256$ m/s

$\Rightarrow f = v / \lambda = (576.7867256 \text{m/s})/ (2.25\text{m}) = 256$ Hz

$\Rightarrow$ Beat frequency = 256 Hz – 250 Hz = 6 Hz

Hence the beat frequency is 6 Hz.

Note the speed of sound in solids, liquids, and ideal gases is given by the following three equations.

$v = \sqrt{[Y/\rho]}$ = speed of sound in solid

$v = \sqrt{[B_{ad}/\rho]}$ = speed of sound in liquid

$v = \sqrt{[\gamma kT/m]}$ = speed of sound in an ideal gas

Transverse Standing Waves: -

10) The A string on a string bass is tuned to vibrate at a fundamental frequency of 60 Hz. If the tension in the string were increased by a factor of four, what would be the new fundamental frequency?

Solution: -

$f_1 = 60$ Hz

F increases to 4F.

$v = \sqrt{[F/\rho]}$

$f_n = n (v/2L)$ n = 1, 2, 3, ...

$\Rightarrow f_1 = \sqrt{[F/\rho]}/ 2L$

$\Rightarrow f_1^* = \sqrt{[4F/\rho]} /2L = 2 \sqrt{[F/\rho]}/ 2L = 2f_1 = 2 \times 60$ Hz = 120 Hz

Hence the new fundamental frequency is $f_1^* = 120$ Hz.

11) The G-string on a guitar has a fundamental frequency of 200 Hz and a length of 0.7 m. This string is pressed against the proper fret to produce the note C, whose fundamental frequency is 300 Hz. What is the distance L between the fret and the end of the string at the bridge of the guitar?

Solution: -

$v = 2Lf_1 = 2 \times 0.7$ m $\times 200$ Hz = 280 m/s

$\Rightarrow L = v / 2f_1` = (280 \text{ m/s}) / (2 \times 300 \text{ Hz}) = 0.46666$ m

$\Rightarrow L = 0.46$ m

Longitudinal Standing Waves, Complex Sound Waves: -

12) The fundamental frequency of a vibrating system is 300 Hz. For each of the following systems, give the three lowest frequencies (excluding the fundamental) at which standing waves can occur: (a) a string fixed at both ends, (b) a cylindrical pipe with both ends open, and (c) a cylindrical pipe with only one end open.

Solution: -

(a) $f_n = n (v/2L)$ n = 1, 2, 3, ...

For the string fixed at both ends, these are called natural frequencies.

(b) $f_n = n (v/2L)$ n = 1, 2, 3, ...

For a tube open at both ends, these are the lowest frequencies.

(c) $f_n = n (v/4L)$ n = 1, 3, 5, ...

These represent lowest frequencies for a tube open at one end only.

$\Rightarrow$ (a) $f_1 = 300$ Hz

$f_2 = 2f_1 = 600$ Hz

$f_3 = 3f_1 = 900$ Hz

$f_4 = 4f_1 = 1200$ Hz

$\Rightarrow$ (b) $f_1 = 300$ Hz

$f_2 = 2f_1 = 600$ Hz

$f_3 = 3f_1 = 900$ Hz

$f_4 = 4f_1 = 1200$ Hz

$\Rightarrow$ (c) $f_1 = 300$ Hz

$f_3 = 3f_1 = 900$ Hz

$f_5 = 5f_1 = 1500$ Hz

$f_7 = 7f_1 = 2100$ Hz

13) A tube of air is open at only one end and has a length of 1.2 m. This tube sustains a standing wave at its third harmonic. What is the distance between one node and the adjacent antinode?

Solution: -

$f_3 = 3f_1$ (third harmonic)

$\Rightarrow$ Distance between one node and an adjacent antinode = d

d = L/n = 1.2 m / 3 = 0.4 m

Hence the distance between one node and an adjacent antinode is d = 0.4 m.

14) Both neon (Ne) and helium (He) are mono-atomic gases and can be assumed to be ideal gases. The fundamental frequency of a tube of neon is 300 Hz. What is the fundamental frequency of the tube if the tube is filled with helium, all other factors remaining the same?

Solution: -

$f_n = n (v/2L)$

$v = \sqrt{[F/\rho]} = \sqrt{[F/(m/L)]}$

$\Rightarrow f_1 (Ne)/ f_1 (He) = \sqrt{[m(He)/ m(Ne)]} = \sqrt{[4.00260/ 20.180]}$

$\Rightarrow f_1 (He) = f_1 (Ne) \times \sqrt{[20.180/ 4.00260]}$

$\Rightarrow f_1 (He) = 300 \text{ Hz} \times \sqrt{[20.180/4.00260]} = 673.6 \text{ Hz}$

$\Rightarrow f_1 (He) = 673.6 \text{ Hz}$

Hence the fundamental frequency of the tube when it is filled with helium, all other factors remaining the same is $f_1 = 673.6$ Hz.

Miscellaneous: -

15) A vertical tube is closed at one end and open to air at the other end. The air pressure is 1.01×10^5 Pa. The tube has a length of 0.9 m. Mercury (mass density = 13,600 kg/ m^3) is poured into it to shorten the effective length for standing waves. What is the absolute pressure at the bottom of the mercury column, when the fundamental frequency of the shortened, air filled tube is equal to the third harmonic of the original tube?

Solution: -

$f_n = n (v/4L)$

$f_3 = 3f_1 = 3 \times (343\text{m/s})/ (4 \times 0.9\text{m}) = 285.8333 \text{ Hz}$

$\Rightarrow v = 2Lf_3 = 343\text{m/s} = 2L \times 285.833 \text{ Hz}$

$\Rightarrow L = (343\text{m/s})/ (2 \times 285.833 \text{ Hz}) = 0.6 \text{ m}$

$\Rightarrow P = \rho gh = 13,600 \text{ kg/m}^3 \times 9.8 \text{ m/s}^2 \times 0.6 \text{ m}$

$P = 0.79968 \times 10^5 \text{ Pa}$

$\Rightarrow P_{absolute} = P_0 + \rho gh = (1.013 + 0.79968) \times 10^5 \text{ Pa}$

$\Rightarrow P_{absolute} = 1.81268 \times 10^5 \text{ Pa}$

Hence the absolute pressure at the bottom of the mercury column is $P_{absolute} = 1.81268 \times 10^5$ Pa.

Appendix A: -

· ·

Area of a Triangle = (1/2)[base b][altitude h] = (1/2)bh
Area of a Square = (side a)^2 = a^2
Area of a Rectangle = [(side a)(side b)] = ab
Area of a Circle = π(radius r)^2 = πr^2
Circumference of a Circle = 2πr
Surface Area of a Sphere = 4π(radius r)^2 = 4πr^2
Volume of a Sphere = (4/3)πr^3
Surface Area of a Cylinder = 2πrh + 2πr^2
Volume of a Cylinder = πr^{2}h
Theorem of Pythagorus: - This holds for a right angled triangle.
a^2 + b^2 = c^2
Quadratic Formula: - x = [- b ± √(b^2 – 4ac)]/2a
Binomial Theorem: -
(a + b)^n = a^n + na^{n-1}b + [n(n – 1)/2!] a^{n-2}b^2 + ... + b^n
 Appendix B: -
Trigonometric Identities and Equations: - These trigonometric identities hold for a right angled triangle, where h is the height, b is the base, and H is the hypotenuse of the given right angled triangle, and θ is the angle that H (the hypotenuse) subtends with b (the base).
Sin θ = h/H Cos θ = b/H Tan θ = h/b
Cosec θ = 1/ [Sin θ] Sec θ = 1/ [Cos θ]
Cot θ = 1/ [Tan θ] Tan θ = [Sin θ]/ [Cos θ]
Sin^2 θ + Cos^2 θ = 1 Sec^2 θ = 1 + Tan^2 θ
Cosec^2 θ = 1 + Cot^2 θ
Sin (α ± β) = Sin α Cos β ± Sin β Cos α
Cos (α ± β) = Cos α Cos β σ Sin α Sin β
· Law of Cosine: -
C^2 = A^2 + B^2 – 2AB Cos α
Law of Sine: -
A / [Sinα] = B / [Sinβ] = C / [Sinγ]

Table of Common Logarithm: -

1	0			2	0.30103	3	0.4771213
1.001	0.0004341			2.01	0.3031961	3.01	0.4785665
1.002	0.0008677			2.02	0.3053514	3.02	0.4800069
1.003	0.0013009			2.03	0.307496	3.03	0.4814426
1.004	0.0017337			2.04	0.3096302	3.04	0.4828736
1.005	0.0021661			2.05	0.3117539	3.05	0.4842998
1.006	0.002598			2.06	0.3138672	3.06	0.4857214
1.007	0.0030295			2.07	0.3159703	3.07	0.4871384
1.008	0.0034605			2.08	0.3180633	3.08	0.4885507
1.009	0.0038912			2.09	0.3201463	3.09	0.4899585
1.01	0.0043214	1.1	0.0413927	2.1	0.3222193	3.1	0.4913617
1.011	0.0047512	1.11	0.045323	2.11	0.3242825	3.11	0.4927604
1.012	0.0051805	1.12	0.049218	2.12	0.3263359	3.12	0.4941546
1.013	0.0056095	1.13	0.0530784	2.13	0.3283796	3.13	0.4955443
1.014	0.006038	1.14	0.0569049	2.14	0.3304138	3.14	0.4969296
1.015	0.006466	1.15	0.0606978	2.15	0.3324385	3.15	0.4983106
1.016	0.0068937	1.16	0.064458	2.16	0.3344538	3.16	0.4996871
1.017	0.007321	1.17	0.0681859	2.17	0.3364597	3.17	0.5010593
1.018	0.0077478	1.18	0.071882	2.18	0.3384565	3.18	0.5024271
1.019	0.0081742	1.19	0.075547	2.19	0.3404441	3.19	0.5037907
1.02	0.0086002	1.2	0.0791812	2.2	0.3424227	3.2	0.50515
1.021	0.0090257	1.21	0.0827854	2.21	0.3443923	3.21	0.506505
1.022	0.0094509	1.22	0.0863598	2.22	0.346353	3.22	0.5078559
1.023	0.0098756	1.23	0.0899051	2.23	0.3483049	3.23	0.5092025
1.024	0.0103	1.24	0.0934217	2.24	0.350248	3.24	0.510545
1.025	0.0107239	1.25	0.09691	2.25	0.3521825	3.25	0.5118834
1.026	0.0111474	1.26	0.1003705	2.26	0.3541084	3.26	0.5132176
1.027	0.0115704	1.27	0.1038037	2.27	0.3560259	3.27	0.5145478
1.028	0.0119931	1.28	0.10721	2.28	0.3579348	3.28	0.5158738
1.029	0.0124154	1.29	0.1105897	2.29	0.3598355	3.29	0.5171959
1.03	0.0128372	1.3	0.1139434	2.3	0.3617278	3.3	0.5185139
1.031	0.0132587	1.31	0.1172713	2.31	0.363612	3.31	0.519828
1.032	0.0136797	1.32	0.1205739	2.32	0.365488	3.32	0.5211381
1.033	0.0141003	1.33	0.1238516	2.33	0.3673559	3.33	0.5224442
1.034	0.0145205	1.34	0.1271048	2.34	0.3692159	3.34	0.5237465

"The Morning Echo"

1.035	0.0149404	1.35	0.1303338	2.35	0.3710679	3.35	0.5250448
1.036	0.0153598	1.36	0.1335389	2.36	0.372912	3.36	0.5263393
1.037	0.0157788	1.37	0.1367206	2.37	0.3747483	3.37	0.5276299
1.038	0.0161974	1.38	0.1398791	2.38	0.376577	3.38	0.5289167
1.039	0.0166156	1.39	0.1430148	2.39	0.3783979	3.39	0.5301997
1.04	0.0170333	1.4	0.146128	2.4	0.3802112	3.4	0.5314789
1.041	0.0174507	1.41	0.1492191	2.41	0.382017	3.41	0.5327544
1.042	0.0178677	1.42	0.1522883	2.42	0.3838154	3.42	0.5340261
1.043	0.0182843	1.43	0.155336	2.43	0.3856063	3.43	0.5352941
1.044	0.0187005	1.44	0.1583625	2.44	0.3873898	3.44	0.5365584
1.045	0.0191163	1.45	0.161368	2.45	0.3891661	3.45	0.5378191
1.046	0.0195317	1.46	0.1643529	2.46	0.3909351	3.46	0.5390761
1.047	0.0199467	1.47	0.1673173	2.47	0.392697	3.47	0.5403295
1.048	0.0203613	1.48	0.1702617	2.48	0.3944517	3.48	0.5415792
1.049	0.0207755	1.49	0.1731863	2.49	0.3961993	3.49	0.5428254
1.05	0.0211893	1.5	0.1760913	2.5	0.39794	3.5	0.544068
1.051	0.0216027	1.51	0.1789769	2.51	0.3996737	3.51	0.5453071
1.052	0.0220157	1.52	0.1818436	2.52	0.4014005	3.52	0.5465427
1.053	0.0224284	1.53	0.1846914	2.53	0.4031205	3.53	0.5477747
1.054	0.0228406	1.54	0.1875207	2.54	0.4048337	3.54	0.5490033
1.055	0.0232525	1.55	0.1903317	2.55	0.4065402	3.55	0.5502284
1.056	0.0236639	1.56	0.1931246	2.56	0.40824	3.56	0.55145
1.057	0.024075	1.57	0.1958997	2.57	0.4099331	3.57	0.5526682
1.058	0.0244857	1.58	0.1986571	2.58	0.4116197	3.58	0.553883
1.059	0.024896	1.59	0.2013971	2.59	0.4132998	3.59	0.5550944
1.06	0.0253059	1.6	0.20412	2.6	0.4149733	3.6	0.5563025
1.061	0.0257154	1.61	0.2068259	2.61	0.4166405	3.61	0.5575072
1.062	0.0261245	1.62	0.209515	2.62	0.4183013	3.62	0.5587086
1.063	0.0265333	1.63	0.2121876	2.63	0.4199557	3.63	0.5599066
1.064	0.0269416	1.64	0.2148438	2.64	0.4216039	3.64	0.5611014
1.065	0.0273496	1.65	0.2174839	2.65	0.4232459	3.65	0.5622929
1.066	0.0277572	1.66	0.2201081	2.66	0.4248816	3.66	0.5634811
1.067	0.0281644	1.67	0.2227165	2.67	0.4265113	3.67	0.5646661
1.068	0.0285713	1.68	0.2253093	2.68	0.4281348	3.68	0.5658478
1.069	0.0289777	1.69	0.2278867	2.69	0.4297523	3.69	0.5670264
1.07	0.0293838	1.7	0.2304489	2.7	0.4313638	3.7	0.5682017

1.071	0.0297895	1.71	0.2329961	2.71	0.4329693	3.71	0.5693739
1.072	0.0301948	1.72	0.2355284	2.72	0.4345689	3.72	0.5705429
1.073	0.0305997	1.73	0.2380461	2.73	0.4361626	3.73	0.5717088
1.074	0.0310043	1.74	0.2405492	2.74	0.4377506	3.74	0.5728716
1.075	0.0314085	1.75	0.243038	2.75	0.4393327	3.75	0.5740313
1.076	0.0318123	1.76	0.2455127	2.76	0.4409091	3.76	0.5751878
1.077	0.0322157	1.77	0.2479733	2.77	0.4424798	3.77	0.5763414
1.078	0.0326188	1.78	0.25042	2.78	0.4440448	3.78	0.5774918
1.079	0.0330214	1.79	0.252853	2.79	0.4456042	3.79	0.5786392
1.08	0.0334238	1.8	0.2552725	2.8	0.447158	3.8	0.5797836
1.081	0.0338257	1.81	0.2576786	2.81	0.4487063	3.81	0.580925
1.082	0.0342273	1.82	0.2600714	2.82	0.4502491	3.82	0.5820634
1.083	0.0346285	1.83	0.2624511	2.83	0.4517864	3.83	0.5831988
1.084	0.0350293	1.84	0.2648178	2.84	0.4533183	3.84	0.5843312
1.085	0.0354297	1.85	0.2671717	2.85	0.4548449	3.85	0.5854607
1.086	0.0358298	1.86	0.2695129	2.86	0.456366	3.86	0.5865873
1.087	0.0362295	1.87	0.2718416	2.87	0.4578819	3.87	0.587711
1.088	0.0366289	1.88	0.2741578	2.88	0.4593925	3.88	0.5888317
1.089	0.0370279	1.89	0.2764618	2.89	0.4608978	3.89	0.5899496
1.09	0.0374265	1.9	0.2787536	2.9	0.462398	3.9	0.5910646
1.091	0.0378248	1.91	0.2810334	2.91	0.463893	3.91	0.5921768
1.092	0.0382226	1.92	0.2833012	2.92	0.4653829	3.92	0.5932861
1.093	0.0386202	1.93	0.2855573	2.93	0.4668676	3.93	0.5943926
1.094	0.0390173	1.94	0.2878017	2.94	0.4683473	3.94	0.5954962
1.095	0.0394141	1.95	0.2900346	2.95	0.469822	3.95	0.5965971
1.096	0.0398106	1.96	0.2922561	2.96	0.4712917	3.96	0.5976952
1.097	0.0402066	1.97	0.2944662	2.97	0.4727564	3.97	0.5987905
1.098	0.0406023	1.98	0.2966652	2.98	0.4742163	3.98	0.5998831
1.099	0.0409977	1.99	0.2988531	2.99	0.4756712	3.99	0.6009729

Natural LogTable:-

N	0	1	2	3	4	5	6	7	8	9
1	0	3z99503	0.019803	0.029559	0.039221	0.04879	0.058269	0.067659	0.076961	0.086178
1.1	0.09531	0.10436	0.113329	0.122218	0.131028	0.139762	0.14842	0.157004	0.165514	0.173953
1.2	0.182322	0.19062	0.198851	0.207014	0.215111	0.223144	0.231112	0.239017	0.24686	0.254642
1.3	0.262364	0.270027	0.277632	0.285179	0.29267	0.300105	0.307485	0.314811	0.322083	0.329304
1.4	0.336472	0.34359	0.350657	0.357674	0.364643	0.371564	0.378436	0.385262	0.392042	0.398776
1.5	0.405465	0.41211	0.41871	0.425268	0.431782	0.438255	0.444686	0.451076	0.457425	0.463734
1.6	0.470004	0.476234	0.482426	0.48858	0.494696	0.500775	0.506818	0.512824	0.518794	0.524729
1.7	0.530628	0.536493	0.542324	0.548121	0.553885	0.559616	0.565314	0.57098	0.576613	0.582216
1.8	0.587787	0.593327	0.598837	0.604316	0.609766	0.615186	0.620576	0.625938	0.631272	0.636577
1.9	0.641854	0.647103	0.652325	0.65752	0.662688	0.667829	0.672944	0.678034	0.683097	0.688135

N	0	1	2	3	4	5	6	7	8	9
2	0.693147	0.698135	0.703098	0.708036	0.71295	0.71784	0.722706	0.727549	0.732368	0.737164
2.1	0.741937	0.746688	0.751416	0.756122	0.760806	0.765468	0.770108	0.774727	0.779325	0.783902
2.2	0.788457	0.792993	0.797507	0.802002	0.806476	0.81093	0.815365	0.81978	0.824175	0.828552
2.3	0.832909	0.837248	0.841567	0.845868	0.850151	0.854415	0.858662	0.86289	0.8671	0.871293
2.4	0.875469	0.879627	0.883768	0.887891	0.891998	0.896088	0.900161	0.904218	0.908259	0.912283
2.5	0.916291	0.920283	0.924259	0.928219	0.932164	0.936093	0.940007	0.943906	0.947789	0.951658

N	0	1	2	3	4	5	6	7	8	9
2.6	0.955511	0.95935	0.963174	0.966984	0.970779	0.97456	0.978326	0.982078	0.98817	0.989541
2.7	0.993252	0.996949	1.00063	1.0043	1.00796	1.0116	1.01523	1.01885	1.02245	1.02604
2.8	1.02962	1.03318	1.03674	1.04028	1.0438	1.04732	1.05082	1.05431	1.05779	1.06126
2.9	1.06471	1.06815	1.07158	1.075	1.07841	1.08181	1.08519	1.08856	1.09192	1.09527
N	0	1	2	3	4	5	6	7	8	9
3	1.09861	1.10194	1.10526	1.10856	1.11186	1.11514	1.11841	1.12168	1.12493	1.12817
3.1	1.1314	1.13462	1.13783	1.14103	1.14422	1.1474	1.15057	1.15373	1.15688	1.16002
3.2	1.16315	1.16627	1.16938	1.17248	1.17557	1.17865	1.18173	1.18479	1.18784	1.19089
3.3	1.19392	1.19695	1.19996	1.20297	1.20597	1.20896	1.21194	1.21491	1.21788	1.22083
3.4	1.22378	1.22671	1.22964	1.23256	1.23547	1.23837	1.24127	1.24415	1.24703	1.2499
3.5	1.25276	1.25562	1.25846	1.2613	1.26413	1.26695	1.26976	1.27257	1.27536	1.27815
3.6	1.28093	1.28371	1.28647	1.28923	1.29198	1.29473	1.29746	1.30019	1.30291	1.30563
3.7	1.30833	1.31103	1.31372	1.31641	1.31909	1.32176	1.32442	1.32708	1.32972	1.33237
3.8	1.335	1.33763	1.34025	1.34286	1.34547	1.34807	1.35067	1.35325	1.35584	1.35841
3.9	1.36098	1.36354	1.36609	1.36864	1.37118	1.37372	1.37624	1.37877	1.38128	1.38379
N	0	1	2	3	4	5	6	7	8	9
4	1.38629	1.38879	1.39128	1.39377	1.39624	1.39872	1.40118	1.40364	1.4061	1.40854
4.1	1.41099	1.41342	1.41585	1.41828	1.4207	1.42311	1.42552	1.42792	1.43031	1.4327
4.2	1.43508	1.43746	1.43984	1.4422	1.44456	1.44692	1.44927	1.45161	1.45395	1.45629
4.3	1.45862	1.46094	1.46326	1.46557	1.46787	1.47018	1.47247	1.47476	1.47705	1.47933

N	0	1	2	3	4	5	6	7	8	9
4.4	1.4816	1.48387	1.48614	1.4884	1.49065	1.4929	1.49515	1.49739	1.49962	1.50185
4.5	1.50408	1.5063	1.50851	1.51072	1.51293	1.51513	1.51732	1.51951	1.5217	1.52388
4.6	1.52606	1.52823	1.53039	1.53256	1.53471	1.53687	1.53902	1.54116	1.5433	1.54543
4.7	1.54756	1.54969	1.55181	1.55393	1.55604	1.55814	1.56025	1.56235	1.56444	1.56653
4.8	1.56862	1.5707	1.57277	1.57485	1.57691	1.57898	1.58104	1.58309	1.58515	1.58719
4.9	1.58924	1.59127	1.59331	1.59534	1.59737	1.59939	1.60141	1.60342	1.60543	1.60744
N	0	1	2	3	4	5	6	7	8	9
5	1.60944	1.61144	1.61343	1.61542	1.61741	1.61939	1.62137	1.62334	1.62531	1.62728
5.1	1.62924	1.6312	1.63315	1.63511	1.63705	1.639	1.64094	1.64287	1.64481	1.64673
5.2	1.64866	1.65058	1.6525	1.65441	1.65632	1.65823	1.66013	1.66203	1.66393	1.66582
5.3	1.66771	1.66959	1.67147	1.67335	1.67523	1.6771	1.67896	1.68083	1.68269	1.68455
5.4	1.6864	1.68825	1.6901	1.69194	1.69378	1.69562	1.69745	1.69928	1.70111	1.70293
5.5	1.70475	1.70656	1.70838	1.71019	1.71199	1.7138	1.7156	1.7174	1.71919	1.72098
5.6	1.72277	1.72455	1.72633	1.72811	1.72988	1.73166	1.73342	1.73519	1.73695	1.73871
5.7	1.74047	1.74222	1.74397	1.74572	1.74746	1.7492	1.75094	1.75267	1.7544	1.75613
5.8	1.75786	1.75958	1.7613	1.76302	1.76473	1.76644	1.76815	1.76985	1.77156	1.77326
5.9	1.77495	1.77665	1.77834	1.78002	1.78171	1.78339	1.78507	1.78675	1.78842	1.79009
N	0	1	2	3	4	5	6	7	8	9
6	1.79176	1.79342	1.79509	1.79675	1.7984	1.80006	1.80171	1.80336	1.805	1.80665
6.1	1.80829	1.80993	1.81156	1.81319	1.81482	1.81645	1.81808	1.8197	1.82132	1.82294

N	0	1	2	3	4	5	6	7	8	9
6.2	1.82455	1.82616	1.82777	1.82938	1.83098	1.83258	1.83418	1.83578	1.83737	1.83896
6.3	1.84055	1.84214	1.84372	1.8453	1.84688	1.84845	1.85003	1.8516	1.85317	1.85473
6.4	1.8563	1.85786	1.85942	1.86097	1.86253	1.86408	1.86563	1.86718	1.86872	1.87026
6.5	1.8718	1.87334	1.87487	1.87641	1.87794	1.87947	1.88099	1.88251	1.88403	1.88555
6.6	1.88707	1.88858	1.8901	1.8916	1.89311	1.89462	1.89612	1.89762	1.89912	1.90061
6.7	1.90211	1.9036	1.90509	1.90658	1.90806	1.90954	1.91102	1.9125	1.91398	1.91545
6.8	1.91692	1.91839	1.91986	1.92132	1.92279	1.92425	1.92571	1.92716	1.92862	1.93007
6.9	1.93152	1.93297	1.93442	1.93586	1.9373	1.93874	1.94018	1.94162	1.94305	1.94448

N	0	1	2	3	4	5	6	7	8	9
7	1.94591	1.94734	1.94876	1.95019	1.95161	1.95303	1.95445	1.95586	1.95727	1.95869
7.1	1.96009	1.9615	1.96291	1.96431	1.96571	1.96711	1.96851	1.96991	1.9713	1.97269
7.2	1.97408	1.97547	1.97685	1.97824	1.97962	1.981	1.98238	1.98376	1.98513	1.9865
7.3	1.98787	1.98924	1.99061	1.99198	1.99334	1.9947	1.99606	1.99742	1.99877	2.00013
7.4	2.00148	2.00283	2.00418	2.00553	2.00687	2.00821	2.00956	2.01089	2.01223	2.01357
7.5	2.0149	2.01624	2.01757	2.0189	2.02022	2.02155	2.02287	2.02419	2.02551	2.02683
7.6	2.02815	2.02946	2.03078	2.03209	2.0334	2.03471	2.03601	2.03732	2.03862	2.03992
7.7	2.04122	2.04252	2.04381	2.04511	2.0464	2.04769	2.04898	2.05027	2.05156	2.05284
7.8	2.05412	2.0554	2.05668	2.05796	2.05924	2.06051	2.06179	2.06306	2.06433	2.0656
7.9	2.06686	2.06813	2.06939	2.07065	2.07191	2.07317	2.07443	2.07568	2.07694	2.07819

N	0	1	2	3	4	5	6	7	8	9
8	2.07944	2.08069	2.08194	2.08318	2.08443	2.08567	2.08691	2.08815	2.08939	2.09063
8.1	2.09186	2.0931	2.09433	2.09556	2.09679	2.09802	2.09924	2.10047	2.10169	2.10291
8.2	2.10413	2.10535	2.10657	2.10779	2.109	2.11021	2.11142	2.11263	2.11384	2.11505
8.3	2.11626	2.11746	2.11866	2.11986	2.12106	2.12226	2.12346	2.12465	2.12585	2.12704
8.4	2.12823	2.12942	2.13061	2.1318	2.13298	2.13417	2.13535	2.13653	2.13771	2.13889
8.5	2.14007	2.14124	2.14242	2.14359	2.14476	2.14593	2.1471	2.14827	2.14943	2.1506
8.6	2.15176	2.15292	2.15409	2.15524	2.1564	2.15756	2.15871	2.15987	2.16102	2.16217
8.7	2.16332	2.16447	2.16562	2.16677	2.16791	2.16905	2.1702	2.17134	2.17248	2.17361
8.8	2.17475	2.17589	2.17702	2.17816	2.17929	2.18042	2.18155	2.18267	2.1838	2.18493
8.9	2.18605	2.18717	2.1883	2.18942	2.19054	2.19165	2.19277	2.19389	2.195	2.19611
N	0	1	2	3	4	5	6	7	8	9
9	2.19722	2.19834	2.19944	2.20055	2.20166	2.20276	2.20387	2.20497	2.20607	2.20717
9.1	2.20827	2.20937	2.21047	2.21157	2.21266	2.21375	2.21485	2.21594	2.21703	2.21812
9.2	2.2192	2.22029	2.22138	2.22246	2.22354	2.22462	2.2257	2.22678	2.22786	2.22894
9.3	2.23001	2.23109	2.23216	2.23324	2.23431	2.23538	2.23645	2.23751	2.23858	2.23965
9.4	2.24071	2.24177	2.24284	2.2439	2.24496	2.24601	2.24707	2.24813	2.24918	2.25024
9.5	2.25129	2.25234	2.25339	2.25444	2.25549	2.25654	2.25759	2.25863	2.25968	2.26072
9.6	2.26176	2.2628	2.26384	2.26488	2.26592	2.26696	2.26799	2.26903	2.27006	2.27109
9.7	2.27213	2.27316	2.27419	2.27521	2.27624	2.27727	2.27829	2.27932	2.28034	2.28136
9.8	2.28238	2.2834	2.28442	2.28544	2.28646	2.28747	2.28849	2.2895	2.29051	2.29152

9.9	2.29253	2.29354	2.29455	2.29556	2.29657	2.29757	2.29858	2.29958	2.30058	2.30158
10	2.30259	2.30358	2.30458	2.30558	2.30658	2.30757	2.30857	2.30956	2.31055	2.31154

"The Morning Echo"

Table of Trigonometric Functions:

x		sin(x)	cos(x)	tan(x)	cot(x)	csc(x)	sec(x)
deg	rad						
0	0	0.0000	1.0000	0.0000			1.0000
1	0.0175	0.0175	0.9998	0.0175	57.2900	57.2987	1.0002
2	0.0349	0.0349	0.9994	0.0349	28.6363	28.6537	1.0006
3	0.0524	0.0523	0.9986	0.0524	19.0811	19.1073	1.0014
4	0.0698	0.0698	0.9976	0.0699	14.3007	14.3356	1.0024
5	0.0873	0.0872	0.9962	0.0875	11.4301	11.4737	1.0038
6	0.1047	0.1045	0.9945	0.1051	9.5144	9.5668	1.0055
7	0.1222	0.1219	0.9925	0.1228	8.1443	8.2055	1.0075
8	0.1396	0.1392	0.9903	0.1405	7.1154	7.1853	1.0098
9	0.1571	0.1564	0.9877	0.1584	6.3138	6.3925	1.0125
10	0.1745	0.1736	0.9848	0.1763	5.6713	5.7588	1.0154
11	0.192	0.1908	0.9816	0.1944	5.1446	5.2408	1.0187
12	0.2094	0.2079	0.9781	0.2126	4.7046	4.8097	1.0223
13	0.2269	0.2250	0.9744	0.2309	4.3315	4.4454	1.0263
14	0.2443	0.2419	0.9703	0.2493	4.0108	4.1336	1.0306
15	0.2618	0.2588	0.9659	0.2679	3.7321	3.8637	1.0353
16	0.2793	0.2756	0.9613	0.2867	3.4874	3.6280	1.0403
17	0.2967	0.2924	0.9563	0.3057	3.2709	3.4203	1.0457
18	0.3142	0.3090	0.9511	0.3249	3.0777	3.2361	1.0515
19	0.3316	0.3256	0.9455	0.3443	2.9042	3.0716	1.0576
20	0.3491	0.3420	0.9397	0.3640	2.7475	2.9238	1.0642
21	0.3665	0.3584	0.9336	0.3839	2.6051	2.7904	1.0711
22	0.384	0.3746	0.9272	0.4040	2.4751	2.6695	1.0785
23	0.4014	0.3907	0.9205	0.4245	2.3559	2.5593	1.0864
24	0.4189	0.4067	0.9135	0.4452	2.2460	2.4586	1.0946
25	0.4363	0.4226	0.9063	0.4663	2.1445	2.3662	1.1034
26	0.4538	0.4384	0.8988	0.4877	2.0503	2.2812	1.1126
27	0.4712	0.4540	0.8910	0.5095	1.9626	2.2027	1.1223
28	0.4887	0.4695	0.8829	0.5317	1.8807	2.1301	1.1326
29	0.5061	0.4848	0.8746	0.5543	1.8040	2.0627	1.1434
30	0.5236	0.5000	0.8660	0.5774	1.7321	2.0000	1.1547
31	0.5411	0.5150	0.8572	0.6009	1.6643	1.9416	1.1666
32	0.5585	0.5299	0.8480	0.6249	1.6003	1.8871	1.1792
33	0.576	0.5446	0.8387	0.6494	1.5399	1.8361	1.1924
34	0.5934	0.5592	0.8290	0.6745	1.4826	1.7883	1.2062
35	0.6109	0.5736	0.8192	0.7002	1.4281	1.7434	1.2208
36	0.6283	0.5878	0.8090	0.7265	1.3764	1.7013	1.2361
37	0.6458	0.6018	0.7986	0.7536	1.3270	1.6616	1.2521
38	0.6632	0.6157	0.7880	0.7813	1.2799	1.6243	1.2690
39	0.6807	0.6293	0.7771	0.8098	1.2349	1.5890	1.2868
40	0.6981	0.6428	0.7660	0.8391	1.1918	1.5557	1.3054
41	0.7156	0.6561	0.7547	0.8693	1.1504	1.5243	1.3250
42	0.733	0.6691	0.7431	0.9004	1.1106	1.4945	1.3456
43	0.7505	0.6820	0.7314	0.9325	1.0724	1.4663	1.3673
44	0.7679	0.6947	0.7193	0.9657	1.0355	1.4396	1.3902
45	0.7854	0.7071	0.7071	1.0000	1.0000	1.4142	1.4142

www,analyzemath.com

x		sin(x)	cos(x)	tan(x)	cot(x)	csc(x)	sec(x)
deg	rad						
46	0.8029	0.7193	0.6947	1.0355	0.9657	1.3902	1.4396
47	0.8203	0.7314	0.6820	1.0724	0.9325	1.3673	1.4663
48	0.8378	0.7431	0.6691	1.1106	0.9004	1.3456	1.4945
49	0.8552	0.7547	0.6561	1.1504	0.8693	1.3250	1.5243
50	0.8727	0.7660	0.6428	1.1918	0.8391	1.3054	1.5557
51	0.8901	0.7771	0.6293	1.2349	0.8098	1.2868	1.5890
52	0.9076	0.7880	0.6157	1.2799	0.7813	1.2690	1.6243
53	0.925	0.7986	0.6018	1.3270	0.7536	1.2521	1.6616
54	0.9425	0.8090	0.5878	1.3764	0.7265	1.2361	1.7013
55	0.9599	0.8192	0.5736	1.4281	0.7002	1.2208	1.7434
56	0.9774	0.8290	0.5592	1.4826	0.6745	1.2062	1.7883
57	0.9948	0.8387	0.5446	1.5399	0.6494	1.1924	1.8361
58	1.0123	0.8480	0.5299	1.6003	0.6249	1.1792	1.8871
59	1.0297	0.8572	0.5150	1.6643	0.6009	1.1666	1.9416
60	1.0472	0.8660	0.5000	1.7321	0.5774	1.1547	2.0000
61	1.0647	0.8746	0.4848	1.8040	0.5543	1.1434	2.0627
62	1.0821	0.8829	0.4695	1.8807	0.5317	1.1326	2.1301
63	1.0996	0.8910	0.4540	1.9626	0.5095	1.1223	2.2027
64	1.117	0.8988	0.4384	2.0503	0.4877	1.1126	2.2812
65	1.1345	0.9063	0.4226	2.1445	0.4663	1.1034	2.3662
66	1.1519	0.9135	0.4067	2.2460	0.4452	1.0946	2.4586
67	1.1694	0.9205	0.3907	2.3559	0.4245	1.0864	2.5593
68	1.1868	0.9272	0.3746	2.4751	0.4040	1.0785	2.6695
69	1.2043	0.9336	0.3584	2.6051	0.3839	1.0711	2.7904
70	1.2217	0.9397	0.3420	2.7475	0.3640	1.0642	2.9238
71	1.2392	0.9455	0.3256	2.9042	0.3443	1.0576	3.0716
72	1.2566	0.9511	0.3090	3.0777	0.3249	1.0515	3.2361
73	1.2741	0.9563	0.2924	3.2709	0.3057	1.0457	3.4203
74	1.2915	0.9613	0.2756	3.4874	0.2867	1.0403	3.6280
75	1.309	0.9659	0.2588	3.7321	0.2679	1.0353	3.8637
76	1.3265	0.9703	0.2419	4.0108	0.2493	1.0306	4.1336
77	1.3439	0.9744	0.2250	4.3315	0.2309	1.0263	4.4454
78	1.3614	0.9781	0.2079	4.7046	0.2126	1.0223	4.8097
79	1.3788	0.9816	0.1908	5.1446	0.1944	1.0187	5.2408
80	1.3963	0.9848	0.1736	5.6713	0.1763	1.0154	5.7588
81	1.4137	0.9877	0.1564	6.3138	0.1584	1.0125	6.3925
82	1.4312	0.9903	0.1392	7.1154	0.1405	1.0098	7.1853
83	1.4486	0.9925	0.1219	8.1443	0.1228	1.0075	8.2055
84	1.4661	0.9945	0.1045	9.5144	0.1051	1.0055	9.5668
85	1.4835	0.9962	0.0872	11.4301	0.0875	1.0038	11.4737
86	1.501	0.9976	0.0698	14.3007	0.0699	1.0024	14.3356
87	1.5184	0.9986	0.0523	19.0811	0.0524	1.0014	19.1073
88	1.5359	0.9994	0.0349	28.6363	0.0349	1.0006	28.6537
89	1.5533	0.9998	0.0175	57.2900	0.0175	1.0002	57.2987
90	1.5708	1.0000	0.0000		0.0000	1.0000	

www.analyzemath.com

"The Morning Echo"

θ	0	$\dfrac{\pi}{6}$	$\dfrac{\pi}{4}$	$\dfrac{\pi}{3}$	$\dfrac{\pi}{2}$
	0	30°	45°	60°	90°
$\sin(\theta)$	0	$\dfrac{1}{2}$	$\dfrac{\sqrt{2}}{2}$	$\dfrac{\sqrt{3}}{2}$	1
$\cos(\theta)$	1	$\dfrac{\sqrt{3}}{2}$	$\dfrac{\sqrt{2}}{2}$	$\dfrac{1}{2}$	0
$\tan(\theta)$	0	$\dfrac{\sqrt{3}}{3}$	1	$\sqrt{3}$	U
$\csc(\theta)$	U	2	$\sqrt{2}$	$\dfrac{2}{\sqrt{3}}$	1
$\sec(\theta)$	1	$\dfrac{2}{\sqrt{3}}$	$\sqrt{2}$	2	U
$\cot(\theta)$	U	$\sqrt{3}$	1	$\dfrac{\sqrt{3}}{3}$	0

Constant	Symbol	Value
acceleration due to gravity	G	9.8 m s-2
atomic mass unit	amu, mu or u	1.66 x10-27 kg
Avogadro's Number	N	6.022 x 1023 mol-1
Bohr radius	a0	0.529 x 10-10 m
Boltzmann constant	K	1.38 x 10-23 J K-1
electron charge to mass ratio	-e/me	-1.7588 x 1011 C kg-1
electron classical radius	re	2.818 x 10-15 m
electron mass energy (J)	mec2	8.187 x 10-14 J
electron mass energy (MeV)	mec2	0.511 MeV
electron rest mass	me	9.109 x 10-31 kg
Faraday constant	F	9.649 x 104 C mol-1
fine-structure constant	▯	7.297 x 10-3
gas constant	R	8.314 J mol-1 K-1
gravitational constant	G	6.67 x 10-11 Nm-2kg-2
neutron mass energy (J)	mnc2	1.505 x 10-10 J
neutron mass energy (MeV)	mnc2	939.565 MeV
neutron rest mass	mn	1.675 x 10-27 kg
neutron-electron mass ratio	mn/me	1838.68
neutron-proton mass ratio	mn/mp	1.0014
permeability of a vacuum	μ0	4π x 10-7 N A-2
permittivity of a vacuum	▯0	8.854 x 10-12 F m-1
Planck constant	H	6.626 x 10-34 J s
proton mass energy (J)	mpc2	1.503 x 10-10 J
proton mass energy (MeV)	mpc2	938.272 MeV
proton rest mass	mp	1.6726 x 10-27 kg
proton-electron mass ratio	mp/me	1836.15
Rydberg constant	r∞	1.0974 x 107 m-1
speed of light in vacuum	C	2.9979 x 108 m/s